DURABLE INEQUALITIES

DURABLE INEQUALITIES

Contextualising Caste-Exclusion, Marginalisation and Reservation in India's North-East

Chunnu Prasad

GYAN

ISBN: 978-81-212-1309-7
Price: ₹ 990/-
First Published, 2015

Published by
Gyan Publishing House
5, Main Ansari Road
Daryaganj, New Delhi-110002
Moble: 9811692060
Fax: 91-11-23285914
E-mail: books@gyanbooks.com

Laser Typesetting: Rajender Vashist, Delhi
Printed at: Chawla Offset Printers, Delhi

Cataloging in Publication Oata—OK
Courtesy: O.K. Agencies (P) Ltd. <docinfo@dkagencies.com>

Chunnu Prasad, author.
Durable inequalities: contextualising caste-exclusion, marginalisation and reservation in India's north-east / Chunnu Prasad.
pages cm
Includes bibliographical references (pages) and index.
ISBN 9788121213097

1. Dalits—India, Northeastern—Social conditions.
2. Marginality, Social—India, Northeastern. 3. Equality—India, Northeastern. 4. Dalits—Civil rights—India, Northeastern.
5. Reverse discrimination—India, Northeastern. 6. India, Northeastern—Social conditions. I. Title.

DOC 305.568809541 23

"After coming in this world, don't live like those small plants which grow up because of excessive rain but wilt under."

–Gautam Buddha

"All men are my children. I desire for my children their welfare and happiness both in this world and the next. That I desire for all men."

–Ashoka

"I have never claimed to be a universal leader of suffering humanity. The problem of the untouchables is quite enough for my slender strength. I do not say that other causes are not equally noble. But knowing that life is short, one can only serve one cause and I have never aspired to do more than serve the Untouchables."

"Educate, Agitate and Organise and have faith in yourself"

"Learn to live in this world with self-respect. You should always cherish some ambition to do something in this world. They alone rise who strive. Some of you nurse the wrong notion that you will not rise in this world. But remember that the age of helplessness has ended. A new epoch has set in. All things are now possible because of your being able to participate in the Politics and Legislatures of this country."

"We are Indians, firstly and lastly"

"Religion is for man and not man for religion"

"Life should be Great, Rather than Long"

"There is nothing fixed, nothing eternal, nothing sanatan; everything is changing, change is the law of life for individuals as well as for society. In a changing society there must be constant revolution of old values."

"Lost rights are never regained by appeals to the conscience of the usurpers, but by relentless struggle.... Goats are used for sacrificial offerings and not lions."

"Unlike a drop of water which loses its identity when it joins the ocean, man does not lose his being in the society in which he lives. Man's life is independent. He is born not for the development of the society alone, but for the development of him self."

"Democracy is not a Form of Government, but a form of social organisation."

–Dr B.R. Ambedkar

"Let us all hope that the dark clouds of racial prejudice will soon pass away, and that in some not too distant tomorrow the radiant stars of love and brotherhood will shine over our great nation with all their scintillating beauty."

–Martin Luther King

Contents

Preface

I wrote this book out of passion. The reason for writing is to identify something which is untouched by parts of the world and brings the voice of the voiceless in the mainstream. I found from the land of Northeast cast is completely excluded from the academic discourse. None of the so-called academia and well renounded writer of India's northeast touched it. The scheduled castes of the Indian States of Assam, Arunachal Pradesh, Meghalaya, Manipur, Mizoram, Nagaland, Tripura and Sikkim is suffering with, multiple backwardness firstly, as a general scheduled caste, secondly, as a regional backwardness/isolation, thirdly, linguistic or migrational exclusion and so on so forth. These populations have been denied their basic constitutional fundamental rights in the region. They are suffering from huge discrimination and exclusion by both the State Government as well as the local inhabitants of the state.

The Central as well as State Government initiated lots of developmental activities to strengthen the political economy of the state and the people, but none of the policies and programmes have any strong inclusive provisions for scheduled castes of these States. These populations largely engaged with the jobs like sweeping, stitching shoes, washing dirty cloths, cleaning toilets, engaged in burial grounds, and all other dirty jobs. Even after getting good education they are not getting jobs and compelled to do their traditional dirty works as doing in other parts of India from centuries.

I hope the work produce would be the first work ever produced on castes issues from the land of northeast. Their is a huge hue and cry on the issue of migration, ethnic conflicts, insergency, and so on so forth, but the issue of castes is totally out of the discource. In India caste is the only issue on which everything working as like planets revolving around the sun, and those who are not taking the issue of caste is at all not taking the issue properly. The simple understanding is that one has to identify the problems, because unless and until if problem not identified there is no solution at all. Lastly, this work brings the various issues related to the problems of the scheduled castes population in the Indian States of Northeast, their constitutional rights as well as right to livelihood. It also suggests some of the solution to the problem and requirement to fill the gap of discrimination done over a period of time to the scheduled caste population in the region.

This piece is largely the collection of paper presented to various universities over a period of time on caste, social exclusion and the question of livelihood in the region as a whole. Before going to begin the chapters let me first thank to the people who really helped me to compile and produce in a concise form. First of all I would like to thanks all those people who are fully devoted and working for the rights and dignity of all those people who are fighting to get their human rights and dignity.

I would like to thank Prof S.K.Thorat, former Chairman, University Grants Commission (UGC) for introducing Centre for the Study of Social Exclusion and Inclusive Policy in various universities to exclusively work on the issues related to Scheduled Castes and Scheduled Tribes. My heartiest thanks goes to all those people who are regularly writing on the issues related to SC's and ST's particularly, Prof Vivek Kumar, Prof Gopal Guru, Prof Valarian Rodrigues, Prof Sudha Pai, Prof Nandu Ram, Prof Kancha Ilahi, Prof Tulshi Ram, Dr Anand Teltumbde, Prof Gail Omvet, Prof Cristofer Jeferlot, Prof Narender Kumar and many more.

I would deeply like to thanks personally to all those friends from Jawaharlal Nehru University, New Delhi, University of Delhi, Delhi, Jamia Milia Islamia, Indian Institute of Technology

(Delhi), New Delhi, Hindu University, Varanasi, Indira Gandhi Institute of Development Research, Mumbai, Aurangabad University, Aurangabad, University of Lucknow, Babasahab Dr Bhim Rao Ambedkar University, Lucknow, Uttar Pradesh, Mangalore University, Mangalore, University of Hyderabad, Osmania University, Hyderabad, Dr B.R. Ambedkar Open University, Hyderabad, Rajiv Gandhi University, Itanagar, Arunachal Pradesh, North Eastern Hill University, Shillong, Meghalaya, Sikkim University, Gangtok, Sikkim, Manipur University, Manipur, Nagaland University, Nagaland, Mizoram University, Mizoram, Tripura University, Tripura, Assam University, Guwahati University, Tezpur University, Dibrugarh University, Assam, Dhaka University, Dhaka, Kathmandu University, Katmandu, Oxford University, United Kingdom, Indane University, United States of America and others with whome I got an opportunities to discuss critically on the issue related to Scheduled Castes of Northeast in particular and India in general.

Lastly, I would like to thank my wife Ms Anuradha Prasad for her suggestion in improving/correction of the work since inception to completion. I would also be thankful to Gyan Publishing House, New Delhi for accepting the manuscript to publish on time.

Chunnu Prasad

Acronyms and Abbreviations

AAPSU	:	All Arunachal Pradesh Student Union
AHD	:	Abor Hill District
AIIMS	:	All India Institute of Medical Sciences
BC	:	Before Christ
BCC	:	Backward Class Commission
BCs	:	Backward Castes
BFT	:	Balipara Frontier Tract
BJP	:	Bharatiya Janata Party
CCS	:	Christian Caste System
CDS	:	Current Daily Status
CP	:	Communist Party
CWS	:	Current Weekly Status
DPM	:	Dalit Panthar Movement
HEI	:	Higher Education Institutes
HSO	:	Hindu Social Order
HVV	:	Hindu Varna Vewesta
IIM	:	Indian Institute of Management
IIT	:	Indian Institute of Technology
LPG	:	Liberalisation, Privatisation and Globalisation
MBC	:	Most Backward Castes
MHA	:	Ministry of Home Affairs
MHD	:	Mishmi Hill District
MMKS	:	Maharashtra Muslim Khatik Samaj
MP	:	Member of Parliament

NABARD	:	National Bank for Agriculture and Rural Development
NBM	:	Non Brahmin Movement
NCDC	:	National Council of Dalit Christians
NEFA	:	North East Frontier Agency
NEFT	:	North Eastern Frontier Tracts
NERI	:	North Eastern Region of India
NFT	:	North Frontier Tracts
NHTA	:	Naga Hills Tuesnsang Area
NSSO	:	National Sample Survey Organisation
OBCs	:	Other Backward Classes
PAP	:	Protected Area Permits
PPAP	:	People's Party of Arunachal Pradesh
PSUs	:	Public Sector Undertakings
RAP	:	Restricted Area Permits
RMs	:	Religious Minorities
SC	:	Scheduled Caste
ST	:	Scheduled Tribe
TCA	:	Trichi Church Association
TFD	:	Tuensang Frontier Division
TFT	:	Tirap Frontier Tract
UNICEF	:	United Nations Children's Fund
UPS	:	Usual Principal Status
UPSS	:	Usual Principal and Subsidiary Status
USA	:	United States of America
UT	:	Union Territory
VHP	:	Viswa Hindu Parishad
WE	:	Western Europe
WPR	:	Work Participation Rate

List of Tables

1

Caste and its Legitimacy

India, a country with an oldest traditions, culture and beauty, has an unwanted, ugly and inhuman structure called *'Caste System'*.[1] The caste system discriminates the human and stratifies them into different groups. According to Manu Dharma, the Hindu religious code of conduct, divides human into four Varna-Brahmin, Kshatriya, Vaisya, Sudra.[2]

There is perhaps no other aspect of Hinduism or Sanatana Dharma, that elicits as much debate and controversy as the subject of India's social order based on its ancient conceptions of Varna, Jati and Kula. Contemporary discussions of the subject tend to be extremely divisive to say the least, and can generate far more heat than light, especially when Hindus attempt to frame a representative narrative of the phenomenon.[3] The fact that much of this narrative has been generated by non-Indic scholarship in the past few centuries further vitiates own understanding of this social order. The influence of colonial scholarship on India is so pervasive that many well-meaning Hindus themselves tend to have a very distorted and incomplete view of this social order.[4] Moreover there are many vested interests who have exploited the fissures that arise naturally within this social organisation for multifarious personal ends, ranging from conversion of Hindus to other faiths, creation of political vote-banks and other forms of personal advancement.

In recent years, caste identities appear to be acquiring a renewed strength and vitality based on caste-based political mobilisation and reservations.[5] After 2011, the Census of India's population once again ask people about their caste affiliation – a question they had not asked for 80 years since 1931, thereby placing caste at the center stage once more. At the same time, governments of many countries stand ready to indict India and its society for what in their view is its continued practice of caste-based discrimination and perceived human rights violations.[6]

Caste has always been central to modern Indian politics. Even the power structure of mediaeval India was based on caste.[7] Caste also operated as the central principle in the distribution of power and material resources in the colonial period. Colonialism in India created a democratic and modernist space; nevertheless this space was also predominantly captured by advantaged groups. The nationalist struggle against the imperial power was aimed at establishing the caste-class hegemony.[8] Non-Brahmin and low-caste movements were active during the colonial era, broadly pursuing two aims: achieving upward caste-class mobility and annihilation of caste.[9]

The caste system played a significant role in determining the content and direction of the processes of political socialisation, political mobilisation and institutionalisation within the framework of modern democracy. The dynamics of caste and class were at the root of the complexity of Indian politics in its functioning. Behind the seemingly religious and communal movements in post-independent India, it was the dynamics of caste-class hegemony that was the real operational factor. Both the anti-caste and the upwardly mobile caste movements are guiding the pro-reservation movement, which aims at upward class mobility of the hitherto excluded castes. The pro-imperialist bourgeois policies of the ruling class and the struggles against these policies are also influenced and shaped by the tensions and contradictions in caste-class dynamics.[10]

Caste is also instrumental in regulating the modern democratic processes and institutions which function through the Panchayati Raj. The rural elites use caste to orient the political process to safeguard their caste-class interests. The implementation of reservation, welfare schemes and political decentralisation in the Panchayati Raj also operate in the caste-class matrix. Consequently, the exploited caste-class groups remain deprived of their right to development. It is only the grass-roots anti-caste movement that can achieve democratisation of such processes and institutions.

Dr Ambedkar in his book from millions to factions, Chapter 20, Vol. 2 says;

> *"Whatever view may be taken of the advantages or disadvantages of caste as a social institution, it is impossible to conceive of any useful discussion of the population questions in India in which caste would not be an important element. Caste is still 'the foundation of the Indian social fabric,' and the record of caste is still 'the best guide to the changes in the various social strata in the Indian Society'. Every Hindu (using the term in its most elastic sense) is born into a caste and his caste determines his religious, social, economic and domestic life from the cradle to the grave. In Western countries the major factors which determine the different strata of society, viz, wealth, education and vocation are fluid and catholic and tend to modify the rigidity of birth and hereditary position. In India spiritual and social community and traditional occupation override all other factors. Thus, where in censuses of western countries, an economic or occupational grouping of the population affords a basis for the combination of demographic statistics; the corresponding basis in the case of the Indian population is the distinction of religion and caste. Whatever view may be taken of caste as a national and social institution, it is useless to ignore it, and so long as caste continues to be used as one of the distinguishing features of an individual's official and social identity, it cannot be claimed that a decennial enumeration helps to perpetuate an undesirable institution."*[11]

The way anti-caste movements, respond to such processes gathers importance largly. The ideology of caste alliance and participation in power has strengthened further a patron-client form of relationship even within political parties and public institutions. Ambedkarism has been reduced to the slogan *'Become the ruling community'*.[12]

Caste and brahminical patriarchy have consistently worked together in maintaining rigid caste-based status and uneven distribution of material resources. As upward caste mobility also strengthens brahminical patriarchy, the caste elites in the backward feudal states have nurtured caste mobs to protect patriarchal traditions. The new caste elites, while achieving class mobility, have maintained their social status by stringent protection of the norms of caste patriarchy. In the states dominated by landlordism, the nexus between caste mobs, the police and the state machinery acts with brutality when cases of inter-caste marriage occur. Against this backdrop, discussion on *'patriarchy and politics of caste'* becomes essential and *khap* is the fine example in India.[13]

There is ample justification in the Gita alone to maintain caste divisions and oppressions; here is Lord Krsna's word:

> *"It is far better to perform one's svadharma (prescribed duties), even though faultily, than another's duties perfectly. Destruction in the course of performing one's own duty is better than engaging in another's duties, to follow another's path is dangerous."*[14]

"According to the three modes of material nature (goodness, passion, ignorance) and the work associated with them, the four divisions of human society (Brahmin/Ksatriya/Vaisya/ Sudra) are created by me. And although I am the creator of this system, you should know that I am yet the nondoer, being unchangeable."[15]

> *"It is better to engage in one's own svadharma (occupation), even though one may perform it imperfectly, than to accept another's occupation and perform it perfectly. Duties prescribed according to one's nature are never affected by sinful reactions."*[16]

Lord Rama would be in complete accord with the above quotes; afterall, he killed an innocent Sudra, Shambuka, only because he was performing austerities which were not prescribed duties for low-castes[17]. The killing of Shambuka appears in the Valmiki Ramayana, Book 7, the 'Uttarakanda' [Final Chapter], sargas 73-76. Three scene-setting sargas are paraphrased, and then the crucial one is presented in full;

> *(73) When Rama is reigning as a virtuous king, a humble aged Brahmin comes to him, weeping, with his dead son in his arms. He says that Rama must have committed some sin, or else his son would not have died. (74) The sage Narada explains to Rama that a Shudra is practicing penances, and this is the cause of the child's death. (75) Rama goes on a tour of inspection in his flying chariot, and finds an ascetic doing austerities, and asks*

who he is. "(76) Hearing the [inquiring] words of Rama of imperishable exploits, that ascetic, his head still hanging downwards [as part of his austerities] answered:— 'O Rama, I was born of a Shudra alliance and I am performing this rigorous penance in order to acquire the status of a God in this body. I am not telling a lie, O Rama, I wish to attain the Celestial Region. Know that I am a Shudra and my name is Shambuka.' As he was yet speaking, Raghava [Rama], drawing his brilliant and stainless sword from its scabbard, cut off his head. The Shudra being slain, all the Gods and their leaders with Agni's followers, cried out, 'Well done! Well done!' overwhelming Rama with praise, and a rain of celestial flowers of divine fragrance fell on all sides, scattered by Vayu. In their supreme satisfaction, the Gods said to that hero, Rama:— 'Thou hast protected the interests of the Gods, O Highly Intelligent Prince, now ask a boon, O beloved Offspring of Raghu, Destroyer of Thy Foes. By thy grace, this Shudra will not be able to attain heaven!'" (583-84).[18]

Caste is a position in society inherited from parents at birth and from which there is no transfer throughout life. The system is at its strongest in India where people of advantaged are respected but those of the disadvantaged—the untouchables who usually work in the most menial occupations. Political dictionary suggest that caste is a group of people bound together through Hindu religious sanctions and rituals. Broadly speaking, the origins of the caste system, first articulated in the *Law Book of Manu* between 200 BC and AD 200, were functional.[19] The four major caste groups (varnas) were characterised according to the social functions they performed. Brahmins were the educators, kshatriyas the producers and warriors, vaishyas the merchants, and shudras the labourers.[20] Tasks perceived as involving pollution were undertaken by the *avarna*, or untouchables. Political dictionary in other sense refers that the castes are further divided into subcastes (*jatis*) which are more important in their impact on daily lives of people. Those belonging to a *jati* form a *biradari* which is the specific sociocultural unit within which caste roles are performed.[21]

Caste in India is a social institution and social stratification deriving sanction from Hindu Religion. Caste system has survived in India more than 3500 years.[22] The word 'Caste' comes from Portuguese word 'Casta' which signifies 'Breed' or 'Race'[23] as

"Membership confined to those who are born of members and include all members so born. The members are forbidden by an inexorable social law to marry outside group. Each group has a special name by which it is called. Several of such small aggregates are again grouped together under one common name"[24].

Caste system was introduced to the Indian history by Aryans who invaded India in BC 1500. The Hierarchical Caste System (HCS) was attributed to God's creation. In the traditional understanding the caste system is derived from Varna system, which has the foundation in Rig-Veda.[25] Mandala describes the creation of different groups from Purusha, the primordial being. *Purushasukta (Hymn of Man in Rig-Veda)* speaks about Varna as the origin of the caste system. The Brahmana was his mouth; both of his arms were Ranjanya (Kshatriya); his thighs became the Vaishya and from his feet the Shudra was produced.[26] The people outside of Chatur Varna were called outcastes. Aryans called them Dasas (Dark people), *Punchama* (fifth order or outcastes) *Avarna, Chandala, Antayas, Shvapaka, Meda etc.*[27]

In Hindu society, caste is still the most powerful factor in determining a person's dignity. The caste system is the result of the Hindu belief in *'Reincarnation and Karma'*. The four castes eventually developed into a social mosaic of more than 3000 sub-castes, with the untouchables at the bottom of the list and actually outside the list. Such a rigid caste system is not found anywhere in the world outside India. A person is born into a caste and once born in that caste, his status is predetermined and immutable. Birth decides one's status and this cannot be altered by any talent the person may develop or wealth the person may accumulate. Similarly, the caste in which a person is born predetermines what vocation the person will pursue. One has no choice.[28]

In Bhagavat Gita reference that it catogorise human beings into compartments which goes like these, *Moya Shristong Chaturvarnam* (Four castes are my creation).[29] The Britannica encyclopedia affirms that the more than 3000 Indian castes are loosely grouped into four varnas- Brahmin, Kshatriya, Vaishya and Shudra. The Hindu religious textbook, in fact the most widely accessed one and Gita states that Lord Krishna is the originator of the four Varnas. So Hindus are expected to aver casteism as a divine arrangement. Literal English translation of the Sanskrit words above is: *"I created four Varnas"*.[30]

Birth decides the occupation of the person in question. Here are the four major castes:

BRAHMINS (the Priestly Caste/Class)

↓

KSHATRIYAS (the Warrior Caste/Class)

↓

VAISYAS (the Trading Caste/Class)

↓

SUDRAS (the Servants Caste/Class)

↓

PANCHAMAS (out Hindu Castes/Class)

Myth and Origin of the Caste System

The BRAHMINS are the priestly class came from the head of God. They are eligible for learning and teaching and perform sacrifices. The others cannot teach and perform sacrifice.

The KSHATRIAS are the warrior class came from the shoulder of God. Their work is to protect the people by waging war against the enemies.

The VAISYAS are the trading class came from the thigh of God. Their work is to trade and feed the above two classes.

The SUDRAS are the servants came from the feet of God and their work as a labourer and artisan to the above three classes. They are not entitled to learn anything.

The PANCHAMAS are the people who remain always out of the Hindu fold. They were never the part of Hindu traditions. They were outcastes and untouchables. Today they are called the Scheduled Castes and Scheduled Tribes. The people who accepted the slavery become caste and those who ran to the forest and protested violently become tribes. As such they do not assign any work.

Other sub-castes are more than 3000 in number, with the *'Untouchables'* or *'Scheduled Castes'* at the bottom and outside.[31] They are the slaves of the above groups and they are absolutely forbidden to learn and teach. In the above circumstances the Scheduled Castes are deprived of:

1. Education;
2. Right to hold assets;
3. Right to hold weapons to protect themselves; and
4. Right to have participation in political process/public sphere freely.

Therefore, they are owned as the property of the caste people. The code of conduct that deprives them of these rights was written more than three thousand years back. One may wonder why this is still in practice. The tragedy is that although untouchability was abolished by law 1950 in India, yet the SC's experience the agony of untouchability very deeply in all walks of life: Social, Economical and Political. One cannot understand the pain of being a Dalit unless he experiences it.[32]

There are also other categories of people who don't come under any of these above caste groups, since they are not considered as human beings. They are called 'the Outcastes' or the 'Untouchables' or the 'Unseeables'. There are hundreds of codes of conduct written for them. Now constitutionally these people call as *'Scheduled Castes.'* Politically they called 'Dalit'[33] which means' has broken, torn, scattered and crushed. Mohandas Karamchand Gandhi called them 'Harijans' which means God's Children,[34] but the word *'Harijans' does* not describe their condition adequately.[35] Latter the word Harijan was opposed by many scholars particulary Dr Bhim Rao Ambedkar.[36] Therefore, the outcaste preferred to call themselves Constitutional identity as *'Scheduled Castes.'*[37]

The term *'Dalit'* has roots in Sanskrit where the root *'dal'* means *'to split, crack, open'*. (This Indo-European root appears in

German and English in the form of *'dal'* or *'tal'*, meaning *'cut'*. In English, *'dale'* is a valley, a cut in the ground; in German, that: a tailor is one who cuts; *'to tell a tale'* is the same as *'to cut a tally'*, the cut-marks made by the shepherd on his staff when counting sheep.[38]

Dalit has come to mean things or persons, who are cut, split, broken or torn asunder, scattered or crushed and destroyed.[39] By coincidence, there is in Hebrew a root 'dal' meaning low, weak, poor. In the Bible, different forms of this term have been used to describe people who have been reduced to nothingness or helplessness.The present usage of the term Dalit goes back to the nineteenth century, when a Marathi social reformer and revolutionary, Mahatma Jyotirao Phule (1826-1890), used it to describe the Outcastes and Untouchables as the oppressed and the broken victims of our caste-ridden society.[40] Under the charismatic leadership of Dr B.R. Ambedkar (1891-1956), this term gained greater importance and popularity. During the 1970s, the followers of the Dalit Panther Movement (DPM) of Maharashtra gave currency to the term Dalit as a constant reminder of their age-old oppression, denoting both their state of deprivation and the people who are oppressed.[41] This term for them is not a mere name or title. For them it has become an expression of hope, the hope of recovering their past self-identity. The term has gained a new connotation with a more positive meaning. It must be remembered that *Dalit does not mean Caste or low-Caste or poor;* it refers to the deplorable state or condition to which a large group of people has been reduced by social convention and in which they are now living.[42]

It has been observed through various studies that Dalits of India is originated from the evil of untouchability.[43] Those communities and their posterities who suffered untouchability in the past are to be considered as Dalits irrespective of religion, and those communities and their ancestors or posterities who never suffered any kind of untouchability shall not be considered as Dalits[44]. It is also correctly said that there is a positive correlation between caste and Dalit poverty; as the poverty of Dalits is due to the caste system and all the backwardness inflicted upon them by the caste system.[45]

Scheduled Castes

The Scheduled Castes (SCs) are official designations given to various groups of historically disadvantaged people. The terms are recognised in the Constitution of India and the various groups are designated in one or other of the categories.[46] SCs are among the most disadvantaged socio-economic groups in India. The Scheduled Castes are called by different names in different parts of the country.[47] These names were given by the caste people as expressions of contempt. They include: Dasa, Dasysa,. Raksasa, Asura, Avarna, Nisada, Panchama, Chandala, Harijan, and Untouchable. Each of these names has a history and background. Besides these names, there are a number of other titles or names which have been given to them at the level of the regional language. For example, Chura in Punjab (North West India), Bhangi or Lal Beghi in Hindi (North India), Mahar in Marathi (Central India), Mala in Telugu, Paraiya in Tamil and Pulayan in Malayalam (South India). These names carry within them the two-term contrast of 'we-the pure' and 'you-the impure'. In response to these insulting labels, the untouchables have chosen to give themselves a name and this is 'Dalit', which refers to the hardship of their condition of life. This name is a constant reminder of the age-old oppression.[48]

The term is also an expression of their hope to recover their past self-identity. If today the Dalits are reduced to a life of abject poverty and treated as polluted human beings, it is the non-Dalit that must be seen as the agent of their dehumanisation.[49] By the British, the Dalits were named 'the Depressed Classes' and 'the Scheduled Castes', in the Scheduled Caste Act of India, 1935.[50]

Hinduism is not the religion of the SC's. To understand the religion of the SC's, one must understand the religion of Mohenjodaro. They had and have to this day the strong concept of a personal transcendent creator God. However, their popular religion gradually degenerated to the worship of malevolent spirits and demigods. They also worshipped the spirits and Mother-goddess. They believed in sorcery. The Aryans worshipped the impersonal phenomena of nature, viz., Prithvi, Varuna, Indra and the Sun. Hermann Goetz states that the Dravidian Siva and Parvati link up with the cult of the moon god and the 'Lady of the Mountain'. Ur K.M. Munshi says that

Shiva, the Dravidian father god with his bull, was known to Harappan civilisation as the lord of creation and Ma, the mother of goddess of the Mediterranean people with lion as her mount, was worshipped in many parts of Asia, though unknown to Vedic Aryans.[51] The Sumerian Moon God, Nannar, is the Sivan of the Dravidians and the multi-armed Ishtar of Ur with her lion is the Kali of the Dravidians. Scholars are now finding that the Sivan of the Dravidians is none other than Adam of the first man.[52]

The trantric forms of worship, human sacrifice, walking on fire, are of Dravidian origin. Besides the above, the Dasyus worshipped demi-gods, demons, trees, animals, etc. The Chamars of northern India worship as gods, Saliya, Purbi, and as demons Vetal, Baital, Chural, Gayal, Paret, Pisach, Masau, Dund etc. The Untouchables of South Bihar have as their gods Surjahi, Barachi Vir, Basumit, Masana and Kunwar. Dr Vidhyarti, the famous anthropologist studying the religion of untouchables, says they follow their own native festivals of Karam puja, Sohrai, Phagua Kadleta, Nawan, Jiutiya, Chhat, etc. It must be noted that all these are etymologically Dravidi gods and Dravidi words.[53]

According to Smritis, the untouchable was prohibited from hearing any Sanskrit scriptures, much less reading or writing them. Molten lead must be poured into his ears if he does - decreed Manu. Basham, the great historian, records, "*It was with the conscious motive of preserving ritual and religious purity that all contact with the untouchables was avoided*".[54] That is why, the SC's were not allowed into any temple in India for the last 3000 years. The reason was clear racial and religious distinctives. The recent opening of some Hindu temples for the SC's is purely a political action to get the votes of the Scheduled Castes. Such move was vehemently opposed by honest Hindu saints like Puri Sankarachary who was bold enough to tell the truth.[55]

The Vedic Aryans and the Dasyu slaves had distinct religions of their own. There was no chance of mixing the two faiths, at any time of history, because most stringent rules of untouchability and isolation. To put it more exactly, it was out of the greatest concern to keep the two faiths separate, that untouchability and isolation were stringently maintained. Therefore, to call a person as Hindu SC's is absurd and irrelevant so far the evidence of migrations is concerned.[56]

Archaeological Evidence

Prehistoric India was inhabited first by the Negritos. The second group that migrated in was the Australoids. The Santals and Bhils belong to the Australoids. The third group that inhabited India was the Mongoloid family. To the present time the Mongoloid have maintained their distinct cultural, racial and religious identities. The fourth and largest group that inhabited ancient India was the Dravidian. Most scholars agree that the Dravidians came into India from the Eastern Mediterranean in the third millennium B.C. By 1400 B.C., the Dravidian civilisation in India extended across the entire land. Munshi says:

> *"The Early Dravidians, who arrived in India prior to 2000 B.C., possessed a highly developed material culture as would appear from their early speech forms and the findings in Mohenjo-daro, Harappa and Lothal".*[57]

Goetz speaks of the Indus Valley Civilisation as ranging from Lothal to Mohenjodaro from 3000 to 1400 B.C., and having cultural connections with Sumer, the earliest known cradle of human civilisation. The Indo-Aryans in the 2nd millennium B.C. migrated from their homeland of Eranvej (the present Russian Turkestan) via Afghanistan into India. Thus, the Aryans moved eastwards, fighting the Dravidians whom they exterminated or enslaved. They overran the open country, stormed the fortified towns (*pur*) of the Indus Valley and slowly migrated eastwards, conquering the whole of Northern India around 1400-1000 B.C.[58] This coincides with the records of Wheeler, the original authority on the Indus Valley Civilisation. These conquests are described in numerous verses of the Rig Veda.[59]

In the Rig Veda, the natives are described as dark-skinned, snub-nosed enemies of alien language and religion. Marshall and Cunningham who did the original archaeological excavation on Indus Civilisation and Yuria Knorozov who did the deciphering of the Indus pictographic writings and authorities such as Madho Sarup Vats, Dikshit, N.C. Majumdar, Rapson, Wheeler, R.D. Banerjee, B.B. Lal point to the fact that the native Black Dravidians were largely exterminated by the light-coloured Aryan invaders, their 'Puram' (meaning fort or town) civilisation was destroyed and those who were not killed were made slaves. When the Aryans began to spread eastward and southward from Punjab, they spread too thin. Therefore, the policy of total annihilation of the Dasyus was found unnecessary as well as impossible. Instead the Dravidians were made domestic and village slaves. In earlier civilisations, slavery or extermination were the only two methods used by most of the conquering races. Therefore, the Dasyus (slaves, now known to us as the scheduled caste) of the Rig Veda were the Dravidians living north of the Vindhya Satpura range and now enslaved by the invading Aryans. The distinguished indologist Basham says:

> *"In the reduction to bondage of the many dasas captured in the battle, we find the origin of Indian slavery".*[60]

Literary Evidence[61]

In all the four strong sources, it find that (Scheduled Castes)[62] Das, Chandala, Avarna, Panchama were reduced by their oppressors to a non-human level, with no identity or dignity.[63]

1. Rigvedas: (1500-1000 B.C.) The earliest available literary source is the Rigveda. Its Purusa sukta hymn talks about the origin of the four Varnas, Brahmanas, Kashatries, Vaisias and Sudras. The Scheduled Castes find no place in it under this name: they are referred as Avarna, Dasa and Dasyus.[64]

2. Upanishads: (800-600 B.C.) by the time Upanishad texts came into existence, the problem of the scheduled caste was becoming deeper and clearer. For example, the famous Chandogys Upanishad not only refers to the first three privileged castes, but also compares Chandala (Outcaste) with a dog and a swine.[65]

3. Ramayana: In the time of Lord Rama's rule, only the privileged three castes were allowed to do 'tapasya' (penance and meditation). Once one Shudra undertook penance in order to attain divinity (dignity). As soon as Lord Rama heard this, he killed the Sudhra for such presumption. If this happened to a Sudhra, one can imagine what would have happend to a Dalit so much lower in status.

4. Mahabharata: It describes the degraded state of the scheduled castes. It is the story of Ekalabya, a tribal boy, who has to lose the thumb of his right hand because he has learnt archery and has come to be no less skilled than Arjuna in this art.[66]

The caste system survived for centuries because the religious leaders transmitted the Hindu scriptures to the common people and attributed the caste system to divine ordinance. Breaking of this system, individually or collectively, was tantamount to breaking the divine law. Painstakingly, every dimension of the divine ordinance of caste was included in the scriptures. The very fine example found in Bhagavad Gita, which is regarded as the noblest of all the scriptures. The caste system thus, become sanctioned by scripture, it came to be accepted even by the outcastes themselves[67].

In the words of Dr B.R. Ambedkar, another ploy to make caste acceptable to all was the strategy of introducing an extensive system of 'graded inferiority', providing everyone with an inferior grade immediately beneath him. Thus, so long as the Brahmin was at the top, with no other caste above him, his superiority over all was secured. Below Brahmin had the Kshatriya - and below him was the Vaisya and below him the Sudra - and the Sudras had the untouchables beneath them. Thus each caste had at least one group beneath them. This compensated for the humiliation of having someone above them. This 'graded inferiority' made the entire system tolerable.

"The world owes a duty to the untouchables as it does to all oppressed people to break their shakles and to set them free".[68]

India's caste system is perhaps the world's longest surviving social hierarchy. A defining feature of Hinduism, caste encompasses a complex ordering of social groups on the basis of ritual purity. A person is considered a member of the caste into which he or she is born and remains within that caste until death, although the particular ranking of that caste may vary among regions and over time. Differences in status are traditionally justified by the religious doctrine of *karma*, a belief that one's place in life is determined by one's deeds in previous lifetimes. Traditional scholarship has described this more than 3,000-year-old system within the context of the four principal varnas, or large caste categories.[69]

In order of precedence the four categories, the Brahmins, the Kshatriyas, the Vaisyas, and the Shudras. A fifth category falls outside the Varna system and consists of those known as 'untouchables', Dalits and later in Constitution scheduled as Scheduled Castes; they are often assigned tasks too ritually polluting to merit inclusion within the traditional Varna system. Within the four principal castes, there are thousands of sub-castes, also called *jatis,* endogamous groups that are further divided among occupational, sectarian, regional and linguistic lines. Collectively all of these are sometimes referred to as 'Caste Hindus' or those falling within the caste system.[70]

The SC's are described as varna-sankara: they are 'outside the system'. So inferior to other castes that they are deemed polluting and therefore 'untouchable'. Even as outcastes, they themselves are divided into further sub-castes. Although 'untouchability' was abolished under Article-17 of the Indian Constitution[71], the practice continues to determine the socio-economic and religious standing of those at the bottom of the caste hierarchy. Whereas, the first four varnas are free to choose and change their occupation. SC's have generally been confined to the occupational structures into which they are born.[72]

Despite the fact that 'untouchability' abolished under India's Constitution in 1950[73], the practice of 'untouchability' the imposition of social disabilities on persons by reason of their birth in certain castes remains very much a part of rural India. 'Untouchables' may not cross the line dividing their part of the village from that occupied by privileged castes. They may not use the same wells, visit the same temples, drink from the same cups in tea stalls, or lay claim to land that is legally theirs. SC children are frequently made to sit in the back of classrooms and ill treatment by the teachers with derogatory words and communities as a whole are made to perform degrading rituals in the name of caste.[74]

Most SC's continue to live in extreme poverty, without land or opportunities for better employment and education. With exception of a minority who have benefited from India's policy of quotas in education and government jobs, SC's are relegated to the most menial of tasks, as manual scavengers, removers of human waste and dead animals, leather workers, street sweepers, and cobblers.[75]

Even in these modern times, all over India the SC's are still treated as untouchables in the eyes of the privileged and even of the ordinary people. Having undergone three thousand years of slavery and discrimination, the SC's find it nearly impossible to get out of this terrible trauma. The general situation of untouchables is miserable but it is more wretched in the case of those untouchables who have become Muslims and Christians because they now suffer severe discrimination in two ways - in society and in the Mosque and Church. Now they are identifying themselves as the Dalit Muslims and Dalit Christians. They bear the stigma of untouchability, a nightmare in every-day life.[76]

The SC community is deeply wounded one, a community that, with the sanction of the prevailing religion, has for centuries been systematically robbed and reduced to a state of empty powerlessness. The caste people on the other hand have risen to power at the cost of the SC's. The conversion of some SC's to Islam and Christianity has served as a motive for the Government of India to deprive them of those constitutional rights and privileges which are enjoyed by SC's who are Hindu, Sikh or Buddhist. Even within the Mosque and Church, the Dalit Muslims and Dalit Christians are robbed by the privileged caste Muslims and Christians in matters of mosque and Church related jobs and benefits.[77]

Most of the key positions in the Mosque and Church are occupied by the Muslims and Christians of the privileged caste. Therefore, Dalit Muslims and Dalit Christians have actually become refugees in their own homeland and in their home Mosque and Church.[78] Dalit Muslims and Dalit Christians represent the victimised masses, completely denied social justice.[79] Against social and economic exploiters, they have no protection. Dalit Muslims and Dalit Christians are the most exploited and oppressed community in India as compare to Hindu Dalits, Sikh Dalits and Buddhist Dalits.[80]

Centuries of oppression have inflicted on the Dalit people and deep psychological wounds, the trauma of low self-esteem. The Dalit cannot go to the village pump or well to draw water as the other villagers do. A Dalit cannot send his boy or girl to the village school where the other boys and girls of the village go. The Dalit cannot set foot in the temple. Dalit men and women or children may not walk in a street where caste people live. In a village restaurant, a Dalit cannot use the same cup as the upper caste people.[81]

Such constant inhuman treatment has a devastating impact on the psyche. This psychic wound has been inflicted on the SC's by others. The cruelty of the caste system is that one is born into that caste or non-caste, in case of the Dalit, and from this there is no escape. However, no matter what one does or achieves. In the eyes of the majority people in India, a Dalit, by the fact of birth alone is forever condemned as an agent of pollution.[82]

Deprived of the constitutional protection ought to have received from government which, in fact, is carrying out atrocious discriminatory policies, the SC's suffer from severe economic disabilities. They cannot aim at higher studies, or aspire to the government scholarships that might lead thereto. Even if, by way of exception, some SC's have managed to acquire the necessary qualifications, they do not get the job. Even within the Church-run institutions, schools and hospitals and such like, the jobs go in favour of the privileged caste people, acting in collusion with the clergy. The share of job opportunities held by the privileged caste people in various institutions is grossly disproportionate to their numbers. Even among the rural population, who are poor indeed, the SC's are cut off from the majority community, and are poorer than the poor themselves. Caste gives no scope for SC's to change their destiny. They are the people of the soil, yet in a so-called democratic system, they have no hope of owning their share of that soil, condemned day after day to grief and despair, to poverty as their immutable condition[83].

With little land of their own to cultivate, SC's men, women, and children numbering in the tens of millions work as agricultural labourers for a few kilograms of rice or Rs 15 to Rs 35 (US$0.38 to $0.88) a day.[84] Most live on the brink of destitution, barely able to feed their families and unable to send their children to school or break away from cycles of debt bondage that are passed on from generation to generation. At the end of day they return to a hut in their SC's colony with no electricity, kilometers away from the nearest water source, and segregated from all non-scheduled castes, known as caste Hindus. They are forbidden by caste Hindus to enter places of worship, to draw water from public wells, or to wear shoes in caste Hindu presence. They are made to dig the village graves, dispose of dead animals, clean human waste with their bare hands, and to wash and use separate tea tumblers at neighbourhood tea stalls, all because due to their caste status they are deemed polluting and therefore 'untouchable'. Any attempt to defy the social order is met with violence or economic retaliation.[85]

Most SC's in rural areas live in segregated colonies, away from the caste Hindus.[86] As part of village custom, SC's are made to render free services in times of death, marriage, or any village function. Most SC's victims of abuse are landless agricultural labourers. As per the 1991 census, 77 per cent of the SC's workforce is in the primary (agricultural) sector of the economy. Those who own land often fall into the category of marginal landowners. Land is the prime asset in rural areas that determines an individual's standard of living and social status. Lack of access to land makes SC's economically vulnerable; their dependency is exploited by privileged and middle caste landlords and allows for many abuses to go unpunished.[87]

No one practices untouchability when it comes to sex. Rape is a common phenomenon in rural areas. Women are raped as part of caste-custom or village tradition. SC girls have been forced to have sex with the village landlord. In rural areas, *"women are induced into prostitution (Devadasi system), which forced on them in the name of religion"*.[88] The prevalence of rape in villages contributes to the greater incidence of child marriage in those areas. Early marriage between the ages of ten years and sixteen years persists in large part because of SC girls' vulnerability to sexual assault by privileged-caste men; once a girl is raped, she becomes unmarriageable. An early marriage also gives parents greater control over the caste into which their children are married.[89]

SC women are also raped as a form of retaliation. Women of SC's and ST's are raped as part of an effort by privileged caste leaders to suppress movements to demand payment of minimum wages, to settle sharecropping disputes, or to reclaim lost land. They are raped by members of the privileged caste, by landlords, and by the police in pursuit of their male relatives. SC women face multiple burdens of caste, class, and gender. SC girls have been forced to become prostitutes for privileged caste patrons and village priests. Sexual abuse and other forms of violence against women are used by landlords and the police to inflict political *'lessons'* and crush dissent within the community.[90]

Table 1.1 Incidence of Crime against the SCs (Under the SC and ST Prevention of Atrocities Act, 1989)

Sr. No.	*State/UT*	*No. of cases reported during the year 2002*	*No. of cases reported during the year 2001*
1.	Madhya Pradesh	6,758	4,432
2.	Uttar Pradesh	5,841	9,764
3.	Rajasthan	5,464	5,915
4.	Andhra Pradesh	1,806	2,020
5.	Odisha	1,274	1,277
6.	Karnataka	1,232	1,214
7.	Gujarat	1,167	1,217
8.	Chhattishgarh	920	902
9.	Tamil Nadu	917	828
10.	Bihar	876	693
11.	Maharashtra	812	797
12.	Kerala	469	499
13.	Jharkhand*	93	155
14.	Uttarakhand	78	132
15.	Haryana	63	68
16.	Punjab	60	56
17.	West Bengal	27	10
18.	Delhi	17	17
19.	Himachal Pradesh	14	17
20.	Goa	2	1
21.	Daman & Diu	2	0
22.	Andaman & Nicobar Islands	1	1
23.	Dadra & Nagar Haveli	1	5
	India	**27,894**	**30,022**

Source: Annual Report on the Scheduled Castes and Scheduled Tribes (Prevention of Atrocities) Act, 1989 for the Year 2002.

Table 1.2: Incidence of Crime against SC's during 1998 to 2001[91]

Crime Head	*1998*	*1999*	*2000*	*2001*
Murder	516	506	526	763
Rape	923	1000	1083	1136
Kidnaping and Abduction	253	228	268	400
Dacoity	49	36	38	41
Robbery	150	109	108	133
Arson	346	337	290	354
Hurt	3809	3241	3497	4547
Crime Against Protection of Civil Rights	724	678	672	633
Crime under POA Act	7443	7301	7386	13113
Others	11425	11657	11587	12201
Total	**25638**	**25093**	**25455**	**33501**

Source: Crime Record of India, National Crime Record Bureau, Ministry of Home Affairs, Government of India, New Delhi, 2000, 2001, 2002, 2003.

Table 1.3: Cases Registered under the PCR Act in 2002

Sr. No.	*State/UT*	*Number of Cases Registered during the Year 2002*	*Per-centage*
1.	Andhra Pradesh	343	65.21
2.	Karnataka	101	19.20
3.	Maharashtra	41	07.80
4.	Puducherry	18	03.42
5.	Madhya Pradesh	07	01.33
6.	Odisha	07	01.33
7.	Himachal Pradesh	03	00.57
8.	Jharkhand	02	00.38
9.	Tamil Nadu	02	00.38
10.	Rajasthan	01	00.19
11.	Delhi	01	00.19
	India	**526**	**100**

Source: Annual Report on the Protection of Civil Rights Act, 1955 for the Year 2002 (Twenty Second Report), Government of India, Ministry of Social Justice and Empowerment.

Due to huge discrimination and exclusion in the social strata and religion Dalits over a period of time attracted to the non-Hindu religions. Buddhism attracted many untouchables because it practised no caste and no untouchability.[92] The Buddhists rejected the authority of the Vedas and condemned blood sacrifice. The egalitarian outlook was viewed with great alarm by the brahminical writings of the time of Yuga Purana, Mahabharata, Patanjali Bhasya, Bana, Manu and others. In spite of the Brahminic elimination of the Buddhism from India, the aspiration of the SC's for an egalitarian faith did not end[93]. The Neo Buddhist movement started from Nagpur in 1956 with Dr B.R. Ambedkar and ten lakhs of his followers' becomes Buddhist must be understood in the light of this background.[94] The quest continues equally into other egalitarian faiths like Kabir Panth, Nanak Panth, etc. Kabir made a great impact on the religious pursuit of the untouchables.[95]

Kabir, while powerfully appealing to the untouchables, equally influenced Sur Das, Tulsi Das and Guru Nanak. The untouchables as a result joined the Kabir Panth and Nanak Panth in great numbers. Another significant impact of the monotheistic bhakti movement among the untouchables was initiated by Jagjivan Das of Lucknow, who was himself initiated by a Fakir. The movement, Satnami, as it was later called, euphorised monotheism with the abolition of all symbolism and castes, though later symbols and castes made partial re-entry.[96] The above monotheistic pietistic egalitarian faiths in a personal god and brotherhood of classless believers are close to the Christian faith.[97] Thus, the untouchable slaves in India, who are non-Aryan by race and religion have in the past 2500 years, voluntarily chosen several egalitarian faiths, that gave them religious and social satisfaction.[98] Under the Indian Constitution caste discrimination and the practice of untouchability were made a criminal offence. However, many thought that caste was an outdated social institution which would wither away has been disappointed. Instead it has remained an important factor in the Indian political system even today.

Notes

1. Christophe Jaffrelot, 2009. Dr Ambedkar's Strategies Against Untouchability and the Caste System, Indian Institute of Dalit Studies, Vol. III, No. 04, New Delhi, pp. 2-16.

2. Generally 'Varna' means colour but in Indian context it is caste.
3. See in details in Vidhu Verma, 2007. Caste and Caste Systems, Varna and Jati: An Overview, Encyclopedia of Women in World History, Oxford University Press, New York.
4. See details in Kumar, Vivek. 2010. 'Teaching Caste and the Hindu Social Order: Dalits in Indian Sociology' in Maitrayee Chaudhuri (eds.), Sociology in India: Intellectual and Institutional Practices, New Delhi: Rawat Publications.
5. Vivek, Kumar, 2005. 'Understanding the Politics of Reservation', Economic and Political Weekly, Vol. XL, No. 9, February 26-March 4, Mumbai, pp. 803-806.
6. See details From Millions to Fractions, Chapter 20, Dr Babasaheb Ambedkar writings and speeches: Vol. 2.
7. Chunnu, Prasad, 2008. Political Economy and Social Exclusion: A Case of Scheduled Castes in Arunachal Pradesh, South India, Journal of Social Sciences, Vol. VI, No. 2, December, pp. 47-58.
8. James Massey, 1997. Down Trodden - The Struggle of India's Dalits for Identity, Solidarity and Liberation, WCC Publication, Geneva, p. 3.
9. John Campbell Oman, 2003. Religious Festivals and Caste System in India, Khana Publishers, New Delhi, p. 42.
10. Rajani Kothari, 1993. Caste in Indian Politics, Oriental Longman Publication, Delhi, 1954 and Baldev Raj Nayar, "Religion and Caste in the Punjab: Sidhwan Bet Constituency", in Myron Weiner and Rajni Kothari (ed.), Indian Voting Behaviour-Studies of the 1962 General Elections, Firma K.L. Mukhopadhayay, Calcutta, 1965.
11. See details in From millions to Fractions, Chapter 20, Dr Babasaheb Ambedkar writings and speeches: Vol. 2.
12. Gail Omvedt, 1995. Dalit Visions : The Anti-Caste Movements and the Construction of an Indian Identity, Oriental Longman, New Delhi, p. 77.
13. Uma Chakravarti, Conceptualising Brahmanical Patriarchy in Early India: Gender, Caste, Class and State, Economic and Political Weekly, Vol. 28, No. 14 (April 3, 1993), pp. 579-585.
14. *Bhagavad-Gita*, 3:35.
15. *Bhagavad-Gita*, 4:13.
16. Bhag*avad-Gita,* 18:47.
17. *Ramayana,* 7:88-89.

18. Hari Prasad Shastri, 1970. The Ramayana of Valmiki, Shanti Sadan, London, 3, pp. 579-85.

19. M.A. Al-Bakhit, L. Bazin, S.M. Cissoko, 2000 (ed.). History of Humanity: From the Seventeenth to Sixteenth Century, Vol. IV, Routledge, UNESCO, pp. 142-145 and George Bühler, translator, The Laws of Manu, (Sacred Books of the East, Vol. 25), http://www.sacred-texts.com/hin/manu/manu01.htm,

20. Nalini, Sinha, 2011. Manu: Social Laws in an edited book by M.P. Singh and Himansu Roy, Indian Political Thought; Themes and Thinkers, Delhi: Pearson, pp. 18-29.

21. For more detail see http://anthro.palomar.edu/status/stat_2.htm

22. Christophe Jaffrelot, 2009. Dr Ambedkar's Strategies Against Untouchability and the Caste System, Indian Institute of Dalit Studies, Vol. III, No. 4, New Delhi, pp. 2-16.

23. Ketkar, History of Caste in India, p. 15.

24. Letter to His Holiness Pope Francis, Vatican, Rome, Italy, Mission of the Church and Dalit Catholic Empowerment, Rev. Dr Fr. S. Lourduswamy, Former Secretary, National CBCI committee for SC/ST http://www.vodintl.org.uk/article/Indian% 20Bishops %20 Memorandum% 20to%20Vatican% 20February%201013.pdf

25. Rig-Veda. X 90.12.

26. Griffith Ralph, The Hymns of Rig-Veda, p. 603.

27. Letter to His Holiness Pope Francis, Vatican, Rome, Italy, Mission of the Church and Dalit Catholic Empowerment, Rev. Dr Fr. S. Lourduswamy, Former Secretary, National CBCI committee for SC/ST http://www.vodintl.org.uk/article/Indian%20 Bishops % 20Memorandum% 20to%20Vatican% 20February% 201013.pdf

28. Himansu Charan Sadangi, 2008. Dalits: The Down Trodden of India, Isha Books, Delhi, pp. 46-47.

29. See detail in Bhagawat Gita - Lord Krihna.

30. *Ibid.*

31. http://www.Dalitchristians.com/Html/Dalit_and_caste.htm

32. See more details of book by S. Akhilesh, 2013. Social Change and Development in India, Gayatri Publication, Rewa, Madhya Pradesh.

33. Dalit is a Marathi word which means a broken or scattered people who are landless or without basic human rights.

34. The word 'Harijan' is coined by Mohan Das Karamchand Gandhi (Mahatma Gandhi).

35. See details in Joan V. Bondurant, 1973. Harijan: Collected Issues of Gandhi's Journal, 1933-1955 (19 Volumes) Garland Publication, New York.
36. Leela Visaria, 'The Harijans' Worsening Plight', Economics and Political Weekly, Vol. IX, No. 5, Feb., 1979.
37. Constitution of India (http://lawmin.nic.in/coi/coiason 29july08.pdf (See more details in The Constitution of India, Government of India, Ministry of Law and Justice)
38. Eleanor Zelliot, 1992. 'From Untouchable to Dalit- Essay on the Ambedkar Movement, Manohar Publications, New Delhi, p. 268.
39. See more details on http://www.Dalitsolidarity.org/Dalits-and-untoucchability.html
40. Niraj, Kumar, 2011. Jothiba Phule: Social Justice in an edited book by M.P. Singh and Himansu Roy, Indian Political Thought; Themes and Thinkers, Delhi: Pearson, pp. 70-92.
41. Ghanshyam, Shah, 2001. 'Dalit Movement and Search for Identify'.in Ghanshyam Shah (ed.), Dalit Identity and Politics, Sage Publication, New Delhi, p. 96.
42. See more details on http://www.Dalitchristians.com/html/Dalitmeaning.htm
43. See more in Untouchability 97, 100, 112, 117–20, 124, 128–32, 189
44. Chunnu, Prasad, 2009. Dalits Struggle for Democratic Space: Bahujan Samaj Party and the Democratisation of Indian Politics", in an edited book by Vivek Kumar, G. Stanley, Jaya Kumar and Tenepali Hari in The Dynamics of Change and Community in the Era of Globalisation: Voices of the Margins, Sunrise Publications, New Delhi, pp. 336-367.
45. Gail Omvedt, 1995. Dalit Visions: The Anti-Caste Movements and the Construction of an Indian Identity, Oriental Longman, New Delhi, p. 77. Also see details in Sukhadeo Thorat and Nidhi Sadana Sabharwal, 2006. Rural Non-Farm Employment of the Scheduled Castes - A Comparative Study, Indian Institute of Dalit Studies, Vol. I, No. 05, New Delhi, pp. 2-31.
46. http://www.in.one.un.org/task-teams/scheduled-castes-and-scheduled-tribes
47. http://www.persmin.nic.in/DOPT/Publication/Handbook OnPersonnelOfficers/ch-11.pdf
48. Ghanshyam, Shah, 2001. 'Dalit Movement and Search for Identify'. in Ghanshyam Shah (ed.), Dalit Identity and Politics, Sage Publications, New Delhi, p. 96.

49. Sukhadeo Thorat and Nidhi Sadana Sabharwal, 2006. Rural Non-Farm Employment of the Scheduled Castes - A Comparative Study, Indian Institute of Dalit Studies, Vol. I, No. 5, New Delhi, pp. 2-31.
50. The Govt. of India (Scheduled Castes) Order, 1936. http://www.anagrasar kalyan.gov.in/compendium/part-1_page9-24.pdf
51. http://www.Dalitchristians.com/Html/faith.htm
52. Himaṇsu Charan Sadangi, 2008. Dalits: The Down Trodden of India, Isha Books, Delhi, pp. 66-198.
53. *Ibid.*
54. *Ibid.*
55. *Ibid.*
56. http://www.saylor.org/site/wp-content/uploads/2011/09/HIST101-Subunit-3.1.2-Aryan-Society-and-Religion-Final.pdf
57. Himansu Charan Sadangi, 2008. Dalits: The Down Trodden of India, Isha Books, Delhi, pp. 60-67.
58. See for details in Romila, Thapar, 2000, ed. India another Millennium, New Delhi: Penguin-Viking.
59. *Ibid.*
60. Himansu Charan Sadangi, 2008. Dalits: The Down Trodden of India, Isha Books, Delhi, pp. 60-67.
61. Sukta 90 in Book X of the Rig Veda tells the story of the myth of creation. It describes the sacrifice of the Purusha (Primeval Man), from whose body the four varnas and the entire universe emerged. When (the gods) divided the Purusha, his mouth became Brahmin, his arms Kshatriya, his thighs Vaishya and Shudra sprang from his feet. See Wendy Doniger (translation, 2005). Some scholars believe that Sukta is a latter-day interpolation into the Rig Veda.
62. See details in Mumtaj Ali Khan, 1980. Scheduled Castes and their Status in India, Uppal Publishing House, New Delhi.
63. *www.Dalitchristians.com/Html/Dalit_and_caste.htm*
64. 6th and 10th Mandala
65. See Chandogya Upanisad, Khanda 10, verse 7.
66. Himansu Charan Sadangi, 2008. Dalits: The Down Trodden of India, Isha Books, Delhi, pp. 60-67.
67. http://www.eaglespace.com/spirit/gita_castesystem.php
68. R.S. Sharma, 1990. Sudras in Ancient India: A Social History of the Lower Order Down, Motilal Banarsidas Publication, Delhi, pp. 191-203.

69. Sanjay, Paswan and Paramanshi, Jaideva, 2003. Encyclopaedia of Dalits in India, Vol. 13, Delhi: Kalpaz Publications, pp. 231-278.
70. See details in Surinder S. Jodhka, 2012. Caste; Oxford India Short Introductions, Oxford University Press, New Delhi.
71. Constitution of India (http://lawmin.nic.in/coi/coiason 29july08.pdf (See more details in The Constitution of India, Government of India, Ministry of Law and Justice).
72. *Ibid.*
73. Constitution of India (http://lawmin.nic.in/coi/coiason 29july08.pdf (See more details in The Constitution of India, Government of India, Ministry of Law and Justice.
74. See details in Sukhadeo Thorat and Narender Kumar, 2008, ed. In Search of Inclusive Policy: Addressing Graded Inequality, IIDS and Rawat Publications, Jaipur.
75. See detail report on Millennium Development Goals and Dalits A Status Report April 2006 National Conference of Dalit Organisations (NACDOR).
76. Satyanarayana, A. "Dalits and Privileged Castes: Essays in Social History", p. 45.
77. http://www.Dalitchristians.com/html/demands.htm
78. See more in The Hindu, Dalit Christians Neglected, May 30, 2013.
79. See details in Valerain, Rodrigues, 2001 "Caste among Muslims and Christians in India", One India One People, August.
80. *Ibid.*
81. Condition of the Untouchables or the Dalits (http://www.dalitchristians.com/html/condition.htm)
82. John, C.B. Webster, 2001. The Dalit Situation in India Today, Spring, pp. 15-17.
83. See details in Kumar, Narender and Rai, Manoj. 2006. Dalit Leadership in Panchayats: A Comparative Study of Four States, Jaipur: Rawat Publications.
84. http://dspace.africaportal.org /jspui/bitstream/123456789/18960/11/Broken% 20People%20Caste%20Violence% 20Against % 20Indias%20 Untouchables%20I%20Summary.pdf?1
85. Broken People, p. 23.
86. See details in Thorat, Sukhadeo and Narender Kumar (ed.). 2008. In Search of Inclusive Policy: Addressing Graded Inequality, Jaipur: Rawat Publications.

87. Sunil Kumar Mishra, 2001. Poverty and Economic Change in Kalahandi. Orissa: The Unfinished Agenda and New Challenges, Journal of Social and Economic Development July - Dec., pp. 246-265
88. See in details in Vidhu Verma, 2007. Caste and Caste Systems, Varna and Jati: An Overview, Encyclopaedia of Women in World History, Oxford University Press, New York.
89. *Ibid.*
90. Human Rights Watch, Broken People: Caste Violence Against India's "Untouchables", 1 April 1999, available at: http://www.refworld.org/docid/3ae6a83f0.
91. Prakash, Louis, 2007. Caste-Based Discrimination and Atrocities on Dalit Christians and the Need for Reservations, Working Paper Series, Indian Institute of Dalit Studies, Vol. II, No. 4, New Delhi, p. 7
92. Himansu Charan Sadangi, 2008. Dalits: The Down Trodden of India, ISHA Books Publication, Delhi, p. 67.
93. Valerain, Rodrigues, 1994. "Between Tradition and Modernity: The Gandhi-Ambedkar Debate," in A.K.Narain, and D.C. Ahir, eds., Dr Ambedkar, Buddhism and Social Change, Delhi, B.R. Publishing, 137-162.
94. A.K. Narain and D.C. Ahir, eds., 1994. Dr Ambedkar, Buddhism and Social Change, Delhi, B.R. Publishing, pp. 137-162.
95. Valerain, Rodrigues, 2011. "Ambedkar on Modernity and Religion", Voices for Equity: Minority and Majority in South Asia, RINDAS International Symposium Series, Ryukoku University, The Centre for the Study of Contemporary India, pp. 3-18.
96. Christophe Jaffrelot, 2009. Dr Ambedkar's Strategies Against Untouchability and the Caste System, Indian Institute of Dalit Studies, Vol. III, No. 04, New Delhi, pp. 2-16.
97. Prakash, Louis, 2007. Caste-Based Discrimination and Atrocities on Dalit Christians and the Need for Reservations, Working Paper Series, Indian Institute of Dalit Studies, Vol. II, No. 4, New Delhi, pp. 4-40.
98. Vidhu Verma, 2010. Reinterpreting Buddhism: Ambedkar on the Politics of Social Action. EPW, Vol. XLV, No. 49, December 4, pp. 56-65.

2

Scheduled Castes of India: An Overview

Government of India released the first set of final data on August 2013 from the population enumeration (Census, 2011) which held in February 2011.[1] It also called the Primary Census Abstract. It pegs the population of Scheduled Castes at 16.6 per cent. The highest SC population, 31.9 per cent of the state's total number, is in Punjab. Lakshadweep has the highest proportion of STs at 94.8 per cent. Besides the SC figures, the Census data pegs the work participation rate at 39.8 per cent. More than 60 per cent of the population does not participate in any economic activity as per the 2011 census record. The social groups are among the most subordinate and poorest in India. The deprivation of these groups is associated with the historical processes of economic and social exclusion and discrimination based on caste.[2]

The total schedules castes population returned in census 2011 is 20,13,78,086. Out of this 15,38,50,562 are in rural areas and 4,75,27,524 in urban areas. In terms of proportion, the scheduled catses population constitute 16.6 per cent of the total population. The proportion during the last census was 16.2 per cent. There has thus been an increase of 20.8 per cent during the last decades. The highest proportion of scheduled castes has been recorded in Punjab (31.9 per cent) and the lowest in Mizoram (0.1 per cent) in 2011 census. The literacy rate in person of the scheduled castes population is 66.1 per cent as compare to 54.7 per cent in 2001 census report. The literacy rate according to 2011 census for rural is 66.8 per cent and for urban it is 76.2 per cent. The male literacy rate is 75.2 per cent whreas females is 56.5 per cent. The rural male literacy is 72.6 per cent and urban is 83.3 per cent whereas the female rural literacy rate is 52.6 per cent and urban is 68.6 per cent.[3]

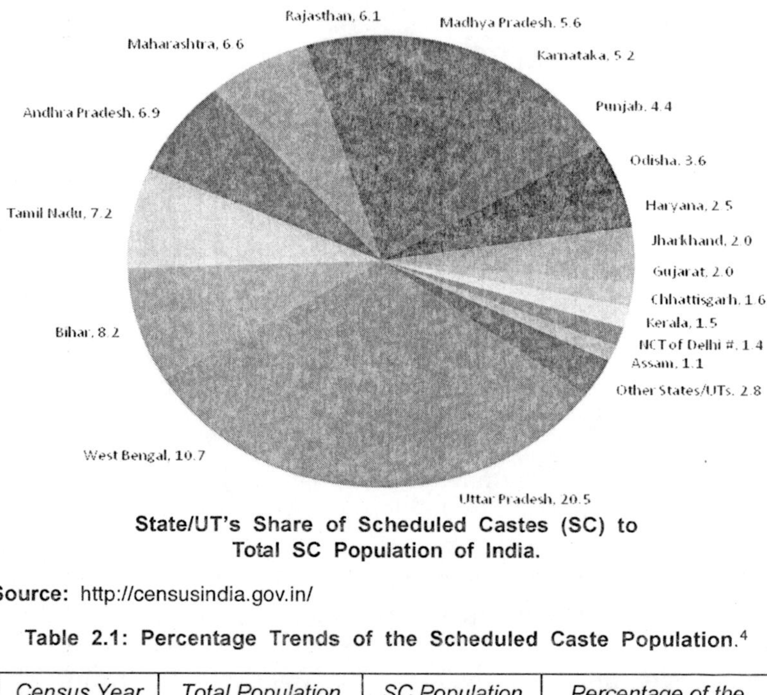

State/UT's Share of Scheduled Castes (SC) to Total SC Population of India.

Source: http://censusindia.gov.in/

Table 2.1: Percentage Trends of the Scheduled Caste Population.[4]

Census Year	*Total Population (in millions)*	*SC Population (in million)*	*Percentage of the SC Population to theTtotal Population*
1961	439.2	64.4	14.7
1971	547.9	80.0	14.6
1981	665.3	104.8	15.7
1991	838.6	138.2	16.5
2001	128.6	166.6	16.2

Source: Primary Census Abstract, Office of the Registrar General, New Delhi, 1961 to 2011.

Table 2.2: Enrolment among School Going Scheduled Caste and Scheduled Tribe Population in States/UTs: 2008-09 (Percentage)[5]

State/Union Territory	*Primary*		*Middle*	
	SC	*ST*	*SC*	*ST*
A & N Islands	0.08	7.10	0.01	7.81
Andhra Pradesh	18.72	10.73	18.36	7.51
Arunachal Pradesh	0.74	77.30	0.67	73.80
Assam	9.31	14.61	10.82	16.45
Bihar	18.52	2.44	13.53	1.55
Chandigarh	8.59	0.12	10.42	0.09
Chhattisgarh	14.98	33.85	14.66	29.11
Dadra & Nagar Haveli	1.7	70.96	2.37	68.56
Daman & Diu	4.0	11.85	5.20	12.36
Delhi	11.02	0.44	10.49	0.32
Goa	2.68	8.51	2.23	9.60
Gujarat	7.16	19.54	7.74	16.50
Haryana	29.37	0.16	26.16	0.16
Himachal Pradesh	28.57	5.63	27.23	5.80
Jammu & Kashmir	8.52	15.81	8.82	11.35
Jharkhand	15.36	31.74	12.99	27.15
Karnataka	19.59	8.09	18.34	7.54
Kerala	11.57	2.42	11.26	1.98
Lakshadweep	0.01	99.23	0.03	99.55
Madhya Pradesh	17.26	23.53	17.56	18.72
Maharashtra	14.79	12.76	14.56	9.47
Manipur	3.20	46.48	3.32	36.62
Meghalaya	1.15	92.53	1.32	90.15
Mizoram	0.47	98.69	0.21	98.96
Nagaland	0.09	95.13	0.05	95.91
Odisha	19.89	29.92	19.65	19.45
Puducherry	18.67	0.15	19.25	0.24
Punjab	50.57	0.14	43.04	0.19
Rajasthan	20.04	15.97	17.98	12.98
Sikkim	7.53	37.45	6.25	36.81
Tamil Nadu	24.42	1.91	24.68	1.71
Tripura	18.99	42.97	22.18	32.58
Uttar Pradesh	27.07	0.61	26.54	0.55
Uttarakhand	26.78	3.30	24.75	3.79
West Bengal	27.16	6.74	27.84	5.25
All India	**19.94**	**11.68**	**19.18**	**9.41**

Source: Elementary Education in India (2008-09); DISE, NUEPA and Ministry of Human Resource Development.

Table 2.3: Literacy Rate by Sex and Residence- India/State/ Union Territory: Census 2011 (Provisional)

Sr No.	India/State/ Union Territory	Literacy Rate (%) (Persons)			Literacy Rate (%) (Males)			Literacy Rate (%) (Females)		
		Total	Rural	Urban	Total	Rural	Urban	Total	Rural	Urban
	States	74.04	68.91	84.98	82.14	78.57	89.67	65.46	58.75	79.92
1.	ANDHRA PRADESH	67.66	61.14	80.54	75.56	70.24	85.99	59.74	52.05	75.02
2.	**ARUNACHAL PRADESH**	**66.95**	**61.59**	**84.57**	**73.69**	**68.79**	**89.45**	**59.57**	**53.78**	**79.04**
3.	**ASSAM**	**73.18**	**70.44**	**88.88**	**78.81**	**76.51**	**91.84**	**67.27**	**64.09**	**85.71**
4.	BIHAR	63.82	61.83	78.75	73.39	71.90	84.42	53.33	50.82	72.36
5.	CHHATTISGARH	71.04	66.76	84.79	81.45	78.20	91.63	60.59	55.40	77.65
6.	GOA	87.40	84.26	89.31	92.81	91.71	93.47	81.84	76.84	84.96
7.	GUJARAT	79.31	73.00	87.58	87.23	83.10	92.44	70.73	62.41	82.08
8.	HARYANA	76.64	72.74	83.83	85.38	83.20	89.37	66.77	60.97	77.51
9.	HIMACHAL PRADESH	83.78	82.91	91.39	90.83	90.48	93.72	76.60	75.33	88.66
10.	JAMMU & KASHMIR	68.74	64.97	78.19	78.26	75.51	84.90	58.01	53.36	70.19
11.	JHARKHAND	67.63	62.40	83.30	78.45	74.57	89.78	56.21	49.75	76.17
12.	KARNATAKA	75.60	68.86	86.21	82.85	77.92	90.54	68.13	59.60	81.71
13.	KERALA	93.91	92.92	94.99	96.02	95.29	96.83	91.98	90.74	93.33
14.	MADHYA PRADESH	70.63	65.29	84.09	80.53	76.64	90.24	60.02	53.20	77.39
15.	MAHARASHTRA	82.91	77.09	89.84	89.82	86.39	93.79	75.48	67.38	85.44
16.	**MANIPUR**	**79.85**	**77.15**	**85.98**	**86.49**	**84.14**	**92.05**	**73.17**	**69.95**	**80.21**
17.	**MEGHALAYA**	**75.48**	**71.15**	**91.33**	**77.17**	**72.83**	**93.17**	**73.78**	**69.45**	**89.49**
18.	**MIZORAM**	**91.58**	**84.31**	**98.10**	**93.72**	**88.35**	**98.67**	**89.40**	**80.04**	**97.54**
19.	**NAGALAND**	**80.11**	**75.86**	**90.21**	**83.29**	**79.49**	**92.11**	**76.69**	**72.01**	**88.10**
20.	ODISHA	73.45	70.78	86.45	82.40	80.41	91.83	64.36	61.10	80.70
21.	PUNJAB	76.68	72.45	83.70	81.48	77.92	87.28	71.34	66.47	79.62
22.	RAJASTHAN	67.06	62.34	80.73	80.51	77.49	89.16	52.66	46.25	71.53
23.	**SIKKIM**	**82.20**	**79.82**	**89.26**	**87.29**	**85.42**	**92.94**	**76.43**	**73.42**	**85.19**
24.	TAMIL NADU	80.33	73.80	87.24	86.81	82.08	91.82	73.86	65.52	82.67
25.	**TRIPURA**	**87.75**	**85.58**	**93.61**	**92.18**	**90.86**	**95.80**	**83.15**	**80.06**	**91.38**
26.	UTTAR PRADESH	69.72	67.55	77.01	79.24	78.48	81.75	59.26	55.61	71.68
27.	UTTARAKHAND	79.63	77.11	85.20	88.33	87.63	89.78	70.70	66.79	80.02
28.	WEST BENGAL	77.08	72.97	85.54	82.67	79.51	89.15	71.16	66.08	81.70
	Union Territories									
1.	A & N ISLANDS	86.27	84.39	89.60	90.11	88.53	92.96	81.84	79.58	85.79
2.	CHANDIGARH	86.43	81.69	86.56	90.54	86.68	90.65	81.38	74.17	81.55
3.	DADRA & NAGAR HAVELI	77.65	65.89	90.86	86.46	78.18	94.81	65.93	51.36	84.86
4.	DAMAN & DIU	87.07	81.51	88.87	91.48	89.71	91.95	79.59	71.97	82.94
5.	LAKSHADWEEP	92.28	91.92	92.38	96.11	95.06	96.40	88.25	88.66	88.13
6.	NCT of DELHI	86.34	82.67	86.43	91.03	90.04	91.05	80.93	74.03	81.10
7.	PUDUCHERRY	86.55	81.02	89.09	92.12	88.49	93.80	81.22	73.82	84.60

Source: Census of India-2011, http://censusindia.gov.in/

Table 2.4: State-wise Dropout Rates of Scheduled Caste (SC) Students in Classes I-V, I-VIII and I-X in India (2005-2006)

States/UTs	*Classes I-V*			*Classes I-VIII*			*Classes I-X*		
	Boys	*Girls*	*Total*	*Boys*	*Girls*	*Total*	*Boys*	*Girls*	*Total*
Andhra Pradesh	25.12	25.86	25.49	62.63	66.47	64.51	68.41	72.20	70.24
Arunachal Pradesh	22.58	42.31	31.58	29.63	46.15	37.74	39.39	42.31	40.68
Assam	58.81	52.28	55.88	70.38	70.50	70.43	73.78	70.14	72.15
Bihar	55.52	55.84	55.64	79.86	80.43	80.06	89.65	92.05	90.52
Chhattisgarh*	25.00	24.77	24.89	-	-	-	-	-	-
Goa	4.02	17.02	10.33	49.32	56.15	52.48	80.00	73.46	76.85
Gujarat	24.14	25.82	24.93	36.40	54.47	44.82	58.34	69.12	63.25
Haryana	7.32	7.80	7.55	27.50	37.33	32.16	60.96	69.28	64.85
Himachal Pradesh	14.82	16.08	15.44	23.95	29.29	26.61	47.64	53.00	50.28
Jammu & Kashmir	-	.	-	12.03	23.99	17.70	56.72	54.66	55.79
Jharkhand*	46.66	51.88	48.83	-	-	-	-	-	-
Karnataka	16.87	22.13	19.47	46.68	54.08	50.26	64.72	67.17	65.87
Kerala	-5.35	-1.89	-3.66	-12.32	-3.87	-8.17	2^51	11.82	16.31
Madhya Pradesh	-0.23	-3.79	-1.85	36.67	51.51	43.28	62.13	71.05	65.92
Maharashtra	12.82	15.41	14.07	41.05	28.83	35.16	53.75	54.88	54.29
Manipur	32.89	21.26	27.26	-15.76	-8.54	-12.28	-3.42	-1.43	-2.47
Meghalaya	49.73	39.74	45.19	65.21	69.14	67.16	73.87	74.63	74.24
Mizoram	5.26	0.00	2.66	-	-	-	-	-	-
Nagaland	-	-	-	-	-	-	-	-	-
Odisha	51.21	42.97	47.87	67.18	68.02	67.55	70.23	73.92	71.87
Punjab	32.02	31.29	31.67	50.65	50.87	50.75	64.51	67.16	65.75
Rajasthan	52.34	52.41	52.37	59.43	71.28	64.34	79.12	88.05	82.74
Sikkim	14.58	5.17	10.02	72.50	59.44	66.69.	86.58	82.91	84.95
Tamil Nadu	1.59	-47.72	-17.42	25.65	11.84	19.49	49.43	43.11	46.50
Tripura	14.13	10.54	12.39	50.42	19.20	35.23	72.89	77.04	74.91
Uttar Pradesh	49.27	55.12	51.35	50.51	66.93	56.70	64.00	86.80	72.56
Uttarakhand	36.44	40.32	38.37	-					-
West Bengal	43.43	50.95	47.05	70.18	73.69	71.77	79.40	82.12	54.66
Andaman & Nicobar Islands	-	-		-	-	-	-		-
Chandigarh	-9.79	-6.77	-8.38	52.31	50.49	51.46	76.51	70.17	73.56
Dadra & Nagar Haveli	9.46	18.46	13.67	6.06	25.42	15.20	29.31	22.64	26.13
Daman & Diu	-9.52	-3.57	-6.72	-29.85	1.72	-15.20	-13.43	0.00	-6.98
Delhi	19.44	16.84	18.27	41.98	48.91	45.77	27.51	20.22	23.90
Lakshadweep	-	-		-	-	-	-	-	-
Puducherry	-2.13	-4.00	-3.04	-18.81	-15.32	-17.04	20.88	17.18	19.05
India	**37.03**	**35.36**	**36.31**	**54.60**	**58.37**	**56.24**	**68.42**	**73.42**	**70.57**

Note: *Dropout rates are shown combined with the respective parent state. : Zero indicates that there is no Drop-Out.

Source: Ministry of Human Resource Development, Govt. of India.

Table 2.5: SC Students in Academic and Professional Courses.[6]

Courses	*SC*
M.A	55,182
M.Sc.	15,328
M.Com	8,956
B.Ed/BT	15,360
Polytechnic	43,511
Engineering	38,935
Medical	16,972
Ph.D	3,133
Total	**1,97,377**

Source: Select Educational Statistics, 2001, 2002. Planning Monitoring and Statistics Division, Ministry of Human Resource and Development, Government of India, New Delhi, 2003, pp. 43-55.

Table 2.6: Households

Indicator	*Absolute*		*Percentage*	
	2001	*2011*	*2001*	*2011*
All Households				
Total	19,35,79,954	24,94,54,252	100.0	100.0
Rural	13,77,73,323	16,85,65,486	100.0	100.0
Urban	5,58,06,631	8,08,88,766	100.0	100.0
Scheduled Caste				
Total	3,25,26,101	4,16,94,816	16.8	16.7
Rural	2,59,83,792	3,18,03,728	18.9	18.9
Urban	65,42,309	98,91,088	11.7	12.2

Source: Primary Census Abstract for Total Population, Scheduled Castes, 2011, Office of the Registrar General and Census Commissioner, India, http://censusindia.gov.in/

Table 2.7: Scheduled Caste Population

Indicator	*Absolute*		*Percentage*		*Growth rate (2001-11)*
	2001	*2011*	*2001*	*2011*	
Total Population					
Total	1,02,86,10,328	1,21,05,69,573	100.0	100.0	17.7
Rural	74,23,02,537	83,34,63,448	100.0	100.0	12.3
Urban	28,63,07,791	37,71,06,125	100.0	100.0	31.7
Scheduled Castes					
Total	16,66,35,700	20,13,78,086	16.2	16.6	20.8
Rural	13,30,10,878	15,38,50,562	17.9	18.5	15.7
Urban	3,36,24,822	4,75,27,524	11.7	12.6	41.3

Source: Primary Census Abstract for Total Population, Scheduled Castes, 2011, Office of the Registrar General and Census Commissioner, India, http://censusindia.gov.in/

The Scheduled Caste households indicated that in 2011 total households is 16.7 per cent as compared to the 2001 household census as about 16.8 per cent. The total rural household is 18.9 per cent and urban is 12.2 per cent in 2011 as compared to rural 18.9 per cent and 11.7 per cent subsequently in 2001. On the other hand the SC population gives different picture when we compare both the 2001 and 2011 census report. The total SC population in 2011 is 16.6 per cent as compare to 2001 in 16.2 per cent with a growth rate of 20.8 per cent. The rural SC population is 18.5 per cent in 2011 and urban is 12.6 per cent. So far the 2001 census is concerned it was 17.9 per cent for rural and 11.7 per cent urban respectively.

Table 2.8: Percentage to Total Population 2011

State/ Union Territory	*Percentage*	*State/Union Territory#*	*Percentage*
Top 5		*Bottom 5*	
Scheduled Castes			
Punjab	31.9	Mizoram	0.1
Himachal Pradesh	25.2	Meghalaya	0.6
West Bengal	23.5	Goa	1.7
Uttar Pradesh	20.7	D & N Haveli	1.8
Haryana	20.2	Daman & Diu	2.5

Source: Primary Census Abstract for Total Population, Scheduled Castes, 2011, Office of the Registrar General and Census Commissioner, India, http://censusindia.gov.in/

Table 2.9: Percentage to Total Population 2011 (Major States)

State/Union Territory	*Percentage*	*State/Union Territory*	*Percentage*
Top 5		*Bottom 5*	
Scheduled Castes			
Punjab	31.9	Gujarat	6.7
West Bengal	23.5	Assam	7.2
Uttar Pradesh	20.7	Jammu & Kashmir	7.4
Haryana	20.2	Kerala	9.1
Tamil Nadu	20.0	Maharashtra	11.8

Major States: States having Population 10 million and above.

Source: Primary Census Abstract for Total Population, Scheduled Castes, 2011, Office of the Registrar General and Census Commissioner, India. http://censusindia.gov.in/

The highest percentage to the total SC population is in the state of Punjab: 31.9 per cent, Himachal Pradesh: 25.2 per cent, West Bengal: 23.5 per cent, Uttar Pradesh: 20.7 per cent and Haryana: 20.2 per cent whereas the less percentage states are Mizoram: 0.1 per cent, Meghalaya: 0.6 per cent, Goa: 1.7 per cent, Dadar and Nagar Haveli: 1.8 per cent and Daman and Diu: 2.5 per cent respectively. On the other hand, the major five states having more than 10 million SC population according to 2011 census is Punjab: 31.9 per cent, West Bengal: 23.5 per cent, Uttar Pradesh: 20.7 per cent, Haryana: 20.2 per cent, Tamil Nadu: 20.0 per cent whereas the less populated states are Gujarat: 6.7 per cent, Assam: 7.2 per cent, Jammu and Kashmir: 7.4 per cent, Kerala: 9.1 per cent and Maharashtra: 11.8 per cent.

Table 2.10: Child Population (0-6 Years)

Indicator	*Absolute*		*Proportion to population*	
	2001	*2011*	*2001*	*2011*
Total Child Population				
Total	16,38,19,614	16,44,78,150	15.9	13.6
Rural	12,63,92,327	12,12,85,762	17.0	14.6
Urban	3,74,27,287	4,31,92,388	13.1	11.5
Scheduled Castes				
Total	2,89,14,095	2,92,00,529	17.4	14.5
Rural	2,39,32,402	2,33,43,549	18.0	15.2
Urban	49,81,693	58,56,980	14.8	12.3

Source: Primary Census Abstract for Total Population, Scheduled Castes, 2011, Office of the Registrar General and Census Commissioner, India, http://censusindia.gov.in/

The total child population from 0-6 years in the year 2011 indicated 13.6 per cent whereas in 2001 it was 15.9 per cent. In 2011, the rural population is 14.6 per cent and the urban is 11.5 per cent whereas in 2001 it was 17.0 per cent for rural and 13.1 per cent for urban. So far the SC population from 0-6 years is concerned; it is 14.5 per cent in 2011 census report as compare to 17.4 per cent in 2001 census report. In 2011, the rural population is 15.2 per cent and the urban population is 12.3 per cent whereas in 2001 the rural population was 18.0 per cent and 14.1 per cent in 2001 census report.

Table 2.11: Sex Ratio and Child Sex Ratio (Females per 1000 Males)

Indicator	*Sex Ratio*		*Child Sex Ratio*	
	2001	*2011*	*2001*	*2011*
Total Population				
Total	933	943	927	919
Rural	946	949	934	923
Urban	900	929	907	905
Scheduled Castes				
Total	936	945	938	933
Rural	939	945	941	936
Urban	923	946	924	922

Source: Primary Census Abstract for Total Population, Scheduled Castes, 2011, Office of the Registrar General and Census Commissioner, India, http://censusindia.gov.in/

The total sex ratio is 943/1000 in 2011 as compare to 933/1000 in 2001. So far the rural sex ratio is concerned it is 949/1000 and urban 929/1000 in 2011 whereas, in 2001 it was 946/1000 in rural and 900/1000 in urban level. So far 2001 census is concerned the child sex ratio in 2011 is 919/1000 as compared to 927/1000 in 2001. The rural child sex ratio in 2011 is 923/1000 and urban is 905/1000 as compared to rural 934/1000 and urban 907/1000 as indicated in 2001 census. So far the SC sex ratio is concerned the total child sex ratio recorded in 2011 is 945/1000 as compared to 936/1000 in 2001. The child sex ratio of the SC

Table 2.12: Sex Ratio

State/ Union Territory	*Sex Ratio*	*State/Union Territory*	*Sex Ratio*
Top 5		*Bottom 5*	
Scheduled Castes			
Kerala	1,057	Mizoram	509
Puducherry	1,056	D & N Haveli	853
Goa	1,015	Chandigarh	872
Andhra Pradesh	1,008	Haryana	887
Tamil Nadu	1,004	NCT of Delhi	889

Source: Primary Census Abstract for Total Population, Scheduled Castes, 2011, Office of the Registrar General and Census Commissioner, India, http://censusindia.gov.in/

is 933/1000 in 2011 but it was 938/1000 in 2001 census. The rural SC population is 945/1000 and urban 946/1000 according to 2011 census whereas it was 939/1000 rural and 923/1000 urban during 2001 census. So far the child sex ratio of SC is concerned the rural population is 936/1000 and urban is 922/1000 in 2011 whereas in 2001 the rural SC child sex ratio was 941/1000 and urban was 924/1000.

The five major states having the highest SC sex ratio in number are Kerala: 1057, Puducherry: 1056, Goa: 1015, Andhra Pradesh: 1008, Tamil Nadu: 1004 and the five major states having lowest SC sex ratio is Mizoram: 509, Dadra and Nagar Haveli: 853, Chandigarh: 872, Haryana: 887 and NCT of Delhi: 889 according to 2011 census report.

The literacy rate among scheduled castes and scheduled tribes remains well below the rest of India's population, but the gap has closed significantly in the last decade. During this period (2001-2011), ST and SC women made the most rapid progress, latest census data reveals. Data released earlier this week shows a 14.6 percentage point increase in literacy among ST and SC women over the decade, compared to a jump of 10 percentage points for non-SC/ST women. The literacy rate of ST men and SC men has jumped by 9.4 and 8.5 percentage points, respectively, compared to just 4.8 percentage points among non-SC/ST men. The pattern of SC and ST women showing a higher increase in literacy holds good across almost all states, and in both rural and urban areas. Of course, the base was very low to start within the case of both women and men in the two communities, compared to the general population.[7]

Table 2.13: Total General Percentage of Literacy Rate among Male and Female

S.No.	*Census Year*	*Total (%)*	*Male (%)*	*Female (%)*
1.	1901	5.35	9.83	0.60
2.	1911	5.92	10.56	1.05
3.	1921	7.16	12.21	1.81
4.	1931	9.50	15.59	2.93
5.	1941	16.10	24.90	7.30
6.	1951	16.67	24.95	9.45
7.	1961	24.02	34.44	12.95
8.	1971	29.45	39.45	18.69
9.	1981	36.23	46.89	24.82
10.	1991	42.84	52.74	32.17
11.	2001	64.83	75.26	53.67
12.	2011	74.04	82.14	65.46

Source: Census of India, 2011, http://censusindia.gov.in/

Table 2.14: Trends in Literacy Rates by Sex in India (per cent)

Particulars	*1981*	*1991*	*2001*	*2011*
Male	56.37	64.13	75.85	82.14
Female	29.75	39.29	54.16	65.46
Total	43.56	52.20	65.38	74.04
Divergence (Male- Female)	26.62	24.84	21.69	16.68

Source: (i) Registrar General of India, Census of India, for relevant years (ii) Socio-Economic Review 2011-2012, Gujarat State, Directorate of Economics and Statistics, Government of Gujarat, Gandhinagar. (iii) http://mpra.ub.uni-muenchen. de/20680

Table 2.15: Literates and Literacy Rate (Persons)

Indicator	*Literates*		*Effective Literacy Rate*	
	2001	*2011*	*2001*	*2011*
Total Population				
Total	56,06,87,797	76,34,98,517	64.8	73.0
Rural	36,17,36,601	48,26,53,540	58.7	67.8
Urban	19,89,51,196	28,08,44,977	79.9	84.1
Scheduled Castes				
Total	7,53,18,285	11,37,59,907	54.7	66.1
Rural	5,58,06,266	8,20,20,232	51.2	62.8
Urban	1,95,12,019	3,17,39,675	68.1	76.2

Source: Primary Census Abstract for Total Population, Scheduled Castes, 2011, Office of the Registrar General and Census Commissioner, India, http://censusindia.gov.in/

The literates and literacy rates is 73.0 per cent in 2011 whereas it was 64.8 per cent in 2001. The rural effective literacy rate is 67.8 per cent and urban is 84.1 per cent according to 2011 census whereas in 2001 it was 58.7 per cent for rural and 79.9 per cent for urban. So far the SC effective literacy rate is concerned the total literate in 2011 is 66.1 per cent whereas it was 54.7 per cent in 2001. The total rural SC literates are 62.8 per cent and urban is 51.2 per cent in 2011 whereas in 2001 the total rural literates were 51.2 per cent and urban 68.1 per cent according to 2001 census report.

Table 2.16: Literacy Rate (Persons)

State/Union Territory	*Literacy rate*	*State/Union Territory*	*Literacy rate*
Top 5		*Bottom 5*	
Scheduled Castes			
Daman & Diu	92.6	Bihar	48.6
Mizoram	92.4	Jharkhand	55.9
Tripura	89.4	Rajasthan	59.7
D & N Haveli	89.4	Uttar Pradesh	60.9
Kerala	88.7	Andhra Pradesh	62.3

Source: Primary Census Abstract for Total Population, Scheduled Castes, 2011, Office of the Registrar General and Census Commissioner, India, http://censusindia.gov.in/

So far the top five states are concerned the highest SC literacy rate according to 2011 census report is Daman and Diu: 92.6 per cent, Mizoram: 92.4 per cent, Tripura: 89.4 per cent, Dadar and Nagar Havelli: 89.4 per cent and Kerala: 88.7 per cent whereas the top five states having lowest SC literacy rate according to 2011 census report is Bihar: 48.6 per cent, Jharkhand: 55.9 per cent, Rajasthan: 59.7 per cent, Uttar Pradesh: 60.9 per cent and Andhra Pradesh: 62.3 per cent respectively.

Table 2.17: Literates and Literacy Rate (Males)

Indicator	*Literates*		*Effective Literacy Rate*	
	2001	*2011*	*2001*	*2011*
Total Population				
Total	33,65,33,716	43,46,83,779	75.3	80.9
Rural	22,34,93,084	28,12,81,531	70.7	77.2
Urban	11,30,40,632	15,34,02,248	86.3	88.8
Scheduled Castes				
Total	4,74,32,887	6,64,76,908	66.6	75.2
Rural	3,58,23,885	4,86,72,140	63.7	72.6
Urban	1,16,09,002	1,78,04,768	77.9	83.3

Source: Primary Census Abstract for Total Population, Scheduled Castes, 2011, Office of the Registrar General and Census Commissioner, India, http://censusindia.gov.in/

The literates and literacy rate of male population in India is 80.9 per cent according to 2011 census whereas it was 75.3 per cent in 2001 census. The rural total literacy rate in 2011 is 77.2 per cent and urban is 88.8 per cent whereas in 2001 the total rural male literacy rate was 70.7 per cent and urban was 86.3 per cent. So far the total male SC literacy rate is concerned it is 72.6 per cent and urban is 83.3 per cent in 2011 census whereas in 2001 it was 63.7 per cent rural and 77.9 per cent urban male literacy rates.

Table 2.18: Literates and Literacy Rate (Females)

Indicator	*Literates*		*Effective Literacy Rate*	
	2001	*2011*	*2001*	*2011*
Total Population				
Total	22,41,54,081	32,88,14,738	53.7	64.6
Rural	13,82,43,517	20,13,72,009	46.1	57.9
Urban	8,59,10,564	12,74,42,729	72.9	79.1
Scheduled Castes				
Total	2,78,85,398	4,72,82,999	41.9	56.5
Rural	1,99,82,381	3,33,48,092	37.8	52.6
Urban	79,03,017	1,39,34,907	57.5	68.6

Source: Primary Census Abstract for Total Population, Scheduled Castes, 2011, Office of the Registrar General and Census Commissioner, India, http://censusindia.gov.in/

The literates and literacy rate of females in India is about 64.6 per cent according to the 2011 census whereas it was 53.7 per cent in 2001 census. The rural total female literacy rate is 57.9 per cent and urban is 79.1 per cent whereas in 2001 it was 46.1 per cent rural and 72.9 per cent urban literacy rate. So far the total female SC literacy rate is concerned it is 56.5 per cent in 2011 whereas in 2001 it was only 41.9 per cent. The total female SC rural literacy rate is 52.6 per cent and 68.6 per cent urban in 2011 census whereas during 2001 rural literacy rate was 37.8 and urban 57.5 per cent subsequently.

Table 2.19: Gender Gap in Literacy Rate

Indicator	*Literacy Rate (Males)*		*Literacy Rate (Females)*		*Gender Gap*	
	2001	*2011*	*2001*	*2011*	*2001*	*2011*
Total Population						
Total	75.3	80.9	53.7	64.6	21.6	16.3
Rural	70.7	77.2	46.1	57.9	24.6	19.3
Urban	86.3	88.8	72.9	79.1	13.4	9.7

contd...

contd...

Indicator	Literacy Rate (Males)		Literacy Rate (Females)		Gender Gap	
	2001	2011	2001	2011	2001	2011
Scheduled Castes						
Total	66.6	75.2	41.9	56.5	24.7	18.7
Rural	63.7	72.6	37.8	52.6	25.9	20.0
Urban	77.9	83.3	57.5	68.6	20.4	14.7

Source: Primary Census Abstract for Total Population, Scheduled Castes, 2011, Office of the Registrar General and Census Commissioner, India, http://censusindia.gov.in/

The gender gap in literacy rate the total male literacy rate is 80.9 per cent as compare to female which is just 64.6 per cent. So far the male and female literacy gender gap is concerned it is 16.3 per cent according to 2011 census report. In 2001, the literacy rate for male was 53.7 per cent and the literacy gender gap was 21.6 per cent. The total rural male literacy rate in 2011 is 77.2 per cent and urban is 88.8 per cent whereas the rural literacy rate for female is 57.9 per cent and urban is 79.1 per cent with a gender gap of rural 19.3 per cent and urban 9.7 per cent. In 2001, the total rural literacy rate for male was 70.7 per cent and urban 86.3 per cent whereas the rural literacy rate for female were 57.9 and urban 79.1 per cent. In the year 2001, the gender gap was 24.6 per cent for rural and 13.4 per cent was for urban respectively.

So far the SC gender gap in literacy rate is concerned the total literacy rate is 75.2 per cent for male and 56.5 per cent for females and the gender gap recorded 18.7 per cent according to 2011 census report. The rural SC male literacy rate according to 2011 is 72.6 per cent and urban 83.3 per cent whereas the SC female rural literacy rate is 52.6 per cent and urban 68.6 per cent. The gender gap between male and female in rural is 20.0 per cent and urban is 14.7 per cent. As compare to 2001 census, the urban SC male literacy rate was 63.7 per cent and urban 77.9 per cent whereas the SC females' rural literacy rate was 37.8 per cent and urban 57.5 per cent respectively. The gender gap between male and female for rural according to 2001 was 25.9 per cent and urban 20.4 per cent.

Table 2.20: Gross Enrolment in Higher Education.[8]

Year	*Gender/Sector*	*Rural*	*Urban*	*Total*
2007-08	Male	13.74	29.81	19.12
	Female	8.36	30.78	15.32
	Total	11.12	30.26	17.31

Source: NSS 64th Round, 2007-08.

Table 2.21: Gross Enrolment Ratio by Social Groups: 2007.[9]

Year 2007-08	*Gender/Social Groups*	*ST*	*SC*	*OBC*	*Others*
Rural	Male	6.25	10.46	13.45	15.81
	Female	3.50	6.00	7.80	9.84
	Total	4.96	8.32	10.73	12.92
Urban	Male	26.61	20.90	25.68	31.79
	Female	24.34	20.26	24.48	33.18
	Total	25.55	20.61	25.13	32.34
Total	Male	9.33	13.36	17.01	21.74
	Female	6.14	9.65	12.37	17.93
	Total	7.74	11.60	14.80	19.93

Source: NSS 64th Round, 2007-08.

Table 2.22: Gross Enrolment Ratio by Religious Groups[10]

Year 2007-08	*Gender/Social Groups*	*Hindu*	*Muslim*	*Chri-stian*	*Sikh*	*Jain*	*Bud-dhist*	*Others*
Rural	Male	14.53	8.43	19.49	9.93	35.66	11.12	6.26
	Female	8.54	5.08	20.89	11.72	15.93	8.88	4.25
	Total	11.64	6.75	20.18	10.79	23.44	9.98	5.23
Urban	Male	33.59	14.83	34.42	28.42	49.24	21.63	16.02
	Female	34.50	11.58	44.32	46.58	74.46	39.38	10.22
	Total	34.00	13.36	39.88	36.45	60.57	30.13	12.54
Total	Male	20.50	11.31	25.30	14.57	47.33	16.27	7.40
	Female	16.08	7.68	31.39	19.50	60.02	22.94	5.19
	Total	18.40	9.56	28.45	16.90	53.44	19.57	6.24

Source: NSS 64th Round, 2007-08.

Table 2.23: Gross Enrolment Ratio across Socio-Religious Groups in 2007-08[11]

Year 2007-08	*Gender*	*ST*	*SC*	*OBC*	*Others*
Hindu	Male	9.01	13.57	18.06	24.11
	Female	5.26	9.07	12.73	19.81
	Total	7.14	11.44	15.53	22.08
Muslim	Male	6.01	14.60	10.53	11.32
	Female	6.82	18.41	7.93	7.58
	Total	6.40	16.42	9.29	9.52
Christian	Male	13.69	15.06	36.31	38.13
	Female	13.25	21.07	40.54	46.18
	Total	13.47	17.84	38.70	42.56
Sikhs	Male	NA	4.28	4.90	21.16
	Female	NA	7.41	14.29	25.19
	Total	NA	5.60	9.95	23.17
Buddhist	Male	3.36	17.92	2.36	4.01
	Female	21.24	25.12	NA	NA
	Total	12.79	21.40	-	-

Source: NSS 64th Round, 2007-08.

Table 2.24: Workers and Work Participation Rate (Persons)

Indicator	*Workers*		*Work Participation Rate*	
	2001	*2011*	*2001*	*2011*
Total Population				
Total	40,22,34,724	48,17,43,311	39.1	39.8
Rural	30,98,35,681	34,85,97,535	41.7	41.8
Urban	9,23,99,043	13,31,45,776	32.3	35.3
Scheduled Caste				
Total	6,73,32,884	8,23,04,605	40.4	40.9
Rural	5,65,26,950	6,52,27,547	42.5	42.4
Urban	1,08,05,934	1,70,77,058	32.1	35.9

Source: Primary Census Abstract for Total Population, Scheduled Castes, 2011, Office of the Registrar General and Census Commissioner, India, http://censusindia.gov.in/

Table 2.25: Work Participation Rate (WPR) (Persons)

State/Union Territory	*WPR*	*State/Union Territory*	*WPR*
Top 5		*Bottom 5*	
Scheduled Castes			
Mizoram	53.4	NCT of Delhi	32.1
Himachal Pradesh	52.1	Daman & Diu	34.3
Andhra Pradesh	50.5	Uttar Pradesh	34.4
Tamil Nadu	49.0	Jammu & Kashmir	34.6
Sikkim	47.6	Haryana	35.1

Source: Primary Census Abstract for Total Population, Scheduled Castes, 2011, Office of the Registrar General and Census Commissioner, India, http://censusindia.gov.in/

Table 2.26: Workers and Work Participation Rate (Males)

Indicator	*Workers*		*Work Participation Rate*	
	2001	*2011*	*2001*	*2011*
Total Population				
Total	27,50,14,476	33,18,65,930	51.7	53.3
Rural	19,87,99,870	22,67,63,068	52.1	53.0
Urban	7,62,14,606	10,51,02,862	50.6	53.8
Scheduled Caste				
Total	4,36,58,975	5,46,19,798	50.7	52.8
Rural	3,53,65,078	4,18,26,734	51.6	52.9
Urban	82,93,897	1,27,93,064	47.4	52.4

Source: Primary Census Abstract for Total Population, Scheduled Castes, 2011, Office of the Registrar General and Census Commissioner, India, http://censusindia.gov.in/

Table 2.27: Workers and Work Participation Rate (Females)

Indicator	*Workers*		*Work Participation Rate*	
	2001	*2011*	*2001*	*2011*
Total Population				
Total	12,72,20,248	14,98,77,381	25.6	25.5
Rural	11,10,35,811	12,18,34,467	30.8	30.0
Urban	1,61,84,437	2,80,42,914	11.9	15.4
Scheduled Caste				
Total	2,36,73,909	2,76,84,807	29.4	28.3
Rural	2,11,61,872	2,34,00,813	32.9	31.3
Urban	25,12,037	42,83,994	15.6	18.5

Source: Primary Census Abstract for Total Population, Scheduled Castes, 2011, Office of the Registrar General and Census Commissioner, India, http://censusindia.gov.in/

Table 2.28: Main Workers

Indicator	*Main Workers*		*Percentage to total workers*	
	2001	*2011*	*2001*	*2011*
Total Population				
Total	31,30,04,983	36,24,46,420	77.8	75.2
Rural	22,91,10,641	24,57,49,270	73.9	70.5
Urban	8,38,94,342	11,66,97,150	90.8	87.6
Scheduled Castes				
Total	4,91,32,343	5,81,83,356	73.0	70.7
Rural	3,99,06,882	4,38,30,622	70.6	67.2
Urban	92,25,461	1,43,52,734	85.4	84.0

Source: Primary Census Abstract for Total Population, Scheduled Castes, 2011, Office of the Registrar General and Census Commissioner, India, http://censusindia.gov.in/

Table 2.29: Marginal Workers

Indicator	*Marginal Workers*		*Percentage to total workers*	
	2001	*2011*	*2001*	*2011*
Total Population				
Total	8,92,29,741	11,92,96,891	22.2	24.8
Rural	8,07,25,040	10,28,48,265	26.1	29.5
Urban	85,04,701	1,64,48,626	9.2	12.4
Scheduled Castes				
Total	1,82,00,541	2,41,21,249	27.0	29.3
Rural	1,66,20,068	2,13,96,925	29.4	32.8
Urban	15,80,473	27,24,324	14.6	16.0

Source: Primary Census Abstract for Total Population, Scheduled Castes, 2011, Office of the Registrar General and Census Commissioner, India, http://censusindia.gov.in/

Table 2.30: Marginal Workers by Period of Work 2011

Indicator	*Marginal Workers*		*Percentage to Marginal Workers*	
	Less than 3 months	*3 to 6 months*	*Less than 3 months*	*3 to 6 months*
Total Population				
Total	2,22,52,784	9,70,44,107	18.7	81.3
Rural	1,98,16,595	8,30,31,670	19.3	80.7
Urban	24,36,189	1,40,12,437	14.8	85.2
Scheduled Castes				
Total	47,07,324	1,94,13,925	19.5	80.5
Rural	42,38,587	1,71,58,338	19.8	80.2
Urban	4,68,737	22,55,587	17.2	82.8

Source: Primary Census Abstract for Total Population, Scheduled Castes, 2011, Office of the Registrar General and Census Commissioner, India, http://censusindia.gov.in/

Table 2.31: Cultivators

Indicator	Cultivators		Percentage to total workers	
	2001	2011	2001	2011
Total Population				
Total	12,73,12,851	11,86,92,640	31.7	24.6
Rural	12,45,34,135	11,49,68,498	40.2	33.0
Urban	27,78,716	37,24,142	3.0	2.8
Scheduled Castes				
Total	1,34,58,018	1,21,44,111	20.0	14.8
Rural	1,32,68,183	1,18,52,590	23.5	18.2
Urban	1,89,835	2,91,521	1.8	1.7

Source: Primary Census Abstract for Total Population, Scheduled Castes, 2011, Office of the Registrar General and Census Commissioner, India, http://censusindia.gov.in/

Table 2.32: Agricultural Labourers

Indicator	Agricultural Labourers		Percentage to total workers	
	2001	2011	2001	2011
Total Population				
Total	10,67,75,330	14,43,29,833	26.5	30.0
Rural	10,24,60,732	13,69,94,451	33.1	39.3
Urban	43,14,598	73,35,382	4.7	5.5
Scheduled Castes				
Total	3,07,13,370	3,78,01,083	45.6	45.9
Rural	2,95,21,444	3,60,10,925	52.2	55.2
Urban	11,91,926	17,90,158	11.0	10.5

Source: Primary Census Abstract for Total Population, Scheduled Castes, 2011, Office of the Registrar General and Census Commissioner, India.

Table 2.33: Household Industry Workers

Indicator	Household Industry Workers		Percentage to total workers	
	2001	2011	2001	2011
Total Population				
Total	1,69,56,942	1,83,36,307	4.2	3.8
Rural	1,21,46,951	1,19,47,619	3.9	3.4
Urban	48,09,991	63,88,688	5.2	4.8
Scheduled Castes				
Total	26,29,912	26,52,919	3.9	3.2
Rural	21,06,600	19,72,691	3.7	3.0
Urban	5,23,312	6,80,228	4.8	4.0

Source: Primary Census Abstract for Total Population, Scheduled Castes, 2011, Office of the Registrar General and Census Commissioner, India, http://censusindia.gov.in/

Table 2.34: Other Workers

Indicator	*Other Workers*		*Percentage to total workers*	
	2001	*2011*	*2001*	*2011*
Total Population				
Total	15,11,89,601	20,03,84,531	37.6	41.6
Rural	7,06,93,863	8,46,86,967	22.8	24.3
Urban	8,04,95,738	11,56,97,564	87.1	86.9
Scheduled Castes				
Total	2,05,31,584	2,97,06,492	30.5	36.1
Rural	1,16,30,723	1,53,91,341	20.6	23.6
Urban	89,00,861	1,43,15,151	82.4	83.8

Source: Primary Census Abstract for Total Population, Scheduled Castes, 2011, Office of the Registrar General and Census Commissioner, India, http://censusindia.gov.in/

The total work participation of the person in 2011 is 39.8 per cent whereas in 2001 it was 39.1 per cent. The total rural work participation is 41.8 per cent. The urban recorded 35.3 per cent in 2011 whereas it was 41.7 per cent rural and 32.3 per cent urban according to 2001 census report. So far the SC work participation rate in person according to 2011 census report is concerned it is 40.9 per cent whereas it was 40.4 per cent in 2001. For rural percentage it is 35.9 per cent according to 2011 census report whereas it was 42.5 per cent rural and 32.1 per cent urban in 2001 census report. So far the top five states having highest SC work participation rate in person according to 2011 census report is Mizoram: 53.4 per cent, Himachal Pradesh: 52.1 per cent, Andhra Pradesh: 50.5 per cent, Tamil Nadu: 49.0 per cent and Sikkim: 47.6 per cent. On the other hand the states with lowest work participation rate in person are NCT of Delhi: 32.1 per cent, Daman and Diu: 34.3 per cent, Uttar Pradesh: 34.6 per cent, Jammu and Kashmir: 34.4 per cent and Haryana: 35.1 per cent according to 2011 census report.

The total male work participation according to 2011 census is 53.3 per cent. The rural participation is 53.0 per cent and urban participation is 53.8 per cent whereas in 2001 the total male work participation rate was 51.7 per cent. The rural participation was 52.1 per cent and urban was 50.6 per cent respectively. So far the total SC male work participation according to 2011 census report is concerned it is 52.8 per cent. The rural work participation is 52.9 per cent and urban is 52.4 per cent whereas in 2001 the SC male work participation rate was 50.7 per cent. The rural work participation rate was 51.6 per cent and urban was 47.4 per cent.

The total female work participation according to 2011 census is 25.5 per cent. The rural work participation is 30.0 per cent and urban is 15.4 per cent whereas in 2001 the total female work participation was 25.6 per cent. The rural work participation was 30.8 per cent and urban was 11.9 per cent respectively. So far the total SC female work participation according to 2011 census report is concerned it is 28.3 per cent. The rural work participation is 31.3 per cent and urban is 28.3 per cent whereas in 2001 the SC female work participation rate was 29.4 per cent. The total rural work participation was 32.9 per cent and urban was 15.6 per cent.

According to 2011 census report the total percentage of workers is 75.2 per cent. The rural percentage to the total workers is 70.5 per cent and urban is 87.6 per cent whereas in 2001 the percentage to total workers was 77.8 per cent. The rural percentage to the total workers was 73.9 per cent and urban was 90.8 per cent. So far the total SC percentage to total workers according to 2011 is concerned it is 70.7 per cent. The rural SC percentage to total workers is 67.2 per cent and urban 84.0 per cent whereas in 2001 the SC percentage to total workers was 73.0 per cent. The rural percentage to total workers was 70.6 per cent and urban was 85.4 per cent.

According to 2011, the total percentage to total marginal workers is 24.8 per cent. The total rural percentage to the total marginal workers is 29.5 per cent and urban 12.4 per cent whereas in 2001 the total percentage to the total marginal workers was 22.2 per cent. The total rural marginal workers were 26.1 per cent and urban was 9.2 per cent. So far the SC percentage to total marginal workers is concerned it is 29.3 per cent according to 2011 census report. The percentage to total marginal rural workers is 32.8 per cent and urban is 16.0 per cent whereas in 2001, the total marginal workers were 27.0 per cent. The percentage to total rural marginal workers was 29.4 per cent and urban was 14.6 per cent respectively.

Table 2.30 indicates the total percentage of marginal workers from three to six month period. According to 2011 census the total three to six month percentage to marginal workers is 81.3 per cent. The rural percentage is 80.7 per cent and urban is 85.2 per cent. The percentage to marginal workers less than three months is 18.7 per cent and the rural percentage is 19.3 per cent and urban is 14.8 per cent. So far the SC marginal worker by period of work is concerned in three to six months it is 80.5 per cent. The rural is 80.2 per cent and urban is 82.8 per cent whereas the marginal worker less than three month period is 19.5 per cent. The rural worker is 19.8 per cent and urban is 17.2 per cent.

In 2011 the total percentage of the cultivator workers is 24.6 per cent whereas the rural cultivator is 33.0 per cent and urban is 2.8 per cent. To compare with 2001 the total percentage of cultivator workers were 40.2 per cent and urban was 3.0 per cent. So far the SC percentage to total cultivator workers according to 2011 is concerned it is 14.8 per cent whereas the rural cultivator worker is 18.2 per cent and urban is 1.7 per cent. To compare with the 2001 census report the percentage to total SC cultivator worker were 20.0 per cent whereas the rural were 23.5 per cent and urban was 1.8 per cent respectively.

According to 2011 census report the total percentage to total agricultural labourers is 30.0 per cent whereas the rural percentage is 39.3 per cent and urban is 5.5 per cent. As compare to 2001 census report the total percentage to total agricultural workers were 26.5 per cent whereas the rural percentage was 33.1 per cent and urban was 4.7 per cent. So far the SC percentage to total agricultural workers according to 2011 census report is concerned it is 45.9 per cent whereas as the rural percentage is 55.2 per cent and urban is 10.5 per cent. As compare to the 2001 census report the total agricultural workers was 45.6 per cent whereas the rural percentage was 52.2 per cent and urban was 11.0 per cent.

The percentage to total household industry workers is 3.8 per cent whereas the rural percentage is 3.4 per cent and urban is 4.8 per cent. As compare to 2001 the percentage to total household industry workers were 4.2 per cent whereas the rural percentage was 3.9 per cent and urban is 5.2 per cent. So far the SC percentage to total household workers is concerned it is

3.2 per cent according to 2011 census report whereas the rural percentage is 3.0 per cent and urban is 4.0 per cent. As compare to 2001 census report the percentage to total household industries workers is concerned it was 3.9 per cent whereas the rural percentage was 3.7 per cent and urban was 4.8 per cent.

The percentage to total other workers is 41.6 per cent whereas the rural percentage is 24.3 per cent and urban is 86.9 per cent. As compare to the 2001 census report the percentage to total other workers were 37.6 per cent whereas the rural percentage was 22.8 per cent and urban was 87.1 per cent. The total SC other workers according to 2011 census report is 36.1 per cent whereas the rural percentage is 23.6 per cent and urban is 83.8 per cent. As compare to 2001 census report the percentage to total other workers were 30.5 per cent. The rural percentage was 20.6 per cent and urban was 82.4 per cent respectively.

Table 2.35: Population Trends for Major Religious Groups in India (1951–2011)

Religious group	*Population % 1951*	*Population % 1961*	*Population % 1971*	*Population % 1981*	*Population % 1991*	*Population % 2001*	*Population % 2011*
Hindu	85%	83.45%	82.73%	82.30%	81.53%	80.46%	79.6%
Muslim	9.9%	10.69%	11.21%	11.75%	12.61%	13.43%	14.2%
Christian	2%	2.44%	2.60%	2.44%	2.32%	2.34%	2.34%
Sikh	1.79%	1.79%	1.89%	1.92%	1.94%	1.87%	1.87%
Buddhist	0.74%	0.74%	0.70%	0.70%	0.77%	0.77%	0.77%
Jain	0.46%	0.46%	0.48%	0.47%	0.40%	0.41%	0.41%
Parsi	0.13%	0.09%	0.09%	0.09%	0.08%	0.06%	0.06%
Animist, others	0.43%	0.43%	0.41%	0.42%	0.44%	0.72%	0.72%

Source: http://en.wikipedia.org/wiki/2011_Census_of_India and Primary Census Abstract for Total Population, Scheduled Castes, 2011, Office of the Registrar General and Census Commissioner, India, http://censusindia.gov.in/

The poverty ratios for different religious groups estimated poverty for five distinct religious groups: Hindus, Muslims, Sikhs, Christians and Jains estimated that in rural-urban Jains and Sikhs, both very small religious groups, have significantly lower poverty rates than the general population in both rural and urban areas. Christians also enjoy very low poverty rates in urban areas though their lead in the rural areas is small. Between Hindus and Muslims, as expected, the latter have higher poverty rates but the difference is far smaller than that between the SC and ST on the one hand and non-scheduled castes on the other.[12]

Table 2.36: Poverty by Religious Groups[13]

Religion	Share in the Polulation	Percent Population Below the Tendulkar Line				Percentage Point Reduction in Poverty	
	2011-12	1993-94	2004-05	2009-10	2011-12	1993-94 to 2004-05	2004-05 to 2011-12
Rural							
Christianity	2.0	44.9	28.7	23.8	22.2	16.1	6.5
Hinduism	83.2	50.5	42.1	33.5	25.6	8.4	16.5
Islam	12.4	53.6	44.5	36.2	26.9	9.1	17.6
Jainism	0.1	24.3	10.6	0.0	0.7	13.7	10.0
Sikhism	1.7	19.8	21.7	11.9	6.2	-1.9	15.5
Total	100.0	50.3	41.8	33.3	25.4	8.5	16.4
Urban							
Christianity	2.7	22.9	14.1	12.9	5.5	8.9	8.6
Hinduism	77.3	29.7	23.1	18.7	12.1	6.6	10.9
Islam	16.8	46.6	41.8	33.9	22.7	4.7	19.1
Jainism	0.7	6.0	2.7	1.7	3.9	3.3	-1.2
Sikhism	1.4	18.6	9.5	14.5	5.0	9.1	4.5
Total	100.0	31.9	25.7	20.9	13.7	6.2	12.0
Rural + Urban							
Christianity	2.2	38.5	24.5	20.5	16.4	14.0	8.1
Hinduism	81.5	45.6	37.5	29.7	21.9	8.1	15.6
Islam	13.6	51.2	43.6	35.4	25.4	7.6	18.2
Jainism	0.3	10.5	4.6	1.5	3.3	5.9	1.4
Sikhism	1.6	19.6	18.9	12.5	5.9	0.6	13.1
Total	100.0	45.7	37.7	29.9	22.0	8.0	15.7

Source: Arvind, Panagariya and Vishal More, Poverty by Social, Religious and Economic Groups in India and Its Largest States 1993-94 to 2011-12, Working Paper No. 2013-02, SIPA School of International and Public Affairs ISERP Institute for Social and Economic Research and Policy, Programme of Indian Economic Policies, Colombia University, p. 8.

To talk about religion is very easy but it is more difficult to define. So many definitions of religion have been framed in the west over the years that even a partial listing would be impractical with varying success they have all struggled to avoid, on the one hand, the Scylla of hard short, particularistic definition and on the other hand, the charybdis of meaningless generalities.

Predictably, western-derived definitions have tended to emphasise the sharp distinction between the religious and non-religious dimensions of culture and sometimes have equated religion with beliefs, particularly belief in a supreme being.[14]

Such definitional usage has had its critics in the west. As early as the late eighteenth century an attempt was made to shift the importance from the conceptual to the intuitive and visceral statement, *Friedrich Schleiermacher* defined religion as, *"feeling of absolute dependence"*- absolute as contrasted to other, relative feelings of dependence, since that time there have been others who have sought to escape formalistic doctrinal definitions and to include the experimental emotive and intuitive factors as well as valuation and ethnical factors.[15] These factors seemed to be truer to the religious person's sense of what religion is like from the inside, to include what William James called *"the enthusiastic temper of espousal"*. Such definitions appear to be more universally applicable to primitive and Asian religious than belief oriented ones.[16]

Discrimination and exclusion of certain groups due to their identity based on social origin, ethnic and religious background, race, colour, gender and nationality is common to several societies. It is well illustrated that the nature and forms of discrimination and social exclusion have undergone changes over time and space. While it has changed to fluid forms, practices of discrimination overwhelmingly exist in the social, economic, political and cultural spheres of every society, irrespective of the existence of legal safeguards and equal opportunity policies. This seeks to extend discussions to the changing nature and forms of discrimination and social exclusion, both in specific and comparative contexts.[17]

Discrimination has multiple ramifications related to exclusion from economic entitlements, basic services and opportunities on one hand and humiliation, subordination, exploitation and denial of citizenship rights on the other. It is well entrenched that discrimination and social exclusion leads to widening of income inequalities, degree of poverty and deprivation by denying equal opportunities and access to resources and services.[18] It is a well known fact that in India religion plays an important role. It cross the entire framework and enters into the personal discourse of each and every individuals of the society. Each and every religion mainly in Indian context is an important source to gets its dominating nature with all forms of exploitation and exclusion. Further Dr Ambedkar says; *"Religion is for man and not man for religion"*.

Constitutional Status of Dalit Muslims and Dalit Christians

Indian law does not provide benefits for *"Dalit Muslims and Dalit Christians"* however; Muslims and Christians have been agitating for the same rights given to Hindus, Buddhist and Sikhs SC's. The Constitution of India, which came into force on 26 January 1950, provides some preferential options to the SC's who for so many centuries have been deprived of their rights in Indian society. It was Dr B.R. Ambedkar; the chief architect of the Indian Constitution, who formulated the provision of compensatory discrimination for SC's of India for their upliftment and connects them to the mailland social structure and society.[19]

Islam entered India almost immediately after its birth in the 7th century A.D. and made its way into different parts of the country.[20] In the south it entered through the present day state of Kerala situated on the Malabar Coast (1).[21] Its carriers were the Arab traders who had been involved in trade activities with India even before the times of Prophet Muhammad. During their numerous voyages to the Malabar region, the Arab traders established matrimonial relationships with the local women and had many progeny from these marriages. This resulted in the spread of Islam to different parts of the region. Many Sufi saints accompanied these traders and under the influence of their preaching and the attraction of an egalitarian faith mainly from Depressed Classes, converted to Islam.[22] A major factor to be borne in mind here is that Islam's first step on Indian soil was not, as many would like to believe, riding on the wave of the sword. In the North, Islam came along with the invasion of Muhammad bin Qasim, a general of Yusuf bin Hajjaj, the governor of Iraq during the Umayyad period.[23] This was followed by the many invasions of Muhammad Ghori and Mahmud Ghazni, both interested merely in the enormous wealth and richness that India offered. The two were never interested in occupying and ruling the land of India. Their main focus was to plunder, pillage and transfer as much wealth as possible to their respective capitals since this was crucial for them to maintain their large armed forces and entourage used in their frequent military campaigns.[24]

The history of Islam in India is well over a thousand years old today. It has blended beautifully into the background of its adopted land and contributed immensely to the formation of a composite Indian culture and the building of the Indian nation. Islam and its practitioners are not a homogeneous entity as is widely believed. In fact, there is a great deal of diversity in the manner in which Islam is practiced and perceived throughout India. This is hardly surprising considering the facts that Islam in India is almost as old as the faith itself and that its followers in different regions of the country represent a myriad of cultures. In this process of adapting to the variety of cultural milieus, Islam has acquired many hues and should not be considered as a monolithic entity. Nevertheless, Muslims in India have responded well to the challenges of living as a minority in a religiously plural society. But this process of assimilation into the Indian society has not been an easy one and the challenges that Muslims of India face today continue to exist with the constantly shifting national and international state of affairs.[25]

Largely, it has seen the people belong to Depressed Classes who converted to Islam in history become either slave or condition gone more pathetic than Hinduism. In this religion caste become again the controller instrument of opportunists *'Molvis'* (priest) of the mosque and *'Asrafs'* (Privileged Caste Indian Muslims).[26] For various historical and customary reasons the Hindu caste system made such a deep impact on Islam in the country that the Muslim even when the weakened the caste system could not escape in completely themselves.[27] Caste system is a social reality of Muslims despite the fact that they are followers of Islam[28] for example,

Abdul Bismillah, Sahitya Academy award winner recounts a tale in his article, *'The Basis of Dalit Muslim Identity'*, which reflects the deep bias of the *Asrafs* (high castes) against the *Arjals* (low castes). He says,

> *"Once I had gone to a friend's village, a Dhobi (washerman) had invited the entire village to his daughter's weeding. The Khan Sahib was enraged by this. They all gave the Nai (Barber) five rupees each. When the Nai was reluctant to take the money, they declared, 'go and tell the Dhobi that if he is so desperate to invite us to a feast then he should send a quarter of meat to each one of our house. We will cook it ourselves and eat it'".*

When author asked to the Khan Sahab about this, he replied, *"Dhobis are the untouchables because they wash the contaminated clothes of menstruating women and that is why he is an untouchable"*.[29]

In fact, some of the castes in Muslim community such as the Bhatiyars considered so low that their name itself is a term of abuse.[30] It is said of the kalal man that even if his son were dying of hunger he would still shout, *'kill the bastard, he is mumbling inanities after drinking too much'*. The Dhobis are considered worse off than the Doms. The saying goes *'eat at the Dom's house but never at the Dhobis'*. The privileged castes among the Muslims even consider some of these marginal castes as *'untouchables'*.[31] Indian Muslim believes in castes but they forget to locate Mohhamed Prophet who was belongs to a tribal (Quarasi) community whom they are following and praying.[32]

Muslim League or Muslim Majliz didn't think about the backward section of the Muslim committee. These political parties tried to earn their vote in the name of religion or by instilling fear of communal parties in the minds of Dalit Muslims thus, limiting the involvement of Dalit Muslims.[33] These parties feared that giving reservations to Dalit Muslims would boost their social and financial status resulting in failure of agenda of the parties and dominations of the Dalits in the politics[34] as Dalits Muslims are more than 85 per cent of the total Muslim populations residing in India. This difference in Muslims relating to their status is not new issue.[35]

In 1946, Abdullah Qayum and Atikurrahman Mansuri Aarabi of Momin party had said that *Muslim League is party of rich Muslims and Pakistan would have no place for Dalit Muslims*. This point was explained by Abdullah Qayum to Dalit Muslims and stopping them by migrating to Pakistan. Later, Jinnah had said that if Dalit Muslims would have supported Muslim League then Pakistan would have extended till Delhi. Even after partition, 25 crore Muslims in India are dominated by just 25 Muslim aristocrats and these aristocrats are discriminating and humiliating other Muslims just in the name of religion.[36]

The conditions of Dalits belonging to other religions are improving day by day, but the condition of Muslim Dalits is just getting worse. The atrocities done against Dalit Muslims are continuing even today, so they have decided to voice against these atrocities on their own.[37]

For purposes of better understanding, the challenges that confront the community today can be categorised into external and internal challenges. The external challenges are those, which emanate from factors that exist outside the community. The most important among these factors would undoubtedly be the Muslims of India being constantly viewed as 'fifth-columnists' are harbouring 'extra-territorial loyalties' and a 'pro-Pakistan sentiment'. Despite having contributed to just about every sphere of life - be it sports, politics, movies and music, fine arts or literature Muslims are still questioned about their role in the growth and development of India. These allegations need to be rebutted by the community, untidily and in a systematic, logical manner. The threat being referred to here is the caste-based discrimination practised by certain sections of Muslims in India.

The Holy Quran says,

"O mankind! We (God) created you from a single pair of male and a female; and made you into peoples and tribes, that you may know each other (not that you may despise each other). Verily the most honoured in the sight of God is (he who is) the most righteous among you".[38]

This verse makes it quite clear that though Islam accepts differentiation based on gender and tribe, it does not recognise social stratification. But in reality, the Muslim community remains diversified, fragmented and as caste-ridden as any other community of India.[39] In fact, the levels of stratification witnessed within the Muslim community of India totally negate this Quranic edict. *Imtiaz Ahmad's seminal work, Caste and Social Stratification Among Muslims in India (1973) and more recently, Ali Anwar's Masawat ki jung: Pasemanzar Bihar ka Pasmanda Musalman (2001)* in Hindi have convincingly demonstrated the reality of caste among Indian Muslims.[40] However, it should be acknowledged that this discriminatory practice among Muslims, observed more in North India than South or any other parts of India, is not as much pronounced, oppressive and widespread as amongst the Hindus. But that is hardly comforting. The fact that discrimination based on caste lines exists within the Muslim community of India is cause enough for consternation.[41]

Most Indian Muslims are descendants of 'untouchable' and 'Backward' caste converts, with only a small minority tracing their origins to Arab, Iranian and Central Asian settlers.[42] Muslims who claim foreign descent assert a superior status for themselves as Ashraf or 'noble'. Descendants of indigenous converts are, on the other hand, commonly referred to contemptuously as Ajlaf or 'base' or 'lowly'. Going by this classification, an overwhelming 85 per cent of Muslim population of India would fall into the Ajlaf category.[43] But conversion to the egalitarian faith of Islam has not helped their cause. The Ajlaf continue to be discriminated against by the Muslim privileged caste. Due to ill-treatment meted out to the Dalit Muslims a movement for recognition of the Dalit Muslims' as scheduled castes, on par with the backward castes in the Hindu society is capturing the ground.[44]

The leaders of this movement have demanded reservations for 'Dalit Muslims' based on the concept of positive discrimination enshrined in Article 341 of the Indian Constitution, which authorises the President to declare certain castes as Scheduled Castes for special benefits.[45] At the same time, one of the leaders of this movement Dr Ejaz Ali, rather curiously, protested the denial of burial rights to lower caste Muslims in Bihar by stating that it was *'against the basic tenets of Islam'* and that there was *'no basis of caste in Islam'*.[46] There is a slight contradiction here. If Dr Ejaz Ali accepts the Islamic teaching that there is no basis for caste in Islam, on what grounds then does he talk about a 'lower caste' Muslim and consequently, reservations for them?

While there is no denying the fact that the despicable custom of discrimination on the basis of a person's birth is prevalent in the Muslims of India, demanding a separate identity and other benefits based on caste is no panacea for this iniquity. This move is fraught with great danger. It will only end up providing another dimension to the already existing divisions within the community. Aren't schisms based on Shi'a-Sunni, Deobandi, Barelwi, Ahl-i-Hadith, Jamaat-i-Islami etc., enough that they are now seeking to create categories like 'Dalit Muslim' and 'forward caste Muslim'? Matters have reached a position where an organisation called the *All India United Muslim Morcha* led by Dr Ejaz Ali has gone ahead and proposed a unique 'give-and-take' formula for securing job reservations for Muslims by removing religious restrictions from Article 341 of the Indian Constitution to include Dalit Muslims in the scheduled caste category.[47]

Now let's look at a hypothetical situation where the reservation system is replicated within the Muslim community of India. To begin with castes that deserves to be categorised as 'Dalit Muslims' need to be identified. This process would present a scenario where a set of Muslims, especially those coming from south India would either say that they are not 'Dalit Muslims' or would express their inability to identify the caste they belong to for the simple reason that they don't have a caste. A few other perplexing situations would be thrown up. How would, for example, a Muslim from Kerala with no caste, react to his fellow 'Dalit Muslim' from Bihar getting a job based on his caste? It would be nothing short of a shock for the Malayalee Muslim who shares his reverence for Allah, his Friday namaz, and belief in Islamic tenets with the Bihari Muslim but still finds that he is different from him (the Bihari Muslim) because he doesn't have a 'caste' - something which has no religious sanction at all! But most importantly, it would become the cause of much heartburn for those 'casteless' and so-called 'non-Dalit' sections of the Muslim community, who would be ineligible to use the benefits of the reservation policy, as they do not meet the caste criteria laid down to avail this privilege. Assuming that caste-based reservation is extended to Muslims too; it is bound to cause further fragmentation within the community.[48]

The bitter truth is that the community needs to square up with caste stratification, howsoever blasphemous, is a reality of the Muslim society in India. This obnoxious practice cannot be wished away. The community has to set its face against it and the only way to fight this inhuman practice is direct action against anyone practising, promoting or legitimising caste-based stratification. Moreover, this state of affairs is not only un-Islamic but also detrimental to the prosperity and security of the Muslim community in India. Under these circumstances, the response of the Muslim community of India to this test should be one that reflects its maturity and age; a response that exhibits the collective wisdom of the community and the noble teachings of the Holy Quran and the Prophet (pbuh).[49]

In response to a Public Interest Litigation (PIL) filed by Akhil under Maharashtra Muslim Khatik Samaj (MMKS), stating that there were Dalits within Muslim community who needed reservation and demanded inclusion in the SC list, the Supreme Court has issued notice to the Centre seeking its reply. Further, the judge referred to the strict dictates of Quran prohibiting practice of any forms of caste system within Islam and it asked the petitioner if Islam permitted caste system.[50] This observation of the apex court has initiated a debate whether there is caste system in Islam or among Muslims? All social scientists agree that though there is no caste system as much in Islam, the Indian Muslim society did develop a hierarchical structure by characterising numerous biraderis. The Quran and the Prophet's sayings are crystal clear that all human beings are equal; all are brothers and sisters of each other.[51]

Historically, a good number of Dalits converted to Islam. But after conversion their socio-economic status remained impoverished, backward and downtrodden. By joining the fold of Islam they did not get such a boost to their talents and abilities that they could face equal competition with all others. They were still treated as Untouchables in the society. Most of them continued with their traditional professions as artisans, peasants and labourers, except when it was considered impure or unacceptable in Shariah. Nevertheless, of late, some of these Muslim caste groups got *islamised*. They also became organised and given themselves Muslim nomenclatures. They identified and associated themselves with Islamic personalities. For example, the butchers designated themselves as Qureshi; the weavers as Ansari; the tailors as Idrisi; the Bhishtis as Abbasi; the vegetable vendors as Raeen; the barbers as Salmani; the carpenters and blacksmiths as Saifi etc. In a democratic state, each socially identifiable group aspires to see its face in the development. Millions of Dalit Muslims, who are occupationally akin to the SCs, demand inclusion in the SC List to enable them to avail the benefits of reservation.[52]

However, some Muslims established superior status for themselves as Ashraf or noble on the basis of their foreign descent, while descendants of indigenous converts are commonly referred as Ajlaf or 'lowly'. Some Islamic jurists too, deviating from Islamic teachings, in the name of *kufu* i.e. parity in marriage between the parties, legitimise castes. Even the Muslim law of marriage recognises the doctrine of kufu[53] in all vital respects including social status and descent, which, in India, means nothing but casteism.

The Sachar Committee Report, on the existence of castes among Indian Muslims, says:

"The present day Muslim society is divided into four major groups

(a) The Ashrafs, who trace their origins to foreign lands.

(b) The privileged caste Hindus who converted to Islam.

(c) The middle caste converts whose occupations are ritually clean.

(d) The converts from the erstwhile Untouchable castes – Bhangi (scavengers), Mehtar (sweeper), Chamar (tanner), Halalkhor (Dom) and so on".[54]

On the level of backwardness, the Sachar report finds that out of every 100 workers about 11 are Hindu OBCs, three are Muslim-general and only one is Muslim OBC[55], whereas the population of OBC Muslims is as much as 75 per cent of the total Muslims' population. Similarly, the Justice Rangnath Misra Commission finds prevalence of castes among various sections of the Indian citizenry. It concludes:

"The caste is in fact a social phenomenon shared by almost all Indian communities irrespective of their religious persuasions".[56]

The Sachar Reports further says:

"The incidence of poverty is highest among Muslim-OBC (38 per cent) followed by Muslim General (35 per cent). Overall, the conditions of Muslim-OBCs are worse than those of Muslim-General. Within the Muslim community a larger percentage of Muslim OBCs fall in low income category as compared to Muslim-General. Within Muslims, Muslim-OBCs are slightly lagging behind the Muslim-General in high income group."[57]

In its recommendation the report says:

"Being at the bottom of the Social hierarchy, the arzals (SCs) are the worst off and need to be handled separately. It would be most appropriate if they were absorbed in the SC list or at least in a separate category."[58]

On the other hand, Justice Misra Commission says that 'the caste system should be recognised as a general social characteristic of the Indian society as a whole, without questioning whether the philosophy and teachings of any particular religion recognise it or not. It further recommends that 'Para 3 of the Constitution (Scheduled Castes) Order 1950 should be wholly deleted by appropriate action so as to completely de-link the Scheduled Caste status from religion'. The denial of reservation to Dalit Muslims by the Presidential Order of 1950 appeared to be with an eye on the balance of power which is tilted in favour of Hindus. Hence, the required amendment will be a step towards secularism.[59]

The Constitution prohibits any discrimination between the citizens. Hence, any religion-based discrimination conflicts with the letter and spirit of the provisions. In the famous Indra Sawhney case the Supreme Court had decided that 'a caste can be and quite often is a social class in India'. Further it conceptualises: 'If it is backward socially, it would be a backward class for the purpose of Article 16(4). Among non-Hindus, there are several occupational groups, sects and denominations, which for historical reasons are socially backward. They too represent backward social collectives for the purpose of Article 16(4). Identification of the backward classes can certainly be done with reference to castes among, and along with, other occupational groups, classes and section of people. Reservation in public employment is specifically covered by Article 16(4) of the Constitution, for any backward class of citizens, which are not adequately represented in the services under the State. Hence, it is expected that the Supreme Court would analyse the issue of reservation of Dalit Muslims keeping in mind the context of Indian Constitution, findings of various commissions and social realities.[60]

Meanwhile, instead of solving the issue of reservation for Dalit Muslims under the carpet it is the duty of the Ulema and community leaders to realise that this group needs special attention and there should be no roadblock in the way of their getting fair share, for they are, as suggested by the Sachar report, 'cumulatively oppressed'. Repeated appeal to the Muslim community to maintain unity in the name of Islam, foregoing the Constitutional benefits, will not be a wise idea. May be some day in the future reservations will be based solely on community's impoverishment, but until then caste-based support seems to be perfectly justified. True, the Muslim community must reject the proposition of fragmentation, but they should apply the same principles of social justice as much within the community as it demands for itself within the nation.[61]

The situation clearly calls for the amendment of the Constitution of India; only then the Dalit Muslims can be included among the scheduled castes.[62] If it happens, it would not be the first time. The relevant part of the Constitution containing the order has already been amended twice: first in 1956 and second in 1990. Through these amendments, Sikhs and Buddhists respectively were included in the Scheduled Caste category and thus they were allowed to avail the benefits of reservation. Hence Dalit Muslims should also be provided with the benefit of reservations and other privileges as scheduled castes as the Presidential Order of 1950 is un-constitutional. The only reason why Dalit belonging to other communities are progressing is due to reservation whereas the condition of Dalit Muslims is turning worse day by day in the lack of same. Atrocities against Dalit Muslim are continuing even today.[63] Dalit Muslims deserve scheduled caste reservation or representation as they are not only engaged in the same profession as Dalit Hindus but also undergo the same social discrimination as their counterpart Dalit Hindus. The status of Dalit Muslims which include Nutt, Bakkho, Khatik, Bhatiyara, Kunjra, Dhunia, Kalal, Dafali, Halakhor, Dhobi, Gorkan, Meershikar, Rangrz, Darji, Mochis, Mukris and Garudis etc. is turning worse day by day.[64]

So far the caste systems among Indian Christians are concerned is attributed to the assimilation of local Hindu practices, which has caused caste distinctions to be retained after conversion.[65] Some Christian groups have adapted the Indian caste system in diverse ways across the subcontinent, often reflecting their own stratification by sect, location, and the castes of their predecessors. Social practices among certain Indian Christians parallel much of the discrimination faced by excluded castes in other religious communities, as well as having features unique to this community.[66] Caste distinctions among Indian Christians are breaking down at about the same rate as those among Indians belonging to other religions. About 80 per cent of Indian Christian is Dalit Christian, members of the Dalit or backward classes.[67]

History of Christinity starts with the history of conversion in India.[68] In the Indian state of Goa, mass conversions were carried out by Portuguese missionaries from the 16th century onwards.[69] The Hindu converts retained their caste practices. The continued maintenance of the caste system among the Christians in Goa is attributed to the nature of mass conversions of entire villages, as a result of which existing social stratification was not affected. The Portuguese colonists, even during the Goan Inquisition, did not do anything to change the caste system. Thus, the original *Hindu Brahamins* in Goa now became *Christian Bamons* and the *Kshatriya* became *Christian noblemen* called *Chardos*.[70] The Christian clergy became almost exclusively Bamon. *Vaishyas* who converted to Christianity became *Gauddos*, and *Shudras*[71] became *Sudirs*. Finally, the Dalits or *"Untouchables"* who converted to Christianity became *Maharas* and *Chamars* (an appellation of the anti-Dalit ethnic slur *Chamaar*). The privileged caste Gaonkar Christians have demanded that only their community be given positions on the Pastoral Council of Goa's Catholic Church.[72]

Christians in Kerala were divided into several communities, including *Syrian Christian* and the so-called *'Latin'* or *'New Rite'* Christians. Syrian Christian tends to be endogamous, and tend not to intermarry with other Christian castes. Also, very rarely are there intermarriages between *Latin Rite Christians* and *New Christians* (converted in the 16th and 19th centuries) in Kerala; the latter were converted mainly from castes where fishing was the traditional occupation. Syrian Christian derive status within the caste system from the tradition that they are converted Namboodiris, who were evangelised by St. Thomas. Others argue however, that the claims were made by the later Christians to obtain special caste status in the prevailing caste system of India. A notable point is that the Namboothiri history claims their origin in Kerala in the seventh century CE, while Christianity in India originated in the first century CE, after St Thomas was speculated to have landed in Kerala at 52 AD. Early writings place them below the level of the matrilineal Nairs and the patrilineal Namboodiris. Following efforts by the

Christian Missionary Society in the 1880s to enhance the rights of *"New Christian"* low-caste converts, and their demands to equal status with *"Syrian Christians"*, some of whom later joined the Syrian Christian community, the *"delicate bonds"* tying Syrian Christians to high-caste Hindus were broken. Anthropologists have noted that the caste hierarchy among Christians in Kerala is much more polarised than the Hindu practices in the surrounding areas, due to the lack of jatis. Also, the caste status is kept even if the sect allegiance is switched (i.e., from Syrian Catholic to Syrian Orthodox).[73]

The cohesion of jatis among caste Christians[74] e.g., Paravas and the strength of caste leadership are noted by scholars to be much stronger than comparable predominantly Hindu castes in Tamil Nadu. Among Catholic Reddys in Andhra Pradesh, Christians prefer marrying Hindu members of their jati, to marrying low caste Christians. In Puduchery, the Eraiyur incident[75], where the Dalits were ostracised, is still fresh in the memory of the Dalit Christians.[76]

Table 2.37: Catholic Data Reveal Discrimination in the Church–2013 Statistics on Population

	Total Number	*Dalit Catholics*	*Percentage*
Total Indian Population	1200 Millions		
Total Christians	25 Millions		
Total Dalit Christians		20 Millions	(65%)
Total Catholics	18 Millions		
Total Dalit Catholics		12 Millions	(65%)
Catholic Dioceses	166		
Catholic Bishops	180	07	
Dalit Bishops			(4%)
Catholic Diocesan Priests	15420		
Dalit Catholic Priests		754	(5%)
Religious Priests	7031		
Dalit Religious Priests		310	(4%)
Religious sisters	65,000		
Dalit Religious sisters		3200	(5%)
Cardinals	06		
Dalit Cardinals		Nil	

Source: Letter to His Holiness Pope Francis, Vatican, Rome, Italy, Mission of the Church and Dalit Catholic Empowerment, Rev. Dr Fr. S. Lourduswamy, Former Secretary, National CBCI committee for SC/ST
http://www.vodintl.org.uk/article/Indian%20Bishops%20Memorandum% 20to% 20Vatican% 20February% 201013.pdf

After the incident, both caste Christians and Dalits were allowed to use the common path to the church and cemetery. Various studies suggests that 75 per cent Catholics are living in South India and the largest Dalit Catholic community reside in Andhra Pradesh, Tamil Nadu, Karnataka, states in South India. In North India and except Tribals and Adivasis communities all the Catholics belong to Dalit Community. Tribals/Adivasi People are not affected by caste system and untouchability. They continue to get all the reservation facilities even after conversion to Christianity.[77]

In the Indian context, the Hindu dominant castes used exactly the same technique that the god an almighty being is also the first constituting element in the western theory of political power, which is very similar to orthodox Hinduism.[78] No doubt, in general, Christianity there is no caste system but in Indian context Christianity have caste system with hierarchy and today's new concept *'Dalit Christian'* is the product of Christian Caste system (CSS). Those depressed caste who converted to Christianity in the paste again come under the trap of caste system.[79]

As we know that the Christian pope (priest) gives the message of equality and goodwill amongst the human beings but it has reported that in Indian state of Tamil Nadu (Trichi Village) Dalit Christians even after death is being discriminated. Dalit Christians are not allowed burying the dead bodies of their relatives in the burial ground of the high caste, which is under the control of the church.[80] Dalit Christians have separate burial grounds different from high caste Christians burial ground. One of the members of the Trichi Church Association (TCA) member (Tamil Nadu) Prof Selwa stated that,

> "the high caste Christians created these differences between Dalit Christian and the high caste Christians in twenty years back and nobody have courage to go against this authority".[81]

National Council of Dalit Christians (NCDC) president Mr Fraclin Sizer shares his pain and told that,

> *"though we are Christians but we do not allow meeting other members of the high castes Christian in the church. Church restricts to marry out of the Dalit Christian community. Even we not allowed participating in the ceremonies of the church.*

We force to stand in a queue in one side of the church", Because of this discrimination and inequality within the Christians (High caste Christians over low caste Christians) NCDC's regularly fighting and demanding reservation for Dalit Christians.[82]

Even those people who converted to Christianity from Hinduism over a period still to leave Hindu identity and its behaviour for example Fr. George Grispert-Sauch emeritus Professor at Vidya Jyoti is a Spanish origin and is now an Indian citizen. He has published two volumes of the writing of Brahmabandhab Upadhya. He says that, Upadhya was among the first to demand complete independence of India from British Raj. Upadhya died in jail on October 1907, a martyr of the freedom struggle like other freedom fighters. He further says that, Upadhya was born in a Hindu Vaishnava family and he converted to Christianity. When asked by a census official whether he remains catholic or protestant he replied, *"Neither, put me down as an Indian Catholic"*. It means he was personally a Hindu by birth and culturally a Christian by faith and religion.[83] He was a Hindu Christian, which means still he believes in the Hindu Varna Vewesta (HVV), which he wanted to, practiced in Christianity.[84]

The plight of the Dalits economic position has been the issue of landlessness. In an agricultural society like India, land is an important consideration. The landed dominant caste had deprived the Dalits of owning land or property of any kind. This is intended to ensure the supply of a stream of continuous and permanent labour force.[85] Landless and dependent, the lower castes lead an economical un-free and penurious life. From the survey, it is culled that 12,086 persons out of 9,000 families sell their labour, and 607 persons have to sell themselves to eke out a living. They are called un-free labourers. Out of the 607 un-free labourers, 243 are indebted to the landowners. Out of 9,000 families, 3744 (41.6 per cent) have taken loans and are indebted to various types of creditors. About 71.23 per cent have borrowed to meet their daily consumer needs. Only 599, out of 9,000 households (6.6 per cent) have savings below Rs 3,000. Thus 93 per cent of the Dalit Christians have no saving at all.[86]

While the majority of the Dalit Christians (around 58 per cent) are able to have three meals a day, over 39 per cent are unable to do so. More than 25 per cent of the families have clothes valued at Rs 100 or less for the whole family, and over 65 per cent have clothes worth less than Rs 200. Hence, 65 per cent of the Dalit Christians have clothes worth less valued less than Rs 39 per head. Over 19 per cent of the Dalit Christians do not own homes. Since nine-tenths of the rural households in the Tamil Nadu have their own homes, 10 per cent of the Dalit Christians have no homes of their own. As of 31/01/1988, 99.4 per cent of the villages in Tamil Nadu have been supplied with electricity. But 67 per cent of the Dalit Christians do not enjoy this facility. Dalit Christian children are prone to attacks of fever. As much as 17.62 per cent of the Dalit Christian children are killed annually by this sickness for which simple medical remedies could be procured. About 4.97 per cent of the Dalit children become victims of dysentery and diarrhoea. All this underscores the extent of poverty and lack of financial means to obtains these simple facilities by Dalit Christians.[87] Needless to say, the economic situation of Dalits leaves much room for improvement.[88]

UNICEF in its report says to be illiterate is to be excluded because when a Dalit was asked why she did not send her son to school, she answered, *"My son is not going to be a collector, so why brother?"* For this Dalit, education is a gateway for status and lucrative employment, which she feels is closed to her kind.[89] The attitude of this woman reflects the position of the Dalits in general. A lack of economic resources of Dalit Christians is one of the main reasons for poverty.[90] The attitude of priests and nuns in Christian schools is not helpful to the cause of the Dalit Christian students. There are also a small percentage of Dalit Christian students who dropped out of school which does not promise them a good future either. Even after completing school they are unable to obtain employment.[91] The distribution of Dalit Christians according to their occupations (1990) is high administrative - 0.62 per cent, lower administrative - 2.68 per cent, professional - 0.60 per cent, teaching - 3.57 per cent, clerical - 1.37 per cent, trade and commerce - 0.75 per cent, transport and public utility - 1.72 per cent, manufacturing, processing and service - 2.26 per cent, construction - 2.80 per cent, own cultivation - 7.29 per cent, agricultural labourers - 54.75 per cent, livestock, forestry etc. - 1.05 per cent, menial - 1.80 per cent, other - 18.74

per cent. There is very less number of IAS or IPS officer from the ranks of the Dalit Christian community. Only those who got reconverted to Hinduism managed to enter into the administrative services. It appears that to be a Dalit Christian is to be excluded from the mainstream of society.[92]

The experience of Dalit Christians is all about powerlessness.[93] Among those who are involved in politics none are given any important position at the national or at state level. There has not been any evidence of Dalit Christian representation either in the Central or State Cabinet. Even at the party rank and file no Dalit Christian is given any importance. Political reservation of seats in Parliament and State Assembly is non-existent.[94] As they have been marginalised in politics, their grievances go unheard, naturally. More than ever, the state wields extraordinary power through the Legislative, Executive and the Judiciary. There is no Dalit Christians either in the legislature, executive or judiciary.[95] The non-representation in these bodies renders the positions of Dalit Christians weak. Finally, the ennui of powerlessness faced by the Dalit Christians in the Church is a matter of deep concern. Out of despair, frustration and confusion, the powerless Dalits may garner and muster enough strength and conviction to fight back. If they do, the struggle could be violent. When violence is the end product, the outcome will be uncertain.[96]

Dalit Christians are severely marginalised in the vocations of Priests and Nuns and in the appointments for any higher authority or positions. Even though Dalit Christians are about 75 per cent in the Catholic Church in the state of Tamil Nadu, South India, only about six per cent among the priests and nuns are Dalits. Similar situation exists in the whole of India. This must be taken up seriously, as it is against the natural and distributive justice and democratic values. Similarly, there are not even about eight Dalit Bishops nearly 150 Catholic Bishops in India. This is again a serious exclusion of the Dalit Christians from the mainstream of the Church even though they form a big majority in the Catholics population. It is a clear proof that the caste-domination is operating at all levels of making the choice, recommendations and decisions for the appointment of Bishops.[97]

Casteism in the Church not only causes the loss of civil or social rights and violates human dignity and basic natural equality.[98] but it also has very adversely affected educational and economic progress for generations. There is violation of the distributive justice to them in the minority institutions themselves. In leading and well-established institutions, Dalit Christians are severely marginalised both in admissions and appointments. In most of these institutions, their representation is only less than 10 per cent. There is lack of policies in these institutions to see that the historically oppressed Dalit Christians get their due share in proportion to their bigger population.[99] By and large the caste authorities of the church disown the Dalit Christians when it comes to sharing such privileges, benefits and facilities. This caste-culture of the Church has very adversely affected the Dalit Christian community in the past more than six decades. Even knowing that the Dalit Christians have been denied the Constitutional safeguards just because they are Christians, they have just neglected their cause. Because of this, a great majority of Dalit Christians are excluded and are living below poverty line.[100]

The local church authorities, institutions and organisations have built up and accumulated financial and material resources and continue to get financial aid from Catholic donors and agencies all over the world, primarily with the appeal to help the underprivileged and the untouchable Dalits and poor people. But these have not really reached them, not their due share and not even a minimum share. There is no transparency and accountability to these people, their leaders or their committees. This has been going on for decades. The cumulative effect of all these have caused enormous damage to the progress of Dalit Christians and have ended in a tragic situation. The Dalit Christians are waiting long for peaceful solution from the Church authorities as well as present political regime. But lack of sincerity and sensitivity towards the core problems cannot lead to a peaceful solution. Peaceful solution consists of sincere, honest and speedy attempts to restore justice and equality to the oppressed and the suffering people. That has to come from the authorities, the powerful and the dominant.[101]

Dalit Christians for the last so many decades asking their fundamental rights which they belong to the same caste and undergo the same age-old torment and oppression as other Dalits. Dalit Christians live under the same system of oppression, deprived of justice and human dignity.[102] The economic condition of Dalit converts is in no way different from that of their counterparts the Dalits who are not converted.[103] Dalit Christians suffer from a high incidence of atrocities and economic and social disabilities owing to the government's reluctance to modify its discriminatory policy on reservation. Christians feel that this religion-based discrimination is in violation of Article 15(1) and contravenes the provisions of Article 15(4) of the Constitution of India. Constitutional principles prohibit discrimination on the grounds of religion, race, caste, sex or place of birth.[104] At stake is the fate of more than 19 million Dalit Christians, who form 70 per cent of the Indian Christians. In the whole country, Indian Christians total 25 million. They are not asking for any expansion of the Scheduled Caste list or any increase in the reservation quota.[105] There was also a call for a separate Church for the Dalits, but during all these developments, the Archbishop never met and interacted with the Dalit community. They also alleged that despite being a part of the Christian faith for the past 60 years, the Dalit Christians continued to be treated as second class citizens.[106]

Without going into details of how enlightened Hindus have dealt with the unconscionable practice of untouchability, one cannot understand the real issues of the castes and Dalit Christians. The Dalits constitute more than 15 per cent of the total Indian population and 20 per cent of the Hindu population.[107]

The Dalit Christians make 65 per cent of the ten million Christians in the South, but less than four per cent of the parishes are entrusted to Dalit priests. There are no Dalits among the 13 Catholic Bishops Council of Tamil Nadu or among the Vicars-general and the Rectors of seminaries and Directors of social assistance centres.[108] The secular intellectual establishment and the Christian community it seems is ignorant about this simmering discontent among the Dalits who converted to the Christian faith hoping to be empowered. And yet, the Dalits still within the Hindu fold have risen to the highest positions in all walks of life including to Rashtrapati Bhavan. Sadly, little has changed in 2006 for the Dalits within the Christian fold. Much noise is also made about the despicable practice of untouchability which is placed at the door of Hindu dharma even though there is no religious sanction for it in the religious content or traditions. Be that as it may but untouchability is not the only form of discrimination faced by the Dalit Christians.[109] There are other forms of discrimination too and, as shown above, these concern their positions in the Christian institutions and also their marriage practices and many more.[110]

Various studies and statistic shows that more than 75 per cent of the Christians in India are Dalits.[111] When Christian missionaries began their work in India in the decades before Independence, their promise of equal treatment and opportunity for all castes became the prime reason for Dalits who find themselves at the socio-economic lowest rung of Hinduism's hierarchy to embrace the missionary message but nothing has worked out and made no escape from caste prejudices.[112]

The expression *"Scheduled Castes"* was used for those people who were kept outside the fourfold Varna (caste) system, and were called Avarnas (casteless). They were called by different names such as, Chandalas, Panchamas or Untouchables. The term Scheduled Caste was used by the British Government to designate all castes and classes previously covered under the term *"Depressed Classes"*. Officially this word was embodied in Section 305 of the Government of India Act, 1935. Later the expression was included in the Government of India (Scheduled Castes) Order, 1936.[113]

The President may with respect to any State or Union Territory, and where it is a State, after consultation with the Governor thereof, by public notification, specify the castes, races or tribes or parts of or groups within castes, races or tribes which shall for the purposes of this Constitution be deemed to be Scheduled Castes in relation to that State or Union territory, as the case may be.[114]

In 1950, while exercising the powers conferred on him in Article 341(1), the President of India promulgated an order known as The Constitution (Scheduled Castes) Order, 1950. This Order of 1950 continued to use the same list used in the Government of India (Scheduled Castes) Order of 1936. The third paragraph of the 1950 Order reads.[115]

Notwithstanding anything contained in paragraph 2, no person who professes a religion different from Hindu shall be deemed to be a member of a Scheduled Caste. This third Paragraph was amended in 1956 and in 1990 in favour of Sikh and Buddhist Dalits.[116]

As a step towards equality, the Constitution of India has provided the SC's with compensatory discrimination or affirmative action, but since 1950 the Government of India has deprived Dalit Muslims and Dalit Christians of such rights. Most Dalit Muslims and Dalit Christians are economically poor, educationally backward, politically powerless and socially outcaste.[117] For this reason the Dalit Muslims and Dalit Christians demand that the Indian Government restore their legitimate rights and cease to discriminate against them on grounds of religion. Dalit Muslims and Dalit Christians should be accorded the same reservation and welfare benefits that are granted to the SC's professing the Hindu, Sikh, and Buddhist religions under the Constitution (Scheduled Castes) Order 1950 as, amended in 1956 and 1990.[118]

Amendment of 1956 in Favour of Dalit Sikhs

Following agitation by Master *Tara Singh*, the Constitution (Scheduled Castes and the Scheduled Tribes) Orders (Amendment) Act, providing for inclusion of Dalit Sikhs in the list of the Scheduled Castes, was passed in 1956.[119] It said;

"Notwithstanding anything contained in para 2, no person who professes a religion different from the Hindu or Sikh religion shall be deemed to be a member of a Scheduled Caste."[120]

Amendment of 1990 in Favour of Dalit Buddhists

In May 1990, to commemorate the centenary of the birth of Dr B.R. Ambedkar, Prime Minister V.P. Singh brought Dalits who converted to Buddhism.[121] into the list of Scheduled Castes. He made representations to Parliament that this change of religion, from Hindu to Buddhist, had not altered their social, economic or educational conditions. The same should be acknowledged in the case of Dalits who become Christians;[122]

> *"Notwithstanding anything contained in para 2, no person who professes a religion different from the Hindu, the Sikh or the Buddhist religion shall be deemed to be a member of a Scheduled Caste."*[123]

The whole debate is if Hindus, Sikhs and Buddhists are being given reservation on the basis of caste and religion, then why not Dalit Muslims and Dalit Christians. In fact, Dalit Muslims and Dalit Christians deserve the same treatment and reservations. There should be a democratic as well as legal solution to the problem. All these vulnerable groups should be included in the framework of reservation so that they could also live as the life of dignity, space to present themselves and get their due share which denied since immemorial.[124]

The very important question comes how have conversion taken place in India? We can examine this in two stages. In medieval period as far as conversion to Islam is concerned it took place mainly due to the caste oppression, as pointed out by Swami Vivekananda[125] what was the religion of Nomads-Pagans? Some social scientists call it Indigenous culture, rather than religion for the phenomenon which was and is practiced by indigenous (Adivasi) people all over the World. Society is always changing. As caste system has been the central part of religion in India many of the dominated castes regularly kept leaving Hinduism to opt for other religions, Jainism, Buddhism, Christianity, Islam and Sikhism. People felt that they are not getting equality and so kept leaving the Hindu fold and embracing other religions. After Lord Buddha's teachings a large chunk of people became Buddhists in the sub-continent. Many felt that the missions are doing service to their community so they changed their faith.[126]

One has to understand that a very small section did convert to Islam due to anticipation for reward by Muslim kings, a smaller section due to fear and a substantial chunk due to the social interaction as seen in the Muslims of Malabar coast and the Muslims of Mewat. Major conversion to Islam during medieval time was due to the influence of Sufi saints, at whose *Dargah* the untouchables could also visit.[127] Since even today one-fourth of the population holds to the norms of untouchability, it is not surprising that some dominated castes do keep deciding to leave the fold of Hinduism.[128] Over time, Ambedkar became increasingly critical of orthodox Hinduism, which he saw as inextricably linked to caste discrimination, and at the Yeola Conversion Conference in 1935, he stated famously, "*I was born as a Hindu but will not die as a Hindu;*" and exhorted his followers to leave Hinduism and join another religion.[129]

So far the conversions to Christianity is concerned it did not begin with the coming of British as propagated by some. Christianity is century's old, entering India with the coming of *St. Thomas* in the first century.[130] Some doubt this version and hold that Christianity came here in fifth century.[131] The Christian missionaries have been working here in the neglected Adivasi areas providing the health and educational services, the appeal of which prompted many an Adivasis-Dalits to embrace this religion. Not to forget here is the point that many a Christian institutions are located in cities, where all sections of society vie to send their children. One can also concede that a few of these missions may be aiming for conversions through their prayer and healing services.[132]

In the present scheme of things if one leaves Hindu fold to embrace Buddhism-Jainism-Sikhism, no problem at all and they are considered to be 'Indian religions. For communalists problem seems to be only with Islam and Christianity! The basic shrewdness is to call religions as national or foreign. As such religions are basically universal not bound by national boundaries. Constituent Assembly had discussed this thread bare and so the right to practice and propagate one's religion is very much there.[133] In the debate the word used is 'converting' others. Where is the place for people volunteering and adopting another religion, like Ambedkar and so many others? In a way it is a way to undermine the conscience of people that somebody is converting them. Where is the place for choice of one's religion in a democratic society believing in 'freedom of religion and conscience'?.[134]

Compensatory discrimination was one of the means chosen to achieve those ends. Its purpose is to promote equalisation by offsetting historically accumulated inequalities. The Government of India has used compensatory discrimination as a means of achieving greater equality by deliberately overcoming some of those historically accumulated disabilities from which Dalits have long suffered.[135] So far various study on Dalit Christians and Dalit Muslims are concerned, there is not a single inclusive policy for these vulnerable groups to claim themselves as the full member of the political community.[136] Scheduled Castes constitute the socially and economically deprived caste groups of the Hindu society. They mainly consist of agricultural labour-ers, cultivators of small land-holdings, artisans, petty labourers and industrial workers. Their geographical distribution provides valuable evidence to-wards the regional dimension of poverty in the country.[137] The Chamars and Pasis of Uttar Pradesh, the Balais of Bengal, the Meghs of Gujarat, the Mahars of Maharashtra, the Malls of Andhra Pradesh and the Adi-Davidas of Tamil Nadu are all toiling Scheduled Castes concentrated in specific regions.

Notes

1. See 2011 Census of India, Governement of India, Ministry of Home Affairs, Office of the Registrar General and Census Commissioner, India, http://censusindia.gov.in/
2. See detail of 2011. Census Report on population, Government of India.
3. http://www.censusindia.gov.in.
4. Sukhadeo Thorat and Chitranjan Senapati, 2006. Reservation Policy in India-Dimensions and Issues, Indian Institute of Dalit Studies, Working Paper Series, Vol. 1, No. 2, New Delhi, p. 3.
5. Selected Socio-Economic Statistics, India, 2011. October 2011, Government of India, Ministry of Statistics and Programme Implementation, Central Statistics Office, Social Statistics Division, New Delhi, p. 79.
6. Prakash, Louis, 2007. Caste-Based Discrimination and Atrocities on Dalit Christians and the Need for Reservations, Working Paper Series, Indian Institute of Dalit Studies, Vol. II, No. 04, New Delhi, p. 6.
7. The Times of India, 10 November 2013. SC/ST takes rapid strides close literacy gap.
8. Khalid Khan and Nidhi Sadana Sabharwal, 2012. Access and Equity in Higher Education: Aspects of Gender, Caste, Ethnicity, Religion, Occupation and Economic Groups in Rural and Urban Areas During Pre and Post Reform Periods, Indian Institute of Dalit Studies, New Delhi, p. 11.
9. *Ibid.*
10. *Ibid.*
11. *Ibid.*
12. Arvind, Panagariya and Vishal More, Poverty by Social, Religious and Economic Groups in India and Its Largest States 1993-94 to 2011-12, Working Paper No. 2013-02, SIPA School of International and Public Affairs ISERP Institute for Social and Economic

Research and Policy, Programme of Indian Economic Policies, Colombia University, p. 8.

13. Sundaram, K. and S. Tendulkar, 2003. "Poverty among social and economic groups in India in 1990s," Economic and Political Weekly 38(50), pp. 5263-5276, Also see in details Arvind, Panagariya and Vishal More, Poverty by Social, Religious and Economic Groups in India and Its Largest States 1993-94 to 2011-12, Working Paper No. 2013-02, SIPA | School of International and Public Affairs ISERP | Institute for Social and Economic Research and Policy, Programme of Indian Economic Policies, Colombia University, p. 7.
14. Eliada, Mircea, 1987. The Encyclopaedia of Religion, Vol. 12, Macmillan Publishing Company, New York, pp. 282-283.
15. Note: citation from D. F. Strauss, 1977. The Christ of Faith and the Jesus of History: A Critique of Schleiermacher's Life of Jesus (1865; ET Philadelphia: Fortress Press), p. 41.
16. *Ibid.*
17. Chunnu Prasad 2007. Issue of Reservation and Quota: A Critical Perspective", Social Action, Vol. 42:3 July-September, pp. 242-258.
18. Prasad, Chunnu 2009. Dalits Struggle for Democratic Space: Bahujan Samaj Party and the Democratisation of Indian Politics, in an edited by Vivek Kumar, G. Stanley, Jaya Kumar and Tenepali Hari in The Dynamics of Change and Community in the era of Globalisation: Voices of the Margins, Sunrise Publication, New Delhi, pp. 336-367.
19. Constitution of India (http://lawmin.nic.in/coi/coiason29july08.pdf (See more details in The Constitution of India, Government of India, Ministry of Law and Justice)
20. Prem Kumar Shinde, 2005. Dalits and Human Rights (Dalits the Broken Future), in Vol. III, ISHA Books, New Delhi, pp. 242-276.
21. Bahauddin, K.M., 1992. Kerala Muslims - the long struggle, Sahitya Pravarthaka Co-op Society, Kottyam.
22. Kurup, K.K.N., 1991. The Sufis and religious harmony in Kerala, in A.A.Engineer (ed.) Sufism and Communal Harmony, Printwell, Jaipur, p. 80.
23. Lal, K.S., 1984. Early Muslims in India, Books and Books, New Delhi, pp. 12-17.
24. See details in Romila Thapar, 2008. The Aryan: Recasting Constructs, Penguin, New Delhi.
25. See details in Murtahin Billah Jasir Fazlie, 1995, (ed.). Muslims in

India: Past and Present, Hindu Chauvinism and Muslims in India, http://www.islamawareness.net/Asia/India/muslims_in_india.html

26. Imtiaj, Ahmad, 1971. Social Stratification among Muslims, The Economic Weekly, Vol. 10, pp. 1093-96.
27. Zillor, Khan, 1968. Caste and Muslim Peasantry in India and Pakistan, Man in India, Vol. 48, pp. 133-148.
28. Imtiaj, Ahmad 2003. The Democratic Problem of the Muslim Community in the edited book by Safdar Imam Quadri and Sanjay Kumar, Marginalisation of Dalit Muslims in Indian Democracy, New Delhi, Deshkal Publication, pp. 1-2.
29. W.H., Mcleod, 1996. The Evolution of the Sikh Community: Five Essays, Delhi, Oxford University Press, p. 87.
30. Imtiaj, Ahmad, 1966. The Ashraf-Ajlaf Dichotomy in Muslim Social Structure in India, IESHR, Vol. 3, No. 3, pp. 268-78.
31. Singh, I.P, 1975. A Sikh Village in M. Singer, Ed. Traditional India: Structure and Change, p. 76.
32. Chunnu, Prasad, 2009. Comparative Context of Discrimination, Social Exclusion and Religion: A Study of Dalit Muslims in India, National Seminar on Socio-Economic and Educational Status of Muslims in Maharastra on 21st to 23rd December by Tata Institute of Social Sciences, Mumbai, Maharashtra.
33. See details in Uadri, Safdar and Kumar Sanjay. 2003. Marginalisation of Dalit Muslims in Indian Democracy. Delhi: Deskhal Publication.
34. See details in P. Muthaiah, 2004. "Politics of Dalit Identity", The Indian Journal of Political Science, Vol. IXI, No. 3, July-Sept. 2004 and Sudha Pai, "Social Capital, Panchayats and Grassroots Democracy: The Politics of Dalit Assertion in Two Districts of Uttar Pradesh" in Dwaipayan Bhattacharyya, Niraja Gopal Joyal, Ishnu N. Mohapatra and Sudha Pai (ed.), Interrogating Social Capital. The Indian Experience, Sachchidananda Publications, New Delhi.
35. By Shameem Ansari, Islam Does Not Discriminate But Muslims Do, June 1, 2009 by Dalitmuslims https://Dalitmuslims.wordpress.com/2009/06/01/islam-does-not-discriminate-but-muslims-do/ and Asghar Ali Engineer Indian Muslims, Fifty Years In Independent India - An Evaluation February 16-28, 2002, http://www.csss-isla.com/arch%20187.htm
36. *Ibid.*
37. *Ibid.*

38. The Holy Quran, Surah al-Hujuraat, verse 13.
39. Alam, Anwar, 2003. Democratisation of Indian Muslims, Economic and Political Weekly, XXXVIII (46) November 15, p. 4881.
40. See in details Ali Anwar's Masawat ki jung: Pasemanzar Bihar ka Pasmanda Musalman, 2001.
41. Anwar, Ali 2001. Masawat ki Jung: Pasemanzar: Bihar ka Pasmanda Musalman (in Hindi), Vani Prakashan, New Delhi, p. 30
42. Sikand, Yoginder 2003. The 'Dalit-Muslims' and the All India Backward Muslim Morcha, Qalandar, http://www.islamin terfaith.org.
43. Anwar, Ali 2001. Masawat ki Jung: Pasemanzar: Bihar ka Pasmanda Musalman (in Hindi), Vani Prakashan, New Delhi, p. 30.
44. See for detail, http://www.islaminterfaith.org/sep2003/ article.html., Sikand, Yoginder 2003) also The 'Dalit-Muslims' and the All India Backward Muslim Morcha.
45. Diwan, Paras, 1979. Constitution of India, Sterling Publishers, New Delhi, p. 70.
46. See for detail, http://www.rediff.com/news/2003/mar/ 06bihar.htm, Sahay, Anand Mohan (2003, March 6), Backward Muslims protest denial of burial also News report in www.rediff.com.
47. Anwar, Ali 2001. Masawat ki Jung: Pasemanzar: Bihar ka Pasmanda Musalman (in Hindi), Vani Prakashan, New Delhi, p. 30
48. Chunnu Prasad, 2009. Comparative Context of Discrimination, Social Exclusion and Religion: A Study of Dalit Muslims in India, National Seminar on Socio-Economic and Educational Status of Muslims in Maharastra on 21st to 23rd December by Tata Institute of Social Sciences, Mumbai, Maharashtra.
49. See details in The Prophet Novel Character, http://d1. islamhouse. com/data/en/ih_books/single/en_The_Prophets_Noble_ Character.pdf
50. *Times of India*, January 26, 2008.
51. In the DV of March 1, 2008, the Editor has rightly said that 'Muslim leaders should not oppose quota for Backward Muslims'. The current debate on the issue in the national and Muslim media establishes the DV analysis of castes among Muslims.
52. *Ibid.*

53. See details in Shemsu Sesen, Khufu Reborn: The Next Chapter in Jean-Pierre Houdin's Work with the Great Pyramid, http://emhotep.net/2011/01/19/structures/pyramids-structures/khufu-reborn-the-next-chapter-in-jean-pierre-houdin%E2%80%99s-work-with-the-great-pyramid/
54. See for detail information of Sachhar Report on Muslims of India, p. 192.
55. *Ibid.*, p. 209.
56. *Ibid.*, Para 16.3.
57. *Ibid.*
58. *Ibid.*
59. Constitution of India (http://lawmin.nic.in/coi/coiason29july08.pdf (See more details in The Constitution of India, Government of India, Ministry of Law and Justice).
60. *Ibid.*
61. See for detail, www.Dalitmuslims.com, Indian Dalit Muslims Voice.
62. Mohammad Shahanshah Ansari, Inclusion of Dalit Muslims in Scheduled Castes: Apex court rekindles hope, 4 August 2009.
63. ncm.nic.in/pdf/report%20Dalit%20%20reservation.pdf
64. Chunnu, Prasad, 2009. Comparative Context of Discrimination, Social Exclusion and Religion: A Study of Dalit Muslims in India, National Seminar on Socio-Economic and Educational Status of Muslims in Maharastra on 21st to 23rd December by Tata Institute of Social Sciences, Mumbai, Maharashtra.
65. Ambedkar, B.R., 1987. Why go for Conversion? Dalit Sahitya Academy, Bangalore, p. 16.
66. http://ishwarsharan.wordpress.com/parts-2-to-9/christian-churches-threaten-Dalit-rights-leela-tampi/
67. http://www.Dalitchristians.com/Html/P_BC_%20Press Release.htm
68. http://www.hinduwisdom.info/Conversion.htm
69. https://mumbailaity.wordpress.com/2011/02/21/caste-system-among-christians/
70. Caste Census in India, Communal Castist Regionalist India, Saturday, July, 2011, http://communalcastistregionalistindian.blogspot.in/2011/07/caste-census-in-india.html
71. Ambedkar, B.R., 1947. Who are the Shudras? Bheem Patrika Publications, p. 145.

72. http://a-mushtaq1114-dp.blogspot.in/2011/12/caste-system-in-india.html
73. See website, http://en.wikipedia.org, article related to Dalit Christians of South India.
74. The term 'caste Christians' is used here purely as a sociological category as used by social scientists to avoid the negative connotations like Dalits and non-Dalits. Instead of using the terms Dalits and non-Dalits, they use the terms Dalits and caste Hindus or general population.
75. Viswanathan. S, 2008. Caste violence at Eraiyur in Tamil Nadu's Villupuram district brings to the fore the issue of discrimination against Dalit Christians, Frontline, Vol. 25, Issue 8, April, pp. 12-25.
76. http://www.Dalitchristians.com/
77. Letter to His Holiness Pope Francis, Vatican, Rome, Italy, Mission of the Church and Dalit Catholic Empowerment, Rev. Dr Fr. S. Lourduswamy, Former Secretary, National CBCI committee for SC/ST http://www.vodintl.org.uk/article/Indian% 20 Bishops %20Memorandum%20to%20Vatican %20February %201013.pdf
78. Prasad, Chunnu 2008. Caste, Social Exclusion and the Question of Livelihood: A Case of Scheduled Castes of Assam and Arunachal Pradesh, National Conference on Economic Reforms in India: Social Exclusion and Social Justice, on 27th to 29th November, Dr B.R. Ambedkar Open University, Hyderabad, Andhra Pradesh.
79. http://www.Dalitchristians.com/
80. Prakash, Louis, 2007. Caste-Based Discrimination and Atrocities on Dalit Christians and the Need for Reservations, Working Paper Series, Indian Institute of Dalit Studies, Vol. II, No. 04, New Delhi, pp. 4-40.
81. Chunnu, Prasad, Social Exclusion and Caste Based Discrimination on Dalit Christians in South India, National Conference, Social Mobility in South India, on 24th and 25th September, 2009 by Department of Sociology, Pondicherry University, Puducherry.
82. Danik Jagran, 4 December, 2006. p. 9.
83. Faleiro, Eduardo 2007. Christianity in India Today, Vol. 5, No. 10, February, p. 3.
84. Chunnu, Prasad, 2009. Social Exclusion and Caste Based Discrimination on Dalit Christians in South India, National Conference, Social Mobility in South India, on 24th and 25th September by Department of Sociology, Pondicherry University, Puducherry.

85. Sukhadeo Thorat, Paul Attewell and Firdaus Fatima Rizvi, 2009. Urban Labour Market Discrimination, Indian Institute of Dalit Studies, Vol. III, No. 01, New Delhi, pp. 2-15.

86. *Ibid.*

87. Prakash, Louis, 2007. Caste-Based Discrimination and Atrocities on Dalit Christians and the Need for Reservations, Working Paper Series, Indian Institute of Dalit Studies, Vol. II, No. 04, New Delhi, pp. 4-40.

88. See website, http://indianhope.free.fr/site_eng/article_5.php3, article related to the discrimination against Dalits Christians in Tamil Nadu, by Aruldoss SJ - SAR News: Bombay - 051, September 19-25, 1992, there is discrimination against Dalits within the Christian Church itself in Tamil Nadu, says a study conduced by Fr Antony Raj SJ, A Dalit Jesuit and Sociologist.

89. Nambissan, G. B. 2006. "Terms of Inclusion: Dalits and the Right to Education" in Kumar, Ravi (ed.), The Crisis of Elementary Education in India, New Delhi: Sage Publications: 225-265

90. Discrimination Against Dalits by Christians, Aruldoss SJ - SAR News: Bombay - 051, September 19-25, 1992, http://indianhope.free.fr/site_eng/article_5.php3

91. *Ibid.*

92. *Ibid.*

93. Prakash, Louis, 2007. Caste-Based Discrimination and Atrocities on Dalit Christians and the Need for Reservations, Working Paper Series, Indian Institute of Dalit Studies, Vol. II, No. 04, New Delhi, pp. 4-40.

94. See in details in Satish Saberwal, 1972. The Reserved Constituency Candidates and Consequences, Economic and Political Weekly, Vol. 7, No. 2 .

95. See details n Kumar, Narender, 2004. Dalit Policies, Politics and Parliament, Shipra Publishers, New Delhi.

96. *Ibid.*

97. Letter to His Holiness Pope Francis, Vatican, Rome, Italy, Mission of the Church and Dalit Catholic Empowerment, Rev. Dr Fr. S. Lourduswamy, Former Secretary, National CBCI committee for SC/ST http://www.vodintl.org.uk/article/Indian%20Bishops%20Memorandum %20to%20Vatican% 20February%201013.pdf

98. R. Chandidas, "How Close to Equality are Scheduled Castes", Economic and Political Weekly. Vol. IV, No. 24, June 14, 1969, pp. 975-979.

99. Chunnu, Prasad, 2009. Social Exclusion and Caste Based Discrimination on Dalit Christians in South India, National Conference, Social Mobility in South India, on 24th and 25th September by Department of Sociology, Pondicherry University, Puducherry. Also see Prakash, Louis, 2007, Caste-Based Discrimination and Atrocities on Dalit Christians and the Need for Reservations, Working Paper Series, Indian Institute of Dalit Studies, Vol. II, No. 04, New Delhi, pp. 4-40.

100. *Ibid.*

101. Madhu Chandra, 60 Years of Constitutional Rights Denied To 20 Millions Indian Dalit Christians, 06 August, 2010, Countercurrents.org.

102. Anis Ansari-on 04/10/2013, Muslim and Christian Dalits are denied their dues, http://gulail.com/religious-discrimination-against-muslim-and-christian-Dalits/

103. Dalits in the Muslim and Christian, Communities, A Status Report on, Current Social Scientific Knowledge, Prepared For The, National Commission for Minorities, Government of India, by Satish Deshpande, with the assistance of, Geetika Bapna, Department of Sociology, University of Delhi.

104. Constitution of India (http://lawmin.nic.in/coi/coiason29july08.pdf (See more details in The Constitution of India, Government of India, Ministry of Law and Justice).

105. Times of India, 8 January, 2009.

106. The New Indian Express dated 31 July 2008.

107. http://a-mushtaq1114-dp.blogspot.in/2011/12/caste-system-in-india.html

108. Massey, John, 1995. Dalits in India, Manohar Publications, New Delhi, p. 82.

109. Prakash, Louis, 2007. Caste-Based Discrimination and Atrocities on Dalit Christians and the Need for Reservations, Working Paper Series, Indian Institute of Dalit Studies, Vol. II, No. 04, New Delhi, pp. 4-40.

110. See website, http://www.mail-archive.com, article related to Dalit Christians Plight.

111. Christian Dalits, A Research on Christian Dalits in India, Summer 2009, http://www.indianet.nl/pdf/christianDalits.pdf

112. *Ibid.*

113. Basu, Durga Das 2004. Introduction to the Constitution of India, Law Publishers, New Delhi, pp. 285-287.

114. http://tribal.nic.in/Content/DefinitionpRrofiles.aspx
115. http://lawmin.nic.in/olwing/coi/coi-english/Const.Pock%202Pg. Rom8Fsss(22).pdf and http://lawmin.nic.in/olwing/coi/coi-english/Const.Pock%202Pg.Rom8Fsss(22).pdf
116. *Ibid.*
117. Constitution of India (http://lawmin.nic.in/coi/coiason29july08.pdf (See more details in The Constitution of India, Government of India, Ministry of Law and Justice)
118. See Constitution of India about the Special Rights given under the Presidential Order, 1950, known as the Constitution (Scheduled Caste) Order, No. 19, 10 August, 1950.
119. Prem Kumar Shinde, 2005 (ed.). Dalit and Human Rights (Dalits: Security and Rights Implecation), Isha Books Publication, New Delhi, pp. 120-125.
120. *Ibid.*
121. Chunnu Prasad, 2014. The Philosophy of Buddhism: Basis of its Existence, in an edited book by P. Chenna Reddy, E. Shiva Nagi Reddy in Bodhisiri, Research India Press, New Delhi, pp. 152-161.
122. Prem Kumar Shinde, 2005 (ed.). Dalit and Human Rights (Dalits: Security and Rights Implecation), Isha Books Publication, New Delhi, pp. 120-125.
123. Basu, Durga Das 2004. Introduction to the Constitution of India, Law Publishers, New Delhi, pp. 79-143.
124. Chunnu, Prasad, 2009. "Social Exclusion and Caste Based Discrimination on Dalit Christians in South India", National Conference, Social Mobility in South India, on 24th and 25th September by Department of Sociology, Pondicherry University, Puducherry.
125. Collected works of Swami Vivekananda, 1893, July 12, 1863 – July 4, 1902, Chicago, p. 330.
126. See for detail in Ram Puniyani, How is Ghar Vapasi Different from Forcible Conversions?, 17, December 2014, http://communalism.blogspot.in/2014/12/how-is-ghar-vapasi-different-from.html
127. *Ibid.*
128. Cited in Zelliot 2013, 147.
129. https://fightagainstuntouchability.wordpress.com/
130. The Encyclopedia of Christinity, Volume 5 by Erwin Fahlbusch. Wm. B. Eerdmans Publishing - 2008. p. 285, http://www.catholictradition.org/Tradition/apostle-thomas.htm

131. Stephen, Andrew Missick, 2000. Mar Thoma: The Apostolic Foundation of the Assyrian Church and the Christians of St. Thomas in India, Journal of Assyrian Academic Studies Vol. XIV, No. 2. pp. 33-61

132. See for detail in Ram Puniyani, How is Ghar Vapasi Different from Forcible Conversions?, 17, December 2014, http://communalism.blogspot.in/2014/12/how-is-ghar-vapasi-different-from.html

133. http://logos.nationalinterest.in/2014/06/constituent-assembly-debate-on-freedom-of-religion/ Constituent Assembly debate on Freedom of Religion Apoorva Tadepalli the fears of the constituent assembly members regarding politicisation of religion have come true, June 25, 2014, IN BLOG.

134. See for detail in Ram Puniyani, How is Ghar Vapasi Different from Forcible Conversions?, 17, December 2014, http://communalism.blogspot.in/2014/12/how-is-ghar-vapasi-different-from.html

135. Chunnu Prasad, 2010. Contextualising Marginalisation and Reservation: An Overview of India's Northeast, National Conference on Movements for Equity in Reservations on 21st to 22nd February by Centre for the Study of Social Systems, Jawaharlal Nehru University, New Delhi and Dalit Information and Education Trust, Hyderabad.

136. Chunnu Prasad, 2008. Rights and the Question of Livelihood: A Case of Scheduled Castes of Arunachal Pradesh", National Seminar on Social Exclusion, Poverty and Livelihood of Marginalised Groups in India-need for effective Inclusive Strategies, on 24th and 25th September, Mangalore University, Karnataka.

137. Sukhadeo Thorat, Paul Attewell and Firdaus Fatima Rizvi, 2009. Urban Labour Market Discrimination, Indian Institute of Dalit Studies, Vol. III, No. 01, New Delhi, pp. 2-15.

3

Mapping Exclusions in Northeast India: Durable Inequalities

The lists of the Scheduled Castes (SC's) are notified in respect of each State and Union Territory separately in pursuance of Articles 341 and 342 of the Constitution of India. These lists are State and area specific and are valid only within the jurisdiction of that State or Union Territory and not outside. In each decennial census since 1951, SC's population has been enumerated. According to the Constitution (Scheduled Castes) Orders (Amendment) Act, 1990, SC's can only belong to Hindu or Sikh or Buddhist religions. No SC list exists for Arunachal Pradesh, Nagaland, Lakshadweep and Andaman and Nicobar Islands after 2001 census due to exclusion/deletion of the category. Consequent to the promulgation of Constitutional Orders/ Amendments from 2002 to 2008 new entries have been added in the SCs lists of 22 and 20 States/UTs respectively. In the SCs list 20 new castes have been added as main SCs in ten States and one Union Territories. The number of main SC's has increased from 1221 to 1241 during the last decade. In addition, 115 sub-entries as synonyms/subgroups/sections have been notified along with the main SCs in 15 states and 3 UTs[1].

The Northeast region comprises of eight states called 'Northeast'. Northeast of India was one political entity named

Assam before the rest of the States were carved out into different sovereign states. The entire Northeast of India has been a pot of amalgamation of different cultures and ethnic groups coming and settling here. Earliest mention of this region was by the Chinese explorer, Chang Kien, in 100 B.C. The Periplus of the Erythrean Sea and Ptolemy's and geography also suggest the same. The Australoids or the pre-Dravidians were the earliest inhabitants of this state. Huen Tsang, Chinese traveller, visited this region in the Seventh century. Assam was the founding state of the Union of India in 1947. At that time, the state comprised the whole of the Northeast region. Subsequently, a number of other Northeastern states were carved out of Assam, starting with Nagaland in 1963 and ending with Arunachal Pradesh in 1972. Northeast of India is the land of Blue Mountains, Green Valleys, large number of Rivers and nestled in the lesser known Easternmost Himalayas. This region is abundant in natural Beauty, Wildlife, Flora and Fauna and its colourful peoples. A blend of which makes it the most beautiful Eco-Tourism destination in South Asia. The Land of Majestic Mountains, crowned with peaks of sapphire blue. The Northeast happens to be the region where the sun rises first in the entire country.

The eight states of Northeast India clockwise Assam, Arunachal Pradesh, Manipur, Meghalaya, Nagaland, Mizoram, Meghalaya, Sikkim and Tripura. It is bordered by Bhutan, Tibet, China, Burma (Myanmar) and Bangladesh. So far the Protected Area Permits (PAP) and Inner-Line Permit (ILP) are concerned only Assam, Meghalaya, Sikkim and Tripura can be visited without it and Indians or any tourists from inside/outside required PAP or ILP to visit some States of North-east.[2] Majority of the peoples in northeast are from plains of Assam, most of them Hindus, Christians, Buddhist, Animist and Muslims. The northeast Indian states have their own problems and cannot be club together. No doubt the issues are very much same but solutions are different because demands and situations are different. This is the reason why one has to see the problems of these states separately.[3]

At present in India the proportion of the Scheduled Caste population constitutes 16.6 per cent of the total population in 2011 Census. The proportion during the last census was 16.2 per cent. Thus, there has been an increase of 0.4 per cent during the last decade. As per 2011 census of India record the Northeast India Region (NIR) in total consist of 30,30,109 (509.3 per cent) Scheduled Caste population.[4]

Table 3.1: Total Scheduled Castes Population of India's Northeast

North-eastern States	*Total SC Population (2011)*	*Male*	*Female*
All India Scheduled Caste Population	20,13,78,372	103535314	97843058
All Scheduled Castes Population in Northeast India as per 2011 Census	3030415	1552965	1477450
Assam	2231321	1145314	1086007
Arunachal Pradesh	6188*		
Manipur	97328	48863	48465
Meghalaya	17355	9157	8198
Mizoram	1218	807	411
Nagaland	NA		
Sikkim	28275	14454	13821
Tripura	654918	334370	320548

*In 2011 Census Report, Government of India, The entire Scheduled Castes Population has been withdrawn.

Note: 'All Scheduled Castes includes figures for unclassified'. Scheduled Castes having 'Nil', return are not shown.

Source: State Primary Census Abstract for Individual Scheduled Caste- 2011. http://censusindia.gov.in/

Table 3.2: Total Scheduled Castes Main Workers in Northeastern States of India

Sl. No.	*State*	*Gender Category*		*Total Number*
		Male	*Female*	
1.	Assam	530874	99658	630532
2.	Manipur	2400	11024	35024
3.	Meghalaya	4142	792	4934
4.	Mizoram	567	38	605
5.	Sikkim	6755	3186	9941
6.	Tripura	162933	27599	190492
7.	Arunachal Pradesh*	Deleted	Deleted	Deleted
8.	Nagaland	NA	NA	NA

* In 2011 Census Report, Government of India, The entire Scheduled Castes Population has been withdrawn.

Note: 'All Scheduled Castes includes figures for unclassified'. Scheduled Castes having 'Nil', return are not shown.

Source: State Primary Census Abstract for Individual Scheduled Caste-2011. http://censusindia.gov.in/

Table 3.3: Total Scheduled Castes Marginal Workers of Northeastern States of India

Sl. No.	State	Gender Category		Total Number
		Male	Female	
1.	Assam	105828	115101	220929
2.	Manipur	2349	7311	9660
3.	Meghalaya	696	601	1297
4.	Mizoram	23	22	45
5.	Sikkim	1517	2002	3519
6.	Tripura	28315	32501	60816
7.	Arunachal Pradesh*	Deleted	Deleted	Deleted
8.	Nagaland	NA	NA	NA

* In 2011 Census Report, Government of India, The entire Scheduled Castes Population has been withdrawn.

Note: 'All Scheduled Castes includes figures for unclassified'. Scheduled Castes having 'Nil', return are not shown.

Source: State Primary Census Abstract for Individual Scheduled Caste- 2011. http://censusindia.gov.in/

Table 3.4: Total Scheduled Castes Non-workers of North Eastern States of India

Sl. No.	State	Gender Category		Total Number
		Male	Female	
1.	Assam	508612	871248	1379860
2.	Manipur	22514	30130	52644
3.	Meghalaya	4319	6805	11124
4.	Mizoram	217	351	568
5.	Sikkim	6182	8633	14815
6.	Tripura	143122	260488	403610
7.	Arunachal Pradesh*	Deleted	Deleted	Deleted
8.	Nagaland	NA	NA	NA

* In 2011 Census Report, Government of India, The entire Scheduled Castes Population has been withdrawn.

Note: 'All Scheduled Castes includes figures for unclassified'. Scheduled Castes having 'Nil', return are not shown.

Source: State Primary Census Abstract for Individual Scheduled Caste- 2011. http://censusindia.gov.in/

Table 3.5: Total Scheduled Castes Literates in Northeast

Sl. No.	*State*	*Gender Category*		*Total Number*
		Male	*Female*	
1.	Assam	826983	662581	1489564
2.	Manipur	35311	29177	64488
3.	Meghalaya	5953	4322	10275
4.	Mizoram	699	315	1014
5.	Sikkim	10491	8707	19198
6.	Tripura	273619	243257	516876
7.	Arunachal Pradesh*	Deleted	Deleted	Deleted
8.	Nagaland	NA	NA	NA

* In 2011 Census Report, Government of India, The entire Scheduled Castes Population has been withdrawn.
Note: 'All Scheduled Castes includes figures for unclassified'. Scheduled Castes having 'Nil', return are not shown.
Source: State Primary Census Abstract for Individual Scheduled Caste- 2011. http://censusindia.gov.in/

Table 3.6: Total Scheduled Castes Other Workers in Northeastern States of India

Sl. No.	*State*	*Gender Category*		*Total Number*
		Male	*Female*	
1.	Assam	51179	36197	87376
2.	Manipur	643	1532	2175
3.	Meghalaya	454	354	808
4.	Mizoram	18	13	31
5.	Sikkim	680	703	1383
6.	Tripura	16995	19691	36686
7.	Arunachal Pradesh*	Deleted	Deleted	Deleted
8.	Nagaland	NA	NA	NA

* In 2011 Census Report, Government of India, The entire Scheduled Castes Population has been withdrawn.
Note: 'All Scheduled Castes includes figures for unclassified'. Scheduled Castes having 'Nil', return are not shown.
Source: State Primary Census Abstract for Individual Scheduled Caste- 2011. http://censusindia.gov.in/

The confusion of caste system begins by the use of the word caste itself. The Indians in their different languages use the word 'Jat' or 'Jati' for any community who have something common like religion, language, origin, similar geographical background, and ethnicity. The Indians also use the word 'Jat' for Varna.[5] The Portuguese who were the first European power to arrive in India distorted the word 'Jat' into English word caste. The British who arrived to India much later after the Portuguese also used the word caste. The British used the word Caste instead of Jat and Varna. And so sometimes in English the caste system is explained in a confusing way according to which, the caste system consists of four castes which are divided into many castes. Sometimes in English the word caste is used for Varna and the word sub-caste for Jat.[6]

Although the caste system is weakening, it is still wields considerable power especially in rural areas. The India that Hindus are born into will largely determine their social standing as well as their career and marriages prospects. Castes are further divided into thousands of *jati,* social communities that are often linked to specific occupation. Surnames often reflect the *jati* that a person belongs to.[7] Out of the four castes, Dalits (formerly known as untouchables) who holds menial jobs such as sweeping and latrine cleaning officially referred to as the Scheduled Castes, the Dalits have also been known as the Depressed Classes, which gives some indication of their status in the society. Most of the Adivasis of the Northeast also fall into the catch-all grouping of Scheduled Castes and Tribes under the Indian Constitution.[8]

So far the basic understanding on the Scheduled Castes and Scheduled Tribes are concerned, historically both of them are belong to the same category called 'Nagas' of Nagamadala. Those who accepted the slavery in the Hindu Social Order (HSO) become untouchables, Dalits and latter notified in the Constitution of India 'Scheduled Castes.[9] On the other hand, those who ran to the forest and rejected the slavery of the Hindu Social Order become tribes, Adivasis and latter notified in the Constitution of India 'Scheduled Tribes.[10]

Over a few decades it has been observed that, Indian cities are suffering with racial attacks, hatred and discrimination towards the northeast people across India at various levels. In order to do so, we need to first of all know the root causes of the problem itself. In fact, the problems of rapes, murders, molestations, sexual harassment, racial discrimination etc. are created by the Indian State (Hindu Social Order) in general and the differences of socio-culture, customs, habits and historical backgrounds of the people in India. The speed in which the State responded with regards to Nirbhaya's gang-raped case of December 12, 2012 was appreciable where those accused were already convicted. However, the same speed or justice has so far not been delivered in cases vis-a-vis Northeast people or in general SC's and ST's. Several cases are still pending in Delhi Court. It took several years to have convicted the 2005 Dhaula Kuan gang-raped of a Mizo girl. On 24 October, 2009, Ramchanphy Hongray, a young Naga girl of 19 years of age from Manipur was murdered in Munirka by one IIT-Delhi Ph.D scholar. However, the accused has not been convicted so far. The question, therefore is, why it has taken such a long years in convicting the accused person where there is *prima facie* evidence that he has deliberately and devilishly strangulated her without any reason? Another example of undelivered justice is the attempted rape and subsequent murder of Reingamphy Awungshi on May 28-29 of 2013 at Chirag Delhi. Brutal murder of Richard Loitam, a second-semester student of Acharya NRV School of Architecture in Bangalore on April 18, 2012 and the mass exodus of Northeast in 2012 from Bengaluru were some of the examples of racial attacks and problems of India. Another example of discrimination was the suicide of Dana Sangma, a niece of Meghalaya Chief Minister, Mukul Sangma after being caught over alleged cheating in Amity University exam in Haryana on 24 April, 2012.[11]

The first and foremost root cause of the problem is the failure of the respective State Governments in providing economic stability and employment to the growing number of youths in Northeast States. It is not a denying fact that due to poor economic conditions and lack of avenues to these growing numbers of youths in their respective home states that has pushed all these youths to mainland India for different types of jobs and employments for their survivals. And most of these poor citizens belong to various tribal communities who have become restless and jobless in their homes due to lack of job avenues, corruption, poor educational infrastructures, discriminations and the unresolved political conflicts in almost all the Northeast States.[12] In most of the Indian cities the populations of the Northeasterners comprised of students, workers (skilled and unskilled) and dropouts school students who can be clubbed as migrants populations. The relevant question is, why so many people have fled their villages and towns and come to live in the mainland Indian cities? The only reason as to why these migrants have fled to these cities is nothing but searching for their survivals as they do not see any hope in their home states for their want. In the process, they are faced with additional hardship of not being readily accepted by their mainland people due to ethno-cultural gap, ways of life, behaviours, attitude, different in food habits, ways of dresses, beliefs, faith and socialisation. This contradiction, thus, resulted into racial discrimination and hatred leading to murder, rape, molestation, physical atrocities, and sexual harassment and so on and so forth.[13]

Centre for North East Studies, Jamia Millia Islamia University in New Delhi, shares;

"The harassment sprouts an uglier, loutish face in the north than in the west of the country (in Mumbai, for instance). "We need to do three things, just three things to curb the kind of brutish harassment people from the North-East are subjected to. People who are convicted in hate crimes against the North-Easterners must be booked under the Scheduled Castes and Scheduled Tribes (Prevention of Atrocities) Act. The law has been used robustly to protect rights of Dalits in Maharashtra — but the police forget that the law includes tribes, too."[14]

The problem of Northeast India cannot be generalised by saying that the Northeastern peoples are targeted because they are from Northeast. To justify this it is necessary to understand the problems of northeast that, why only Tribals and Dalits are being target and not the non-tribal of Northeastern States. So far the problems are concerned it could be seen from the angles of castes/tribes and link it to the Hindu Caste System (HCS) and practices. If we see it in the glass of castes/tribes one can easily reached to the core bone of contention. The tribal's of the Northeastern states are of majority tribal migrants moving to the major cities of India as compare to any other states. Most of the tribal who are migrating from these states are Assam, Arunachal Pradesh, Manipur, Nagaland and Sikkim. No doubt people from Tripura, Mizoram, Meghalaya also migrating but their numbers are less as compare to the other Northeastern states.

As a social science student for me it is very difficult to understand why one section of society is discriminating other sections. If we study the scale of migration it has been observed since independence that people of all the states migrates to all the parts of India. They easily lived and earn their livelihood.[15] To generalise the problems of migrants one has also try to understand the fabrics of migration when North Indian migrants were discriminated in the states of Assam and Maharashtra[16] and received same kind of treatments particularly the Tribals and Dalits are concerned. There is also some kind of thought that if you do not respect the people of other state they also do not respect you. So it is two way process and this has to be kept in mind very strongly. Every time people of Bihar and Eastern Uttar Pradesh has been killed in Assam and badly beaten and treated in the states of Maharashtra.[17]

Overall the problems we found is not the problems of Northeastern states in general rather it is a problem of caste/ tribes mentality which is strongly rooted in the Indian brahaminical minds since the invasion of Aryans from Central Asia.[18] Unless and until we do not recognised it i.e., caste/ tribes problem there won't be a solution. This could also be historicised to understand the problems why Northeast India is on the target since independence and before. This has been targeted because most of the states are inhabitants of tribal's and of non-Hindus. So to bring out any solution simply generalising the issues by saying that this is the problems with the Northeastern people in the cities of India will take nowhere to the solution. The problems could be seen on the angle of caste/tribes atrocities and to be booked under the Scheduled Castes and Scheduled Tribes (Prevention of Atrocities) Act.[19]

There is widespread scholarly consensus that the social groups that suffered in the past continue to suffer and they are ill-equipped to meet the challenges of these drastic changes. Similarly the increasing awareness and mobilisation among various marginalised groups are giving rise to numerous social movements and upheavals.[20] All these factors point at the immediate need to comprehend the situation theoretically and to evolve adequate policy frameworks to address the challenges effectively. Hence this attempt is to engage these issues theoretically as well as empirically. It proposes theoretically to address the continuous perpetuation of social exclusion of the marginalised sections especially Scheduled Castes and Scheduled Tribes to empirically assess the implications of economic reforms and the recent changes seen in India's Northeast. So far the term social exclusion is concerned it was coined in France during 1974 and has gained wide currency in recent years particularly to the South Asian Countries very strongly. Today there is a common feeling and understanding among social scientists and political anthropologist on the definite features of social exclusion and the means by which it perpetuate poverty and inequality of marginalised and socially disadvantaged groups. But the term *"Social exclusion"* has been examined mainly in Western Europe (WE) and United States of America (USA) and other developed countries and appropriate policies have been working to fight social exclusion in these countries.[21] Although developing countries including India has initiated some very strong strategies to fight social exclusion and discrimination through Constitution. No doubt there is a clear absence of comprehensive policy frame work but it largely addresses the issue of caste/tribes, poverty and livelihood questions of marginalised sections in the contemporary Indian society within the framework of social exclusion. These issues are extremely significant in the context of economic reforms initiated in the early 1990s as these reforms brought about drastic changes in the traditional economic and social structures of Indian society.[22]

Amaratya Sen in his understanding about exclusion largely covered with economic perspection which is not over all fit into the excluded communities in India as a whole. No doubt his understanding on capability deprivation has strong importance in the field of studying exclusion. He sees exclusion in the perspectives of active and passiveness. He accepts that the landlessness is similarly an instrumental deprivation.[23] A family without land in a peasant society may be deeply handicapped. Landlessness can also help to generate economic and social deprivations.[24] The distinction between constitutive relevance and instrumental importance is only one of the distinctions that can be fruitfully used to understand and analyse the nature and reach of social exclusion.[25] Another potentially useful distinction is between active and passive exclusion for example, immigrants or refugees are not given a usable political status, it is an active exclusion, and this applies to many of the deprivations from which minority communities suffer in Europe and Asia and elsewhere. However, the deprivation comes about through social processes in which there are no deliberate attempt to exclude; the exclusion can be seen as a passive kind.[26] A good example is provided by poverty and isolation generated by a sluggish economy and a consequent accentuation of poverty. Both active and passive exclusions may be important, but they are not important in the same way.[27] Sometimes an active exclusion can bring about other exclusionary consequences that were not part of the plan of exclusion but nevertheless are results of the directly aimed exclusion, even though they may not have the status of refugees raise an intensely important case of social exclusion. Political exclusion is largely seen in the parts of the settled immigrants who do not have voting rights and participation in the process of government formation. In case of settled immigrants, political right to vote denied because of the difficulties and delays in acquiring citizenship. This keeps them outside the political process in a systematic way—this is clearly an active exclusion.[28]

India is the largest democracy in the world and working on the largest Constitution of the world. Democracy is not something which defined by Abraham Lincoln viz. of the people, by the people and for the people but it is something very deep meaning suggested by Dr Ambedkar, Democracy means equal representation in every sector, and its citizen should get a dignified life based on the principle of liberty, equality and fraternity.[29]

For Bottmore "democracy implies substantial degree of equality among men in the sense that inequality of wealth of social rank or of education and accesses to knowledge should not be so considerable as to result in permanent subordination of some groups of men to others in any of the various spheres of social life or to create great inequalities in the actual exercises of political rights".[30]

Rousseau was one of the earliest thinkers to uphold this point of view, "I conceived", he said "*that there are two kind of inequality among the human beings one which I can call natural or physical, because it is established by nature and consists in a difference of age, health, bodily strength and the qualities of the mind or of the soul and another which may be called moral or political inequality, because it depends upon a kind of convention and established or at least authorised by the consent of men. This latter consist of the different privileges which some men enjoy to the prejudice of others; such as that of being more rich, more honoured, more powerful or even in a position to exact obedience".*[31] So here the basic understanding is that the first type of inequality is designed by the nature and the second type of inequality is man made.

Inequality in society is to be eliminated, according to liberal philosophy by abolishing discrimination and upholding the principles of 'equality of opportunity'. The universal declaration of Human Rights under Article 2 proclaims that;

> *"every one is entitled to all rights and freedom set forth in the declaration without distinction of any kind such as race, colour, sex, language, religion, political or other opinion, birth or other social origin, property, birth or other status".*[32]

The Constitution of India makes a specific provision for reservation of seats in the legislative bodies and in the appointments to services at the union and the state levels for certain classes/castes. Article 15 (1) which states that 'the state shall not discriminate against any citizen or ground only of *religion, race, caste, sex, place of birth* or any of them' also provides in clause (4) of the same articles, nothing in this article or in clause (2) of the Article 29 shall prevent the state from making any special provision for the advancement of any socially and educationally backward classes of citizens or for the Scheduled Castes (SC) and Scheduled Tribes (ST).[33] Accordingly Constitution makes necessary provisions in Articles 14 to 17, 23, 25 to 30, 38, 46 and 330 to 342. It is, however, to be noted that Dr B. R. Ambedkar who is acknowledged as the principal architect of the Constitution had an important role to play in determining and incorporating the reservation policy in the Constitution of India.[34]

On the day when Indian Constitution was adopted Dr Babasaheb Ambedkar said on the 26th January 1950:

> *"We are going to enter into a life of contradiction. In politics we will have equality and in social and economic life we will have inequality. In politics we will be recognising the principle of one-man one vote and one vote one value. In our social and economic life we shall, by reason of our social and economic structure,*

continue to deny the principle of one-man one value. How long shall we continue to live this life of contradiction? How long shall we continue to deny equality in our social and economic life? If we continue to deny it for long, we will do so only putting our political democracy in peril. We must remove this contradiction at the earliest possible movement or else those who suffer from inequality will blow up the structure of political democracy which the constituent assembly so laboriously built up".[35]

About 72 per cent of rural SC population resides in the seven states of Andhra Pradesh, Bihar, Madhya Pradesh, Maharashtra, Rajasthan, Uttar Pradesh and West Bengal. As far as STs are concerned, Chhattisgarh, Gujarat, Jharkhand, Madhya Pradesh, Maharashtra, Odisha and Rajasthan account for 70 per cent of the tribal population in rural India. The growth of SC and ST population in India has been higher in over three per cent per annum over the decades while that of 'overall social groups' has been on declining. The growth of SC population has been on rise since 1981 while that of STs and all social groups have been declining. The gender differences in literacy have still existed in all social classes. The literacy of females among SCs has been growing faster than that of STs. The backwardness of the states is also reflected in literacy levels. In states like Assam, Bihar, Kerala and Uttarakhand, the literacy rates among SCs and STs are very close. Though drop-out rates have been falling, they are still high. The gender disparity has reduced considerably at the primary stage.[36]

The landlessness among various social groups has been reducing and there has been increase in the concentration of marginal holdings. The percentage of households with less than one hectare is relatively more among STs compared to SCs. The shares of marginal holdings in operated area for different social groups in various states are low which can be interpreted as an indicator of economic inequality within each group. The gender disparities in landholdings are evident in all farm size categories. Landlessness among ST households is observed mainly in Arunachal Pradesh (11.2 per cent), Kerala (14.3 per cent) and Mizoram (19.5 per cent). While among SCs, it is high in Arunachal Pradesh (73.1 per cent) and Lakshadweep (100.0 per cent). Poverty among SCs has declined almost at the rate of one per cent per annum during the last two decades, while such decline among STs is about 0.8 per cent per annum. Poverty levels among STs had gone up during the 11-year period ending with 2004-05 in Andhra Pradesh, Gujarat, Kerala, Maharashtra, Madhya Pradesh, Odisha and Punjab. The coverage of SC's and ST's Shelf Helf Groups (SHGs) for financial assistance under Swarnajayanti Gram Swarozgar Yojana (SGSY) was also lower. Under Mahatma Gandhi National Rural Employment Guarantee Act MGNREGA, the share of SCs and STs in employment was more than share in population; a welcome sign.[37]

Table 3.7: State-wise Scheduled Caste and Scheduled Tribe Population (2009-10)-Rural

States/UT		Scheduled Castes			Scheduled Tribes		
State/UT		Males	Females	Persons	Males	Females	Persons
1..	Andhra Pradesh	57.58	60.21	117.80	19.27	18.09	37.36
2.	Arunachal Pradesh	0.08	0.07	0.15	3.36	2.97	6.33
3.	Assam	14.47	12.97	27.43	18.41	16.62	35.03
4.	Bihar	86.68	79.31	165.99	8.79	8.87	17.66
5	Chhattisgarh	13.37	13.41	26.78	34.26	34.02	68.28
6.	Goa	0.10	0.08	0.18	1.80	1.82	3.62
7.	Gujarat	18.10	16.09	34.20	42.20	38.30	80.50
8.	Haryana	22.90	19.84	42.74	0.16	0.16	0.32
9.	Himachal Pradesh	8.05	8.07	16.12	1.66	1.59	3.25
10.	Jammu & Kashmir	3.49	3.17	6.66	1.11	0.97	2.08
11.	Jharkhand	18.39	17.84	36.23	35.56	30.92	66.48
12.	Karnataka	35.10	34.66	69.76	12.43	13.58	26.01
13.	Kerala	13.44	13.59	27.03	2.34	2.71	5.05
14.	Madhya Pradesh	54.97	51.30	106.26	69.21	67.49	136.70
15.	Maharashtra	44.28	41.10	85.38	34.68	34.13	68.81
16.	Manipur	0.20	0.18	0.38	3.78	3.48	7.26
17.	Meghalaya	0.10	0.11	0.22	9.66	8.93	18.59
18.	Mizoram	0.02	0.02	0.04	2.15	1.95	4.10
19.	Nagaland	0.01	0.03	0.04	3.77	3.59	7.36
20.	Odisha	31.63	31.71	63.34	34.27	34.84	69.11
21.	Punjab	34.23	32.08	66.32	0.39	0.28	0.68
22.	Rajasthan	47.94	48.82	96.77	40.31	37.33	77.64
23.	Sikkim	0.17	0.19	0.37	0.90	0.70	1.60
24.	Tamil Nadu	39.77	44.96	84.73	2.24	1.84	4.09

contd...

contd...

States/UT		Scheduled Castes			Scheduled Tribes		
State/UT		Males	Females	Persons	Males	Females	Persons
25.	Tripura	3.25	3.24	6.49	4.73	4.09	8.82
26.	Uttarakhand	6.91	7.13	14.03	1.77	2.13	3.90
27.	Uttar Pradesh	185.80	170.33	356.13	2.83	2.82	5.65
28.	West Bengal	86.77	78.44	165.21	18.85	18.72	37.56
Union Territories							
29.	A & N Islands	0.00	0.00	0.00	0.15	0.14	0.28
30.	Chandigarh	0.40	0.49	0.89	0.00	0.00	0.00
31.	D & N Haveli	0.04	0.05	0.09	0.85	0.76	1.62
32.	Daman & Diu	0.05	0.04	0.09	0.24	0.17	0.40
33.	Delhi	1.49	2.17	3.66	0.13	0.00	0.13
34.	Lakshadweep	0.00	0.00	0.00	0.11	0.12	0.23
35.	Puducherry	0.48	0.51	1.00	0.00	0.00	0.00
All-India		**830.28**	**792.22**	**1622.49**	**412.38**	**394.11**	**806.49**

Section-10: Scheduled Castes and Scheduled Tribes, Table 10.1: State-wise Scheduled Caste (SC) and Scheduled Tribe (ST) Population (2009-10) -Rural
Source: GOI, NSSO, Primary data (2009-10), Rural Development Statistics, Scheduled Castes and Scheduled Tribes

Table 3.8: Literacy Rates* of Scheduled Caste and Scheduled Tribe Persons–Sex-wise - Rural (2009-10)

State / UT	Scheduled Castes			Scheduled Tribes		
	Male	Females	Persons	Males	Females	Persons
Andhra Pradesh	61.7	44.6	52.9	56.9	39.2	48.3
Arunachal Pradesh	78.2	75.6	77.1	76.4	67.4	72.1
Assam	89.1	76.3	83.0	84.3	76.6	80.5
Bihar	54.3	29.1	42.5	67.9	45.0	57.0
Chhattisgarh	89.0	72.9	80.9	75.0	58.5	66.9
Goa	100.0	72.1	83.8	98.8	60.0	78.6
Gujarat	74.2	51.3	63.5	74.2	52.7	63.5
Haryana	77.1	52.6	65.6	77.4	42.2	58.9
Himachal Pradesh	84.8	70.9	77.9	81.8	61.4	71.7
Jharkhand	66.4	45.5	56.0	64.4	43.0	54.6
Jammu & Kashmir	79.5	63.4	71.7	51.9	18.9	36.5

contd...

contd...

State / UT	*Scheduled Castes*			*Scheduled Tribes*		
	Male	*Females*	*Persons*	*Males*	*Females*	*Persons*
Karnataka	65.3	46.7	56.1	65.4	40.6	52.8
Kerala	93.8	81.6	87.6	94.3	82.0	87.0
Madhya Pradesh	78.5	55.2	67.3	65.6	47.8	56.9
Maharashtra	88.2	68.7	78.8	76.3	56.1	66.1
Manipur	87.0	68.0	77.2	90.5	78.8	84.9
Meghalaya	100.0	100.0	100.0	95.4	94.4	94.9
Mizoram	42.1	41.3	41.6	97.8	95.6	96.8
Nagaland	100.0	100.0	100.0	93.8	90.6	92.2
Odisha	74.0	55.8	64.8	62.3	42.5	52.2
Punjab	70.7	56.4	63.7	90.5	84.9	88.0
Rajasthan	69.9	43.6	56.8	66.0	38.0	52.4
Sikkim	90.0	80.9	85.2	89.9	81.9	86.3
Tamil Nadu	75.6	58.7	66.6	55.8	39.2	48.8
Tripura	91.0	78.2	84.7	85.6	70.6	78.5
Uttar Pradesh	72.7	46.4	60.0	49.9	38.6	44.3
Uttaranchal	87.6	66.4	76.8	75.8	64.2	69.7
West Bengal	78.7	62.5	70.9	74.4	57.7	65.8
A & N Islands	--	--	--	76.9	85.2	80.6
Chandigarh	76.3	92.7	84.8	--	--	--
D & N Haveli	100.0	86.5	92.7	78.4	49.8	65.3
Daman & Diu	100.0	100.0	100.0	99.2	83.9	93.4
Delhi	90.1	60.1	74.0	100.0	--	100.0
Lakshadweep	--	--	--	97.1	88.1	92.5
Puducherry	80.4	56.0	67.8	--	--	--
India	**73.0**	**52.1**	**62.8**	**70.7**	**52.1**	**61.6**

*age 7 years and above persons.

Source: Government of India, NSSO, Primary Data (2009-10).

Table 3.9: Level of General Education - Rural Males (Persons of age 15 years and above) (2004-05 and 2009-10)

	(%) Level of General Educ-ation	*2004-05*				*2009-10*				
		ST	*SC*	*OBC*	*All*	*ST*	*SC*	*OBC*	*Others*	*All*
Not literate	45.8	40.7	**31.2**	21.5	32.0	35.8	**33.1**	25.3	17.4	26.0
Literate & up to primary	29.3	27.7	**28.0**	26.6	27.7	26.4	**27.6**	25.2	23.3	25.3
Middle	14.5	17.2	**20.1**	20.8	19.1	18.3	**19.7**	21.3	20.9	20.5
Secondary	5.5	7.6	**10.8**	15.0	10.7	11.1	**10.9**	15.0	18.6	14.7
Higher Secondary	2.8	3.9	**5.3**	8.1	5.5	5.7	**5.4**	8.0	11.2	8.0
Diploma/ Certificate	0.4	0.6	**1.1**	1.4	1.0	0.6	**0.5**	1.1	1.3	1.0
Graduate & above	1.7	2.2	**3.4**	6.5	3.8	2.2	**2.7**	4.2	7.2	4.5
Overall	**100.0**	**100.0**	--	**100.0**	**100.0**	**100.0**	**100.0**	**100.0**	**100.0**	**100.0**

Source: Government of India, NSSO, Report No. 516, Employment and Unemployment Situation among Social Groups in India, 61st Round, (July 2004 – June 2005), October 2006 and NSSO, Primary Data (2009-10).

Table 3.10: Level of General Education - Rural Females (Persons of age 15 years and above) (2004-05 and 2009-10)

	%e Level of General Educat-ion	*2004-05*				*2009-10*				
		ST	**SC**	**OBC**	**All**	**ST**	**SC**	**OBC**	**Others**	**All**
Not literate	71.5	68.5	**60.1**	43.4	58.5	58.3	**58.1**	51.4	36.6	49.8
Literate and up to primary	16.4	16.6	**19.1**	25.2	19.9	21.8	**20.1**	20.8	25.2	21.9
Middle	7.7	8.5	**11.4**	14.9	11.3	10.3	**11.6**	13.5	16.3	13.5
Secondary	2.5	3.5	**5.5**	9.1	5.7	5.7	**6.3**	8.1	11.2	8.2
Higher Secondary	1.3	1.8	**2.5**	4.4	2.7	2.7	**2.6**	4.0	6.7	4.2
Diploma/ Certificate	0.1	0.4	**0.5**	0.6	0.5	0.3	**0.2**	0.4	0.5	0.4
Graduate & above	0.5	0.7	**0.9**	2.6	1.3	0.9	**1.1**	1.8	3.5	2.0
Overall	**100.0**	**100.0**	**100.0**	**100.0**	**100.0**	**100.0**	**100.0**	**100.0**	**100.0**	**100.0**

Source: Government of India, NSSO, Report No. 516, Employment and Unemployment Situation among Social Groups in India, 61st Round, (July 2004 – June 2005), October 2006 and NSSO, Primary Data (2009-10).

Table 3.11 : Distribution of Households According to Land Possession – State-wise (Rural) (2004-05) Scheduled Castes (SC)%

S.No.	State/UT	Size of land Possessed (Hec.)				of HHs with less than one hectare	
		% Landless Households	0.001-1.00	1.01-2.00	2.01-4.00	4.01 & above	
1.	Andhra Pradesh	4.2	86.3	5.4	3.2	0.90	90.5
2.	Arunachal Pradesh	73.1	26.9	0	0	0	100.0
3.	Assam	0.40	73	17.1	8.1	1.4	73.4
4.	Bihar	2.4	91.7	4.4	1.1	0.3	94.1
5.	Chhattisgarh	0.50	77	10.2	7.3	5.1	77.5
6.	Delhi	0	100	0	0	0	100.0
7.	Goa	8.4	91.6	0	0	0	100.0
8.	Gujarat	5.2	85.6	5.4	3.5	0.3	90.8
9.	Haryana	3.9	92.5	2.6	0.8	0.3	96.4
10.	Himachal Pradesh	0.3	88.8	8.5	2.1	0.3	89.1
11.	Jammu & Kashmir	0	80.6	16.6	2.1	0.7	80.6
12.	Jharkhand	0.7	93.3	5.0	0.9	0.2	94.0
13.	Karnataka	3.7	82.2	8.1	4.4	1.5	85.9
14.	Kerala	2.6	97.5	0	0	0	100.1
15.	Madhya Pradesh	4.5	70	15.8	8.1	1.6	74.5
16.	Maharashtra	3.0	82.9	7.8	4.1	2.1	85.9
17.	Manipur	4.6	68.2	25.5	0	1.7	72.8
18.	Meghalaya	0	42.2	18.4	15.3	24.1	42.2
19.	Mizoram	0	0	0	0	0	0.0
20.	Nagaland	0	0	0	0	0	0.0
21.	Odisha	5.8	82.4	9.6	1.3	0.9	88.2
22.	Punjab	0.7	96.8	1.1	1.4	0.1	97.5
23.	Rajasthan	2.6	69.9	11.8	9.7	6.1	72.5
24.	Sikkim	15.5	84.4	0	0	0	99.9
25.	Tamil Nadu	1.8	93.8	3.5	0.70	0.2	95.6
26.	Tripura	3.7	92.2	3.5	0.40	0.2	95.9
27.	Uttarakhand	3.8	93.5	1.6	1.2	0	97.3
28.	Uttar Pradesh	1.9	88.9	7.1	1.8	0.3	90.8
29.	West Bengal	1.9	92.1	5.4	0.6	0	94.0
30.	A & N Islands	0	0	0	0	0	0.0
31.	Chandigarh	0.2	99.8	0	0	0	100.0
32.	D & N Haveli	0	0	0	0	0	0.0
33.	Daman & Diu	0	94.3	5.7	0	0	94.3
34.	Lakshadweep	100.0	0	0	0	0	100.0
35.	Puducherry	0	98.9	1.1	0	0	98.9
	India	2.7	86.9	6.7	2.7	1.00	89.6

Source: Government of India, NSSO, Report No. 516, Employment and Unemployment Situation among Social Groups in India, 61st Round, (July 2004- June 2005), October 2006.

Table 3.12: Poverty among SCs and STs – Rural and Urban India (1983-84, 1993-94, 1999-2000, 2004-05 and 2009-10)

Year	*SC*		*ST*		*Others*		*Total*	
	Rural	*Urban*	*Rural*	*Urban*	*Rural*	*Urban*	*Rural*	*Urban*
1983-84	58.1	56.5	63.8	54.2	37.0	39.1	45.6	42.2
1993-94	48.1	49.9	52.2	42.4	31.3	30.6	37.1	33.7
1999-2000	36.2	38.6	45.9	34.8	21.6	20.6	27.1	23.7
2004-05 (Revised Estimates)	52.7	40.0	61.9	35.0	26.2	15.8	41.8	25.7
2009-10	43.5	33.0	47.1	28.8	21.1	11.9	33.8	20.9

Sources: Government of India, Planning Commission, Eleventh Five Year Plan, 2007-2012, Volume I, Inclusive Growth and NSSO primary data 2009-10.

Table 3.13: Poverty Ratios among SCs and STs – State-wise 1993-94 and 2004-05 – Rural

S.No.	*State*	*1993-94*			*2004-05*				
		SC	*ST*	*All*	*SC*	*ST*	*OBC*	*Others*	*Total*
1.	Andhra Pradesh	26.02	25.66	15.92	15.4	30.5	9.5	4.1	32.3
2.	Assam	45.38	41.44	45.01	27.7	14.1	18.8	25.4	36.4
3.	Bihar	70.66	69.75	58.21	64.0	53.3	37.8	26.6	55.7
4.	Gujarat	32.26	31.20	22.18	21.8	34.7	19.1	4.8	39.1
5.	Haryana	46.56	41.55	28.02	26.8	--	13.9	4.2	24.8
6.	Himachal Pradesh	36.89	63.94	30.34	19.6	14.9	9.1	6.4	25.0
7.	Jammu & Kashmir	--	--	30.34	5.2	8.8	10.0	3.3	14.1
8.	Karnataka	46.36	37.33	29.88	31.8	23.5	20.9	13.8	37.5
9.	Kerala	36.43	37.34	25.76	21.6	44.3	13.7	6.6	20.2
10.	Maharashtra	51.64	50.38	37.93	44.8	56.6	23.9	18.9	47.9
11.	Madhya Pradesh	45.83	56.69	40.64	42.8	58.6	29.6	13.4	53.6
12.	Odisha	48.95	71.26	49.72	50.2	75.6	36.9	23.4	60.8
13.	Punjab	22.08	27.00	11.95	14.6	30.7	10.6	2.2	22.1
14.	Rajasthan	38.38	46.23	26.46	28.7	32.6	13.1	8.2	35.8
15.	Tamil Nadu	44.05	44.37	32.48	31.2	32.1	19.8	19.1	37.5

contd...

contd...

S.No.	State	1993-94			2004-05				
		SC	ST	All	SC	ST	OBC	Others	Total
16.	Uttar Pradesh	58.99	37.11	42.28	44.8	32.4	32.9	19.7	42.7
17.	West Bengal	45.29	61.95	40.80	29.5	42.4	18.3	27.5	38.2
18.	Chhattisgarh	--	--	--	32.7	54.7	33.9	29.2	55.1
19.	Jharkhand	--	--	--	57.9	54.2	40.2	37.1	51.6
20.	Uttarakhand	--	--	--	54.2	43.2	44.8	33.5	35.1
	All – India	**48.11**	**51.94**	**37.27**	**36.8**	**47.2**	**26.7**	**16.1**	**42.0**

—: Not Available.

1. The estimates are based on the methodology outlined in the Report of the Expert Group on Estimation of Proportion and number of poor.
2. The Poverty line for all population is used for SCs and STs.
3. All India Poverty ratios are worked out from the NSS distribution of persons and (implicit) All India Poverty Line.

Source: GOI, Planning Commission, Eleventh Five Year Plan, 2007-2012, Vol. I, Inclusive Growth.

At the National level, the poverty ratio for each social group in rural as well as urban areas in 2011-12 is lower as compare to 2009-10. The percentage point reduction in poverty has been larger for each social group in the second period (2004-05 to 2011-12) than the first (1993-94 to 2004-05). It is also demonstrate that growth acceleration has translated in broad-based benefits. The percentage point reduction in the SC poverty in both rural and urban areas and during both periods has been larger than for the population as a whole. For the ST, the decline is larger in both rural and urban areas in the second period but not the first. Finally, being physically embedded within the mainstream of the economy, the SC has experienced larger percentage point reduction in poverty than the ST who predominantly lives in the remote rural areas.

As we know that the Hindu society are segregated into compartmental units on the basis of their birth and parental vocation. Each compartmental unit is a caste.[38] The caste system is the steel frame of Hinduism. It was more ancient than the Vedas.[39] The system is undemocratic and authoritarian. It is a rare setup in which economic imperialism; political tyranny and social fascism are inseparably fused together.[40]

Table 3.14: Poverty by Social Groups, 1993-94 to 2011-12[41]

Social Groups	*Share in Population*	*Percent Population Below the Tendulkar Line*				*Percentage Point Poverty Reduction*	
Rural							
ST	11.1	65.9	62.3	47.4	45.3	3.7	16.9
SC	20.8	62.4	53.5	42.3	31.5	8.6	22.0
OBC	45.0	44.0	39.8	31.9	22.7	9.0	17.1
FC	23.0		27.1	21.0	15.5		11.6
ALL	100.0	50.3	41.8	33.3	25.4	8.5	16.4
Urban							
ST	3.5	41.1	35.5	30.4	24.1	5.6	11.4
SC	14.6	51.7	40.6	34.1	21.7	11.1	18.8
OBC	41.6	28.2	30.6	24.3	15.4	5.8	15.2
FC	40.3		16.1	12.4	8.1		8.0
ALL	100.0	31.9	25.7	20.9	13.7	6.2	12.0
Rural + Urban							
ST	8.9	63.7	60.0	45.6	43.0	3.7	17.0
SC	19.0	60.5	50.0	40.6	29.4	9.6	21.5
OBC	44.1	39.5	37.8	30.0	20.7	8.1	17.1
FC	28.0		23.0	17.6	12.5		10.5
ALL	100.0	45.7	37.7	29.9	22.0	8.0	15.7

Source: Arvind, Panagariya and Vishal More, Poverty by Social, Religious and Economic Groups in India and Its Largest States 1993-94 to 2011-12, Working Paper No. 2013-02, SIPA, School of International and Public Affairs ISERP Institute for Social and Economic Research and Policy, Programme of Indian Economic Policies, Colombia University, p. 7.

In the words of J. H. Hutton, "*no comparable institution to be seen elsewhere has anything like the complexity elaboration the rigidity of caste in India*".[42]

Considering the general disabilities experienced by the underprivileged communities, the chief framer of the Indian Constitution Dr B.R. Ambedkar wrote specific provisions in the Constitution to enable them to achieve accelerated development. Articles 15, 16, 17, 19, 23, 29, 35, 38A, 46, 164, 244, 244A, 275, 320 (4), 330, 331, 332, 333, 334, 335, 338, 339, 340, 342, 371A, 371B and 371C respectively of the Indian Constitution aiming at promoting and safeguarding the interest of the SCs, STs and Backward Castes (BCs).[43]

The historic Poona Pact was the result of fast-unto-death of Mohandas Karamchand Gandhi and Congress, which watered down the continuous struggle and everlasting dream of separate electorate of Dr Bhimrao Ramji Ambedkar for the Deprived Classes in the legislature.[44] The Congress pressurised for joint electorates instead of separate electorate. Dr Ambedkar was dissatisfied and disappointed with the Poona Pact.[45] The India Charter Act, 1935 is known as second Constitution of India. The universal adult franchise was the outcome of 1935 Act, while restricted franchise was prevailed before 1935.[46] The provisions of reservations to SCs and STs in education and employment were included in Charter Act of 1935. Dr Ambedkar firmly believed that an independent political power is needed to secure and safeguard the interests of Depressed Classes in separate electorate. But M.K. Gandhi and Congress rejected the aspirations of Dr Ambedkar for joint electorate, which makes the political representatives of the illiterate Untouchables.[47]

In 1946 British Government announced to frame Constitution of India in Cabinet Mission Plan. People's representatives were elected to Constituent Assembly for drafting the Constitution. As we know Dr Ambedkar dissatisfied and disappointed with Poona Pact (1932).[48] He strongly desired to enter into Constituent Assembly to secure and safeguard the interests of Depressed Classes.[49]

. In order to accomplish his aspirations, he contested election to enter in Constituent Assembly from Bombay constituency, but he lost the election.[50] Next time he again entered in Constituent Assembly from Jaisur and Khulna from Bengal with the help of the Chandals and Namosudras of Bengal.[51]

In 1946, the interim government was formed under the leadership of Pt. Jawaharlal Nehru. The Congress under the chairmanship of Sardar Vallabhbhai Patel abolished reservations in education and in services to Depressed Classes, which they achieved in Indian Government Act, 1935. Sardar Vallabhbhai Patel declared the abolition of reservation as *"Red letter's day"*. Dr Ambedkar condemned this action as *"Dead letter's day"*.[52] But for vote bank politics Congress continued reservation in politics for Depressed Classes. Congress Dalit leader Babu Jagjivan Ram along with 30-Congress Dalit Member of Parliaments (MPs) supported the Congress interim government decision to abolish the reservation.[53] But one of Congress MP from Andhra Pradesh Naggappa supported Dr Ambedkar on the issue of reservation. Vallabhbhai Patel pressurised Naggappa on the advice of core Congress committee to withdraw his support to Dr Ambedkar. Despite the pressure of the Congress Party Naggappa wholeheartedly enhanced his support to Dr Ambedkar. As a result, Naggappa was expelled from the Congress Party.[54] After the unfortunate partition of the India in 1947, the Congress deliberately manipulated to transfer the Jaisur and Khulna constituency to East Pakistan from where Dr Ambedkar represented, though the constituency consisted majority Buddhist and Hindus.[55] The question arises why the congress deliberately manipulated to transfer the Jaisur and Khulna constituency to East Pakistan? Why Congress could not tolerate Dr Ambedkar's presence and representation in the constituent assembly.[56]

Dr Ambedkar deliberately made efforts to enter into Constituent Assembly in order to safeguard the interests of SCs, STs, OBCs and RMs.[57] In this regard he approached British to seek their help to enter into Constituent Assembly. Consequently, British insisted M.K.Gandhi and Congress to accommodate Dr Ambedkar into Constituent Assembly and threatened M.K. Gandhi and Congress that if you want independence to India, enter Dr Ambedkar into Constituent Assembly. As a result Congress pressurised Mr Jayakar to vacate Poona constituency to accommodate Dr Ambedkar.[58]

After a prolonged struggle, Dr Ambedkar finally entered into Constituent Assembly on 9th July 1947. Consequently, British Government announced on 10th July 1947 that they are going to transfer the political power to India on 15th august 1947. Dr Ambedkar himself drafted the Constitution as the six member of Drafting Committee and its members never actively cooperated in the drafting of the Constitution. That's why Indian Constitution is considered as the brainchild of Dr Ambedkar. He has been considered as the architect of Indian Constitution. Dr Ambedkar incorporated the provisions of reservation in education to .SCs and STs under the provision of the Article 15(4) of the Constitution as fundamental right and secures the reservation in employment under the provision of article 16(4) as a Constitutional right. He also strived to secure the interests of OBCs by inserting the provision of Article 340 to have a Statuary Commission to decide the criteria of social and educational backwardness, so that reservation will be implemented on the basis of the report of the Backward Class Commission (BCC) in the spheres of education and employment. Some special provisions were also incorporated under Articles 25 and 26 to secure the Religious Freedom or Freedom of Religion as the Fundamental Right to the religious minorities.[59]

The first history of reservation starts with the establishement of schools and starting of scholarships for the untouchables first time in the country by Chhatrapati Shahu Maharaj of Kolhapur. He granted special scholarship and established special boarding houses for untouchable students. In 1885, the Madras Government framed a grant-in-aid code to regulate financial aid to educational institutions, providing special facilities to student's belongings to the Depressed classes. In 1921, the Madras State Legislative Council passed a resolution for higher representations of non-Brahmins in the government services. Over a period of time five broad categories and earmarking separate quota for each category. In 1921, the ruler of the Mysore State, Krishna Raja Wodeyar introduced the reservation in government jobs for the non-Brahmins. The Madras Presidency also made similar reservations, in the government jobs on the basis of reservations granted by the Mysore state to bring social equity in the society. During British period they had provided reservation of seats for the Muslims in legislatures. Untouchables were recognised as a separate group through the Communal Award of 1932.[60] That was strengthened by the Poona Pact were provided reservation of seats in legislatures. The Government of India Act, 1935, for the first time made the special provisions for these castes. Hence, they came to be known as the Scheduled Castes. However, the reserving a quota of jobs was taken up in 1942, which was revised in 1946. In 1919 the phrase 'Depressed Classes' was brought into official language by the Montague-Chelmsford Reforms.The Constitution-makers incorporated provisions of reservation meant for the special care and advancement of untouchables and tribals. In administrative language, they are called Scheduled Castes and Scheduled Tribes. An Articles 15 and 17 of the Constitution does away with the discrimination and exclusion of the untouchables. Article 17 of the Constitution declares that untouchability is abolished and its practice in any form is forbidden.[61] Various Articles of the Constitution declares that the State shall promote with special care the educational and economic interest of the weaker sections, in particular the

Scheduled Castes and the Scheduled Tribes, and shall protect them from injustice and exploitation.[63] Article 16 of the Constitution provides for protective discrimination in favour of Backward Classes which in the opinion of the state, is not adequately represented in the services.[63]

In the words of Dr Ambedkar, "*untouchability is abolished legally according to the Constitution. But I see, before my own eyes, my people are ill-treated, humiliated, assaulted, their houses burnt, our women are targeted and sexually harassed. These are happenings of the day in our country. The laws alone cannot establish their rights and livelihood. People should unite and struggle for their rights along with democratic minded sections.*"[64]

Position of SCs, STs and Reservation Policy Under Various Regimes Since 1947

In 1960s, and 1970s, the Congress Government did not show any interest in the enhancement of the training and educational skills of SCs and STs. A look around will show the horrendous deprivation in the matter of employment, not with standing the Constitution providing reservation for Dalits and backward classes. The backlog of vacancies for Dalits even after the 50 years is appalling. Thus there are 70 per cent of backlog vacancies in Group-A jobs and even 45 per cent of vacancies in Group- D jobs. In the public sector, it is more shocking that the backlog of the vacancies is 88 per cent. The Backlog of positions of SCs and STs are reported to be about a million in various government services.[65] The representation of SCs and STs in Central Government services as on 01.01.1998.

Table 3.15: Representation of SC/STs in Central Government Services as on 1.1.1997[66]

Group	*Total*	*SC*	*Percentage*
A	60,067	6,135	10.21
B	94,111	11,649	12.38
C	19,59,477	3,14,995	16.08
D (Excluding Sweepers	8,18,748	1,76,368	21.54
Sweepers	15,51,137	61,149	39.42
Total (Excluding Sweepers)	29,32,403	5,09,149	17.36
Total (Including Sweepers)	30,87,540	5,70,296	18.47

Source: Department of Personnel and Training. Quoted in National Commission for Scheduled Castes and Scheduled Tribes, Fifth Report 1998-99, p.130.

Table 3.16: Position as per Information Received up to 30.06.1999[67]

Group	*Total*	*SC*	*Per-centage*	*ST*	*Per-centage*
A	49749	4888	9.83	1497	3.01
B	62722	6926	11.04	1745	2.78
C	1048390	178787	17.05	62232	5.94
D (Excluding Sweepers)	637333	122345	19.20	48679	7.64
Sweepers	73590	43845	62.30	3401	4.62
Total (Excluding Sweepers)	1798194	312946	17.40	114153	6.35
Total (Including Sweepers)	1871784	358791	19.17	117554	6.28

Source: Ministry of Personal, Public Grievances and Petition (1997)

According to Article 338 of the Constitution, first National Commission for SCs and STs was setup on July 21, 1978 to study the socio-economic conditions of SCs and STs and to fill up the vacancies. This Commission submitted its report that consisted many recommendations for the upliftment of SCs and STs, but the Congress regime fully did not implemented the recommendations of this commission.

Post Independence Scenario of Reservation for OBCs

While drafting the Constitution, OBCs realised that the Congress had done nothing for them and approached Dr Ambedkar to secure their interests and requested him to lead the movement. In order to consider their request and realising the actual position of OBCs, he incorporated Article 340 in the Indian Constitution to secure the interests of OBCs. Under the obligation of the Constitution of Article 340, Congress Government set up Kaka Kalelkar Commission on 29th January 1953 for investigating the conditions of OBCs. Kaka Kalelkar Commission submitted its report on 30th March 1955 with some recommendations. Kaka Kalelkar Commission identified 2399 backward castes out of that 837 Castes were identified as Most Backward Castes (MBC). The followings are some of the important recommendations of the Kalelkar Commissions:[68]

(a) Undertaking caste-wise enumeration of population in the census of 1961;

(b) Relating social backwardness of a class to its low position in the traditional caste hierarchy of Indian society;

(c) Treating all women as a class as "backward";

(d) Reservation of 70 per cent seats in all technical and professional institutions for qualified students of backward classes; and

(e) Reservation of vacancies in all government services and local bodies for other backward classes.

The commission in its final report recommended "*caste as the criteria*" to determine backwardness. But this report was not accepted by the Congress government as it feared that the backward classes excluded from the caste and communities selected by the commission may not be considered and would be swamped by the multitude and would hardly receive special attention. As Commission submitted its report on 30th March 1955, Congress government had not shown any interest so far the implementation of Article 340 is concerned[69] and never tried any alternatives to the aftermath of Kaka Kalelkar Committee till 1977.[70]

Table 3.17: Percentage of Reservation for the SC's, ST's and OBC's iin Government Services[71]

Mode of Appointments	*Fixed Percentage of Reservation for the Social groups*		
	SC	*ST*	*OBC*
Direct recruitment on an all India basis by open competition (i.e., through the Union Public Service Commission or by means of written competitiv e test held by Service Selection Committee or any other authority)	15	7.5	27
Direct recruitment on an all India basis otherwise than (a) above i .e., by Service Selection Committee or any other authority by not conducting a written competitive test	16.2/3	7.5	27
Direct recruitment to Class III and IV posts (Group C and D posts), which normally attract candidates from a locality or region	Generally, in proportion to the population of the SCs, the STs, and the OBCs in the respective States/UTs		
Posts filled by promotion in Groups or services in which the element of direct recruitment, if any, does not exceed 75 per cent. Through limited departmental competitive examinations in Groups A, B, C, and D By Selection from Group B to the lower rung or category in Group A or Groups B, C, and D On the basis of seniority subject to fitness in Groups A,B, C, and D			

Source: Annual Report, Ministry of Personal, Public Grievances and Pensions, Government of India, New Delhi, 2002-2003, Chapter 5, Paragraph 5-2.

The aspirations of OBCs were not materialised because they were not organised and nothing has been done for them during the period of 1953 to 1977. In 1977, Congress lost its power and Janata Government came into power and set up a Backward Class Commission under the Chairmanship of B.P. Mandal on 1st January 1979. The Mandal Commission identified 3743 Backward Castes in terms of social and educational backwardness. Mandal Commission officially stated that 52 per cent of population belongs to Backward Castes and 52 per cent of posts in central services must be reserved for OBCs in education and employment.[72] The Commission suggested forty recommendations. According to 13.11 recommendation of Mandal Commission, the population of OBCs, both Hindus and Non-Hindus is around 52 per cent of total population of India. Accordingly 52 per cent of all posts under the Central Government should be reserved for them. But this provision may go against the law laid down in a number of Supreme Court judgments wherein it has been held that the total quantum of reservation under Articles 15 (4) and 16 (4) of the Constitution should be below 50 per cent.[73] In view of this the proposed reservation of OBCs would have to be pegged at figure when added to 22.5 per cent reservation for OBCs that remains below 50 per cent. In view of these legal constraints the commission is obliged to recommend a reservation of 27 per cent only even though their population is almost twice this figure. The commission submitted its report on December 1980. When the Mandal Commission submitted its report to the Janata government, by that time Janata Government was lost and Congress again came into power. When Congress regained power in 1980 general elections Mrs Indira Gandhi became Prime Minister and rejected the Mandal Commission's Report and shown no interest into implementation of Mandal Commission's Report.[74]

Under the Non-Brahmin Movement, a tremendous pressure was exerted on the V.P. Singh Government to implement the Mandal Commission Report. The Non-Brahmin Movement (NBM) triumphed in bringing consciousness to Non-Brahmins and consistently pressurising the government for the effective implementation of Mandal Report. V.P. Singh came into power in 1989 with the support of Bharatiya Janata Party (BJP) and Communists Party (CP). In such a situation V. P. Singh announced the implementation of Mandal Commission's Report in 1990. But, BJP withdrew its support from V.P. Singh government on the pretext of the Ram Mandir issue. As a result, V.P.Singh government fell. But after assuming power in 1991, the Congress government adopted new economic policy under the programme of *Liberalisation, Privatisation and Globalisation* (LPG),[75] instead of implementing Mandal Commission Report.[76] The new economic policy completely undermined and neglected the spirit of reservation of SCs, STs and OBCs. The new economic policy i.e., LPG was introduced to curtail the reservation. In this process, hundreds of government and semi-government Public Sector Undertakings (PSUs) were privatised by the Congress government of the day and lacks of jobs meant for the SC's, ST's and OBCs were snatched from their hands.[77] This was the biggest betrayal by the Congress Government, which was working in tandem with other parties like the Communists and BJP to harm the interests of the SC's, ST's, OBC's and RMs.[78]

So far the question of reservation in the Higher Educational Institutions (HEI) for OBC's are concerned it created huge hue and cry in 2006.[79] The Medical students of All India Institutes of Medical Sciences (AIIMS), Indian Institute of Technology (IIT's) and Indian Institute of Managements (IIM's) beat the streets of Delhi. On the other side the pro-reservation group also came out of their houses to counter anti-reservation groups. While on the face of it, the conflict has the making of another 1990, Mandal-II that is different from Mandal-I in many ways. The essential differences lies not in the fact that Mandal-I ideals with reservation in HEI of the country instead of jobs, V.P. Singh went in for. If we see BJP's reaction on the question of OBC's reservation in the HEI, they do not have choice to oppose because today the largest supporter of BJP is OBC, particularly from the Northern Belt. For Congress, in today's scenario has the same condition like BJP i.e., Congress plays a card of 'Quota' to bring OBC's under the 'Vote Bank Net'.

It is a well-known fact that caste plays a prominent role in India. However, it appears there is no authentic data on caste-wise population after independence. Caste-wise population differs from report to report. Even the policy-makers are in dilemma about the authentic data of caste-wise population and they are still dependent on and refer the caste-based census of

1931 for administrative purposes. However, the ratio of population is a relevant consideration in fixing the quantum of reservation, budget allocating and framing of policies for the emancipation of weak, particularly, Backward Communities. In this regard it is indisputable that the population of OBCs exceeds 27 per cent and SCs and STs constitute more than 22.5 per cent. However, confining 27 per cent reservation to OBCs, and 22.5 per cent to SCs and STs is meaningless, deceive and conspiracy to keeping them away from the benefits. It is, therefore necessary that, the quantum of reservation must be fixed on par with the ratio of population. The ceiling of not more than 50 per cent fixed in the case of Inder Sawhney vs. Union of India popularly known as Mandal Commission case [1992 Supp. (3) SCC 217] is to be reconsidered for revision in the prevalence of socio-economic conditions of the country. Why should the more than 75 per cent of population to be confined to the benefits of 50 per cent only and why the meager sections comprising less than 25 per cent to enjoy the 50 per cent of benefits.[80]

Assam

Assam one of the most prominent states in India and has been involved in the political and the social issues of the nation since a long time. Assam was a prominent province even during the British rule in India and among the few provinces to retain their name and structure after independence. The state has undergone many changes with respect to territories and areas within its boundaries over the years. The state and its leader played a prominent rule in India's freedom struggle. The state is known for its scenic beauty and wildlife. The city of Dispur is the capital of Assam. The Population of Assam according to the 2011 census stands at about 31 million, making it the 14th most populated state in India. The state makes up about 2.5 per cent of the country's population a figure that has gone up since the last census in 2001. The state is spread over an area of about 78000 sq. km. making it the 16th largest state in the country in terms of area. The density of population per sq. km. is about 397 and is fairly equal to the national average.[81] The state has a growth rate of about 17 per cent which is again very close to the national growth rate of about 17 per cent. The population of the state is rising considerably due to rapid efforts towards development and progress. The literacy rate in the state is about

73 per cent a figure that has improved tremendously in the last few years due to the consistent efforts of the government. The sex ratio in Assam exceeds the national average by a good 30 points and is one of the better states in the country with respect to the sex ratio. The statistics in the Assam Census 2011 reveal facts that can be instrumental in planning for a better development plan for the state. The largest city in the state of Assam is Dispur while Guwahati is the capital city of the Assam. The languages spoken in the Assam state includes Assamese, Bodo and Karbi. In total Assam state comprises 27 districts. Assam (Asom), the land of tea and gateway to the northeast is a verdant land of the eternal blue hills, a treasure of flora and fauna. The word Assam is derived from the Sanskrit word "Asom" meaning 'peerless'. The ancient history refers to Assam as Pragjyotishpur, until in 1228, the Ahoms from North Thailand invaded this land and established a kingdom, which came to be known as Assam. The society in Assam is not just a conglomeration of diverse racial and cultural elements but a composite whole arising out of the integration and synthesis of all of them. Indeed, Assam has been a curious melting pot into which have gone the tribal and the non-tribal and the exotic, making for a delightful fare with wonderful mixed flavour. The majority of the population in the plains is made up of Hindus speaking the Aryan Assamese language.[82] But the Aryan racial strain is prominent only in the privileged castes; most of the other castes are of the Mongoloid stock. The Satras (seat of the religious head Satradhikar) and Namghars (house of names or Prayer hall) plays an important role in the life of an average Assamese and have acted as religious as well as cultural institutions. Majority of the tribal groups belong to the Tibeto-Burmese family. The colourful people of Assam consist of Bodo-Kacharis, Rabha and Hajongs, Tiwas (lalung), Misings, Sonowal Kacharis, Deuris, Karbis, Dimasa Kacharis, Rengma Naga, Zemi Naga, Kukis and the Hmars. In Assam, the line between the tribal and the non-tribal is pretty thin and the so-called non-tribal Assamese Hindu society retains many elements, which are patently 'tribal' by orthodox Hindu standards. More than fourty per cent of Assam's population is thought to be of migrant origin. During the six hundred years of ruling, the Ahom Dynasty managed to keep the kingdom, independent from

Mughal, invaders of India before the British, as well as other invaders though Mughal attacked Assam seventeen times. During this era, the Assamese society was exogenous. The British entered Assam in 1824 as tea planters, which was the starting point of the destruction of Ahom Dynasty. The fairs and festivals in this sparsely populated state are essentially an opportunity for people from far and wide to converge and see the culture of the land.[83]

Assam, a strategic border state of India, witnessed the influx of migrants since the British period from then East Bengal, now Bangladesh. The influx was largely engineered by the British, given the economic rationale of cheap labour that the migrants provided for the sprawling tea estates in Assam. However, this issue of migration assumed political and communal overtones after independence, and continues to be an issue of concern.

As per details from Census 2011, Assam has population of 3.12 crores, an increase from figure of 2.67 crore in 2001 census. Total population of Assam as per 2011 census is 31,205,576 of which male and female are 15,939,443 and 15,266,133 respectively. In 2001, total population was 26,655,528 in which males were 13,777,037 while females were 12,878,491. The total population growth in this decade was 17.07 per cent while in previous decade it was 18.85 per cent. The population of Assam forms 2.58 per cent of India in 2011. In 2001, the figure was 2.59 per cent. Literacy rate in Assam has seen upward trend and is 72.19 per cent as per 2011 population census. Of that, male literacy stands at 77.85 per cent while female literacy is at 63.00 per cent. In 2001, literacy rate in Assam stood at 63.25 per cent of which male and female were 75.23 per cent and 51.85 per cent literate respectively. In actual numbers, total literates in Assam stands at 19,177,977 of which males were 10,568,639 and females were 8,609,338. Total area of Assam is 78,438 sq. km. Density of Assam is 398 per sq km which is higher than national average 382 per sq km. In 2001, density of Assam was 340 per sq km, while nation average in 2001 was 324 per sq km. Sex Ratio in Assam is 958 i.e., for each 1000 male, which is below national average of 940 as per census 2011. In 2001, the sex ratio of female was 932 per 1000 males in Assam.[84]

The total SC population of Assam according to 2011 Census is 22,31,321 persons constituting 7.1 per cent of the total population of the state. The state has registered 10 per cent decadal growth of SC population in 1991-2011. There are sixteen (16) notified SCs, and all have been enumerated in 2011 Census. Kaibartta (31.0 per cent) and Namasudra (28.3 per cent) and are the two major SCs in the state sharing more than half of the total population. Patni (8.1 per cent), Jhalo (3.6 per cent), Muchi (3.4 per cent), Sutradhar (2.9 per cent), Bhuinmali (3.1 per cent), Hira (2.4 per cent), Dhupi (2.3), Brittial Bania (2.2 per cent), and Jalkeot (1.1 per cent) also have sizeable population in the state. SCs namely, Lalbegi, Mahara, Dugla, Mehtar, and Bansphor each accounts for less than one per cent.

Table 3.18: Scheduled Caste Population of Assam (Asom)

Sl.No.	*Name of the Scheduled Caste*	*Total Population*	*Proportion to the total SC Population*
	All Scheduled Castes	**2231321**	**100 per cent**
1.	Bansphor	16359	0.7
2.	Bhuinmali	69535	3.1
3.	Bittal Bania	50598	2.2
4.	Dhupi	52431	2.3
5.	Dugla	7991	0.3
6.	Hira	55300	2.4
7.	Jalkeot	24774	1.1
8.	Jhalo	80376	3.6
9.	Kaibartta	693219	31.0
10.	Lalbegi	790	0.0
11.	Mahara	1822	0.0
12.	Mehtar	8835	0.3
13.	Muchi	77643	3.4
14.	Namasudra	631542	28.3
15.	Patni	181904	8.1
16.	Sutradhar	66303	2.9

Source: Census of India, 2011, http://censusindia.gov.in/

Among the districts, Nalbari (26.98 per cent), Naogaon (11.93 per cent), Cachar (11.87 per cent), Karimganj (7.07 per cent), Marigaon (5.28 per cent), are the main SC concentrated districts in Assam, each having more than 05 per cent SC population. These five districts together share 63.13 per cent of the total SC population of the state.[85]

Table 3.19: District-wise SC's Population of Assam

Sl. No	State/District	Total Population (Districtwise)					Per-cent-age
	ASSAM (Asom)	Total	Rural	Urban	Male	Female	
		2231321	1825761	405560	1145314	1086007	100
1.	Kokrajhar	29570	23747	5823	15386	14184	1.32
2.	Dhubri	70395	39929	30466	36359	34036	3.15
3.	Goalpara	45094	32886	12208	22999	22095	2.02
4.	Bongaigaon	82784	67460	15324	42513	40271	3.71
5.	Barpeta	95320	73946	21374	49165	46155	4.27
6.	Kamrup	107827	88975	18852	55237	52590	4.83
	Kamrup Main	101789	33499	68290	52106	49683	4.56
7.	Nalbari	60216	54232	5984	30654	29562	26.98
8.	Darrang	40260	28746	11514	20566	19694	1.80
9.	Marigaon	117841	109307	8534	60194	57647	5.28
10.	Nagaon	266350	228530	117173	136473	129877	11.93
11.	Sonitpur	109130	94692	14438	55817	53313	4.88
12.	Lakhimpur	81840	74891	6949	41689	40151	3.66
13.	Dhemaji	44225	40524	3701	23006	21219	1.98
14.	Tinsukia	37688	25286	12402	19443	18245	1.68
15.	Dibrugarh	58876	41396	17480	30517	28359	2.63
16.	Sibsagar	42347	34483	7864	21568	20779	1.89
17.	Jorhat	88665	72434	16231	45194	43471	3.97
18.	Golaghat	62298	56152	6146	31807	30491	2.79
19.	Karbi Anglong	44961	39936	5025	23436	21525	2.01
20.	Cachar	264897	216090	48807	136051	128846	11.87
21.	Karimganj	157890	144169	13721	81384	76506	7.07
22.	Dima Hasan	4337	1885	2452	2340	1997	0.19
23.	Hailakandi	70659	65736	4923	36369	34290	3.16
24.	Chirang	35135	31362	3773	18105	17030	1.57
25.	Baksa	73083	71382	1701	37534	35549	3.27
26.	Udalguri	37844	34086	3758	19402	18442	1.69

Source: Office of the Registrar General of India, 2011 Census of India, Government of India, http://censusindia.gov.in/

Table 3.20: Literacy Rate among Major SCs of Assam

Sl.No.	Name of the Scheduled Caste	Total	Male	Female	Percentage
	All SC Literates in Assam	1489564	826983	662581	100
1.	Bansphor	8751	5144	3637	0.58
2.	Bhuinmali, Mali	49361	26913	22448	3.31
3.	Brittial Bania, Bania	38738	20988	17750	2.60
4.	Dhupi, Dhobi	39165	21437	17728	2.62
5.	Dugla, Dholi	4526	2581	1945	0.30
6.	Hira	39102	21263	17839	2.62
7.	Jalkeot	16783	9366	7417	1.12
8.	Jhalo, Malo, Jhalo-Malo	45905	26870	19035	3.08
9.	Kaibartta, Jaliya	486064	264733	221331	32.63
10.	Lalbegi	497	279	218	0.03
11.	Mahara	1224	784	440	0.08
12.	Mehtar, Bhangi	5576	3169	2407	0.37
13.	Muchi, Rishi	41206	24595	16611	2.76
14.	Namasudra	390772	222135	168637	26.23
15.	Patni	135345	72485	62860	9.08
16.	Sutradhar	44320	24849	19471	2.97

Source: Census of India, 2011, http://censusindia.gov.in/

The total literacy among the SCs is 1489564 out of which 826983 are male and 662581 are females. The highest literacy among all the 16 SC's are Kaibarta (486064) and Namosudra (390772) and the lowest is among Lalbegi (997) and Mahara (1224).

The percentage of SC workers to total population Work Participation Rate (WPR) is 38.15 per cent, which is lower than the aggregated average for SCs at national level. Out of the total workers, 74.0 per cent have been recorded as main workers and 25.94 per cent as marginal workers. The female WPR is only 19.77 per cent, which is lower than their male counterparts 55.59 per cent. The total main workers among SCs, 46.40 per cent have been recorded for female and 83.3 per cent are for male on the other hand the total female marginal workers are 53.59 per cent whereas 16.62 per cent are male.[86]

Table 3.21: Distribution of Total, Main and Marginal Workers among SC's (Assam)

T/M/F	Total Workers (Percentage to Total Population)	Main Workers (Percentage to Total Workers)	Marginal Workers (Percentage to Total Workers)
Total	851461 (38.15%)	630532 (74.0%)	220929 (25.94%)
Male	636702 (55.59%)	530874 (83.3%)	105828 (16.62%)
Female	214759 (19.77%)	99658 (46.40%)	115101 (53.59%)

Source: Office of the Registrar General of India, 2011 Census of India, http://censusindia.gov.in/

Table 3.22: Main Workers by Industrial Category among SC's of Assam (Asom)

Sl. No.	Name of the Scheduled Caste	Main Workers	Cultivators	Agricultural Labourers	Household Industry Workers	Other Workers	Percentage
	All Scheduled Castes	630532	196729	56590	29907	347306	100
1.	Bansphor	4689	133	106	63	4387	0.74
2.	Bhuinmali	19337	3646	1750	963	12978	3.06
3.	Bittal Bania	14445	3205	810	831	9599	2.29
4.	Dhupi, Dhobi	14991	2486	1124	1160	10221	2.37
5.	Dugla	2214	329	221	53	1611	0.35
6.	Hira	14545	4936	1178	1390	7041	2.30
7.	Jalkeot	7172	1477	517	399	4779	1.13
8.	Jhalo	23144	4963	1530	799	15852	3.67
9.	Kaibartta	195209	64489	14910	7949	107861	30.95
10.	Lalbegi	243	49	14	4	176	0.03
11.	Mahara	681	49	48	8	576	0.10
12.	Mehtar, Bhangi	2451	138	76	18	2219	0.38
13.	Muchi, Rishi	23596	3541	3018	869	16168	3.74
14.	Namasudra	179085	72179	18797	8888	79221	28.40
15.	Patni	46205	13416	5314	1222	26253	7.32
16.	Sutradhar	19621	3894	1765	1866	12096	3.11

Source: Census of India, 2011, http://censusindia.gov.in/

Overall the total main workers among SC's in Assam (Asom) are 630532, out of which 196729 are cultivators, 56590 are agricultural labourers, 29907 are household industry workers and 347306 are other workers. Among all the 16 SC's the highest main workers are Kaibarta and Namasudra. The total main workers among Kaibarta are 195209, out of which 64489 are cultivators, 14910 are agricultural labourers, 7949 are household industry workers and 107861 are other workers. On the other hand, the total main workers among Namasudra are 179085, out of which 72179 are cultivators, 18797 are agricultural labourers, 8888 are household industry workers and 79221 are other workers.

Table 3.23: Marginal Workers by Industrial Category among SC's of Assam (Asom)

Sl.No.	*Name of the Scheduled Caste*	*Marginal Workers*	*Cultivators*	*Agricultural Labourers*	*Household Industry Workers*	*Other Workers*	*Per-cent-age*
	All Scheduled Castes	220929	50340	59301	23912	87376	100
1.	Bansphor	907	67	76	74	690	3.95
2.	Bhuinmali	5945	858	1439	776	2872	2.69
3.	Bittal Bania	5009	1315	1210	741	1743	2.26
4.	Dhupi, Dhobi	4713	518	1270	698	2227	2.13
5.	Dugla, Dholi	662	38	114	30	480	0.29
6.	Hira	7704	1673	2353	1558	1709	3.48
7.	Jalkeot	2288	310	496	472	1010	1.03
8.	Jhalo, Malo	7020	1620	1426	517	3457	3.17
9.	Kaibartta, Jaliya	71907	21564	17782	7773	24788	32.54
10.	Lalbegi	57	9	16	2	30	0.0
11.	Mahara	127	14	29	4	80	0.0
12.	Mehtar, Bhangi	595	103	72	23	397	0.2
13.	Muchi, Rishi	7388	934	1876	386	4192	3.34
14.	Namasudra	60594	14431	19547	6137	20479	27.42
15.	Patni	14203	2428	3959	920	6896	6.42
16.	Sutradhar	6420	935	2284	616	2585	2.90

Source: Census of India, 2011, http://censusindia.gov.in/

Overall the total marginal workers among SC's in Assam (Asom) are 220929, out of which 50340 are cultivators 59301 are agricultural labourers, 23912 are household industry workers and 87376 are other workers. Among all the 16 SC's the highest marginal workers are Kaibarta and Namasudra. The total marginal workers among Kaibarta are 71907, out of which 21564 are cultivators, 17782 are agricultural labourers, 7773 are household industry workers and 24788 are other workers. On the other hand the total marginal workers among Namasudra are 60594, out of which 14431 are cultivators, 19547 are agricultural labourers, 6137 are household industry workers and 20479 are other workers.

Table 3.24: Non-workers among SC's of Assam (Asom)

Sl. No.	*Name of the Scheduled Caste*	*Total Non-workers*	*Male*	*Female*	*Per-cen-tage*
	All Scheduled Castes	1379860	508612	871248	100
1.	Bansphor	10763	4284	6479	0.78
2.	Bhuinmali	44253	15943	28310	3.20
3.	Bittal Bania	31144	11322	19822	2.25
4.	Dhupi, Dhobi	32727	11610	21117	2.37
5.	Dugla	5115	1866	3249	0.37
6.	Hira	33051	12462	20589	2.39
7.	Jalkeot	15314	5606	9708	1.10
8.	Jhalo	50212	18012	32200	3.63
9.	Kaibartta	426103	158999	267014	30.88
10.	Lalbegi	490	195	295	0.03
11.	Mahara	1014	382	632	0.07
12.	Mehtar, Bhangi	5789	2256	3533	0.41
13.	Muchi, Rishi	46659	17738	28921	3.38
14.	Namasudra	391863	143179	248684	28.39
15.	Patni	121496	42881	78615	8.80
16.	Sutradhar	40262	14429	25833	2.91

Source: Census of India, 2011, http://censusindia.gov.in/

Overall the total non-workers among SC's in Assam (Asom) are 1379860, out of which 50812 are males and 871248 are females. Among all the 16 SC's the highest non-workers are Kaibarta and Namasudra. The total non-workers among Kaibarta are 426103 out of which 158999 are males and 267014 are females.

On the other hand the total non-workers among Namasudra are 391863, out of which 143179 are males and 248684 are females.

Arunachal Pradesh

Arunachal Pradesh is the land of breathtakingly beautiful sunrises between sky rocketing mountains, sparkling rivers, lakes, and ample of snow. It is the Arunachal Pradesh; the vast expanse of rolling plains, hills, and beautiful water bodies at the far eastern edge of India. India shows diversity in every aspect, including its population distribution. Arunachal Pradesh is the Indian state with the least population density, with just over 13 lakhs of people living in the vast area of over 80,000 kilometers square. The population density of Arunachal Pradesh is even less than 20 people per kilometer square of area, according to Arunachal census of 2011. Population growth rate is more than 25 per cent here, but has shown decrement since the last census. Literacy in this state, however, is far more disappointing. With only over 60 per cent of literate citizens, it is one of the two states in India having lowest literacy. On the positive side, the literacy has increased since the last survey by more than 10 per cent. Additionally, the increase in female literacy is greater than that in males. Though large in size, the state of Arunachal has far less area urbanised; making most of the population lives in rural areas. Whatever small urban areas exist, the gender ratio found in those is dissatisfactory, whereas the sex ratio in villages shows above 900 females per 1000 males. As vibrant is the land, so are the people living in it. Arunachal population speaks above 50 dialects in total owing to the cultural diversity. Yet, the official language is English. The state capital is Itanagar. Some other major cities like Bomdila, Bhismaknagar, and Bhalukpong are worth visiting. Numerous tribes reside in the state each following their own cultures and ceremonies. Owing to wide tourism opportunities due to the Buddhist monasteries and cultural fests, the state has been gradually progressing. The capital city which is also the largest city in the state of Arunachal Pradesh is Itanagar. The languages spoken in the Arunachal Pradesh state includes English. In total Arunachal Pradesh state comprises 16 districts.[87]

There are twenty six major tribes and a number of sub-tribes inhabiting in all the sixteen districts. Most of these communities are ethnically similiar having derived from the original common stock but geographical isolation from each other has brought amongst them certain distinctive characteristics in language, dress, religion, tradition and customs. Broadly speaking the people have been divided into three cultural groups on the basis of their socio-religious backgrounds. The Monpas and Sherdukpens of Twang and West Kemeng districts follow the lamastic tradition of Mahayana Buddhism.[88] Noted for their religious beliefs, the villages of these communities have highly decorated 'Gompas'. Though largely agriculturist, many of these people is also pastoral and breeds herds of Yak and mountain Sheep. Culturally similiar to them are the Membas and Khambas who live in the high mountains along the northern borders, Khamptis and Singphos inhabiting the eastern part of the State are Buddhists of Hinayana sect. They are said to have migrated from Thailand and Burma long ago. The second group of people are the Adis, Akas, Apatanis, Bungnis, Nishis, Mishmis, Mijis, Thangsos etc. who worship the Sun and Moon God (Dony Polo). Their religious rituals largely coincide with the phases of agricultural cycles. They invoke nature deities and make animal sacrifices. Adis and Apatanis extensively practice wet-rice cultivation and have a considerable agricultural economy. Apatanis are also famous for their paddy-cum-fish culture. They have specialised over centuries in harvesting two crops of fish along with each crop of paddy.[89] The third group comprises Noctes and Wanchos, adjoining Nagaland in the Tirap district. These are hardy people known for their structured village society in which the gereditary village chief still plays a vital role. The Noctes also practise elementary form of Vaishnavism.[90]

Arunachal Pradesh the land of rising sun is unfamiliar to the other parts of the world is dominated by scheduled tribe population. These tribals have constituted a separate endogamous community with its own mountain territory, customs and traditional and extremely different from other tribal communities, of India in particular and the rest of the world in general. The Indian state of Arunachal Pradesh has approximately 6,188 (0.6 per cent) scheduled castes population according to 2001 census report and as per NSSO 2009 report population has increased to 0.15 per cent are suffering from multiple backwardness, first as a general scheduled caste, second as isolation and third as as regional backwardness. These populations have been denied their basic fundamental rights in the region and suffering from huge discrimination and exclusion by both the state government as well as the local population of the state.[91]

Before going to focus the problem let me bring some of the brief ethnographic information about the state which is unknown to the world. When we talk about the history of Arunachal Pradesh, it goes back to hundreds of years into mists of tradition and myth. Local tradition regards the country around Sadiya as the ancient Vidarbha. Ancient Puranas have many references to the region. History of Arunachal Pradesh can be traced only when Ahoms Kings began to rule Assam in the 16th century. The British took possession of Assam in 1838. British government had brought Arunachal Pradesh also under their administrative control.[92]

Though the history of the growth of political process in Arunachal Pradesh dates back to 1875 when the British India Government started to define the administrative jurisdiction by drawing an Inner-Line in relation to the Frontier Tribes inhabiting the North Frontier Tracts (NFT), the area was kept outside the preview of regular laws of the country. Thereafter the British followed the policy of gradual penetration to bring more areas under normal administration. By the year 1946, the North East Frontier Tracts (NEFT) were recognised into four frontiers tracts namely, Sadiya, Lakhimpur, Tirap and Sela Sub-Agency and Subansiri area and administrated by the Governor of Assam in his discretion. By virtue of the Indian Independence Act 1947 the government of Assam assumed administrative jurisdiction over NEFT and the Governor of Assam was divested of his discretionary powers.[93]

The Government of Assam administered the NEFT during the period of 15th August 1947 to 26th January 1950. After India's independence, a sub-committee headed by Gopinath Bordoloi was appointed by the Constituent Assembly of India to recommend the future pattern of administration of the NEFT. The Bordoloi Committee recommended that since the administration has been satisfactorily established over sufficiently wide areas, the Government of Assam should take over that area by the strength of a notification. But for various considerations, particularly problem of communication and defiance, Government of India decided to administer NEFT as "Exclusive Area" through Governor of India. In the year 1950, the plain portions of these tracts namely, Balipara Frontier Tract (BFT), Tirap Frontier Tract (TFT), Abor Hill District (AHD) and Mishimi Hill Districts (MHD) were transferred to the Government of Assam.[94] In 1951, the units of the tracts were reconstituted again and Tuensang Frontier Division (TFD) was created which latter merged with Nagaland. The remaining portion of the tracts after the introduction of the North East Frontier (Administration) Regulation 1954 was designated as the North East Frontier Agency (NEFA). Thereafter the administration was brought under Ministry of External Affairs (MEA) and in August 1965, it was brought under the supervision and control of the Ministry of Home Affairs (MHA). It remains so, till the attainment of Union Territory status by Arunachal Pradesh in 1972, under the 27th Constitutional Amendment Act of 1971.[95]

It was only in 1975 that the virtue of the enactment of 37th Constitutional Amendment Act 1975 that the Pradesh Council was constituted as a separate Legislative Assembly and Lt. Governor was appointed as the head of the Union Territory of Arunachal Pradesh. The Pradesh Council becomes provisional Legislative Assembly having 23 members during 1975 to 1978. The first elected Legislative Assembly constituting of 33 members (30 elected members and 3 nominated) was formed on 4th March 1978, which lasted only for about 20 months. In November 1979, the Assembly was dissolved and President's rule was imposed which continued till January 1980. The second general election was held in January 1980, the third general election for Legislative Assembly was held simultaneously with the general election for the eighth Lok Sabha in December 1984 and the Assembly was continued till January 1986.[96]

On 20th February 1987, Statehood was conferred on Arunachal Pradesh under the 55th Constitutional Amendment Act of 1986, and becomes the 25th State of the Union of India. In fact, the evolution and formation of Arunachal Pradesh is a tribute to the farsighted tribal policy formulated by 'Verrier Elwin' in its stage. Arunachal Pradesh in its area-wise is the largest state in the North Eastern Region of India (NERI) around 83,743 sq. km, having not more than fourteen lakh population. It forms a complex hill system of Shivalik and Himalayan origin and is criss-crossed by numerous rivers and streams. The state shares a total of 1630 km's of international boundary with neighbouring countries; 1030 km with China, 160 km with Bhutan and 440 km with Myanmar. The Mc-Mohan Lines define the International Boundary between India and China. Administratively the state is divided into sixteen districts. Capital of the state is Itanagar in Papumpare District. Itanagar is named after Ita Fort, meaning Fort of bricks, which was built by Ahom Kings in 14th century A.D. The Hindu influences penetrated along the Brahmaputra up to the Dibang Valley. Sacred Centres sprung up between 11th and 13th centuries. The ruins of the Bhishmark site have reportedly been located in the Dibang Valley and those of Parsuram Kund in Lohit District.[97]

Table 3.25: Total Population in the Districts of Arunachal Pradesh (2011)

S.No.	*Districts Ranking wise (2011)*	*Total Population*	*Total Per cent*
1	Papumpare	176385	12.76
2.	Changlang	147951	10.70
3.	Lohit	145538	10.53
4.	West Siang	112272	8.12
5.	Tirap	111997	8.10
6.	East Siang	99019	7.16
7.	Kurung Kurey	89717	6.49
8.	West Kameng	87013	6.29
9.	Uppar Subansiri	83205	6.02
10.	Lower Subansiri	82839	5.99
11.	East Kameng	78413	5.67
12.	Lower Dibang Valley	53986	3.90
13.	Tawang	49950	3.61
14.	Uppar Siang	35289	2.55
15.	Anjaw	21089	1.53
16.	Dibang Valley	7948	0.57

Source: Office of the Registrar General of India, 2011 Census of India, Government of India, http://censusindia.gov.in/

Arunachal Pradesh has twenty six major tribes with a number of sub-tribes. The major tribes are Adi, Apatani, Bugun, Galo, Hrusso, Jingpho, Khamba, Koro, Mcmba, Mcyor, Mishmi (including Idu, Taroon and Kaman), Monpa, Nyishi (including Bangru, and Puroik), Sajolang, Sartang, Sherdukpen, Tagin, Tai

Khamti (including Khamyang), Yobin, Tangshang (including Muklam, Lonchang, Tutsa, Tikhak, Howoi, Longri, Mungrey, Mushung, Lungphi, Joglai Ngaimong, Ponthai, Khalak, Lungkhai liallry, Chellim, Sheehu, Shiangwal, Rcra, Shiangte, Lowchang, Dohe, Moitai, Hatseng Gajee, Gaja, Kochong, Laki, Gallong, Chamehang, Ringkhu, Shohra, Bowngtai, Rourong of Changlang district and Nocte, Wanchoo and Tutsa of Tirap district). Chakmas and Hajongs also included in the census as the population of Arunachal Pradesh.[98] Arunachal Pradesh have 16 castes like Bansphor, Bhummali or Mali, Brittial, Dhupi or Dhobi, Dugla or Dholi, Hira, Jalkeot, Jhalo, Malo or Jhalo-Malo, Kaibartta or Jaliya, Lalbegi, Machara, Mehtar or Bhangi, Muchi or Rishi, Namasudra, Patni, Sutradhar.[99]

Most of the communities of the state believe in traditional tribal religion. Important aspects of tribal religion are the observance of various festivals, ancestral worship and taboos. The beliefs in malevolent and benevolent spirits and deities and rituals performed by the concept of the supreme beings or god (called various as Ske, Matai, Rang, Rangkuwa by different communities), constitute the animistic tribal religions. Donyi-Poloism is the major tribal religion of Arunachal Pradesh. It has a vast mythology with all its mundane and supernatural elements. Donyi-Polo is a combination of two terms Donyi means 'Sun' and Polo means 'Moon'. Donyi is the source of power and energy for living beings, which cannot be disputed scientifically and philosophically. Thus, Donyi-Polo, the spiritual source and symbol is believed to be the supreme power governing the universe.

A festival is the day or a period of celebration and an essential part of the socio-cultural life of the people. Festivals reflect the customs, traditions and lifestyle of the people. Like other parts of the India, in Arunachal Pradesh also festivals are celebrated with great joy, enthusiasm and most importantly, with a feeling of togetherness. The festivals of Arunachal Pradesh serve a two fold purpose—A thanks giving ceremonies in homage to God and for his gifts of good crops and freedom. Animal sacrifice is a common ritual in most of the festivals of Arunachal Pradesh.[100]

The political system of Arunachal Pradesh may be defined as a part of the total process, which engaged in the maintenance or establishment of social order or social equilibrium among the Arunachalees. It essentially consists of the activities connected with the political institutions of the area, in its broadest sense, a political system of institutionalised customs by which law, order and peace are maintained in a society. The traditional forms of government govern almost all the communities of Arunachal Pradesh.[101] The Dr Diying Ering Committee introduced modern democratic norms in Arunachal Pradesh by providing the people an opportunity to exercise their rights for franchise. Till 1967, Arunachal Pradesh was represented in the Lok Sabha by a member nominated by the President of India. The first general election was held on January 3, 1980 for the formation of a Legislative Assembly during its tenure as a Union Territory (UT). At that time there was only two political parties, namely, the Congress (I) and People's Party of Arunachal Pradesh (PPAP), a new entrant in the political arena of the state, so far two Assembly and Parliamentary elections have taken place and the people have taken part without any fear or compulsion.[102]

So far the politics of reservation in the state is concerned it is 80 per cent for ST and 20 per cent for general category (here general includes all the people from other than Arunachalees viz. SC/ST/OBC/Women/Others of other state). Before 1964, the ratio of reservation in the state was 50:50, i.e., 50 per cent reserved for ST and 50 per cent for the General (Non-Arunachalees). Over a period of time strong movement, protest took place on the question of reservation with the refugee problem in the state and developmental issues. All Arunachal Pradesh Student Union (AAPSU) one of the most popular and powerful student organisation with popular village support, started demanding the 100 per cent reservation for ST in the state.[103] Many months have been engaged to discuss on the related matter and due to huge pressure Government of India, Government of Arunachal Pradesh agreed to provide 80 per cent reservation to the Arunachalees (ST) and another 20 per cent left for general public.

As per details from Census 2011, Arunachal Pradesh has population of 13.84 lakhs, an increase from figure of 10.98 lakh in 2001 census. Total population of Arunachal Pradesh as per 2011 census is 1,383,727 of which male and female are 713,912 and 669,815 respectively. In 2001, total population was 1,097,968 in which males were 579,941 while females were 518,027. The total population growth in this decade was 26.03 per cent while in previous decade it was 26.21 per cent. The population of Arunachal Pradesh forms 0.11 per cent of India in 2011. In 2001, the figure was 0.11 per cent. Literacy rate in Arunachal Pradesh has seen upward trend and is 65.38 per cent as per 2011 population census. Of that, male literacy stands at 72.55 per cent while female literacy is at 53.52 per cent. In 2001, literacy rate in Arunachal Pradesh stood at 54.34 per cent of which male and female were 65.43 per cent and 40.23 per cent literate respectively. In actual numbers, total literates in Arunachal Pradesh stands at 766,005 of which males were 439,868 and females were 326,137. Total area of Arunachal Pradesh is 83,743 sq. km. Density of Arunachal Pradesh is 17 per sq km which is lower than national average 382 per sq km. In 2001, density of Arunachal Pradesh was 13 per sq km, while nation average in 2001 was 324 per sq km. Sex Ratio in Arunachal Pradesh is 938 i.e. for each 1000 male, which is below national average of 940 as per census 2011. In 2001, the sex ratio of female was 901 per 1000 males in Arunachal Pradesh. Lot of viewers are asking us to provide religion's data of Arunachal Pradesh state.[104]

As per 2001 census 6,188[105] persons listed as the SC's population constituting 0.6 per cent of the total population of the state discriminated and excluded various rights like right to get trading license in their own name to do business, right to job in the government sectors and other basic rights. In 1971 Census, total SC population was 339. The number has steadily increased in subsequent Censuses. In 1981 Census, the total SC population was 2,919. This became 4,052 in 1991 Census. In 2001 Census, the SC population in Arunachal Pradesh increase further to 6,188 persons. The state has registered 52.7 per cent decadal growth of its SC population in 1991-2001 Census.[106] Individual SC wise, Namasudra (21.6 per cent), Kaibartta (21.4 per cent), and Dhupi (11.1 per cent) are the major SC's in the state of Arunachal Pradesh. They together constitute about 55 per cent of the total SC population of the state. Six SC's namely, Mahara, Patni, Jhalo, Hira, Dugla, and Lalbegi are small in numbers and have less than hundred populations each.[107]

Table 3.26: Scheduled Castes Population, 2001

Sl. No.	*Name of the Scheduled Caste*	*Total population*	*Proportion to the total SC population*
	All Scheduled Castes	6,188	100 per cent
1.	Namasudra	1,334	21.6
2.	Kaibartta or Jaliya	1,327	21.1
3.	Dhupi or Dhobi	688	11.1
4.	Brittial	496	8.0
5.	Mehtar or Bhangi	409	6.6
6.	Jalkeot	331	5.3
7.	Muchi or Risi	275	4.4
8.	Sutradhar	247	4.0
9.	Bansphor	193	3.1
10.	Bhuinmali or Mali	137	2.2
11.	Dugla or Dholi	NA	NA
12.	Hira	NA	NA
13.	Jhalo, Malo or Jhalo-Malo	NA	NA
14.	Lalbegi	NA	NA
15.	Machara	NA	NA
16.	Patni	NA	NA

Note: In 2011 census Report Scheduled Castes population has been removed by the government.

Source: Office of the Registrar General of India, 2011 Census of India, Government of India, http://censusindia.gov.in

More than half of the SC population has been reported to be living in urban areas. Out of these three main SC's, Dhupi (Dhobi) has recorded the highest 61 per cent urban population, followed by Namasudra (57.4 per cent) and Kaibartta (29.2 per cent). The sex ratio of total SC population in the state is 724, which is quite low. Out of these three main SC's, the Dhupi has recorded the lowest sex ratio of 658. The state has recorded child sex ratio (0-6 age group) of 938, which is exactly at per to the national average for SC's (938). Namasudra have recorded more female children in their population of 0-6 with child sex ratio of 1049. The child sex ratio is, however, low among Kaibartta (813) and Dhupi (820). In 2001 Census, 67.6 per cent of the SC population of the state has been recorded as literate, with male and female literacy being 76.3 per cent and 55 per cent respectively.

Kaibartta has recorded the highest literacy rate of 77.5 per cent. Dhupi and Namasudra are at par each having above 69 per cent literacy rate. The percentage of workers to total population (WPR) among the SC's is low at 38.4 per cent. More than half (56.6 per cent) of the male population have been returned as workers, while the female WPR is low at 13.2 per cent. Out of the total workers, an overwhelming 90.2 per cent are main workers, with 93.3 per cent males and 71.6 per cent females as main workers.[108]

Table 3.27: Distribution of Total, Main and Marginal Workers among SC's

Percentage of Workers			
T/M/F	*Total Workers*	*Main Workers*	*Marginal Workers*
Total	2,375 (38.4 %)	2,142 (90.2%)	233 (9.8%)
Male	2,033 (56.6%)	1,897 (93.3%)	136 (6.7%)
Female	342 (13.2%)	245 (71.6%)	97 (28.4%)

Source: Office of the Registrar General of India, 2011 Census of India, Government of India, http://censusindia.gov.in

The SC's in Arunachal Pradesh are not primarily dependent on agricultural pursuits. Merely 13.4 per cent of the total SC main workers have been recorded as cultivators, 1.2 per cent agricultural labourers, and two per cent in household industry. Thus, a high of 83.4 per cent of the total main workers among SC's have been recorded under industrial category of "other works". Dhupi has recorded the lowest 2.4 per cent of their main workers in agriculture (i.e. cultivators and agricultural labourers), followed by Namasudra (15.9 per cent). However, it is a high of 41.8 per cent among Kaibartta. As regarding marital status, 52.8 per cent of the SC's are never married, 45.2 per cent married, 1.7 per cent widowed, and the remaining 0.2 per cent divorced/separated. Kaibartta has recorded a high of 3.3 per cent widowed in their population. The overwhelming majority of the SC's in Arunachal Pradesh are Hindus.[109]

As we know the ST's of Arunachal Pradesh are protected by the Constitution under different provisions. We also know that the part of north-eastern states are included in the 5th and 6th Scheduled of the Constitution and have been given special status and rights to protect the tribal culture, tradition, religion etc.[110]

In case of Arunachal Pradesh the Bengal Regulation Act, 1873 (inner-line regulation) checks and stop outsiders to enter in the state freely without proper inner line pass.[111] But we also know that the SC's of this country have also being protected by the Constitution whose conditions are worse than any other community. There are different safeguards, laws, articles which protects the SC's from all types of exploitation, exclusion, discrimination and injustice physically or physiologically.

It is constitutionally correct that the Arunachal Pradesh is a tribal dominated state so if ST's are getting eighty per cent reservation in the state is at all not a problem, let these people should get eighty per cent reservation in jobs government or private, State Assembly etc, but the problem lies in that twenty per cent, which is creating problem in the state to those SC's who born or migrated fifty years before. Parents who migrated and their children's born, adopted state's culture and identity should be given justice in any cost on humanitarian ground as well as legally. SC's in Arunachal Pradesh is coming under the general category which is really a big issue to be dealt with. The SC's in the state are no doubt are the migrants, but they migrated before fifty years settled and mixed with the soil of Arunachal, and adopted Arunachal's culture and identity, it is correctly to be related with the theory propounded by a well known physiologist Nimmi Hutnic who opines that, A+B=C, in which A=Different identity, B=Different identity, C=Adopted one identity. In this A, belongs to the different identity B, belongs to the different culture which gives result C. It means A belongs to different culture and identity, B belongs to different culture and identity, and over a period of time they developed or adjust with new identity i.e., C.[112] My point here is that the scheduled castes posses the same position in the Indian states of Arunachal Pradesh. The people behave more like Arunachalese, food habit have changed, language changed, identity has changed and share more commonality with the tribals of the region are more sufferer as they suffering in other states in the other parts of India in the state. They are mostly landless, jobless and due to no other option and opportunities they engaged themselves into their traditional dirty works.

The problem here is the people who migrated before fifty years back, settled in the environment, spent their whole life and cannot be treated in the general category, or to be more specify cannot be included in the 20 per cent. Because if you open 20 per cent for general and include SC population in that 20 per cent is never the less doing injustice to them and snatching their rights to get their representation in all sectors which they are facing today one as regional backwardness and another as untouchables. When government open 20 per cent for general the out state population belongs to preveleged castes getting good education, good financial background are benefiting more or all the twenty per cent who never been the part of the state. The very simple submission to the problem is only that the SC's of Arunachal Pradesh who born and grown up in the region is that, they should be given reservation in the state in that twenty per cent. At least five per cent should be reserved for these marginalised groups who are one of the most backward landless groups in the state. The demand is not in that 80 per cent but the demand is in that twenty per cent that is five per cent seats are to be reserved for the SC population who born in the state and mixed with its culture, tradition and environment. In any case this population cannot be treated as general because these populations are landless; doing all the dirty works in the state long back before fifty years and their children's continuing as usual has to be protected. These populations in any case should be given five per cent reservations in the government jobs, and representation in the Assembly and other sector for their upliftman to minimise the injustice. Government of Arunachal Pradesh have all information about the SC population about their condition, but even knowing everything, the State Government behaving like unknown, and not trying to understand their problems which is really to be criticised strongly. Even after knowing that the SC population's condition is so worse, and not taking any step to implement any policies and programmes for their upliftment. In place of doing any welfare activities the Government of Arunachal Pradesh cancelling trading licenses of these populations, charging heavy taxes on different occupations, which is creating problem to earn their livelihood, the Government of Arunachal Pradesh, Government of India and all the Student organisations should think on this line and work out for the SC's problem in state and support to implement at least five per cent reservation for them in different sector to fill the gap of injustice done over a period of time so far.[113]

The Central as well as State Government initiated lots of developmental activities to strengthen the political economy of the state and the people, but none of the policies and programmes have any inclusive provisions for scheduled castes of Arunachal Pradesh. The initiative like the encouragement of the establishment of industrial undertakings in the private and cooperative sectors for the sustainable development of the state, employment opportunities and gainful self-employment in industrial and allied sectors,[114] tourism, medical services, educational services etc. A programme for the development of infrastructure facilities, inter-alia including the establishment of Industrial Estates, Industrial Growth Centers, Integrated Infrastructure Development Centers, strengthening of existing Industrial Estates, Export Promotion Industrial Parks, Export Promotion Zones, Border trade, Reserves of minerals explored and exploited commercially through appropriate agencies. Government made special efforts for development of local entrepreneurial, managerial and technical skills. For this purpose, special training and educational programmes, put on a sound economic and commercial footing and ensure smooth flow of credit for new industrial projects to village industries and rural artisans. For this the District Industries Centers and financial institutions work in close cooperation.[115] State Level Industrial Empowered Committee comprising of the concerned Secretaries and representatives from banking and financial Institutions formed to grant the requisite clearances and facilitate the establishment of industries from a single window. This Empowered Committee headed by the Minister of Industries and meet as often as necessary.

National Bank for Agriculture and Rural Development (NABARD) has identified more than 10 sectors for development, which included sectors like Agriculture, Fish rearing and processing, Rural Retail Trade, Sericulture and Silk Textile Fiber products, Construction, Small plantation products, Handloom, Handicrafts products in cane and Bamboo and wood. These activities are to be developed for creation of additional employment in the rural areas. All relevant Departments associated in the implementation of these schemes. The State Government gradually vacates economic space for the private and cooperative sectors and the public and state sectors to be economic players to generate employment among tribals and women. The State Government reserve 33 per cent of industrial sheds, development plots in Industrial Area/Estate/Growth Centre etc for women.[116] Non of the any policy has been attached to the SC and because of it the SC's of Arunachal Pradesh engaged with the traditional jobs like sweeping, stitching shoes, washing dirty cloths, cleaning toilets, engaged in burial grounds, and all other dirty jobs. Even after getting good education they are not getting jobs in the state due to injustice they engaged themselves and compelled to do their traditional dirty works as doing in other parts of India from centuries. One has to know that it was only by the efforts of Babasaheb Dr Bhim Rao Ambedkar[117] SC's, ST's and OBC's of India availing all kind of opportunities vis-a-vis, education, jobs or overall talked of social justice.

Manipur

Manipur the Meitei-lon speaking state of Manipur resides on the far north-eastern edge of the map of India. The landscapes filled with brilliant greenery complemented with the crystal-like water, kayaks in the lakes, and waterfalls in hills, seem to be a common sight in Manipur. The gifted land of Manipur also has a growing population of over 25 lakhs, residing in a vast area of about 20000 square kilometer. The population density of the state is very low, which makes it one of the least population density areas, in the northeast corner of India. Here, the population growth rate is less than 20 per cent. The state also ranks first within the northeastern Indian states, when it comes to the sex ratio. It has a good gender proportion of above 900 females in 1000 males, according to the Manipur census 2011. Literacy has greatly increased in this state as compared to the previous census, with around 10 per cent increment rate. It's noteworthy, that literacy in females has increased more than that in males. The ratio of urban to rural population is approximately 3:7 in Manipur, which is better in terms of urbanisation as compared to the rest of north-eastern regions. Imphal is the largest city in the state, which is also its capital. The official language spoken here is Meiteilon. The culture of Manipur is enriched with so many facets, that it is difficult to discuss all of them at once. But when it comes to Manipur, it will be criminal not to mention the 'Manipuri Raslila', which is the native traditional dance form. The dance is a treat to eyes both with the moves and the costumes. Mukna is a popular sport, which is a kind of wrestling. Other than these, many state-wide recreational activities like boat races and festivals ensue. The capital city which is also the largest city in the state of Manipur is Imphal. The languages spoken in the Manipur state includes Manipuri. In total Manipur state comprises nine districts.[118]

As per details from Census 2011, Manipur has population of 25.7 lakhs, an increase from figure of 22.94 lakh in 2001 census. Total population of Manipur as per 2011 census is 2,570,390 of which male and female are 1,290,171 and 1,280,219 respectively. In 2001, total population was 2,293,896 in which males were 1,161,952 while females were 1,131,944. The total population growth in this decade was 12.05 per cent while in previous decade it was 30.02 per cent. The population of Manipur forms 0.21 per cent of India in 2011. In 2001, the figure was 0.22 per cent. Literacy rate in Manipur has seen upward trend and is 79.21 per cent as per 2011 population census. Of that, male literacy stands at 86.06 per cent while female literacy is at 71.73 per cent. In 2001, literacy rate in Manipur stood at 70.53 per cent of which male and female were 80.33 per cent and 61.46 per cent literate respectively. In actual numbers, total literates in Manipur stands at 1,768,181 of which males were 960,015 and females were 808,166. Total area of Manipur is 22,327 sq. km. Density of Manipur is 115 per sq. km. which is lower than national average 382 per sq. km. In 2001, density of Manipur was 103 per sq. km., while nation average in 2001 was 324 per sq km. Sex Ratio in Manipur is 992 i.e., for each 1000 male, which is below national average of 940 as per census 2011. In 2001, the sex ratio of female was 978 per 1000 males in Manipur.[119] The total SC population is 97328.[120] There are seven notified SCs and all of them have been enumerated in 2011 Census.[121]

The Lois represents 87.8 per cent of the total SC population of the state. The population of Lois has increased from 11,234 persons in 1981 to 29,037 in 1991 and 51,668 in 2001 to 85,543 in 2011 Census. Patni (3.7 per cent) and Namasudra (3.8 per cent) are the other SCs having more than 3,000 populations in 2011 Census. Yaithibi, Sutradhar, Dhupi, and Muchi, the remaining four SCs of the state, are small in number.

Table 3.28: Scheduled Caste Population of Manipur, 2011 Census Report

Sl.No.	*Name of the Scheduled Caste*	*Total Population*	*Proportion to the total SC Population*
	All Scheduled Castes	97328	100 per cent
1.	Dhupi, Dhobi	122	0.1
2.	Lois	85543	87.8
3.	Muchi, Ravidas	190	0.1
4.	Namasudra	3747	3.8
5.	Patni	3664	3.7
6.	Sutradar	92	0.0
7.	Yaithibi	1532	1.5

Source: Office of the Registrar General of India, 2011 Census of India, http://censusindia.gov.in/

Table 3.29: Districtwise SC's Population of Manipur

Sl. No	*State/District*	*Total Population of District Wise*					*Per-cen-tage*
	MANIPUR	*Total*	*Rural*	*Urban*	*Male*	*Female*	
		97042	*47563*	*49479*	*48714*	*48328*	*0.05*
1.	Senapati	714	711	3	387	327	0.73
2.	Tamenglon	22	18	4	15	3	0.02
3.	Churachanpur	443	424	19	244	199	0.45
4.	Bishnupur	22113	21834	279	11085	11028	22.78
5.	Thoubal	40593	4397	36196	20137	20456	41.83
6.	Imphal West	16530	11711	4819	8308	8222	17.03
7.	Imphal East	15839	7815	8024	8055	7784	16.32
8.	Ukhrul	248	154	94	160	88	0.25
9.	Chandel	540	499	41	321	219	0.55

Source: Office of the Registrar General of India, 2011 Census of India, http://censusindia.gov.in/

The SC population of Manipur is primarily concentrated in Thoubal district, which accounts for 41.83 per cent of the total SC population of the state. Other two districts having sizeable proportion of SC population are Bishnupur (22.78 per cent), Imphal West (17.03 per cent) and Imphal East (16.32 per cent).[122]

Table 3.30: Literacy Rate among Major SCs of Manipur

Sl. No.	*Name of the Scheduled Caste*	*Total*	*Male*	*Female*	*per-Cen-tage*
	All SC Literates in Manipur	64488	35311	29177	100
1.	Dhobi	101	79	22	0.01
2.	Lois	56879	30863	26016	88.20
3.	Ravidas	136	99	37	0.21
4.	Namasudra	2474	1419	1055	3.83
5.	Patni	2276	1243	1033	3.52
6.	Sutradhar	69	41	28	0.10
7.	Yaithibi	959	521	438	1.48

Source: Census of India, 2011, http://censusindia.gov.in/

The Lois has recorded the highest literacy (56879) followed by Namasudra (2474) and Patni (2276). The least literates are Dhobi (101) and Sutradhar (0.10) among the seven identified SC's.

The percentage of SC workers to total population (WPR) is 45.91 per cent. Out of this total workers, 78.38 per cent have been recorded as main workers and 21.6 per cent as marginal workers. The female WPR at 37.83 per cent as compare to their male counterparts 53.92 per cent on the other hand the female main workers are 60.12 per cent whereas male percentage are 91.08 per cent. The marginal workers in female are 39.8 per cent is quite highest as compare to male counterpart which is 8.91 per cent.[123]

Table 3.31: Distribution of Total, Main and Marginal Workers among SC's (Manipur)

T/M/F	*Total Workers (Percentage to Total Population)*	*Main Workers (Percentage to Total Workers)*	*Marginal Workers (Percentage to Total Workers)*
Total	44684 (45.91%)	35024 (78.38%)	9660 (21.6%)
Male	26349 (53.92%)	24000 (91.08%)	2349 (8.91%)
Female	18335 (37.83%)	11024 (60.12%)	7311 (39.8%)

Source: Office of the Registrar General of India, 2011 Census of India, http://censusindia.gov.in/

Scheduled Castes are largely concentrated to the districts of Sekmai, Imphal and Thoubal of Manipur. As such there is no discrimination as compare to earlier they had. They have reservation like other scheduled castes of India but this only in paper. Today other Manipuris do not look down because scheduled castes are very strong to handle any situation.

Before two decades scheduled caste population was look down as the lower category of the society but when they moved to these districts in majority they emerged as the strong community in the Manipur society. This becomes only possible due to the Christian missionaries. Largely they converted to Christianity where they got educational opportunities to unite into very strong groups. They firmly engaged in their own business in the settled areas. They engaged in fields, small shops and local market goods selling's.

Table 3.32: Main Workers by Industrial Category among SC's of Manipur

Sl. No.	*Name of the Scheduled Caste*	*Main Workers*	*Cultivators*	*Agricultural Labourers*	*Household Industry Workers*	*Other Workers*	*Percentage*
	All Scheduled Castes	35024	14618	2712	1845	15849	100
1.	Dhupi, Dhobi	70	3	-	4	63	0.01
2.	Lois	31014	12451	2368	1547	14648	88.62
3.	Muchi, Ravidas	94	24	5	1	67	0.26
4.	Namasudra	1311	754	84	197	276	3.74
5.	Patni	1050	662	126	27	235	2.99
6.	Sutradar	44	17	-	1	26	0.1
7.	Yaithibi	589	310	63	40	176	1.68

Source: Census of India, 2011, http://censusindia.gov.in/

Overall the total main workers among SC's in Manipur are 35024, out of which 14618 are cultivators, 2712 are agricultural labourers, 1845 are household industry workers and 15849 are other workers. Among all the seven SC's the highest main workers are Lois. The total main workers among Lois are 31014, out of which 12451 are cultivators, 2368 are agricultural labourers, 1547 are household industry workers and 14648 are other workers.

Table 3.33: Marginal Workers by Industrial Category among SC's of Manipur

Sl. No.	*Name of the Scheduled Caste*	*Marginal Workers*	*Cultivators*	*Agricultural Labourers*	*Household Industry Workers*	*Other Workers*	*Percentage*
	All Scheduled Castes	9660	2756	3317	1412	2175	100
1.	Dhupi, Dhobi	4	-	2	1	1	0.04
2.	Lois	8604	2456	2998	1185	1965	89.06
3.	Muchi, Ravidas	8	-	2	-	6	0.0
4.	Namasudra	434	90	134	162	48	4.49
5.	Patni	315	81	93	45	96	3.26
6.	Sutradar	5	3	-	-	2	0.05
7.	Yaithibi	84	50	19	6	9	0.86

Source: Census of India, 2011, http://censusindia.gov.in/

Overall the total marginal workers among SC's in Manipur are 9660, out of which 2756 are cultivators, 3317 are agricultural labourers, 1412 are household industry workers and 2175 are other workers. Among all the seven SC's the highest marginal workers are Lois. The total marginal workers among Lois are 8604, out of which 2456 are cultivators, 2998 are agricultural labourers, 1185 are household industry workers and 1965 are other workers.

Table 3.34: Non-workers among SC's of Manipur

Sl. No.	*Name of the Scheduled Caste*	*Non-workers*	*Male*	*Female*	*Percentage*
	All Scheduled Castes	52644	22514	30130	100
1.	Dhupi, Dhobi	48	21	27	0.09
2.	Lois	45925	19729	26196	87.23
3.	Muchi, Ravidas	88	32	56	0.16
4.	Namasudra	2002	745	1257	3.80
5.	Patni	2299	870	1429	4.36
6.	Sutradar	43	18	25	0.08
7.	Yaithibi	859	362	497	1.63

Source: Census of India, 2011, http://censusindia.gov.in/

Overall the total non-workers among SC's in Manipur are 52644, out of which 22514 are males and 30130 are females. Among all the seven SC's the highest non-workers are Lois. The total non-workers among Lois are 45925 out of which 19729 are males and 26196 are females.

Meghalaya

Meghalaya the land of dwelling clouds and the Hills reaching to the clouds, waterfalls, crystal clear lakes, caves and forests are the nature's signatures on the land of Meghalaya. The far Indian state spreads over about a small area of 20000 sq. km. There are only about 100 people living in a sq. km. of area in Meghalaya, making it a low density region. Approximately 30 lakhs of population reside in the naturally gifted land, which makes the state of Meghalaya one of the states in India with lowest population. In spite of the low density and population of Meghalaya, it is worth noticing that, the state has a rapid population growth rate, and has the third fastest growing population in India, according to the Meghalaya census 2011. The gender ratio in Meghalaya ranks average along with many other states. But there has been a definite increase in the ratio, since the 2001 census, which means the number of females in the state's been increasing. The state has a low literacy rate, but has grown by over 10 per cent in the last decade. At the same time, the percentage of female literacy has been drastically increased. So, females aren't so far behind the other gender when it comes to letters. As with many north-east states of India, lack of urbanisation exists here as well. About 80 per cent population lives in the rural area while only a small portion has moved to the urban land. But maybe that's why this part of the country is rich in culture and nature even today, without the cosmopolitan mix. Shillong is the well known capital of Meghalaya. Another important part of Meghalaya is Cherapunjee, which boasts a grand rainfall every year, making it the rainiest place. The culture of Meghalaya possesses a nice blend of folktales, the Khasi language, colourful festivities and ethnic dance forms and equally colourful attires. The capital city which is also the largest city in the state of Meghalaya is Shillong. The languages spoken in the Meghalaya state includes Khasi, Pnar, Garo, Hindi and English. In total Meghalaya state comprises seven districts.[124]

As per details from Census 2011, Meghalaya has population of 29.67 lakhs, an increase from figure of 23.19 lakh in 2001 census. Total population of Meghalaya as per 2011 census is 2,966,889 of which male and female are 1,491,832 and 1,475,057 respectively. In 2001, total population was 2,318,822 in which males were 1,176,087 while females were 1,142,735. The total population growth in this decade was 27.95 per cent while in previous decade it was 29.94 per cent. The population of Meghalaya forms 0.25 per cent of India in 2011. In 2001, the figure was 0.23 per cent. Literacy rate in Meghalaya has seen upward trend and is 74.43 per cent as per 2011 population census. Of that, male literacy stands at 75.95 per cent while female literacy is at 71.88 per cent. In 2001, literacy rate in Meghalaya stood at 62.56 per cent of which male and female were 71.18 per cent and 50.43 per cent literate respectively. In actual numbers, total literates in Meghalaya stands at 1,785,005 of which males were 913,879 and females were 871,126. Total area of Meghalaya is 22,429 sq. km. Density of Meghalaya is 132 per sq km which is lower than national average 382 per sq km. In 2001, density of Meghalaya was 103 per sq km, while nation average in 2001 was 324 per sq km. Sex Ratio in Meghalaya is 989 i.e., for each 1000 male, which is above national average of 940 as per census 2011. In 2001, the sex ratio of female was 975 per 1000 males in Meghalaya.[125]

Meghalaya has got a very small Scheduled Caste (SC) population of just 17355 persons as per 2011 Census. The list of SCs of Assam is applicable to Meghalaya. As such, sixteen communities are notified as SCs in the state. The SC population of Meghalaya being that of migrants from neighbouring states like Assam and West Bengal, exhibits a skewed demographic trend. Individual SC wise, Namasudra having 3,376 persons is numerically the largest group among the SCs in Meghalaya, followed by Jhalo (1155), Muchi (1155), Kaibarta (1143) and Patni (1039). The rest of the thirteen SCs are small in size having less than one thousand persons each. Out of these, six SCs namely, Hira, Mahara, Dugla, Lalbegi, Jalkeot each have less than hundred populations.[126]

Table 3.35: Scheduled Caste Population of Meghalaya, 2011 Census Report

Sl.No.	Name of the Scheduled Caste	Total Population	Proportion to the total SC Population
	All Scheduled Castes	17355	
1.	Bansphor	250	1.4
2.	Bhuinmali, Mali	383	2.2
3.	Brittial Bania, Bania	308	1.7
4.	Dhupi, Dhobi	598	3.4
5.	Dugla, Dholi	57	0.3
6.	Hira	61	0.3
7.	Jalkeot	39	0.2
8.	Jhalo, Malo, Jhalo-Malo	1895	10.9
9.	Kaibartta, Jaliya	1143	6.5
10.	Lalbegi	10	0.0
11.	Mahara	26	0.1
12.	Mehtar, Bhangi	541	3.1
13.	Muchi, Rishi	1155	6.6
14.	Namasudra	3376	19.4
15.	Patni	1039	5.9
16.	Sutradhar	285	1.6

Source: Office of the Registrar General of India, 2011 Census of India, http://censusindia.gov.in/

Table 3.36: Districtwise SC's Population of Meghalaya (2011)

Sl. No.	State/District	SC Population					
	Meghalaya	Total		Rural		Urban	
		Male	Female	Male	Female	Male	Female
1.	West Garo Hills	4535	4275	3197	3052	1338	1223
2.	East Garo Hills	304	205	128	87	176	118
3.	South Garo Hills	188	131	109	82	79	49
4.	West Khasi Hills	93	75	83	62	10	13
5.	Ribhoi	329	261	279	225	50	36
6.	East Khasi Hills	2924	2718	1566	1488	1358	1230
7.	Jaintia Hills	784	533	724	491	60	42

Source: Office of the Registrar General of India, 2011 Census of India, http://censusindia.gov.in/

As regards district-wise distribution, majority of the SC population are concentrated in the West Garo Hills (4535) and East Khasi Hills (2924) districts Jaintia Hills (784), Ribhoi (329), South Garo Hills (304), West Garo Hills (188), West Khasi Hills (93) districts.[127] Among SCs, the highest literacy is among Namasudra (1519) followed by Jhalo-Malo (1133), Kaibarta (774), Muchi (583), Patni (470), Dhobi (399), Mehtar (377), Mali (253), Bansphore (142), others SC's are less than 100 literacy.

Table 3.37: Literacy Rate among Major SCs of Meghalaya

Sl.No.	*Name of the Scheduled Caste*	*Total*	*Male*	*Female*	*Per-cent-age*
	All SC Literates in Meghalaya	10275	5953	4322	100
1.	Bansphor	142	84	58	1.32
2.	Bhuinmali, Mali	253	139	114	2.46
3.	Brittial Bania, Bania	245	138	107	2.38
4.	Dhupi, Dhobi	399	233	166	3.88
5.	Dugla, Dholi	22	14	8	0.21
6.	Hira	40	19	21	0.38
7.	Jalkeot	34	18	16	0.33
8.	Jhalo, Malo, Jhalo-Malo	1133	643	490	11.02
9.	Kaibartta, Jaliya	774	458	316	7.53
10.	Lalbegi	7	6	1	0.06
11.	Mahara	20	12	8	0.19
12.	Mehtar, Bhangi	377	195	182	3.66
13.	Muchi, Rishi	583	366	217	5.67
14.	Namasudra	1519	881	638	14.78
15.	Patni	470	296	174	4.57
16.	Sutradhar	224	134	90	2.18

Source: Census of India, 2011, http://censusindia.gov.in/

The percentage of SC workers to total population (WPR) is 35.90 per cent, out of the total workers, 79.18 per cent has been recorded as main workers and 20.81per cent as marginal workers. The female WPR is only 16.99 per cent, which is lower than their male counterparts 52.83 per cent.[128] The total female SC workers are 56.85 per cent whereas the male main workers is 85.61 per cent on the other hand the total marginal female SC workers is 43.14 per cent which is quit higher than male counterpart which is 14.38 per cent.

Table 3.38: Distribution of Total, Main and Marginal Workers among SC's (Meghalaya)

T/M/F	*Total Workers (Percentage to Total Population)*	*Main Workers (Percentage to Total Workers)*	*Marginal Workers (Percentage to Total Workers)*
Total	6231 (35.90%)	4934 (79.18%)	1297 (20.81%)
Male	4838 (52.83%)	4142 (85.61%)	696 (14.38%)
Female	1393 (16.99%)	792 (56.85%)	601 (43.14%)

Source: Office of the Registrar General of India, 2011 Census of India, http://censusindia.gov.in/

Table 3.39: Main Workers by Industrial Category among SC's of Meghalaya

Sl. No.	*Name of the Scheduled Caste*	*Main Workers*	*Culti-vators*	*Agricultural Labourers*	*House-hold Industry Workers*	*Other Workers*	*Per-cen-tage*
	All Scheduled Castes	4934	389	336	117	4092	100
1.	Bansphor	64	-	2	-	62	1.29
2.	Bhuinmali, Mali	117	15	4	7	91	2.37
3.	Brittial Bania, Bania	93	4	2	5	82	1.88
4.	Dhupi, Dhobi	149	14	13	-	122	3.01
5.	Dugla, Dholi	19	5	3	-	11	0.38
6.	Hira	16	3	1	1	11	0.32
7.	Jalkeot	14	-	-	-	14	0.28
8.	Jhalo, Malo, Jhalo-Malo	518	26	20	5	467	10.28
9.	Kaibartta, Jaliya	383	28	18	4	331	7.78
10.	Lalbegi	2	-	-	-	2	0.04
11.	Mahara	11	-	1	-	10	0.22
12.	Mehtar, Bhangi	162	3	1	-	158	3.28
13.	Muchi, Rishi	258	15	8	5	230	5.22
14.	Namasudra	916	63	117	12	724	18.56
15.	Patni	269	27	17	15	210	5.45
16.	Sutradhar	81	-	-	5	76	1.64

Source: Census of India, 2011, http://censusindia.gov.in/

Overall the total main workers among SC's in Meghalaya are 4934, out of which 389 are cultivators, 336 are agricultural labourers, 117 are household industry workers and 4092 are other workers. Among all the 16 SC's the highest main workers are Namasudra, Jhalo and Kaibarta. The total main workers among Namasudra are 916, out of which 63 are cultivators, 117 are agricultural labourers, 12 are household industry workers and 724 are other workers. The total main workers among Jhalo are 518, out of which 26 are cultivators, 20 are agricultural labourers, five are household industry workers and 467 are other workers. On the other hand, the total main workers among Kaibarta are 383, out of which 28 are cultivators, 18 are agricultural labourers, four are household industry workers and 331 are other workers.

Table 3.40: Marginal Workers by Industrial Category among SC's of Meghalaya

Sl.No.	Name of the Scheduled Caste	Marginal Workers	Culti-vators	Agricultural Labourers	House-hold Industry Workers	Other Workers	Per-cent-age
	All Scheduled Castes	1297	77	349	63	808	100
1.	Bansphor	21	-	1	3	17	1.61
2.	Bhuinmali, Mali	8	-	2	1	5	0.61
3.	Brittial Bania, Bania	8	2	-	1	5	0.61
4.	Dhupi, Dhobi	43	1	19	-	23	0.0
5.	Dugla, Dholi	-	-	-	-	-	0.0
6.	Hira	3	-	1	-	2	0.23
7.	Jalkeot	3	-	1	-	-	0.23
8.	Jhalo, Malo, Jhalo-Malo	106	8	51	4	43	8.17
9.	Kaibartta, Jaliya	76	4	8	-	64	5.85
10.	Lalbegi	-	-	-	-	-	0.0
11.	Mahara	-	-	-	-	-	0.0
12.	Mehtar, Bhangi	5	-	-	-	5	0.38
13.	Muchi, Rishi	114	3	46	14	51	8.78
14.	Namasudra	262	17	102	-	143	20.20
15.	Patni	154	4	15	16	119	11.87
16.	Sutradhar	15	1	3	2	9	1.15

Source: Census of India, 2011, http://censusindia.gov.in/

Overall the total marginal workers among SC's in Meghalaya are 1297, out of which 77 are cultivators, 349 are agricultural labourers, 63 are household industry workers and 808 are other workers. Among all the 16 SC's the highest marginal workers are Namasudra, Patni, Muchi, Jhalo and Kaibarta. The total marginal workers among Namasudra are 262, out of which 17 are cultivators, 102 are agricultural labourers and 143 are other workers. The total marginal workers among Patni are 154, out of which four are cultivators, 15 are agricultural labourers, 16 are household industry workers and 119 are other workers. The total marginal workers among Muchi are 114, out of which three are cultivators, 46 are agricultural labourers, 14 are household industry workers and 51 are other workers. The total marginal workers among Jhalo are 106, out of which eight are cultivators, 51 are agricultural labourers, four are household industry workers and 43 are other workers. On the other hand the total marginal workers among Kaibarta are 76, out of which four are cultivators, eight are agricultural labourers and 64 are other workers.

Table 3.41: Non-workers among SC's of Meghalaya

Sl.No.	*Name of the Scheduled Caste*	*Non-workers*	*Male*	*Female*	*Per-Cen-tage*
	All Scheduled Castes	11124	4319	6805	100
1.	Bansphor	165	67	98	1.48
2.	Bhuinmali, Mali	258	98	160	2.31
3.	Brittial Bania, Bania	207	83	124	1.86
4.	Dhupi, Dhobi	406	141	265	3.64
5.	Dugla, Dholi	38	15	23	0.34
6.	Hira	42	16	26	0.37
7.	Jalkeot	22	7	15	0.19
8.	Jhalo, Malo, Jhalo-Malo	1271	456	815	11.42
9.	Kaibartta, Jaliya	684	262	422	6.14
10.	Lalbegi	8	4	4	0.07
11.	Mahara	15	6	9	0.13
12.	Mehtar, Bhangi	374	156	218	3.36
13.	Muchi, Rishi	783	294	489	7.03
14.	Namasudra	2198	831	1367	19.75
15.	Patni	616	262	354	5.53
16.	Sutradhar	189	75	114	1.69

Source: Census of India, 2011, http://censusindia.gov.in/

Overall the total non-workers among SC's in Meghalaya are 11124, out of which 4319 are males and 6805 are females. Among all the 16 SC's the highest non-workers are Namasudra, Jhalo, Muchi and Kaibarta. The total non-workers among Namasudra are 2198 out of which 831 are males and 1367 are females. The total non-workers among Jhalo are 1271 out of which 456 are males and 851 are females. The total non-workers among Muchi are 783 out of which 294 are males and 489 are females. On the other hand the total non-workers among Kaibarta are 684, out of which 262 are males and 422 are females.

Mizoram

Mizoram is one of the north eastern states of India, and like its sister states its rich in every aspect of nature and culture, dense forests, lush green hills and lots of bamboo everywhere, pristine waterfalls and transparent lakes present great tourism opportunities. Spreading of a small population of about 10 lakhs over an area of 20000 sq. km., has led to a low population density of about 50 per sq. km., which makes Mizoram the third state in India with the lowest population density, as shown by the Mizoram state census done in 2011. The density has increased in last 10 years. Population growth rate, however, has decreased by approximately 10 per cent and currently stands at about 20 per cent. The percentage of literate population is in the 90's, and has also been subjected to positive increment. Increase in female literacy is more than double of that in males. The gender ratio has also undergone a positive change and is increasing slowly. The child sex ratio, on the other hand, has significantly increased. The distribution of population is equal in rural and urban areas. In urban areas, the gender ratio has a perfect a score, which means there are as many females as males. Literacy in urban areas is naturally high. The official language Mizo is widely spoken in the state of Mizoram, which is the language of the hill folks. English is also widely used, as is the case with most north-eastern states of India. Aizawal is the main city in Mizoram and it's also the state capital. As with most of the land, bamboo has found its way in Mizoram's culture as well. The exclusive dance forms of Mizoram use bamboo for a special effect. The attires of Mizo people are colourful kimono style drapes with native beaded jewellery. All in all, the state presents a great blend of cultures. The capital city which is also the largest city in the state of Mizoram is Aizawal. The languages spoken in the

Mizoram state includes Mizo. In total Mizoram state comprises eight districts.[129]

As per details from Census 2011, Mizoram has population of 10.97 lakhs, an increase from figure of 8.89 lakh in 2001 census. Total population of Mizoram as per 2011 census is 1,097,206 of which male and female are 555,339 and 541,867 respectively. In 2001, total population was 888,573 in which males were 459,109 while females were 429,464. The total population growth in this decade was 23.48 per cent while in previous decade it was 29.18 per cent. The population of Mizoram forms 0.09 per cent of India in 2011. In 2001, the figure was 0.09 per cent. Literacy rate in Mizoram has seen upward trend and is 91.33 per cent as per 2011 population census. Of that, male literacy stands at 93.35 per cent while female literacy is at 86.72 per cent. In 2001, literacy rate in Mizoram stood at 88.80 per cent of which male and female were 92.53 per cent and 86.75 per cent literate respectively. In actual numbers, total literates in Mizoram stands at 848,175 of which males were 438,529 and females were 409,646. Total area of Mizoram is 21,081 sq. km. Density of Mizoram is 52 per sq km which is lower than national average 382 per sq km. In 2001, density of Mizoram was 42 per sq km, while nation average in 2001 was 324 per sq km. Sex Ratio in Mizoram is 976 i.e., for each 1000 male, which is below national average of 940 as per census 2011. In 2001, the sex ratio of female was 938 per 1000 males in Mizoram.[130]

Table 3.42: Scheduled Caste Population of Mizoram, 2011 Census Report

Sl.No.	*Name of the Scheduled Caste*	*Total Population*	*Proportion to the total SC Population*
	All Scheduled Castes	1218	
1.	Bansphor	45	3.6
2.	Bhuinmali, Mali	54	4.4
3.	Brittial Bania, Bania	67	5.5
4.	Dhupi, Dhobi	91	7.4
5.	Dugla, Dholi	27	2.2
6.	Hira	48	3.9
7.	Jalkeot	2	0.1
8.	Jhalo, Malo, Jhalo-Malo	10	0.0
9.	Kaibartta, Jaliya	18	1.4

contd..

contd...

Sl.No.	Name of the Scheduled Caste	Total Population	Proportion to the total SC Population
10.	Lalbegi	14	1.1
11.	Mahara	36	2.9
12.	Mehtar, Bhangi	21	1.7
13.	Muchi, Rishi	235	19.2
14.	Namasudra	136	11.1
15.	Patni	70	5.7
16.	Sutradhar	48	3.9

Source: Office of the Registrar General of India, 2011 Census of India, http://censusindia.gov.in/

Table 3.43: District-wise SC's Population of Mizoram

Sl. No.	State/District	SC's Population					
	MIZORAM	Total		Rural		Urban	
		Male	Female	Male	Female	Male	Female
1.	Mamit	42	9	31	7	11	2
2.	Kolasib	59	25	12	5	47	20
3.	Aizawl	388	239	36	10	352	229
4.	Champhai	16	1	9	1	7	-
5.	Serchhip	20	12	8	5	12	7
6.	Lunglei	125	53	38	27	87	26
7.	Lawngtlai	105	41	68	29	37	12
8.	Saiha	52	31	7	5	45	26

Source: Office of the Registrar General of India, 2011 Census of India, http://censusindia.gov.in/

Mizoram has very small SC population of 1218 persons as per 2011 Census. As such, sixteen communities are notified as SCs in the state. In 1961 Census, there were only five individuals in the state's total SC population, which increased to 82 in 1971 Census, 135 in 1981 Census, and 691 in 1991 Census. In 2001 SC population has recorded decline in absolute number from the previous Census figure. This may be due to the fact that SCs in the state has no permanent residence and they move from one place to another within and outside the state resulting in fluctuation in their number. In 2011 Census, of the total 1218 SC population, Muchi (Rishi) have return with the highest population

(19.2 per cent), followed by Namasudra (11.1 per cent), Dhupi (7.4 per cent), Patni (5.7 per cent), Brital Bania (5.5 per cent), Bhumali (4.4 per cent), Hira (3.9 per cent), Sutradhar (3.9 per cent), Bashphor (3.6 per cent), Dhupi (2.2 per cent).

Table 3.44: Literacy Rate among Major SCs of Mizoram

Sl.No.	Name of the Scheduled Caste	Total	Male	Female	Per-cen-tage
	All SC Literates in Mizoram	1014	699	315	100
1.	Bansphor	38	26	12	3.74
2.	Bhuinmali, Mali	50	29	21	4.93
3.	Brittial Bania, Bania	59	29	30	5.81
4.	Dhupi, Dhobi	83	55	28	8.18
5.	Dugla, Dholi	17	13	4	1.67
6.	Hira	45	25	20	4.43
7.	Jalkeot	1	1	-	0.09
8.	Jhalo, Malo, Jhalo-Malo	10	9	1	0.98
9.	Kaibartta, Jaliya	17	13	4	1.67
10.	Lalbegi	9	5	4	0.88
11.	Mahara	31	25	6	3.05
12.	Mehtar, Bhangi	19	11	8	1.87
13.	Muchi, Rishi	169	130	39	16.66
14.	Namasudra	111	80	31	10.94
15.	Patni	54	46	8	5.32
16.	Sutradhar	42	32	10	4.14

Source: Census of India, 2011, http://censusindia.gov.in/

Table 3.45: Distribution of Total, Main and Marginal Workers among SC's (Mizoram)

T/M/F	Total Workers (Percentage to Total Population)	Main Workers (Percentage to Total Workers)	Marginal Workers (Percentage to Total Workers)
Total	650 (53.36%)	605 (93.07%)	45 (6.92%)
Male	590 (7311%)	567 (96.10%)	23 (3.89%)
Female	60 (14.59%)	38 (63.33%)	22 (36.66%)

Source: Office of the Registrar General of India, 2011 Census of India, http://censusindia.gov.in/

Table 3.46: Main Workers by Industrial Category among SC's of Mizoram

Sl.No.	Name of the Scheduled Caste	Main Workers	Cultivators	Agricultural Labourers	Household Industry Workers	Other Workers	Per-cent-age
	All Scheduled Castes	605	23	17	5	560	100
1.	Bansphor	22	-	1	-	21	3.63
2.	Bhuinmali, Mali	26	-	-	-	26	4.29
3.	Brittial Bania, Bania	20	1	-	-	21	3.30
4.	Dhupi, Dhobi	43	-	-	-	43	7.10
5.	Dugla, Dholi	10	-	-	-	10	1.65
6.	Hira	19	1	1	-	17	3.14
7.	Jalkeot	2	-	-	-	2	0.33
8.	Jhalo, Malo, Jhalo-Malo	8	-	-	-	8	1.32
9.	Kaibartta, Jaliya	7	-	-	-	7	1.15
10.	Lalbegi	7	-	-	-	7	1.15
11.	Mahara	26	1	1	2	22	4.29
12.	Mehtar, Bhangi	14	-	-	-	14	2.31
13.	Muchi, Rishi	110	16	6	-	88	18.18
14.	Namasudra	78	-	4	-	74	12.80
15.	Patni	46	-	-	-	46	7.60
16.	Sutradhar	27	2	-	-	25	4.46

Source: Census of India, 2011, http://censusindia.gov.in/

Overall the total main workers among SC's in Mizoram are 605, out of which 23 are cultivators, 17 are agricultural labourers, five are household industry workers and 560 are other workers. Among all the 16 SC's the highest main workers are Muchi and Namasudra. The total main workers among Muchi are 110, out of which 16 are cultivators, six are agricultural labourers and 107861 are other workers. On the other hand the total main workers among Namasudra are 78, out of which 4 are agricultural labourers and 74 are other workers.

Table 3.47: Marginal Workers by Industrial Category among SC's of Mizoram

Sl.No.	Name of the Scheduled Caste	Main Workers	Cultiv-ators	Agricultural Labourers	Household Industry Workers	Other Workers	Perc-entage
	All Scheduled Castes	45	4	10	-	31	100
1.	Bansphor	1	-	-	-	1	2.22
2.	Bhuinmali, Mali	-	-	-	-	-	0.0
3.	Brittial Bania, Bania	-	-	-	-	-	0.0
4.	Dhupi, Dhobi	-	-	-	-	-	0.0
5.	Dugla, Dholi	2	-	-	-	2	4.44
6.	Hira	7	3	-	-	4	15.55
7.	Jalkeot	-	-	-	-	-	0.0
8.	Jhalo, Malo, Jhalo-Malo	-	-	-	-	-	0.0
9.	Kaibartta, Jaliya	2	-	-	-	2	4.44
10.	Lalbegi	-	-	-	-	-	0.0
11.	Mahara	1	-	-	-	1	2.22
12.	Mehtar, Bhangi	-	-	-	-	-	0.0
13.	Muchi, Rishi	4	1	2	-	1	8.88
14.	Namasudra	3	-	2	-	1	6.66
15.	Patni	3	-	-	-	3	6.66
16.	Sutradhar	1	-	-	-	1	2.22

Source: Census of India, 2011, http://censusindia.gov.in/

Overall the total marginal workers among SC's in Mizoram are 45, out of which four are cultivators, 10 are agricultural labourers and 31 are other workers. Among all the 16 SC's the highest marginal workers are Hira and Muchi. The total marginal workers among Hira are seven, out of which three are cultivators four are other workers. On the other hand the total marginal workers among Muchi are 4, out of which 1 are cultivators, 2 are agricultural labourers and 1are other workers.

Table 3.48: Non-workers among SC's of Mizoram

Sl.No.	*Name of the Scheduled Caste*	*Non Workers*	*Male*	*Female*	*Per-cent-age*
	All Scheduled Castes	568	217	351	100
1.	Bansphor	22	11	11	3.87
2.	Bhuinmali, Mali	28	9	19	4.92
3.	Brittial Bania, Bania	45	13	32	7.92
4.	Dhupi, Dhobi	48	19	29	8.45
5.	Dugla, Dholi	15	6	9	2.64
6.	Hira	22	6	16	3.87
7.	Jalkeot	17	4	13	2.99
8.	Jhalo, Malo, Jhalo-Malo	2	1	1	0.35
9.	Kaibartta, Jaliya	9	5	4	1.58
10.	Lalbegi	7	3	4	1.23
11.	Mahara	9	2	7	1.58
12.	Mehtar, Bhangi	7	1	6	1.23
13.	Muchi, Rishi	121	55	66	21.30
14.	Namasudra	55	15	40	9.68
15.	Patni	21	7	14	3.69
16.	Sutradhar	20	12	8	3.52

Source: Census of India, 2011, http://censusindia.gov.in/

Overall the total non-workers among SC's in Mizoram are 568, out of which 217 are males and 351 are females. Among all the 16 SC's the highest non-workers are Muchi and Namasudra. The total non-workers among Muchi are 121 out of which 55 are males and 66 are females. On the other hand the total non-workers among Namasudra are 55, out of which 15 are males and 40 are females.

The percentage of SC workers to total population is 53.36 per cent. The total 93.07 per cent have been recorded as main workers and 6.92 per cent as marginal workers. The female WPR at 14.59 per cent as compare to the male counterpart 73.11 per cent whereas the total female main workers are 63.33 per cent whereas it is 96.10 per cent for male. On the other hand the marginal SC female workers are 36.66 per cent which is quite high as compare to the male counterpart as 3.89 per cent.

Nagaland

Nagaland named because the people residing there are called Nagas. Its population is widely diverse, and has 16 tribes living in the state. The mostly Christian population of Nagaland draws its culture from many other neighbouring regions. The state of Nagaland is one of the least populated states of India, and ranks 25th population wise, owing to its population of less than 20 lakhs. The population of Nagaland is spread over an area of over 15000 kilometer square, with a population density of just over 100 in one sq km of area, as shown by the Nagaland census 2011. What really sets the state apart from others in India is the growth rate of population in Nagaland. Where, many other states have fallen prey to the population explosion, Nagaland has not only reduced the previous growth rate of above 60 per cent, but it has also brought it to less than zero. This negative growth rate has greatly helped control the population in Nagaland. The growth rate is still above 60 in the urban areas, and far too less in the rural areas. The gender ratio in Nagaland's population however is the least as compared to other north-eastern states. The sex ratio is greater in the rural population as compared to urban. Literacy in Nagaland has undergone an extremely positive improvement in the last decade. From the initial literacy of only 60 per cent, it has risen to about 80 per cent according to census 2011. Urban population is less as compared to the rural. The state has only one airport in its biggest city, Dimapur. The state capital of Nagaland is Kohima. It is one of the few states in India to have English as its official language. Due to the variation in its culture, about 20 languages are spoken in the state, Nagamese being the widely used one. The largest city in the state of Nagaland is Kohima while Dimapur is the capital city of the Nagaland. The languages spoken in the Nagaland state includes English. In total Nagaland state comprises 11 districts.[131]

As per details from Census 2011, Nagaland has population of 19.79 lakhs, decrease from figure of 19.90 lakh in 2001 census. Total population of Nagaland as per 2011 census is 1,978,502 of which male and female are 1,024,649 and 953,853 respectively. In 2001, total population was 1,990,036 in which males were 1,047,141 while females were 942,895. The total population growth in this decade was -0.58 per cent while in previous decade it was 64.41 per cent. The population of Nagaland forms 0.16 per cent of India in 2011. In 2001, the figure was 0.19 per cent. Literacy rate in Nagaland has seen upward trend and is

79.55 per cent as per 2011 population census. Of that, male literacy stands at 82.75 per cent while female literacy is at 70.01 per cent. In 2001, literacy rate in Nagaland stood at 66.59 per cent of which male and female were 76.04 per cent and 56.87 per cent literate respectively. In actual numbers, total literates in Nagaland stands at 1,342,434 of which males were 723,957 and females were 618,477. Total area of Nagaland is 16,579 sq. km. Density of Nagaland is 119 per sq km which is lower than national average 382 per sq km. In 2001, density of Nagaland was 120 per sq km, while nation average in 2001 was 324 per sq km. Sex Ratio in Nagaland is 931 i.e. for each 1000 male, which is below national average of 940 as per census 2011. In 2001, the sex ratio of female was 909 per 1000 males in Nagaland.[132]

Nagaland, covers an area of 16,488 sq. km. is encircled by Assam in the north and west, by Burma and Arunachal Pradesh in the east, and Manipur in the South. The state is predominantly dominated by Naga communities and hence, it forms a single cultural region generally definable by common cultural and linguistic traditions. This state was carved out of the territories that were earlier known as Naga Hills - Tuesnsang Area (NHTA), through the State of Nagaland Act, 1962. It was inaugurated on 1st December, 1963 by the then President of India, Dr S. Radhakrishnan. The entire Naga inhabited area may be described as one culture area, on account of several ethno-historical factors. There are 14 tribes in Nagaland. The traditional faith, religious beliefs and practices of Naga tribes show signs of being animistic. There is a belief of a supreme creator of mankind, and many deities, ghosts and spirits of trees, rivers and hills. There are priests and medicine-men who placate these spirits, banish those who give diseases, attract those who help and guard, and also take the lead in the rites and festivals, which stimulate the processes of agriculture. Among the Naga tribes (Chang, Sangtam, Khiamngan), there is a belief that the soul, after death, goes down a narrow path to the land of the dead that is guarded by a spirit with whom it must struggle. Most Naga tribes regard the ultimate ancestors of man and the tiger, as very intimately associated. The ancient Kachari capital, Dimapur is one of the important sites of megalithic culture. The ruins appear to be contemporaries with the Kachari civilisation, established before the Ahom invasion in the

Thirteenth century A.D. There are evidences of Hindu influence on most of them, though these are predominantly non-Aryan. Today 85 per cent of the people are Christians.[133]

Without a shadow of doubt, there is class division between the rich consisting mostly of ministers in their favoured workers and the poor who are countless. There is a Class division in Naga Society and no one has to remind us of that. Without doubt yes. An elite political class sits at the top. An inflated middle class employed with the government forms another class. And a poor and agriculture class in the rural areas. But class consciousness is somewhat diluted by the 'community' society that we have. There is big gap between rich and poor. Political set up is dominated by the rich and bureaucrats. Power and powerless is measured by economic and political influence. Though there is no such thing as caste system in Nagaland but class certainly exist. A Naga is judged by the wealth one possess and not the values anymore. Rich people are becoming richer and there is a vast difference in the economic conditions amongst the Nagas. Because of the fact that the people and the government tend to categorise the tribe and the high level officers and leaders look down upon the poor section of the people. Unfortunately, Nagas have created the gap so wide in which on can can see the difference. This difference is because of the sharing of opportunity which the lower class do not get their share. The reason is best known by everyone. Definitely Nagas have a division among the have and have-nots. Those in the privileged class have made everything there is as their own. Especially the govt set ups is so corrupted that they have grasp everything for them. To evaluate any society's economy and per capita it is necessary to see how many have and how many don't have. The question here is how come those in Government jobs having a well run private business too. Those in the power to manipulate the government policies give chances to their near and dear ones only, be it subsidairies, fund allocation, contractual works, work permits, etc. The have nots are left behind getting nothing. In another 15 years or so, are going to see Nagas begging in roadsides like what one see in big cities. Where will the sustenance come if there is no equal share of opportunisties?

Everyone and anyone who deserve are held with higher respect which is due to them. But this does not belittle the respect that we Nagas have for each other as human beings. There never has been any sort of rigid class division among the Nagas. This is what sets us apart from the rest. In place of caste division Nagas have tribalism, corruption, factionalism and nepotism. Nagas generally are not rich but have wealth. It's the few people who have converted this wealth into riches to have a comfortable lifestyle. But the majority of the Nagas are depending only on government jobs and letting their wealth go to waste. This means only those in government jobs become rich because the rest of the society is busy trying to get government jobs and are doing nothing with what they already have. Nagas don't have a class system, but over dependency on government jobs means only those in government are classified as rich. The Naga society is an agrarian one which is self-sufficient. But in modern times, the society has not moved from self-sufficiency to mass production and so there is no additional income which means no purchasing power. The difference in purchasing power is being interpreted as class system. Only if Nagas would move from self-sufficiency to mass production, the issue of class system will not be discussed in this way.[134]

Sikkim

The state of Sikkim enveloped by the Himalayas, is a home to one of the world's highest peaks, Kanchenjunga, and as with most of the Himalayan region, Sikkim is rich in life variety and natural beauty, making it a sought after tourist destination. Sikkim draws its culture from its fellow neighbours which are Nepal, Bhutan and Tibet and so many dialects are spoken here. The cuisine, music and other recreational activities like festivals are also influenced by Sikkim's border-mates. The Sikkim census of 2011 says population of Sikkim is the least in all of India. This thinly populated state has a population of mere six lakhs, and has grown by approximately one lakh since the last census. The state of Sikkim is also the second smallest state in India, and thus, the population density here isn't as low as you'd expect it to be. The density is less than 100 in Sikkim, and has undergone significant increment. The population growth rate is another factor indicating the population status. In Sikkim, the growth rate of population has considerably reduced to just above

10 per cent. Percentage of literates however, has increased by about 20 per cent, which is a huge leap toward progress. Increase in female literacy also tells an optimistic story. The gender ratio in Sikkim is quite alarming, and has not shown significant increase in last 10 years. It shows only around 800 females for every 1000 males. As with most north-eastern states in India, the land has not been developed largely. Hence, only over 20 per cent of the population of Sikkim lives in cities. The capital city Gangtok is also the largest one in Sikkim. Population growth in urban and rural areas shows too contrasts a picture. While, city population is growing at an alarming rate of above 150 per cent, the rural population isn't growing at all, but is decreasing. The languages spoken in the Sikkim state includes Nepali, Bhutia, Lepcha, Limbu, Newari, Kulung, Gurung, Manggar, Sherpa, Tamang and Sunwar. In total Sikkim state comprises four districts.[135]

As per details from Census 2011, Sikkim has population of 6.11 lakhs, an increase from figure of 5.41 lakh in 2001 census. Total population of Sikkim as per 2011 census is 610,577 of which male and female are 323,070 and 287,507 respectively. In 2001, total population was 540,851 in which males were 288,484 while females were 252,367. The total population growth in this decade was 12.89 per cent while in previous decade it was 32.98 per cent. The population of Sikkim forms 0.05 per cent of India in 2011. In 2001, the figure was 0.05 per cent. Literacy rate in Sikkim has seen upward trend and is 81.42 per cent as per 2011 population census. Of that, male literacy stands at 86.55 per cent while female literacy is at 66.39 per cent. In 2001, literacy rate in Sikkim stood at 68.81 per cent of which male and female were 77.38 per cent and 59.63 per cent literate respectively. In actual numbers, total literates in Sikkim stands at 444,952 of which males were 251,269 and females were 193,683. Total area of Sikkim is 7,096 sq. km. Density of Sikkim is 86 per sq km which is lower than national average 382 per sq km. In 2001, density of Sikkim was 76 per sq km, while nation average in 2001 was 324 per sq km. Sex Ratio in Sikkim is 890 i.e. for each 1000 male, which is below national average of 940 as per census 2011. In 2001, the sex ratio of female was 875 per 1000 males in Sikkim. Lot of viewers are asking us to provide religion's data of Sikkim state.[136]

Sikkim the beautiful hill state lies on the eastern tip of the Himalayas bordered by Bhutan, Nepal and Tibet; it is famous for Kanch-Endzonga, at 598 mtrs, which is third highest mountain in the world. Being second smallest state in India, Sikkim covers 7,096 sq kms and measures 110 kms from north to south and 64 kms from east to west. It encompasses the privileged valley of Teesta river, a tributary of the Brahmaputra. The watershed forms the borders with Tibet and Nepal. Rangit and Rangpo rivers form the border with West Bengal. Sikkim is separated from Nepal in the west by the Singalila range while Donngkya range is the border to the north and north-east. Sikkim is broadly divided into four districts. The east district with capital city of Gangtok is the hub of all administrative activity. The famous Rumtek Monastery, the Dharma Chakra Centre and the seat of his Holliness Gyalwa Karmapa, all are located here. Other places of interest include the Tsomgo Lake and the Nathula Pass. A most beautiful district, the North District is an abundance of the natural splendour and Alpine scenery. During spring time, the meadows are alive with exotic wild flowers that cover the valley in charming hues. The hot springs and tribal customs and culture here are very attractive. The West District offers the ultimate in adventure. From white water rafting on the foaming Teesta and Rangit, to trekking through thick Rhododendron forests- the district offers it all. A breathtaking view of Mt Kanch-Endzonga can be had from Pelling that has developed as a major tourist attraction. The sacred lake of Khechiperi also lies close to Pelling. The Osuth District is home to some of the oldest monasteries in the state. Adventure treks to Maenam and Tengdong Hill originate from Rawangla. The region is also just-right for mountain biking and nature watching. Sikkim's local name 'Denzong', which means the 'Valley of Rice' is apt, since rice is the main crop here.[137]

All one needs is to be reasonably fit and in good shape. The unrivalled high altitude Alpine treks of Dzongri at 128000 ft and Goechala at 18000 ft, are both breathtaking and awe-inspiring. Also, if one is inclined for some white water action, the rivers Teesta and Rangit beckon. Sikkim Tourism organises river rafting packages through recognised tour operators. Besides these, facilities are also available for mountain biking and rock climbing, with instructors from the Sonam Gyatso Mountaineering Institute in Gangtok. *Maghe Sankranti Mela:* A three day holy festival of the Hindus celebrated along the river banks with huge fairs. *Bumchu:* It is held in the month of January/February in the monastery of Tashiding. The abbot of the monastery unveils a pot of holy water and foretells the future of the state. *Losar* festival is held around the festive month of February to celebrate and welcome the Tibetan New Year with feasting and merry-making. *Saga Dawa Held* during the month of May, this festival celebrates the triple blessed day of Buddha's Birth, Enlightenment and Maha parinirvan in most of important monasteries in Sikkim. *Pang Lhabsol Unique* to Sikkim, this festival worships the snow peaks of Mount Kanchendzonga. An important feature of the celebration is the warrior dance with its intricate steps and leaps accompanied by martial war-cries. *Tendong Lho Rum Faat:* This festival celebrates the event, when according to legend, the Thedong Hill had risen to save the Lepchas, during a great flood. *Dasain:* It is the main festivals of Hindu Nepalese in Sikkim. It signifies the victory of good over evil. The elders of the family apply 'Tika' on the young and bless them. Tihaar This festival is celebrated as the festival of lights with the lighting of lamps accompanied with traditional carols called Deusi and Bhakti. *Losoong Festival:* This Bhutia festival marks the end of harvest season and also the end of the Tibetan year. It is celebrated with religious dances (Chaams) in the monasteries of Tsug Lakhang, Phodongand Rumtek along with family gatherings, feasting and archery contests. *East District:* The capital city Gangtok is located here and it is the hub of all government activities. The world famous Rumtek Monastery, the Dharma Chakra center and the seat of His Holiness, the Gyalwa Karmapa is located here in addition to the alpine Tsomgo lake and Nathula Pass.[138]

The West District offers all adventure activities. River rafting, trekking, mountaineering etc begin here. The rivers Teesta and Rangeet attract white water rafting revelers in large numbers. *North District:* The famous Shingbha Rhododendron sanctuary as well as the Khangchendzonga National Park is located here. During spring time, the meadows of Yumthang abound with wildflowers, which carpet the valley in a riot of colours. The Hot Springs and rich tribal culture and customs are other attractions. *South District:* Most famous monasteries are located here. A 108 ft high image of the patron saint of Sikkim, Guru Padmashambhava is situated near the district headquarters at

Namchi. Ravangla Base Camp offers trekking upto Maenam and Tendong Hill here. Varsey Rhododendrons Sanctuary is also located here.[139]

Total SC population of Sikkim as per 2011 Census has been recorded as 28275. In Sikkim, four communities are notified as SCs, and all of them have been enumerated at 2011 Census. The Kami and Damai are the major SCs. They together have 94.1 per cent of the total SC population of the state. Majhi are small in number with only 338 populations.[140]

Table 3.49: Scheduled Caste Population of Sikkim, 2011 Census Report

Sl.No.	*Name of the Scheduled Caste*	*Total Population*	*Proportion to the total SC Population*
	All Scheduled Castes	28275	
1.	Damai (Nepali)	8714	30.8
2.	Kami	17911	63.3
3.	Majhi (Nepali)	338	1.1
4.	Sarki (Nepali)	798	2.8

Source: Office of the Registrar General of India, 2011 Census of India, http://censusindia.gov.in/

Table 3.50: Districtwise SC's Population of Sikkim

Sl. No.	*State/District*	*Total Population (District wise)*					*Per-cen-tage*
	Sikkim	*Total*	*Rural*	*Urban*	*Male*	*Female*	
		28275	20335	7940	14454	13821	0.01
1.	North District	982	804	178	536	446	3.47
2.	West District	5935	5663	272	3117	2818	20.99
3.	South District	6053	5042	1011	3058	2995	21.40
4.	East District	15305	8826	6479	7743	7562	54.12

Source: Office of the Registrar General of India, 2011 Census of India, http://censusindia.gov.in/

The SC population has higher concentration in East District (54.12 per cent), followed by South (21.40 per cent) and West (201.99 per cent) Districts. The North district accounts for a small percentage of SCs (3.47 per cent). The SC population in the state is predominantly rural; only 12.1 per cent live in urban areas. The highest urban population has been recorded among Damai, while the lowest is among Majhi.

As per 2001 Census, the sex ratio of total SC population is 967, which is well above the national average of 936. The child sex ratio (0-6 age group) of 960 for SCs in the state is also higher than the aggregated national average (938) for SCs. Among Damai, sex ratio of population (987) and child sex ratio (1045) are higher than the state's average for the respective categories. Majhi has recorded low sex ratio of population (927) and a very low child sex ratio (429), which is insignificant due to their small number.

According to 2001 Census, 63 per cent of the SCs in Sikkim are literate with male and female literacy rate of 70 and 55.7 per cent respectively. The gender gap in literacy is quite conspicuous. The Damai with 67.5 per cent literacy is on top, followed by Majhi (66.9 per cent), Kami (61.5 per cent) and Sarki (54.3 per cent).[141]

Table 3.51: Literacy Rate among Major SCs of Sikkim

Sl.No.	*Name of the Scheduled Caste*	*Total*	*Male*	*Female*	*Percentage*
	All SC Literates in Sikkim	19198	10491	8707	100
1.	Damai (Nepali)	6129	3299	2830	31.92
2.	Kami	12013	6577	5436	62.57
3.	Majhi (Nepali)	200	110	90	1.04
4.	Sarki (Nepali)	488	275	213	2.54

Source: Census of India, 2011, http://censusindia.gov.in/

The percentage of workers to total population (WPR) is 47.60 per cent among SCs. Out of the total workers, 73.85 per cent has been recorded as main workers and 26.15 per cent as marginal workers. The female WPR at 37.53 per cent is conspicuously lower than that of male 57.22 per cent. Although overwhelming workers among males are main workers 81.66 per cent, the percentage of female main workers at 61.41 per cent is also significant. On the other hand the female marginal workers are 38.58 per cent which is quite higher to the male counterpart as 18.33 per cent.[142]

Table 3.52: Distribution of Total, Main and Marginal Workers among SC's (Sikkim)

T/M/F	*Total Workers (Percentage to Total Population)*	*Main Workers (Percentage to Total Workers)*	*Marginal Workers (Percentage to Total Workers)*
Total	13460 (47.60%)	9941 (73.85%)	3519 (26.15%)
Male	8272 (57.22%)	6755 (81.66%)	1517 (18.33%)
Female	5188 (37.53%)	3186 (61.41%)	2002 (38.58%)

Source: Office of the Registrar General of India, 2011 Census of India, http://censusindia.gov.in/

Table 3.53: Main Workers by Industrial Category among SC's of Sikkim

Sl. No.	Name of the Scheduled Caste	Main Workers	Cultivators	Agricultural Labourers	Household Industry Workers	Other Workers	Percentage
	All Scheduled Castes	9941	2918	714	299	6010	100
1.	Damai (Nepali)	3053	654	239	100	2060	30.71
2.	Kami	6296	2078	441	179	3598	63.33
3.	Majhi (Nepali)	121	15	3	4	99	1.21
4.	Sarki (Nepali)	289	127	23	5	134	2.90

Source: Census of India, 2011, http://censusindia.gov.in/

Overall the total main workers among SC's in Sikkim are 9941, out of which 2918 are cultivators, 714 are agricultural labourers, 299 are household industry workers and 6010 are other workers. Among all the four SC's the highest main workers are Kami and Damai. The total main workers among Kami are 6296, out of which 2078 are cultivators, 441 are agricultural labourers, 179 are household industry workers and 3598 are other workers. On the other hand the total main workers among Damai are 3053, out of which 654 are cultivators, 239 are agricultural labourers, 100 are household industry workers and 2060 are other workers.

Table 3.54: Marginal Workers by Industrial Category among SC's of Sikkim

Sl. No.	Name of the Scheduled Caste	Marginal Workers	Cultivators	Agricultural Labourers	Household Industry Workers	Other Workers	Per-Centage
	All Scheduled Castes	3519	1113	881	142	1383	100
1.	Damai (Nepali)	1066	264	279	51	472	30.29
2.	Kami	2262	792	559	74	837	64.27
3.	Majhi (Nepali)	28	8	7	-	13	0.79
4.	Sarki (Nepali)	90	35	26	-	29	2.55

Source: Census of India, 2011, http://censusindia.gov.in/

Overall the total marginal workers among SC's in Sikkim are 3519, out of which 1113 cultivators, 881 are agricultural labourers, 142 are household industry workers and 1383 are other workers. Among all the four SC's the highest marginal workers are Kami and Damai. The total marginal workers among Kami are 2262, out of which 792 are cultivators, 559 are agricultural labourers, 74 are household industry workers and 837 are other workers. On the other hand the total marginal workers among Damai are 1066, out of which 264 are cultivators, 279 are agricultural labourers, 51 are household industry workers and 472 are other workers.

Table 3.55: Non-workers among SC's of Sikkim

Sl.No.	*Name of the Scheduled Caste*	*Non Workers*	*Male*	*Female*	*Per centage*
	All Scheduled Castes	14815	6182	8633	100
1.	Damai (Nepali)	4595	1869	2726	31.01
2.	Kami	9353	3945	5408	63.13
3.	Majhi (Nepali)	189	79	110	1.27
4.	Sarki (Nepali)	419	180	239	2.82

Source: Census of India, 2011, http://censusindia.gov.in/

Overall the total non-workers among SC's in Sikkim are 14815, out of which 6182 are males and 8633 are females. Among all the four SC's the highest non-workers are Kami and Damai. The total non-workers among Kami are 9353 out of which 3945 are males and 5408 are females. On the other hand the total non-workers among Damai are 4595, out of which 1869 are males and 2726 are females.

Tripura

Tripura resides at the far north-eastern corner of India. It has spread over a small expanse of about 10,000 sq km, which makes it one of the smallest states in India. Big things come in small packages. And the state of Tripura proves that again. With a rich and colourful historical background and equally vibrant culture, the state of Tripura shines on the map of India. Although small in area, its population density of about 300 ranks medium as compared to other states. Also the population is growing at satisfactory rate according to 2011 Tripura census, which is great for the state progress and in population wise, the state ranks 22nd in India, with around three lakh people residing in it. The remote state has also shown rapid growth in its literacy rate since the previous census. The previous growth rate of about 60-80 per cent has been raised to 80-90 per cent, with subsequent increase in female literacy. Although females are comparatively less in number as compared to the male count, efforts are being taken to balance the gender ratio, which is currently above 900. Due to lack of urbanisation, the population residing in rural area is more as compared to the urban land. About 3/4th of population lives in villages. But, it is noteworthy, that the population growth in villages is far less as compared to the urban areas. Agartala is the state capital of Tripura, and also one of the very few urban regions. Dharmanagar, Udaipur, Badharghat are some other popular towns of Tripura. The culture of Tripura is a mix of numerous other civilisations, including Bengali and Manipuri. The language widely spoken is mostly Bengali. The people of Tripura are widely famous for their attires, which include vibrant combination of red, white and green complemented with bold ethnic jewellery. The capital city which is also the largest city in the state of Tripura is Agartala. The languages spoken in the Tripura state includes Bengali and Tripuri. In total Tripura state comprises four districts.[143]

As per details from Census 2011, Tripura has population of 36.74 lakhs, an increase from figure of 32 lakh in 2001 census. Total population of Tripura as per 2011 census is 3,673,917 of which male and female are 1,874,376 and 1,799,541 respectively. In 2001, total population was 3,199,203 in which males were 1,642,225 while females were 1,556,978. The total population growth in this decade was 14.84 per cent while in previous decade it was 15.74 per cent. The population of Tripura forms 0.30 per cent of India in 2011. In 2001, the figure was 0.31 per cent. Literacy rate in Tripura has seen upward trend and is 87.22 per cent as per 2011 population census. Of that, male literacy stands at 91.53 per cent while female literacy is at 78.98 per cent. In 2001, literacy rate in Tripura stood at 73.19 per cent of which male and female were 82.42 per cent and 64.33 per cent literate respectively. In actual numbers, total literates in Tripura stands at 2,804,783 of which males were 1,501,369 and females were 1,303,414. Total area of Tripura is 10,486 sq. km. Density of Tripura is 350 per sq km which is lower than national average 382 per sq km. In 2001, density of Tripura was 305 per sq km, while nation average in 2001 was 324 per sq km. Sex Ratio in Tripura is 960 i.e., for each 1000 male, which is below national average of 940 as per census 2011. In 2001, the sex ratio of female was 950 per 1000 males in Tripura. Lot of viewers are asking us to provide religion's data of Tripura state.[144]

Tripura, the second smallest state in the country, is almost surrounded by Bangladesh. Inspite of having 19 tribes, the majority of the population of Tripura is Bengali. Situated in one of the remotest corner of the country, Tripura is one of the best potential places that cater the taste of everything from palaces to lakes and hill station.[145]

The ancient history of Tipperah or Tripura is shrouded with mystery. We come to learn from Rajamal that more than 150 tribal kings ruled Tripura since the legendary period and King Ratnapha got the title "Manikya" from the Lord of Gauda. But recent readings of Tripura Coins have proved that Ratna had his two predecessors, Maha Manikya and Dharma Manikya. Hence, it is perhaps reasonable to conclude that with Mahamanikya, the historical period of the "Manikya" Dynasty started, which continued till 1949. The history of the rulers of Tripura in medieval period is the story of continual fights, particularly with the Sultans of Bengal. During the British period, some English officials were eager to occupy Tripura, but it was opposed by others. However, the office of the British Political Agent of Tripura was created in 1871. After the death of Birbikram Kishore Manikya in May 1947, a Council of Regency under the leadership of his widowed wife Maharani Kanchanprava Devi took over the charge of the administration on behalf of the minor prince. The Regent's rule came to an end on September 9, 1947, when due to popular pressure; the agreement of Merger of Tripura with the Indian Union was signed by the Maharani on 15th October 1949. Finally, Tripura became a full-fledged State in January 1972. The original inhabitants of the land, i.e. the hill people were noted for their tolerance and passive obedience. It is only in the 19th century that they started protesting against the oppressive Feudal System. There are only four predominant communities in Tripura professing different religious beliefs-Hindus, Muslims, Buddhists and Christians. Most of the tribal people have their own tribal customs and beliefs but in a broader sense of the religion they are believed to be followers of Hinduism. They worship elements such as the god of water, the god of fire, the god of forests, the god of earth etc. A trace of their old faith is found in their present practice of striking a bamboo in the ground during religious festivals and worshipping it. Sacrifices form an important part of their religion; the buffaloes, pigs, goats and fowls being the animals ordinarily used for this purpose. Most of the modern members of the ruling family of Tripura were great patrons of art and literature and had great regard for eminent scholars of the country. Maharaja Dharmamanikya is said to have inaugurated the rajmala, a verse chronicle of the royal house. Tripura, a neighbouring state, have had a spiritual contact with Bengal for well over a few centuries and this contact became all the more significant during the period due to Tagore's continued association with the ruler and his benign influence over them. Teachers were brought from Mithila for the spread of Music in the State. A flute made of Muli Bamboo of Tripura was very famous. There are also their own improvised musical instruments like Sarinda, Chougpreng and Samu (flute) etc. made of bamboo and strings. The songs are mostlly related to their days work and different songs are sung on different occasions. Dancing in Tripura has always been in complementary lines with Music and it has always been a very popular aspect of cultural functions. The Garia dance is very popular among the Tripuris.[146]

The total SC population of Tripura as per 2011 Census is 654918. Out of which these 334370 is recorded male population and 320548 are female. There are thirty one notified SCs, and all have been enumerated in 2011 Census. The Namasudra with (109687) account highest SC population of the state, followed by Dhoba (28853), Mali (28003), Chamar (6781), Dhuli (4791), Patni (3619), Gour (3488) and Sabar (2262).

Table 3.56: Scheduled Caste Population of Tripura, 2011 Census Report

Sl.No.	*Name of Scheduled Caste*	*Total*		*Rural*		*Urban*	
		Male	*Female*	*Male*	*Female*	*Male*	*Female*
1.	Bagdi	243	267	196	219	47	48
2.	Bhuimali	149	123	129	105	20	18
3.	Bhunar	84	94	61	59	23	35
4.	Chamar, Muchi	6781	6798	2313	2126	4468	4672

contd...

contd...

Sl.No.	Name of Scheduled Caste	Total		Rural		Urban	
		Male	Female	Male	Female	Male	Female
5.	Dandasi	4	1	-	-	4	1
6.	Dhenuar	33	32	21	18	12	14
7.	Dhoba	28853	27660	20068	19234	8785	8426
8.	Dum	21	20	13	10	8	10
9.	Ghasi	108	96	101	91	7	5
10.	Gour	3488	3366	3238	3118	250	248
11.	Gur	57	29	48	28	9	1
12.	Jalia Kaibarta	54792	52057	36080	33798	18712	18259
13.	Kahar	193	164	141	111	52	53
14.	Kalindi	59	76	56	73	3	3
15.	Kan	15	12	15	10	-	2
16.	Kanda	1318	1256	1201	1138	117	118
17.	Knough	28	21	23	18	5	3
18.	Keot	153	149	147	143	6	6
19.	Khadit	11	7	7	7	4	-
20.	Kharia	745	664	712	639	33	25
21.	Koch	419	396	394	374	25	22
22.	Koir	55	47	51	38	4	9
23.	Kol	544	535	514	505	30	30
24.	Kora	58	59	53	56	5	3
25.	Kotal	7	2	4	1	3	1
26.	Mahisyadas	78371	74663	56249	53288	22122	21375
27.	Mali	28003	27006	18424	17773	9579	9233
28.	Mehtor	927	924	93	83	834	841
29.	Musahar	178	149	126	99	52	50
30.	Namasudra	109689	105578	72129	68998	37560	36580
31.	Patni	3619	3616	1283	1311	2336	2305
32.	Sabar	2262	2167	1959	1877	303	290
33.	Dhuli, Sabdakar, Badyakar	4791	4553	3390	3199	1401	1354
34.	Natta, Nat	827	816	591	607	236	209

Source: Census of India, 2011, http://censusindia.gov.in/

Table 3.57: District-wise SC's Population of Tripura

Sl. No.	*State/District*	*Total Population (Districtwise)*					*Per-centage*
		Total	*Rural*	*Urban*	*Male*	*Female*	
	Tripura	654918	437993	216925	334370	320548	0.39
1.	West Tripura	338094	186463	151631	172522	135572	51.62
2.	South Tripura	140168	111464	28704	72012	68156	21.40
3.	Dhalai	61688	50539	11149	31461	30227	9.41
4.	North Tripura	114968	89527	25441	58375	56593	17.55

Source: Office of the Registrar General of India, 2011 Census of India, Government of India, http://censusindia.gov.in/

West Tripura district houses more than half of the state total SC population (51.62 per cent), followed by South Tripura (21.40 per cent), and North Tripura (17.55 per cent). The district Dhalai covers the remaining (9.41 per cent) SCs of the state. Among the major SCs in the state, Namasudra has highest SC population (16766) followed by Mahisyadas (125362), Chamar (9899), Jalia (85577), Dhoba (45893), Mali (43539) and Patni (5688). On the other hand Dandasi (5) and Kotal (9) has recorded lower literacy.

Table 3.58: Literacy Rate among Major SCs of Tripura

Sl. No.	*Name of the Scheduled Caste*	*Total*	*Male*	*Female*	*Per-centage*
	All SC Literates in Tripura	516876	273619	243257	100
1.	Bagdi	331	164	167	0.06
2.	Bhuimali	198	118	80	0.03
3.	Bhunar	131	66	65	0.02
4.	Chamar, Muchi	9898	5221	4677	1.91
5.	Dandasi	5	4	1	0.00
6.	Dhenuar	54	29	25	0.01
7.	Dhoba	45893	24286	21607	8.87
8.	Dum	31	17	14	0.00
9.	Ghasi	160	87	73	0.03
10.	Gour	4808	2590	2218	0.93
11.	Gur	61	42	19	0.01
12.	Jalia Kaibarta	85577	45548	40029	16.55
13.	Kahar	252	143	109	0.04

contd...

contd...

Sl. No.	Name of the Scheduled Caste	Total	Male	Female	Per-centage
14.	Kalindi	95	45	50	0.01
15.	Kan	22	13	9	0.00
16.	Kanda	1775	969	806	0.34
17.	Knough	34	18	16	0.00
18.	Keot	209	114	95	0.04
19.	Khadit	10	7	3	0.00
20.	Kharia	763	424	339	0.01
21.	Koch	576	315	261	0.11
22.	Koir	73	39	34	0.01
23.	Kol	755	410	345	0.14
24.	Kora	76	43	33	0.01
25.	Kotal	6	5	1	0.00
26.	Mahisyadas	125362	66130	59232	24.25
27.	Mali	43539	22660	20879	8.42
28.	Mehtor	1419	743	676	0.27
29.	Musahar	257	150	107	0.04
30.	Namasudra	167666	88978	78688	32.4
31.	Patni	5688	2974	2714	1.10
32.	Sabar	2223	1247	976	0.43
33.	Dhuli, Sabdakar, Badyakar	6792	3600	3192	1.31
34.	Natta, Nat	1264	646	618	0.24

Source: Census of India, 2011, http://censusindia.gov.in/

As among all SCs, the percentage of workers to total population (WPR) is 33.37 per cent, out of the total workers, 75.00 per cent have been recorded as main workers and 24.19 per cent marginal workers. The female WPR at 18.73 per cent is conspicuously lower than male 57.19 per cent. The overwhelming workers among males are main workers 85.19 per cent on the other hand the female SC marginal workers are 54.11 per cent as compare to the male counterpart which is 14.80 per cent.[147]

Table 3.59: Distribution of Total, Main and Marginal Workers among SC's (Tripura)

T/M/F	Total Workers (Percentage to Total Population)	Main Workers (Percentage to Total Workers)	Marginal Workers (Percentage to Total Workers)
Total	251308 (38.37%)	190492 (75.80%)	60816 (24.19%)
Male	191248 (57.19%)	162933 (85.19%)	28315 (14.80%)
Female	60060 (18.73%)	27559 (45.88%)	32501 (54.11%)

Source: Office of the Registrar General of India, 2011 Census of India, http://censusindia.gov.in/

Table 3.60: Main Workers by Industrial Category among SC's of Tripura

Sl. No.	Name of the Scheduled Caste	Main Workers	Cultiv-ators	Agricultural Labourers	House-hold Industry Workers	Other Wor-kers	Per-centa ge
	All Scheduled Castes	190492	29684	34643	4472	1355	100
1.	Bagdi	168	3	25	2	138	0.08
2.	Bhuimali	86	18	5	-	63	0.04
3.	Bhunar	55	5	4	1	45	0.02
4.	Chamâr, Muchi	4470	129	222	101	4018	2.34
5.	Dandasi	4	-	-	-	4	0.0
6.	Dhenuar	20	2	3	1	14	0.01
7.	Dhoba	16544	2478	3169	276	10621	8.68
8.	Dum	15	1	1	1	12	0.0
9.	Ghasi	97	18	45	-	34	0.05
10.	Gour	2152	184	660	19	1289	1.12
11.	Gur	38	1	6	-	31	0.01
12.	Jalia Kaibarta	31089	5094	4689	441	20865	16.32
13.	Kahar	120	9	11	-	100	0.06
14.	Kalindi	17	1	2	-	14	0.0
15.	Kan	13	-	4	-	9	0.0
16.	Kanda	845	58	207	4	576	0.44
17.	Knough	16	-	5	-	11	0.0
18.	Keot	128	6	23	2	97	0.06
19.	Khadit	11	2	1	-	8	0.0
20.	Kharia	499	38	116	12	333	0.06
21.	Koch	285	32	198	3	52	0.14
22.	Koir	28	1	1	1	25	0.01
23.	Kol	51211	25	1	475	71	26.88
24.	Kora	36	3	18	-	15	0.01
25.	Kotal	4	-	-	-	4	0.0
26.	Mahisyadas	44064	8693	8273	7572	26341	23.13
27.	Mali	15250	1973	2212	266	10799	8.00
28.	Mehtor	556	2	14	-	540	2.85
29.	Musahar	136	4	32	2	98	0.07
30.	Namasudra	61879	9728	12459	2395	37297	32.48
31.	Patni	2179	139	223	21	1796	1.14
32.	Sabar	1304	80	377	6	841	0.68
33.	Dhuli, Sabdakar, Badyakar	2559	267	470	23	1799	1.34
34.	Natta, Nat	472	31	96	5	340	0.24

Source: Census of India, 2011, http://censusindia.gov.in/

Overall the total main workers among SC's in Tripura are 190492, out of which 29684 are cultivators, 34643 are agricultural labourers, 4472 are household industry workers and 1355 are other workers. Among all the 34 SC's the highest main workers are Namasudra, Kol, Mahisyadas and Jalia Kaibarta. The total main workers among Namasudra are 61879, out of which 9728 are cultivators, 12459 are agricultural labourers, 2395 are household industry workers and 37297 are other workers. The total main workers among Mahisyadas are 44064, out of which 8693 are cultivators, 8273 are agricultural labourers, 7572 are household industry workers and 26341 are other workers. On the other hand, the total main workers among Jalia Kaibarta 31089, out of which 5094 are cultivators, 4689 are agricultural labourers, 441 are household industry workers and 20865 are other workers.

Table 3.61: Marginal Workers by Industrial Category among SC's of Tripura

Sl. No.	Name of the Scheduled Caste	Marginal Workers	Cultiv-ators	Agricultural Labourers	House-hold Industry Workers	Other Workers	Per-centage
	All Scheduled Castes	60816	3578	16079	4473	36686	100
1.	Bagdi	38	-	9	-	29	0.06
2.	Bhuimali	24	1	5	1	17	0.03
3.	Bhunar	33	2	1	2	28	0.05
4.	Chamar, Muchi	865	26	51	67	721	1.42
5.	Dandasi	1	-	-	-	-	0.0
6.	Dhenuar	7	-	2	-	5	0.0
7.	Dhoba	5314	258	1563	377	3116	8.73
8.	Dum	4	-	-	1	3	0.0
9.	Ghasi	9	-	1	-	8	0.0
10.	Gour	771	57	236	12	466	1.26
11.	Gur	6	-	-	-	6	0.0
12.	Jalia Kaibarta	9516	633	2646	536	5701	15.64
13.	Kahar	24	-	5	1	18	0.03
14.	Kalindi	45	7	1	-	37	0.07
15.	Kan	-	-	-	-	-	0.0
16.	Kanda	306	9	84	10	203	0.50
17.	Knough	3	-	1	-	2	0.0

contd...

contd...

Sl. No.	Name of the Scheduled Caste	Marginal Workers	Cultiv-ators	Agricultural Labourers	House-hold Industry Workers	Other Workers	Per-cent-age
18.	Keot	13	1	-	2	10	0.02
19.	Khadit	-	-	-	-	-	0.0
20.	Kharia	183	-	39	9	135	0.30
21.	Koch	86	5	60	5	16	0.14
22.	Koir	12	2	6	1	3	0.01
23.	Kol	71	2	5	-	64	0.11
24.	Kora	19	-	4	-	15	0.03
25.	Kotal	2	-	-	-	2	0.0
26.	Mahisyadas	13851	1113	4017	660	8061	22.77
27.	Mali	4227	228	817	230	2952	6.95
28.	Mehtor	69	-	2	3	64	0.11
29.	Musahar	28	1	11	1	15	0.04
30.	Namasudra	21453	1060	5547	2073	12773	35.27
31.	Patni	544	10	83	34	417	0.89
32.	Sabar	587	9	249	14	315	0.96
33.	Dhuli, Sabdakar, Badyakar	772	22	157	23	570	0.26
34.	Natta, Nat	165	2	16	13	134	0.27

Source: Census of India, 2011, http://censusindia.gov.in/

Overall the total marginal workers among SC's in Tripura are 60816, out of which 3578 cultivators, 16079 are agricultural labourers, 4473 are household industry workers and 36686 are other workers. Among all the 34 SC's the highest marginal workers are Namasudra, Mahisyadas and Jalia Kaibarta. The total marginal workers among Namasudra are 21453, out of which 1060 are cultivators, 5547 are agricultural labourers, 2073 are household industry workers and 12773 are other workers. The total marginal workers among Mahisyadas are 13851, out of which 1113 are cultivators, 4017 are agricultural labourers, 660 are household industry workers and 8061 are other workers. On the other hand the total marginal workers among Jalia Kaibarta are 9516, out of which 633 are cultivators, 2646 are agricultural labourers, 536 are household industry workers and 5701 are other workers.

Table 3.62: Non-workers among SC's of Tripura

Sl. No.	Name of the Scheduled Caste	Non Workers	Male	Female	Per-centage
	All Scheduled Castes	403610	143122	260488	100
1.	Bagdi	304	113	191	0.07
2.	Bhuimali	162	59	103	0.04
3.	Bhunar	90	31	59	0.02
4.	Chamar, Muchi	8244	2984	5260	2.04
5.	Dandasi	-	-	-	0.0
6.	Dhenuar	38	15	23	0.0
7.	Dhoba	34655	11872	22783	8.58
8.	Dum	22	7	15	0.0
9.	Ghasi	98	42	56	0.02
10.	Gour	3931	1650	2281	0.97
11.	Gur	42	23	19	0.01
12.	Jalia Kaibarta	66244	23435	42809	16.41
13.	Kahar	213	87	126	0.05
14.	Kalindi	73	22	51	0.01
15.	Kan	14	6	· 8	0.0
16.	Kanda	1423	602	821	0.35
17.	Knough	30	15	15	0.0
18.	Keot	161	70	91	0.03
19.	Khadit	7	2	5	0.0
20.	Kharia	727	335	392	0.18
21.	Koch	444	199	245	0.11
22.	Koir	62	25	37	0.01
23.	Kol	496	191	305	0.12
24.	Kora	62	18	44	0.01
25.	Kotal	3	2	1	0.0
26.	Mahisyadas	95119	33209	61910	23.56
27.	Mali	35532	12353	23179	8.80
28.	Mehtor	1226	508	718	0.30
29.	Musahar	163	67	96	0.04
30.	Namasudra	131935	46959	84976	32.68
31.	Patni	4512	1500	3012	1.11
32.	Sabar	2538	1110	1428	0.62
33.	Dhuli, Sabdakar, Badyakar	6013	2181	3832	1.48
34.	Natta, Nat	1006	341	665	0.24

Source: Census of India, 2011, http://censusindia.gov.in/

Overall the total non-workers among SC's in Tripura are 403610, out of which 143122 are males and 260488 are females. Among all the 34 SC's the highest non-workers are Namasudra, Mahisyadas and Jalia Kaibarta. The total non-workers among Namasudra are 131935 out of which 46959 are males and 84976 are females. The total non-workers among Mahisyadas are 95119 out of which 33209 are males and 61910 are females. On the other hand the total non-workers among Jalia Kaibarta are 66244, out of which 23435 are males and 42809 are females.

The survey has been conducted in all the States/UTs by covering all the districts. The field work for the second survey was launched from July, 2011 in phases and by the first fortnight of August, 2011 the field work had started in most of the States/ UTs. The field work was completed in most of the States/UTs by the end of January, 2012. A sample of 1,28,298 households has been covered, out of which 81,430 households are in the rural sector and the remaining 46,868 households in the urban sector. From the households covered, 6,29,753 members are surveyed out of which 4,03,271 members reside in rural households and rest 2,26,482 in the urban households. The labour force estimates based on all the four approaches have been derived. The four approaches are Usual Principal Status (UPS) approach, Usual Principal and Subsidiary Status (UPSS) approach, Current Weekly Status (CWS) approach and Current Daily Status (CDS) approach. A fixed reference period of Agriculture Year 2010-11 i.e. July, 2010 to June, 2011 is used to derive the estimates based on usual status approach. For current weekly and current daily status approach, the week comprising of seven days preceding the date of the survey is taken as the reference period. As the field work was spread over six to seven months period in most of the States/UTs, and since the CDS and CWS estimates are based on the week preceding the date of survey, the seasonal variations would not get captured in the CDS and CWS estimates. All the labour force related tables are generated state-wise/ gender-wise/sector-wise/social-group wise. The labour force estimates are derived for the persons of age 15 years and above. Based on the survey results, 50.8 per cent or majority of the households are found to be having self-employment as the major source of income under agricultural and non-agricultural activities. In the rural areas, 11.1 per cent households are estimated to be having regular/wage salary earning as major source of income. In the urban areas, 42.3 per cent households are estimated to be having regular wage/salary earnings as the major source of income followed by 34.4 per cent households under self-employment category. The Labour Force Participation Rate (LFPR) is estimated to be 52.9 per cent under the UPS approach at All India level. In the rural sector the LFPR is estimated to be 54.8 per cent as compared to 47.2 per cent in the urban sector under the UPS approach. Female LFPR is significantly lower as compared to male LFPR under the usual principal status approach. At All India level, female LFPR is estimated to be 25.4 per cent as compared to 77.4 per cent in male category.[148] LFPR based on all the four approaches for the northeastern states are as below:

Table 3.63: Distribution of HHS by Social Groups in Rural and Urban Sector

Social Group	*Rural*	*Urban*	*Rural + Urban*
Scheduled Castes	220	144	200
Scheduled Tribes	105	37	87
Other Backward Classes	415	384	407
General	260	436	306

Source: Report on employment and unemployment survey 2011-12, Ministry of Labour and Employment, Government of India, Chandigarh.

Table 3.64: Per 1000 distribution for persons of age 15 years and above by broad activity status according to different approaches Assam (Rural+Urban)

	Employed force			*Unemployed*			*Not in labour force*		
	Male	*Female*	*Person*	*Male*	*Female*	*Person*	*Male*	*Female*	*Person*
UPS	777	118	485	31	27	29	193	854	485
UPSS	800	190	530	24	21	23	176	789	447
CDS	737	134	471	39	38	38	224	828	491
CWS	787	191	523	29	49	38	184	759	438

Source: Report on employment and unemployment survey 2011-12, Ministry of Labour and Employment, Government of India, Chandigarh, p. 39.

Table 3.65: Per 1000 distribution for persons of age 15 years and above by broad activity status according to different approaches Assam (Rural)

	Employed force			*Unemployed*			*Not in labour force*		
	Male	*Female*	*Person*	*Male*	*Female*	*Person*	*Male*	*Female*	*Person*
UPS	792	111	490	34	26	31	174	863	479
UPSS	817	193	541	27	19	23	156	789	436
CDS	744	130	473	37	33	35	218	837	492
CWS	801	192	532	26	42	33	172	767	435

Source: Report on employment and unemployment survey 2011-12, Ministry of Labour and Employment, Government of India, Chandigarh, p. 40.

Table 3.66: Per 1000 distribution for persons of age 15 years and above by broad activity status according to different approaches Assam (Urban)

	Employed force			*Unemployed*			*Not in labour force*		
	Male	*Female*	*Per-son*	*Male*	*Female*	*Per-son*	*Male*	*Female*	*Per-son*
UPS	709	152	463	14	33	23	277	814	515
UPSS	719	175	479	11	33	21	270	791	500
CDS	706	152	461	46	59	52	148	789	487
CWS	721	191	487	44	85	62	235	724	451

Source: Report on employment and unemployment survey 2011-12, Ministry of Labour and Employment, Government of India, Chandigarh, p.41.

Table 3.67: Per 1000 distribution for persons of age 15 years and above by broad activity status according to different approaches Arunchal Pradesh (Rural+Urban)

	Employed force			*Unemployed*			*Not in labour force*		
	Male	*Female*	*Per-son*	*Male*	*Female*	*Per-son*	*Male*	*Female*	*Per-son*
UPS	748	271	540	10	60	32	242	428	669
UPSS	762	271	548	10	60	32	228	669	420
CDS	707	274	519	6	60	30	286	665	452
CWS	748	343	571	10	60	32	242	597	397

Source: Report on employment and unemployment survey 2011-12, Ministry of Labour and Employment, Government of India, Chandigarh, p. 36.

Table 3.68: Per 1000 distribution for persons of age 15 years and above by broad activity status according to different approaches Arunchal Pradesh (Rural)

	Employed force			*Unemployed*			*Not in labour force*		
	Male	*Fe-male*	*Per-son*	*Male*	*Fem-ale*	*Per-son*	*Male*	*Fe-male*	*Per-son*
UPS	778	226	562	14	-	9	208	774	430
UPSS	778	226	562	14	-	9	208	774	430
CDS	707	233	521	8	-	5	285	767	474
CWS	778	377	621	14	-	9	208	623	371

Source: Report on employment and unemployment survey 2011-12, Ministry of Labour and Employment, Government of India, Chandigarh, p. 37.

Table 3.69: Per 1000 distribution for persons of age 15 years and above by broad activity status according to different approaches Arunachal Pradesh (Urban)

	Employed force			*Unemployed*			*Not in labour force*		
	Male	*Female*	*Person*	*Male*	*Female*	*Person*	*Male*	*Female*	*Person*
UPS	708	312	515	4	115	58	288	572	426
UPSS	741	312	515	4	115	58	288	572	410
CDS	708	312	515	4	115	58	288	572	426
CWS	708	312	515	4	115	58	288	572	426

Source: Report on employment and unemployment survey 2011-12, Ministry of Labour and Employment, Government of India, Chandigarh, p. 38.

Table 3.70: Per 1000 distribution for persons of age 15 years and above by broad activity status according to different approaches Manipur (Rural+Urban)

	Employed force			*Unemployed*			*Not in labour force*		
	Male	*Female*	*Person*	*Male*	*Female*	*Person*	*Male*	*Female*	*Person*
UPS	782	639	703	52	25	37	166	337	260
UPSS	782	661	715	52	25	37	166	314	248
CDS	705	487	585	52	25	37	243	485	378
CWS	788	621	696	52	25	37	160	354	267

Source: Report on employment and unemployment survey 2011-12, Ministry of Labour and Employment, Government of India, Chandigarh, p. 81.

Table 3.71: Per 1000 distribution for persons of age 15 years and above by broad activity status according to different approaches Manipur (Rural)

	Employed force			*Unemployed*			*Not in labour force*		
	Male	*Female*	*Person*	*Male*	*Female*	*Person*	*Male*	*Female*	*Person*
UPS	802	688	738	58	27	40	140	285	221
UPSS	802	712	752	58	27	40	140	261	208
CDS	717	525	609	58	27	40	225	449	350
CWS	809	669	732	58	27	40	134	304	229

Source: Report on employment and unemployment survey 2011-12, Ministry of Labour and Employment, Government of India, Chandigarh, p. 82.

Table 3.72: Per 1000 distribution for persons of age 15 years and above by broad activity status according to different approaches Manipur (Urban)

	Employed force			Unemployed			Not in labour force		
	Male	Female	Person	Male	Female	Person	Male	Female	Person
	605	-	322	-	-	-	395	1000	678
	605	-	322	-	-	-	395	1000	678
	605	-	322	-	-	-	395	1000	678
	605	-	322	-	-	-	395	1000	678

Source: Report on employment and unemployment survey 2011-12, Ministry of Labour and Employment, Government of India, Chandigarh, p. 83.

Table 3.73: Per 1000 distribution for persons of age 15 years and above by broad activity status according to different approaches Meghalaya (Rural+Urban)

	Employed force			Unemployed			Not in labour force		
	Male	Female	Per-son	Male	Female	Per-son	Male	Female	Per-son
UPS	769	445	575	-	-	-	231	555	425
UPSS	769	542	633	-	-	-	231	458	367
CDS	678	440	535	-	-	-	322	560	465
CWS	750	490	594	-	-	-	250	560	406

Source: Report on employment and unemployment survey 2011-12, Ministry of Labour and Employment, Government of India, Chandigarh, p. 84.

Table 3.74: Per 1000 distribution for persons of age 15 years and above by broad activity status according to different approaches Meghalaya (Rural)

	Employed force			Unemployed			Not in labour force		
	Male	Female	Per-son	Male	Female	Per-son	Male	Female	Per-son
UPS	907	438	603	-	-	-	93	562	397
UPSS	907	573	691	-	-	-	93	427	309
CDS	822	433	570	-	-	-	178	567	430
CWS	907	498	642	-	-	-	93	502	358

Source: Report on employment and unemployment survey 2011-12, Ministry of Labour and Employment, Government of India, Chandigarh, p. 85.

Table 3.75: Per 1000 distribution for persons of age 15 years and above by broad activity status according to different approaches Meghalaya (Urban)

	Employed force			Unemployed			Not in labour force		
	Male	Female	Per-son	Male	Female	Per-son	Male	Female	Per-son
UPS	587	460	523	-	-	-	413	540	477
UPSS	587	470	527	-	-	-	413	530	473
CDS	490	456	473	-	-	-	510	544	527
CWS	544	470	506	-	-	-	456	530	494

Source: Report on employment and unemployment survey 2011-12, Ministry of Labour and Employment, Government of India, Chandigarh, p. 86.

Table 3.76: Per 1000 distribution for persons of age 15 years and above by broad activity status according to different approaches Mizoram (Rural+Urban)

	Employed force			Unemployed			Not in labour force		
	Male	Female	Per-son	Male	Female	Per-son	Male	Female	Per-son
UPS	717	653	686	6	-	3	277	347	311
UPSS	774	765	770	-	-	-	226	235	230
CDS	747	694	721	6	-	3	246	306	275
CWS	752	718	735	6	-	3	242	282	261

Source: Report on employment and unemployment survey 2011-12, Ministry of Labour and Employment, Government of India, Chandigarh, p. 87.

Table 3.77: Per 1000 distribution for persons of age 15 years and above by broad activity status according to different approaches Mizoram (Rural)

	Employed force			Unemployed			Not in labour force		
	Male	Female	Per-son	Male	Female	Per-son	Male	Female	Per-son
UPS	785	744	765	-	-	-	215	256	235
UPSS	815	807	811	-	-	-	185	193	189
CDS	843	833	838	-	-	-	157	167	162
CWS	845	855	850	-	-	-	155	145	150

Source: Report on employment and unemployment survey 2011-12, Ministry of Labour and Employment, Government of India, Chandigarh, p. 88.

Table 3.78: Per 1000 distribution for persons of age 15 years and above by broad activity status according to different approaches Mizoram (Urban)

	Employed force			Unemployed			Not in labour force		
	Male	Female	Person	Male	Female	Person	Male	Female	Person
UPS	626	522	577	14	-	8	359	478	416
UPSS	719	704	712	-	-	-	281	296	288
CDS	619	494	560	14	-	8	366	506	433
CWS	626	522	577	14	-	8	359	478	416

Source: Report on employment and unemployment survey 2011-12, Ministry of Labour and Employment, Government of India, Chandigarh, p. 89.

Table 3.79: Per 1000 distribution for persons of age 15 years and above by broad activity status according to different approaches Nagaland (Rural+Urban)

	Employed force			Unemployed			Not in labour force		
	Male	Female	Person	Male	Female	Person	Male	Female	Person
UPS	712	100	423	42	35	39	246	865	538
UPSS	714	100	424	40	35	38	246	865	538
CDS	691	121	423	-	-	-	309	879	577
CWS	720	127	440	-	-	-	280	873	560

Source: Report on employment and unemployment survey 2011-12, Ministry of Labour and Employment, Government of India, Chandigarh, p. 90.

Table 3.80: Per 1000 distribution for persons of age 15 years and above by broad activity status according to different approaches Nagaland (Rural)

	Employed force			Unemployed			Not in labour force		
	Male	Female	Person	Male	Female	Person	Male	Female	Person
UPS	725	150	470	73	72	72	202	778	458
UPSS	725	150	470	73	72	72	202	778	458
CDS	684	142	444	-	-	-	316	858	556
CWS	736	153	477	-	-	-	264	847	523

Source: Report on employment and unemployment survey 2011-12, Ministry of Labour and Employment, Government of India, Chandigarh, p. 91.

Table 3.81: Per 1000 distribution for persons of age 15 years and above by broad activity status according to different approaches Nagaland (Urban)

	Employed force			*Unemployed*			*Not in labour force*		
	Male	*Female*	*Per-son*	*Male*	*Female*	*Per-son*	*Male*	*Female*	*Per-son*
UPS	695	50	372	5	-	2	300	950	626
UPSS	700	50	374	-	-	-	300	950	626
CDS	700	101	399	-	-	-	300	899	601
CWS	700	101	399	-	-	-	300	899	601

Source: Report on employment and unemployment survey 2011-12, Ministry of Labour and Employment, Government of India, Chandigarh, p. 92.

Table 3.82: Per 1000 distribution for persons of age 15 years and above by broad activity status according to different approaches Sikkim (Rural+Urban)

	Employed force			*Unemployed*			*Not in labour force*		
	Male	*Female*	*Per-son*	*Male*	*Female*	*Per-son*	*Male*	*Female*	*Per-son*
UPS	713	324	539	59	88	72	228	587	389
UPSS	758	458	624	14	62	36	228	479	341
CDS	783	333	581	14	61	35	203	606	384
CWS	807	404	626	14	72	40	180	524	334

Source: Report on employment and unemployment survey 2011-12, Ministry of Labour and Employment, Government of India, Chandigarh, p. 102.

Table 3.83: Per 1000 distribution for persons of age 15 years and above by broad activity status according to different approaches Sikkim (Rural)

	Employed force			*Unemployed*			*Not in labour force*		
	Male	*Female*	*Per-son*	*Male*	*Female*	*Per-son*	*Male*	*Female*	*Per-son*
UPS	777	403	600	66	17	43	157	581	358
UPSS	843	558	708	-	4	2	157	438	290
CDS	843	411	638	-	9	4	157	579	357
CWS	843	489	675	-	17	8	157	494	317

Source: Report on employment and unemployment survey 2011-12, Ministry of Labour and Employment, Government of India, Chandigarh, p. 103.

Table 3.84: Per 1000 distribution for persons of age 15 years and above by broad activity status according to different approaches Sikkim (Urban)

	Employed force			*Unemployed*			*Not in labour force*		
	Male	*Female*	*Person*	*Male*	*Female*	*Person*	*Male*	*Female*	*Person*
UPS	574	80	385	43	312	146	382	608	469
UPSS	574	146	410	43	246	121	382	608	469
CDS	652	89	436	44	223	113	304	688	452
CWS	727	137	501	43	246	121	230	618	378

Source: Report on employment and unemployment survey 2011-12, Ministry of Labour and Employment, Government of India, Chandigarh, p. 104.

Table 3.85: Per 1000 distribution for persons of age 15 years and above by broad activity status according to different approaches Tripura (Rural+Urban)

	Employed force			*Unemployed*			*Not in labour force*		
	Male	*Female*	*Person*	*Male*	*Female*	*Person*	*Male*	*Female*	*Person*
UPS	791	205	512	24	84	52	185	711	436
UPSS	792	278	547	23	81	51	185	640	402
CDS	716	230	484	75	64	70	210	706	446
CWS	787	260	536	39	81	59	174	659	405

Source: Report on employment and unemployment survey 2011-12, Ministry of Labour and Employment, Government of India, Chandigarh, p. 108.

Table 3.86: Per 1000 distribution for persons of age 15 years and above by broad activity status according to different approaches Tripura (Rural)

	Employed force			Unemployed			Not in labour force		
	Male	Female	Person	Male	Female	Person	Male	Female	Person
UPS	802	205	517	20	87	52	178	707	431
UPSS	802	285	555	20	85	51	178	630	394
CDS	736	234	496	75	66	71	189	700	433
CWS	798	265	544	37	84	60	166	650	397

Source: Report on employment and unemployment survey 2011-12, Ministry of Labour and Employment, Government of India, Chandigarh, p. 109.

Table 3.87: Per 1000 distribution for persons of age .15 years and above by broad activity status according to different approaches Tripura (Urban)

	Employed force			*Unemployed*			*Not in labour force*		
	Male	*Female*	*Per-son*	*Male*	*Female*	*Per-son*	*Male*	*Female*	*Per-son*
UPS	677	202	456	60	43	52	263	756	492
UPSS	677	202	456	60	43	52	263	756	492
CDS	487	189	349	74	36	56	439	775	595
CWS	677	202	456	60	43	52	263	755	491

Source: Report on employment and unemployment survey 2011-12, Ministry of Labour and Employment, Government of India, Chandigarh, p. 110.

Overall this could be concluded by saying that there is a need to focus more on the part of education, health, security and opportunity of livelihood in more inclusive manner so that the tag of disadvantage and marginalisation could be removed from the political society. Even after independence, almost all the National Political Parties used SCs, STs and OBCs for their vote-banks and never implemented reservation fully since independence. A huge backlog of vacancies has been created in educational institutions and services for SCs, STs, OBCs and Religion Minorities (RMs) under various political regimes.[149] From the benefits cited since independence it is obvious that reservation is helping by improving socio-economic status reflected in better financial condition and better career options. The reservation policy has open up a number of avenues for social and economic mobility. It has raised the general level of consciousness of the deprived sections by teaching them self-respect and dignity. It has brought the underprivileged section of the society into the mainstream and thereby enlarged the human resource base. It has accelerated the process of rectifying the efforts of historical injustice. But even after six decades of independence reservation policy which is in the Constitution for the underprivileged sections including SCs, STs, OBCs and Religious Minorities (Including Buddhists but excluding Muslims, Sikhs, Christians) not implemented fully by the Nationalist Parties who ruled this country for more than six decades.[150]

The pre and post-strategies are required to take the implementation of reservations are also needed among educationists to suggest ways in which reservation lead to the empowerment of the beneficiaries. A country whose one-quarter of population remains deprived, oppressed and uneducated is a handicapped even though the country engaged with scientific and economic activities. Education is the one means of equality and employment is another way to improve the condition of the under privileged sections of the society.[151]

The basic question comes in mind, why one or we are talking about reservation or correctly representation. The very simple argument is that India is the largest democracy in the world, and working since 1947, but still its people do not have proper representation in the public as well private sectors.[152] (Education, employment, land, industries etc.) Why having such a largest Constitution and largest democracy, people fighting for their basic fundamental rights from each and every corner of the country. The preamble itself starts with the word *Liberty, Equality. Fraternity, Justice, Socialist, Secularism, Democratic, Republic* and so on so forth.[153] the basic point to be focus is that these all talks about the equality, which means equal representation, equal opportunities, equality of justice, equal treatment to all its citizens. Fundamental rights are made to provide the basic rights to all its citizens irrespective of *caste, creed, language, class, religion, tradition, sex* etc, to get basic human dignity. If country like India always talking about democracy and believes in social Justice and its people do not have basic dignity of life, then it is baseless to say that in India democratic institutions are working at all.

Notes

1. State Primary Census Abstract for Individual Scheduled Caste and Scheduled Tribes- 2011.
2. Chunnu Prasad, (2007). Arunachal Pradesh and the Inner-Outer Line Regulation of 1873-1874 of North East Frontier Agency, Third World Impact, Vol. XVIII, No.173, January-March, pp. 15-19.
3. *Ibid.*
4. Constitution of India (http://lawmin.nic.in/coi/coiason29july08.pdf (See more details in The Constitution of India, Government of India, Ministry of Law and Justice).
5. http://allaboutindiageography.wikispaces.com/Caste+ System+by+Hilal

6. The Confusing Caste System, http://adaniel.tripod.com/confusion.htm

7. Joe, Bindloss, 2009. Northeast India, Lonely Planet, Publication Ltd., Delhi, pp. 43-44.

8. *Ibid.*

9. See details in Kumar, Vivek. 2010 b. 'Teaching Caste and the Hindu Social Order: Dalits in Indian Sociology' in Maitrayee Chaudhuri (eds.), Sociology in India: Intellectual and Institutional Practices, New Delhi: Rawat Publications.

10. Constitution of India (http://lawmin.nic.in/coi/coiason29july 08.pdf (See more details in The Constitution of India, Government of India, Ministry of Law and Justice).

11. Yaronsho Ngalung, President, The Morung Erxpress, The Hao Research Initiative.

12. *Ibid.*

13. *Ibid.*

14. Sanjay, Hajarika, Director, Centre for North East Studies, Jamia Millia Islamia University in New Delhi,http://www.mid-day.com/articles/is-india-no-country-for-people-from-north-eastern-states/15081090#sthash.fiJWCrsv.dpuf .

15. Chunnu, Prasad, Naxalism Fighting for what: "Question of Exclusion, Dignity and Livelihood", in an edited book by Pradeep Basu in Discourse on Naxalite Movement (1967-2009); Insights into Radical Left Politics, Setu Prakasan, Kolkatta, 2010, pp. 238-251.

16. Chunnu Prasad, 2012. Conceptualising Migration in the Era of Globalisation: A Brief Overview of the problems and Challenges in an edited book by Hokip in Indian Politics: Problems, Issues and Challenges, New wave, New Delhi, pp. 1-16.

17. *Ibid.*, pp. 1-16.

18. Romila Thapar, The Aryan Question Revisited Transcript of lecture delivered on 11th October 1999, at the Academic Staff College, JNU (http://ascjnu.tripod.com/aryan.html). Also see details in Romila Thapar, 2008, The Aryan: Recasting Constructs, Penguin, New Delhi.

19. http://www.mid-day.com/articles/is-india-no-country-for-people-from-north-eastern-states/15081090#sthash.fiJWCrsv.dpuf

20. Surinder S. Jodhka and Tanvi Sirari, 2012. In the Footsteps of Ambedkar: Mobility, Identity and Dalit Initiatives for Change Mobility, Indian Institute of Dalit Studies, New Delhi, pp. 2-39.

21. Chunnu Prasad, 2012. Exclusion of Excluded Dalits in Nepal: A Case of Hill, Madhesi and Terai Region", in an edited book by B.C. Upreti and Uddhab Pd. Pyakurel in Contemporary Nepal: Reflections on Emerging Political and Social Issues and Trends, Kalinga Publications, New Delhi, pp. 81-90.
22. See details in Dipankar Gupta, Interrogating Caste: Understanding Hierarchy and Difference in Indian Society, Penguin Books, New Delhi, 2000.
23. Ann, Nevil, 2007. Amartya K. Sen and Social Exclusion, Development in Practice, Volume. 17, Number. 2, pp. 249-255.
24. De Haan, Arjan, 1998, Social Exclusion: An Alternative for the Study of Deprivation?, IDS, Bulletin 29 (1), pp. 10-19
25. Amartya K. Sen, Social Exclusion, Development in Practice, Vol. II, No. 2, pp. 249-253.
26. *Ibid.*
27. Amartya Sen, Social exclusion: Concept, application, and scrutiny, Harvard University Social Development Papers No. 1, Office of Environment and Social Development Asian Development Bank June 2000.
28. *Ibid.*
29. B.R. Ambedkar: Writing and Speeches, Vol. 9, p. 168, Lokhande. G. S., B.R. Ambedkar: A Study in Social Democracy p. 23
30. T.B. Bottmore, 1994. Elites and society, C.A.Watta and Co., Ltd. London, p. 122.
31. J.J.Rousseau, A Dissertation on the origin and foundation of the inequality of mankind, (everyman's edition) quated in T.B. Bottmore, p. 122.
32. Sharma, B.B.V and Reddy, K. Madhusudan (ed.) 1982. Reservation Policy in India, Light and Life Publishers, New Delhi, p. 62.
33. Constitution of India (http://lawmin.nic.in/coi/coiason29july08.pdf (See more details in The Constitution of India, Government of India, Ministry of Law and Justice)
34. *Ibid.*, p. 122.
35. Dr B.R.Ambedkar's address to the constituent assembly, November 25, 1949. Sharma, B.A.V and Reddy K.Madusudha, op., cit., p.227.
36. Rural Development Statistics Scheduled Castes and Scheduled Tribes, GOI, NSSO, Primary data (2009-10).
37. *Ibid.*
38. Sundaram, K. and S. Tendulkar, 2003. "Poverty among social and economic groups in India in 1990s," Economic and Political Weekly

38(50), pp. 5263-5276. Also see in details Arvind, Panagariya and Vishal More, Poverty by Social, Religious and Economic Groups in India and Its Largest States 1993-94 to 2011-12, Working Paper No. 2013-02, SIPA (School of International and Public Affairs ISERP), Institute for Social and Economic Research and Policy, Programme of Indian Economic Policies, Colombia University, p. 7.

39. A.R Desai, 1990. Social Background of Indian Nationalism, Popular Prakeshan, Bombay, p. 243.

40. *Ibid.*

41. J.J. Hutson, 1951. Caste in India: Its Nature, Function and Organisation, OUP, p. 56.

42. The Constitution of India, Government of India, Ministry of law and Justice (Article related to reservation and welfare for weaker section of the society).

43. Satyanarayana P, Reservation and Attitudes of Political Parties in (ed.) Sharma, B.A.V and Reddy, K. Madhusudan (1982) Reservation Policy in India, Light and Life Publilishers, New Delhi, p. 122.

44. Ravindar Kumar, 1985. Gandhi, Ambedkar and the Poona Pact, XX Occasional Papers in History and the Society, Nehru Memorial Museum and Library, New Delhi: Mimeo.

45. Dr B.R. Ambedkar (1945), What Gandhi and Congress have done to Untouchables, Bombay: Thacker abd Co., p. 85.

46. *Ibid.*, p. 71.

47. B.R. Ambedkar, 1943. Mr.Gandhi and the Emancipation of the Untouchables, Jullundhar: Bheem Patrika Publication, pp. 30-31.

48. Dr B.R. Ambedkar, 1945. What Gandhi and Congress have done to Untouchables, Bombay: Thacker abd Co., p. 87.

49. Dr Bhimrao R. Ambedkar, Dr Ambedkar with the Simon Commission (Indian Statutory Commission) STATEMENT "C", concerning the safeguards for the protection of the interests of the Depressed Classes as a minority in the Bombay Presidency and the changes in the composition of and the guarantees from the Bombay Legislative Council necessary to ensure the same under Provincial Autonomy, on behalf of the Bahishkrita Hitakarini Sabha (Depressed Classes Institute of Bombay) to the Indian Statutory Commission 29th May 192 Damodar Hall Parel, Bombay-12 India. (http://www.ambedkar.org/ambcd/14C.%20 Dr%20Ambedkar%20with%20the% 20Simon%20Commission% 20C. htm)

50. Publications Division, Government of India, Constitutent Assembly Debates Vol. VII, p. 33-37 and 42-43.
51. Moon Vasant (ed.) (1979), Writings and Speeches of Dr Ambedkar, Bombay: Education Department, Government of Maharastra, Vol.13, XXVI.
52. Dr B.R. Ambedkar 1945. What Gandhi and Congress have done to Untouchables, Bombay: Thacker abd Co., p.85.
53. Sanharanand, Shastri, My Memories and Experiences of Babasaheb Dr Ambedkar, Ch-15, Gaziabad: New Rajnagar Publication, pp. 163-165.
54. Meesaalati, Chaluvali, 1998. Isthihaasa Mattu Bhavishya (Reservation Movement, History and Future) Collected Action of Essays, Ed. By Krishnamurthy Chamaram, President, BVS, Mysore: Justice Publication, No. 46, p. 31.
55. See details in http://www.mulnivasibahujanbharat.org/PDF/Mulnivasi%20Bahujan%20Bharat%20-%20Apr-2006.pdf and http://www.old.bamcef.org/, http://www.ambedkartimes.com/Bamcef. htm
56. *Ibid.*
57. Upendra Baxi, 1984. Legislative Reservation for Social Justice: Some Thoughts on India's Unique Experiment, in R.B. Goldman and J.Wilson, (ed.), Independence to Statehood: Managing Ethnic Conflict: Five African and Asian States, London: H Pinter, pp. 221-223.
58. See details in Omvedt, Gail, Ambedkar: Towards an Enlightened India, Publishers: Penguin Books India, 2004, See more https://babasahebambedkar.wordpress.com/2010/11/16/how-dr-ambedkar-enter-constitution-assembly/,http://lawandothe rthings. blogspot.in/2009/05/yesterday-at-election-rally-in-new.html
59. The Constitution of India, Ministry of law and Justice (Article 340 related to OBC reservation and their welfare).
60. Ambedkar, B.R. 97, 100, and Communal Award (1932) 117–18, and Gandhi 129–30 http://www.ambedkar.org/bamcef/journal/aug02/comaward.html, https://sites.google.com/site/cabinetm ission plan/b-r-ambedkar-on-communal-representation-1909-1947
61. Christophe Jaffrelot, 2009. Dr Ambedkar's Strategies Against Untouchability and the Caste System, Indian Institute of Dalit Studies, Volume III, No. 04, New Delhi, pp. 2-16.
62. See details in Ghanshyam Shah, 1975. Politics of the Scheduled Castes and Scheduled Tribes, Vora and Co. Publishers, Bombay.

63. Sandanshiv, D.N. Reservations for social Justice – A Socio-Constitutional Approach, Current Law Publishers, Bombay – 6.1986, Galarter Mare, Untouchability and the Law – The Untouchables in Contemporary India and The Constitution of India, Government of India, Ministry of law and Justice (Article related to reservation and welfare for weaker section of the society).

64. P. Sampath, 2010. Experiences of Struggles Against Untouchability in Tamilnadu, The Marxist, XXVI 1, January–March, p. 45.

65. Rajandar Sachar, Reservation for Dalits in Private Sector, National Seminar on Reservation in Private Sectors: Prospects and MoDalities, Aug 4-5, 2005 in Dr Babasaheb Ambedkar National Institute of Social Sciences, Mhow, p. 42.

66. Prakash, Louis, 2007. Caste-Based Discrimination and Atrocities on Dalit Christians and the Need for Reservations, Working Paper Series, Indian Institute of Dalit Studies, Vol. II, No. 04, New Delhi, p. 5

67. Ministry of Personal, Public Grievances and Petition (1997), Overview of Reservation Policy, National Seminar on Reservation in Private Sectors: Prospects and MoDalities, Aug 4-5, 2005 in Dr Babasaheb Ambedkar National Institute of Social Sciences, Mhow, p. 17.

68. See Kaka Kalelkar Commission Report Submitted to the Government of India on OBC, 1955.

69. The Constitution of India, Government of India, Ministry of law and Justice, (Article-340 related to reservation and welfare for Other Backward Class.

70. *Ibid.*

71. Sukhadeo Thorat and Chitranjan Senapati, 2006, Reservation Policy in India-Dimensions and Issues, Indian Institute of Dalit Studies, Working Paper Series, Vol. 1, No. 2, New Delhi, p. 10.

72. See B.P.Mandal Commission Report Submitted to The Government of India on OBC, 1990.

73. http://shodhganga.inflibnet.ac.in/bitstream/10603/1869/14/15_appendix.pdf

74. http://www.simplydecoded.com/wp-content/uploads/2013/01/Mandal-commission-report.pdf

75. Sunil Guha, 1994. Towards Industrial Dynamism and Harmony, Oxford and IBH Publishing Co. Pvt. Ltd., p. 65.

76. Ruddar Dut, K.P.M. Sundharam, 2009. Indian Economy, S. Chand and Company Ltd., New Delhi, p. 226 and Planning Commission,

Second Five Year Plan (1956), Government of India Publication, New Delhi, p. 29.

77. Public Enterprises Survey, Government of India, Vol, I, New Delhi, 2007, p. 48.
78. Public Enterprises Survey n-p. 12 and Public Enterprises Survey, 2009-10 p. 18.
79. Chanana, Karuna, 1992. Accessing Higher Education: the Dilemma of Schooling Women, Minorities, Scheduled Castes and Scheduled Tribes in Contemporary India, Higher Education p. 62.
80. D. V. Rao and Dr P. Lakshmi, 2011, Legal Aspect of Caste Census, Mulnivasi Organiser, New Delhi
81. See details in http://assam.gov.in/
82. The Aryan Hindu Assamese are the people who migrated long back from other parts of India to the land of Asssam and captured land and other resources, married local Assamese tribals and considered as the insiders or the original inhabitants of Assam.
83. See details in http://assam.gov.in/
84. http://www.census2011.co.in/census/state/assam.html
85. Office of the Registrar General of India, 2011 Census of India, Government of India
86. State primary census abstract for individual scheduled castes-2011, Census of India, 2011, Government of India.
87. See details in http://arunachalpradesh.gov.in/
88. Chunnu, Prasad, The Philosophy of Buddhism: Basis of its Existence, in an edited book by P. Chenna Reddy, E. Shiva Nagi Reddy in Bodhisiri, Research India Press, New Delhi, 2014, pp. 152-161.
89. Chunnu Prasad, Traditional Knowledge and Sustainable Agriculture: A Study of Apatani Tribes in Arunachal Pradesh, National Conference on 26th to 28th December, 2008 by Head Department of Anthropology, University of Delhi, Delhi
90. See details in http://arunachalpradesh.gov.in/
91. Chunnu, Prasad, 2006. "Arunachal Pradesh Denies the Rights to Scheduled Caste in the State", Radical Humanist, Vol. 433, April: 33-34.
92. Chunnu Prasad, 2007. Natural Resource Management and Sustainable Development: A Study in Arunachal Pradesh, Social Action, Vol. 58, April-June, pp. 200-207.
93. Chunnu Prasad, 2007. Arunachal Pradesh and the Inner-Outer Line Regulation of 1873-1874 of North East Frontier Agency,

Third World Impact, Vol. XVIII, No. 173, January-March, p. 15-19.

94. N. Osik, 1999. Modern history of Arunachal Pradesh-1825 to 1997, Himalayan Publication, Itanagar, pp. 57-62. See details in http://arunachalpradesh.gov.in/

95. *Ibid.*

96. *Ibid.*

97. Chunnu Prasad 2007. Natural Resource Management and Sustainable Development: A Study in Arunachal Pradesh, *op. cit.*, pp. 200-207.

98. See books S. K. Singh, People of India: Arunachal Pradesh and articles by S. Dutta, Deepak K.Singh and Chunnu Prasad on the issue related to the Chakmas and Hajongs of Arunachal Pradesh in detail.

99. See SC/ST Modification order 1956 and inserted by Act 69 of 1986, Also see the Scheduled Caste Population of Arunachal Pradesh, 2001.

100. Chunnu Prasad, 2007. Natural Resource Management and Sustainable Development: A Study in Arunachal Pradesh, op. cit., pp. 200-207.

101. Chunnu Prasad, 2008. Chakma Refugees in Arunachal Pradesh: Question of Identity and Citizenship, Eastern Anthropologist, Vol. 61, No. 1, January-March, pp. 95-104.

102. *Ibid.*

103. Chunnu Prasad 2007. Student Movement in Arunachal Pradesh: A Case of Chakma-Hajong Refugee Problem, Economic and Political Weekly, Vol. XLII, No.15, April 14-20, pp. 1373-1379.

104. http://www.census2011.co.in/census/state/arunachal.html

105. The recent census 2001, by the Government of India on Arunachal Pradesh produced the 60:40 proportion of population (60 per cent belongs to Tribal and 40 per cent belongs to Non Tribals) which is not at all a problem, but the most shocking part is the Scheduled Caste population in the state. According to the 2001 census Arunachal Pradesh which included in the 6th Scheduled in the Indian Constitution have total 6,188 SC Population out of which 3590 are males and 2598 are females and these populations denies their rights of representation in the state. The rights like right to get trading license in their own name to do business, right to job in the government sectors and other basic rights.

106. See detail information of the Office of the Registrar General, India about the Scheduled Caste Population of Arunachal Pradesh, 2001.

107. *Ibid.*

108. *Ibid.*

109. *Ibid.*

110. Fifth Schedule (Article 244(1)) – This provides for the administration and control of Scheduled Areas and Scheduled Tribes (areas and tribes needing special protection due to disadvantageous conditions). Sixth Schedule (Articles 244(2) and 275(1))— Provisions for the administration of tribal areas in Assam, Meghalaya, Tripura, and Mizoram.

111. Chunnu, Prasad (2007), Arunachal Pradesh and the Inner-Outer Line Regulation of 1873-1874 of North East Frontier Agency, op. cit., pp. 15-19.

112. See book by Nimmi, Hutnic (1991), Ethnic Minority Identity, Clarendon Press, Oxford on melting pot theory.

113. Chunnu Prasad, 2006. Radical Humanist, Vol. 433, May, pp. 33-34.

114. Hundred per cent equity ownership of an industrial unit by entrepreneurs allowed for a maximum period of thirty years by the end of which period such equity holding reduced to forty nine per cent, the remaining fifty one per cent held by a local Arunachal Tribal entrepreneur or a group of local tribal entrepreneurs or the state government, if it considers necessary to do so. Outside entrepreneurs allow holding land on lease for a period of thirty years, after which the lease renewed for a further period of thirty days and the consideration for the lease in the form of annual or lump sum payments or as equity. (The lease used as security for loans from financial institutions.) Development of all industries encouraged. Industries based on locally available raw materials, Textiles (handlooms and power looms) and handicrafts, Electronics and knowledge based industries, Industries based on non- timber forest produce and etc.

115. Information published by the State Information department, Government of Arunachal Pradesh on the political economy of the state.

116. *Ibid.*

117. Dr Bhim Raoramaji Ambedkar, who fought, sacrificed and worked for both the Scheduled Castes and Scheduled Tribes of India and made various Constitutional provisions to protect the rights of

these populations to minimise the gap of injustice, discrimination, exclusion which has been done centuries over centuries. Being Scheduled tribes dominated state, Arunachal Pradesh discriminating and excluding Scheduled Castes from getting all opportunities.

118. See details in http://manipur.gov.in/
119. http://www.census2011.co.in/census/state/manipur.html
120. *Ibid.*
121. Source: Office of the Registrar General, India, 2011.
122. *Ibid.*
123. Source: Office of the Registrar General, India
124. See details in http://meghalaya.gov.in:8080/megportal/
125. http://www.census2011.co.in/census/state/meghalaya.html
126 Source: Office of the Registrar General, India, http://censusindia.gov.in/
127. *Ibid.*
128. *Ibid.*
129. See details in *www.mizoram.gov.in/*
130. http://www.census2011.co.in/census/state/mizoram.html
131. See details in http://nagaland.nic.in/
132. http://www.census2011.co.in/census/state/nagaland.html
133. *Ibid.*
134. http://www.morungexpress.com/weekly_poll_result/17223.html
135. See details in https://www.sikkim.gov.in/portal
136. http://www.census2011.co.in/census/state/sikkim.html
137. *Ibid.*
138. *Ibid.*
139. *Ibid.*
140. Office of the Registrar General, India.
141. Source: Office of the Registrar General, India.
142. *Ibid.*
143. See details in http://tripura.gov.in/
144. http://www.census2011.co.in/census/state/tripura.html
145. See details in http://tripura.gov.in/
146. See details in http://tripura.gov.in/

147. *Ibid.*

148. *Ibid.*

149. http://karnmk.blogspot.in/2014/08/backlog-of-vacancies-for.html

150. For more details see Arun R. Swamy, Hindu Nationalism-What Religion Got to Do With it?, Asia Pasific Centre for Security Studies, March-2003, pp. 1-17.

151. Chunnu Prasad, 2009. "Dalits Struggle for Democratic Space: Bahujan Samaj Party and the Democratisation of Indian Politics", in an edited book by Vivek Kumar, G. Stanley, Jaya Kumar and Tenepali Hari in The Dynamics of Change and Community in the Era of Globalisation: Voices of the Margins, Sunrise Publication, New Delhi, pp. 336-367.

152. Sukhadeo Thorat, Prasant Negi and Aryama, 2006. Reservation in the Private Sector-Issues, Concerns and Prospects, Indian Institute of Dalit Studies, Working Paper Series, Vol. 1, No. 1, New Delhi, pp. 2-52.

153. See Preamble of the Constitution of India (http://lawmin.nic.in/coi/coiason29july08.pdf (See more details in The Constitution of India, Government of India, Ministry of Law and Justice).

4

Safeguards through Constitution: Theory to Practice

The whole debate on rights is about social justice. Social justice is a concept that has fascinated philosophers ever since Plato in *"The Republic"* formalised the argument that an ideal state would rest on four virtues *wisdom, courage, moderation* and *justice*.[1] The addition of the word social is to clearly distinguish Social Justice from the concept of Justice as applied in the law-state-administered systems, which label behaviour as unacceptable and enforce a formal mechanism of control. It may produce results that do not match the philosophical definitions of social justice - and from more informal concepts of justice embedded in systems of public policy and morality.[2] This may differ from culture to culture and therefore lack universality. Social justice is also used to refer to the overall fairness of a society in its divisions and distributions of rewards and burdens and, as such, the phrase has been adopted by political parties with a redistributive agenda.[3] Social Justice derives its authority from the codes of morality prevailing in each culture.[4]

By gathering together into bands and communities, humans seek to gain strength and to address their vulnerabilities which, in turn, create the potential to develop into more complex and evolving civilisations. If simple survival is to be transformed into long-term security, something more than co-ordinating the contribution of everyone's skills will be required. A social organisation will be needed to resolve disputes and offer physical security against attack. The achievement of community aims will depend upon the co-ordination of many functional specialisations (such as farmers for food, soldiers for protection and rulers for resource management) and a willingness of community members to sacrifice some personal freedom for the greater good. So, would defining or administering justice become one of these specialisations and, as such, be the exclusive responsibility of any one class of citizens? People will not accept the surrender of any of their freedoms unless they perceive real benefits flowing from their decisions. The key factor is likely to be the emergence of a consensus that the society is working in a fair way, i.e., both that individuals are allowed as much freedom as possible given the role they have within the society and that the rewards compensate adequately for any loss of freedom. Hence, true social justice is attained only through the harmonious co-operative effort of the citizens who, in their own self-interest, accept the current norms of morality as the price of membership in the community.[5]

The next major impetus for the development of the concept came from Christianity. Thomas Aquinas (1225-1274) says,

> *"Justice is certain rectitude of mind whereby a man does what he ought to do in the circumstances confronting him".*[6]

As a theologian, Aquinas believed that justice is a form of natural duty owed by one person to another and not enforced by any human-made law.[7] This reflects the Christian view that, before god, all people are equal and must treat each other with respect. Hence, the framework of the argument shifts to require obedience to natural principles of morality to satisfy a duty owed to god, and the outcome of social justice is driven by the tenets of morality embedded in the religion.[8]

John Locke (1632-1704), an early theologist utilitarian argued that people have innate natural goodness and beauty, and so, in the long run, if individuals rationally pursue their private happiness and pleasure, the interests of the society or the general welfare will be looked after fairly. Locke characterised most of Christianity as utilitarian since believers see utility in rewards in the afterlife for their actions on earth.[9]

Immanuel Kant (1724-1804) on the other hand, believs that actions are morally right if they are motivated by duty without regard to any personal goal, desire, motive, or self-interest. Kant's moral theory is, therefore, deontological and based on the concept of abject selflessness. In his view, the only relevant feature of moral law is its universalisability.[10]

In the latter part of the twentieth century, the concept of social justice has largely been associated with the political philosopher John Rawls (1921-2002) who draws on the utilitarian insights of Bentham and Mill, the social contract ideas of Locke, and the categorical imperative ideas of Kant.[11] His first statement of principle was made in *A Theory of Justice* (1971) where he proposed that,

"Each person possesses an inviolability founded on justice that even the welfare of society as a whole cannot override. For this reason justice denies that the loss of freedom for some is made right by a greater good shared by others".

His views are definitively restated in Political Liberalism (1993), where society is seen, "as a fair system of co-operation over time, from one generation to the next". All societies have a basic structure of social, economic, and political institutions, both formal and informal. In testing how well these elements fit and work together, Rawls based a key test of legitimacy on the theories of social contract. To determine whether any particular system of collectively enforced social arrangements is legitimate he argued that one must look for agreement by the people who are subject to it. Obviously, not every citizen can be asked to participate in a poll to determine his or her consent to every proposal in which some degree of coercion is involved, so we have to assume that all citizens are reasonable. Rawls constructed an argument for a two-stage process to determine a citizen's hypothetical agreement:[12]

- the citizen agrees to be represented by X for certain purposes; to that extent, X holds these powers as a trustee for the citizen;
- X agrees that a use of enforcement in a particular social context is legitimate; the citizen, therefore, is bound by this decision because it is the function of the trustee to represent the citizen in this way.

This applies to one person representing a small group (e.g. to the organiser of a social event setting a dress code) as equally as it does to national governments which are the ultimate trustees, holding representative powers for the benefit of all citizens within their territorial boundaries, and if those governments fail to provide for the welfare of their citizens according to the principles of justice, they are not legitimate. To emphasise the general principle that justice should rise from the people and not be dictated by the law-making powers of governments, Rawls asserted that,

> *"There is a general presumption against imposing legal and other restrictions on conduct without sufficient reason. But this presumption creates no special priority for any particular liberty".*[13]

This is support for an unranked set of liberties that reasonable citizens in all states should respect and uphold - to some extent, the list proposed by Rawls matches the normative human rights that have international recognition and direct enforcement in some nation states where the citizens need encouragement to act in a more objectively just way. Social justice as conceived by Rawls is an apolitical philosophical concept.[14] The concept of social justice may hold some or all of the following beliefs:

- Historical inequities insofar as they affect current injustices should be corrected until the actual inequities no longer exist or have been perceptively "negated".
- The redistribution of wealth, power and status for the individual, community and societal good.
- It is government's (or those who hold significant power) responsibility to ensure a basic quality of life for all its citizens.

According to the advocates of equal opportunity all citizens should get equal social and political benefits. On the other hand the proponents of special opportunity demand that protective discrimination policy should be used for certain sections of the society. This policy is meant to provide certain benefits and special opportunities to the weaker sections of the society.[15] Justice is action in accordance with the requirements of some law. Whether these rules are grounded in human consensus or societal norms, they are supposed to ensure that all members of society receive fair treatment. Issues of justice arise in several different spheres and play a significant role in causing, perpetuating, and addressing conflict. Just institutions tend to instill a sense of stability, well-being, and satisfaction among society members, while perceived injustices can lead to dissatisfaction, rebellion, or revolution. Each of the different spheres expresses the principles of justice in its own way, resulting in different types and concepts of justice: *distributive, procedural, retributive, and restorative.* These types of justice have important implications for socio-economic, political, civil, and criminal justice at both the national and international level.[16]

Distributive, or economic justice, is concerned with giving all members of society a "fair share" of the benefits and resources available. However, while everyone might agree that wealth should be distributed fairly, there is much disagreement about what counts as a "fair share". Some possible criteria of distribution are equity, equality, and need. Procedural, is concerned with making and implementing decisions according to fair processes that ensure "fair treatment". Rules must be impartially followed and consistently applied in order to generate an unbiased decision. Those carrying out the procedures should be neutral, and those directly affected by the decisions should have some voice or representation in the decision-making process.[17]

Retributive appeals to the notion that people deserve to be treated in the same way they treat others. It is a retroactive approach that justifies punishment as a response to past injustice or wrong doing. The central idea is that the offender has gained unfair advantages through his or her behaviour, and that punishment will set this imbalance straight. However, because there is a tendency to slip from retributive justice to an emphasis on revenge, some suggest that restorative justice processes are more effective. While a retributive justice approach conceives of transgressions as crimes against the state or nation, restorative justice focuses on violations as crimes against individuals. It is concerned with healing victim's wounds, restoring offenders to law-abiding lives, and repairing harm done to interpersonal relationships and the community.[18]

The Indian Constitution provides a detailed insight into the entire government structure, basic rights and duties of the citizen and special provisions relating to certain classes are included in Part XVI (16). From Article 330 to Article 342, the special provisions have been clearly indicated in the Constitution for Scheduled Castes and Scheduled Tribes of India.[19]

As we know Dr B.R. Ambedkar drafted most of the parts of the constitution. He deeply studied the possible need of all the sections of the society and brought inclusive policies and provisions for certain sections of the society who has been denied basic rights to recognise as human beings and live with dignity. In the Constitution of India, the Preamble (as amended in 1976) declares the State to be "Secular", and this is of special relevance for the religious minorities. Equally relevant for them, especially, is the prefatory declaration of the Constitution in its Preamble that all citizens of India are to be secured liberty of thought, expression, belief, faith and worship and equality of status and of opportunity.[20]

The Constitution of India has provided two types of safeguards—general and specific to safeguard various interests of the minorities. In the first category are those provisions that are equally enjoyed by both groups. The provisions ensure justice-social, economic and political equality to all. The second category consists of provisions meant specifically for the protection of particular interests of minorities.[21]

1. People's right to equality before the law and equal protection of the laws;
2. Prohibition of discrimination against citizens on grounds of religion, race, caste, sex or place of birth;
3. Authority of State to make any special provision for the advancement of any socially and educationally backward classes of citizen (besides the Scheduled Castes and Scheduled Tribes);
4. Citizens' right to equality of opportunity in matters relating to employment or appointment to any office under the State - and prohibition in this regard of discrimination on grounds of religion, race, caste, sex or place of birth;
5. Authority of State to make any provision for the reservation of appointments or posts in favour of any backward class of citizens which, in the opinion of the State, is not adequately represented in the services under the State;

6. People's freedom of conscience and right to freely profess, practice and propagate religion - subject to public order, morality and other Fundamental Rights;
7. Authority of State to make law for regulating or restricting any economic financial, political or other secular activity which may be associated with religious practice, and for providing for social welfare and reform;
8. Authority of State to make laws for throwing open of Hindu, Sikh, Jain or Buddhist religious institutions of a public character to all classes and sections of the respective communities;
9. Sikh community's right of wearing and carrying of *kirpans;*
10. Right of every religious denomination or any section thereof - subject to public order, morality and health - to establish and maintain institutions for religious and charitable proposes, manage its own affairs of religion, and own and acquire movable immovable property and administer it in accordance with law;
11. People's freedom as to payment of taxes for promotion of any particular religion;
12. People's freedom as to attendance at religious instruction or religious worship in educational institutions wholly maintained, recognised, or aided by the State;
13. Right of any section of the citizens to conserve its distinct language, script or culture;
14. Restriction on denial of admission to any citizen, to any educational institution maintained or aided by the State, on grounds only of religion, race, caste, language or any of them;
15. Right of all Religious and Linguistic Minorities to establish and administer educational institutions of their choice; and
16. Freedom of Minority-managed educational institutions from discrimination in the matter of receiving aid from the State.

Part IV of the Constitution of India, containing non-justifiable Directive Principles of State Policy, includes the following provisions having significant implications for the Minorities:[22]

1. Obligation of the State to endeavor to eliminate inequalities in status, facilities and opportunities amongst individuals and groups of people residing in different areas or engaged in different vocations;
2. Obligation of State to endeavor to secure for the citizens a uniform civil code throughout the territory of India;
3. Obligation of State to promote with special care the educational and economic interests of "the weaker sections of the people" (besides Scheduled Castes and Scheduled Tribes); and
4. Obligation of State to take steps for prohibiting the slaughter of cows and calves and other milch and draught cattle.

Part IV-A of the Constitution, relating to Fundamental Duties, applies in full to all citizens, including those belonging to Minorities and of special relevance for the Minorities are the following provisions in this Part:[23]

1. Citizens' duty to promote harmony and the spirit of common brotherhood amongst all the people of India transcending religious, linguistic and regional or sectional diversities; and
2. Citizens' duty to value and preserve the rich heritage of our composite culture.

Some other provisions of the Constitution having special relevance and implications for the Minorities are:[24]

1. Official obligation to pay out of the consolidated funds of the States of Kerala and Tamil Nadu 46.5 and 13.5 lakh rupees respectively to the local Dewasom Funds for the maintenance of Hindu temples and shrines in the territories of the erstwhile State of Travancore-Cochin;
2. Special provision relating to the language spoken by a section of the population of any State;
3. Provision for facilities for instruction in mother-tongue at primary stage;
4. Provision for a Special Officer for Linguistic Minorities and his duties;
5. Special provision with respect to Naga religious or social practices, customary law and procedure, and administration

of civil and criminal justice involving decisions according to Naga customary law;

6. Identical special provision for the Mizos; and
7. Provision relating to continuation in force of pre-Constitution laws until altered or repealed or amended by a competent legislature or other competent authority.

Part III of the Constitution gives certain fundamental rights. Some of these rights are common to all the citizens of India including minorities. These rights are enshrined in the discriminations suffered by the oppressed sections of the society including SC's and ST's over great period of time has led to the concept of protective discrimination to safeguard their interests. The main reason behind protective discrimination is to provide the necessary facilities to the deprived sections and to bring them to the mainstream society. These two classes were placed beyond the bounds of the larger society, the scheduled tribes on account of their isolation in particular ecological riches and the scheduled castes on account of the segregation imposed on them by the rules of pollution.[25]

There are certain clauses in the Constitution which aims at providing equality of opportunity to all by prohibiting discrimination and to remove disparities between privileged and underprivileged classes. However, the state faced with the dilemma that this would mean that in the society characterised by the distinctions on the basis of caste, religion only who are better positioned than the rest would get all the benefits and the backward and depressed classes will remain sidelined. In order to overcome this, state has the special responsibility of giving equal rights to the communities through protective discrimination. There are many provisions in the Constitution:[26]

Article 14: This ensures equality before law and equal protection of law.

Article 15: This prohibits discrimination on any ground i.e. religion, race, caste, sex, place of birth.[27]

(1) The State shall not discriminate against any citizen on grounds only of religion, race, caste, sex, place of birth or any of them.

(2) No citizen shall, on grounds only of religion, race, caste,

sex, place of birth or any of them, be subject to any disability, liability, restriction or condition with regard to-

(a) access to shops, public restaurants, hotels and places of public entertainment; or

(b) the use of wells, tanks, bathing ghats, roads and places of public resort maintained wholly or partly out of State funds or dedicated to the use of the general public.

(3) Nothing in this article shall prevent the State from making any special provision for women and children.

(4) Nothing in this article or in clause (2) of Article 29 shall prevent the State from making any special provision for the advancement of any socially and educationally backward classes of citizens or for the Scheduled Castes and the Scheduled Tribes.

Article 16(2): No citizen shall, on grounds only of religion, race, caste, sex, decent, place of birth, residence, or any of them be ineligible for, or discriminate against in respect of, any employment or office under the state.

Article 16(4): Nothing in this article shall prevent state from making any provisions for the reservation of appointments or posts in favour of any backward class of citizen which, in the opinion of the state is not adequately represented in the services under the state.

Article 16(4)A: Nothing in this article shall prevent the state from making any provision for reservation in matters of promotion, with consequential seniority, to any class or classes of posts in the service under the state in favour of the scheduled castes and the scheduled tribes, which in the opinion of the state, are not adequately represented in the services under the state.

Article 17: Untouchability is abolished and its practiced in any form is forbidden, the enforcement of any disability arising out of untouchability, shall be an offence punishable in accordance with law.

Article 21: No person shall be deprived of his life or personal liberty except the procedure established by law.

Article 25: This ensures freedom of conscience and the right freely to profess, practice and propagate religion.

Article 26: This ensures a right to manage religious institutions, religious affairs, subject to public order, morality and health.

Article 29: Gives minorities a right to conserve their language, script or culture.

It provides for the protection of the interests of minorities by giving them a right to establish and administer educational institutions of their choice. The State is directed not to discriminate against minorities institutions in granting aid.[28]

Article 46: The state shall promote with special care the educational and economic interest of the weaker sections of the people, and in particular, of the scheduled castes and the scheduled tribes.

Art 164(1): According to this article in states of Bihar, MP and Orissa there shall be a Minister in charge of tribal welfare who may in addition be in charge of the welfare of the scheduled castes and backward classes.

Article 243: Seats shall be reserved for the scheduled castes and scheduled tribes in the panchayats.

Article 243(2): Not less than one-third of the total number of seats reserved under Clause-(1) shall be reserved for women belonging to the scheduled castes and scheduled tribes.

Article 243(3): Not less than one-third (including the number of seats reserved for women belonging to the scheduled castes and scheduled tribes) of the total number of seats to be filled by direct election in every panchayats shall be reserved for women and such seats may be allotted by rotation to different constituencies in a panchayats.

Article 243(4): The offices of the chairpersons in the panchayats at the village or any other level shall be reserved for the scheduled castes and scheduled tribes and women in such a manner as the legislature of the state any by law.

Article 243T: Seats shall be reserved for the scheduled castes and scheduled tribes in every municipality and the number of seats so reserved shall bear, as nearly as may be, the same proportion to the total number of seats to be fulfilled by direct election in the municipality as the population of the scheduled caste in the municipal areas or of the scheduled tribes in the municipal areas bears to the total population of the of that area as such seats may be allotted by rotation to different constituencies in a municipality.

Article 243 T(2): Not less than one–third of the total number of seats reserved under Clause (1) shall be reserved for the women belonging to the scheduled castes and scheduled tribes.

Article 243T(3): Not less than one-third of the (including the number of seats reserved for women belonging to the scheduled castes and scheduled tribes) of the total number of seats to be filled by direct election in every municipality shall be reserved for women and such seats may be allotted by rotating to different constituencies in a municipality.

Art 244(1): Regarding administration of scheduled areas and tribal areas - (1) The provisions of the Fifth Schedule shall apply to the administration and control of the Scheduled areas and Scheduled tribes in any state other than the state of Assam, Meghalaya, Tripura and Mizoram. (2) The provisions of the sixth schedule shall apply to the administration of the tribal areas in the state of Assam, Meghalaya, Tripura and Mizoram.

Art 244(A): Formation of an autonomous state comprising certain tribal areas in Assam and creation of local legislature or Council of Ministers or both thereof. Parliament may by law form within the state of Assam an autonomous state comprising (whether wholly or part) all or any of the tribal areas.

Art 275: Provided that there shall be paid out of consolidated fund of India as grants-in-aid of the revenues of a state such capital and recurring sums as may be necessary to enable the state to meet the costs of such schemes of development as may be undertaken by the state with the approval of the Government of India for the purpose of promoting the welfare of the scheduled tribes in that state or raising the level of administration of the scheduled areas therein to that of the administration of the rest of the areas in that state. Further provided that there shall be paid out of the Consolidated Fund of India as grant-in-aid of the revenues of the state of Assam sum capital and recurring.[29]

Article 330: Reservation of seats for the scheduled castes and scheduled tribes in the House of People;

(a) Seats shall be reserved for scheduled castes.

(b) The scheduled tribes except the scheduled tribes except the scheduled tribes in the autonomous districts of Assam.

(c) The scheduled tribes in the autonomous districts in Assam.

Article 330(2): The number of seats reserved in any state or Union territory for the scheduled castes and scheduled tribes under clause-(1) shall bear, as nearly as many be the same proportion of the total number of seats allotted to that states or union territory in the House of the People as the population of the scheduled castes in the states or union territory of the scheduled tribes in the state or union territory or part of the state or union territory, as the case may be in respect of which seats are so reserved, bears to the total population of the state or union territory.

Article 332: Reservation of seats for Scheduled Castes and Scheduled Tribes in the Legislative Assemblies of the States;

(a) (1) Seats shall be reserved for the Scheduled Castes and the Scheduled Tribes, except the Scheduled Tribes in the autonomous districts of Assam, in the Legislative Assembly of every State.

(b) (2) Seats shall be reserved also for the autonomous districts in the Legislative Assembly of the State of Assam.

(c) (3) The number of seats reserved for the Scheduled Castes or the Scheduled Tribes in the Legislative Assembly of any State under Clause-(1) shall bear, as nearly as may be, the same proportion to the total number of seats in the Assembly as the population of the Scheduled Castes in the State or of the Scheduled Tribes in the State or part of the State, as the case may be, in respect of which seats are so reserved, bears to the total population of the State.

(d) (3A) Notwithstanding anything contained in Clause-(3), until the taking effect, under Article 170, of the readjustment, on the basis of the first census after the year 2000, of the number of seats in the Legislative Assemblies of the States of Arunachal Pradesh, Meghalaya, Mizoram and Nagaland, the seats which shall be reserved for the Scheduled Tribes in the Legislative Assembly of any such State shall be,

(e) (a) if all the seats in the Legislative Assembly of such State in existence on the date of coming into force of the Constitution (Fifty-seventh Amendment) Act, 1987 (hereafter in this clause referred to as the existing Assembly) are held by members of the Scheduled Tribes, all the seats except one;

(f) (b) in any other case, such number of seats as bears to the total number of seats, a proportion not less than the number (as on the said date) of members belonging to the Scheduled Tribes in the existing Assembly bears to the total number of seats in the existing Assembly.

(g) (3B) Notwithstanding anything contained in clause-(3), until the re-adjustment, under article 170, takes effect on the basis of the first census after the year 2000, of the number of seats in the Legislative Assembly of the State of Tripura, the seats which shall be reserved for the Scheduled Tribes in the Legislative Assembly shall be, such number of seats as bears to the total number of seats, a proportion not less than the number, as on the date of coming into force of the Constitution (Seventy-second Amendment) Act, 1992, of members belonging to the Scheduled Tribes in the Legislative Assembly in existence on the said date bears to the total number of seats in that Assembly.

(h) (4) The number of seats reserved for an autonomous district in the Legislative Assembly of the State of Assam shall bear to the total number of seats in that Assembly a proportion not less than the population of the district bears to the total population of the State.

(i) (5) The constituencies for the seats reserved for any autonomous district of Assam shall not comprise any area outside that district.

(j) (6) No person who is not a member of a Scheduled Tribe of any autonomous district of the State of Assam shall be eligible for election to the Legislative Assembly of the State from any constituency of that district.

Article 334: Reservation of seats and special representation to cease after sixty years, notwithstanding anything in the forgoing provisions of this part, the provision of the Constitution related to:

Article 334a: The reservation of seats for the scheduled castes and scheduled tribes in the House of the People in the Legislative Assemblies of the states by nomination.

Article 335: Claims of scheduled castes and scheduled tribes to services and posts. The claim of the members of the scheduled castes and scheduled tribes shall be taken into consideration, consistently with the maintenance of efficiency of administration, in the making of appointments to services or posts in connection with the affairs of the Union or of a state:

Provide nothing in this article shall prevent in making of any provision in favour of the member of the scheduled castes and scheduled tribes for relaxation in qualifying marks in any examination or lowering the standards of evaluation, for reservation in matters or promotion to any class or classes of services or posts in connection with the affairs of the Union of a State.

Article 338: There shall be a commission for scheduled castes or known as the National Commission for the Scheduled Castes. Commission looks into the matters of the problems and caste based discrimination against scheduled castes, and work for the safeguards of the scheduled castes.

Article 338A: There shall be a commission for scheduled tribes or known as the National Commission for the Scheduled Tribes. Commission looks into the matters of the problems and caste based discrimination against scheduled tribes, and work for the safeguards of the scheduled tribes.

Article 339: Control of the Union over the administration of Scheduled castes and Scheduled tribes.

Article 340: Appointment of a commission by the President to investigate the conditions of backward classes.

Article 341: Power of the President to specify the castes, races or tribes or posts of or groups within castes, races or tribes as scheduled castes.

Article 341(1): The President may with respect to any state or union territory, and where it is a state, after consultation with the Governor thereof, by public notification, specify the castes, race, or tribes, or part of or groups within castes, races or tribes which shall for the purpose of this Constitution be deemed to be scheduled castes in relation to that state or Union Territory, as the case may be.

Article 341(2): Parliament may by law include in or exclude from the list of scheduled castes specified in a notification issued under clauses (1) any caste, race or tribe or part of or group within any caste, race or tribe, but save as aforesaid a notification issues under the said clauses shall not be varies by any subsequent notification.

Art 342: Power of the President to specify the tribes or tribal communities or parts of or groups within tribes or tribal communities as scheduled tribe.

Article 342(1): The President may with respect to any state or union territory, and where it is a state, after consultation with the Governor thereof, by public notification, specify the tribes, or tribal communities or parts of or groups within tribes or tribal communities which shall for the purpose of this Constitution be deemed to be scheduled castes in relation to that state or Union Territory, as the case may be.

Article 342(2): Parliament may by law include in or exclude from the list of scheduled tribes specified in a notification issued under clauses (1) any caste, race or tribe or part of or group within any tribal community, but save as aforesaid a notification issues under the said clauses shall not be varies by any subsequent notification.

Article 342T(4): The offices of chairpersons in the municipalities shall be reserved for the scheduled castes and scheduled tribes and women in such a manner as the legislature of the state may by law provided

Article 350(A): Directs the State to provide facilities for instruction in the mother tongue at the primary stage of education.

Art 350(B): Special officer for linguistic minorities

Apart from the various provisions made in the Constitution of India the Central and State government made various provisions for the upliftment of the SC, ST and OBC communities to bring them to the mainstream India. No doubt there are political and bureaucratic delays in the policy implementation but still it has made positive support for upliftment.

Despite the constitutional prohibitions and laws, most of the Scheduled Castes and Scheduled Tribes (Prevention of Atrocities) Act of 1989, violence and injustices against untouchables continue today, particularly in rural areas of India. So far caste and Hinduism is concerned it is the two sides of same coin, strongly interrelated and interconnected. One cannot separate caste from Hinduism. Many scholars pointed if caste system detached from Hinduism, it will disappear from this universe.[30] India no doubt is the country of unreal representation practically, but constitutionally it talks of equality and protective representation. When we talk of India, it is one of the worse nation-state on caste discrimination and exclusion where people belong to SC/ST/OBC's even not recognised above animals.

India could be seen from the perspectives of exclusion and discrimination and questions the authenticity of reservation policy for the excluded community and their livelihood. The focus is to highlight how the people who are controlling the so-called democratic system and managing reservation policies according to their choice and suitability. The 10 per cent of privileged section of the Indian society enjoying more than 50 per cent reservation/quota policy and in this argument follows mainly in two ways, firstly what is caste reservation and its brief understanding, secondly, how reservation is a policy of exclusion through inclusion and lastly how one could lost their status once migrate from one state to another.

It has been observed by 2011 census that four states account for nearly half of the country's Scheduled castes population. Uttar Pradesh stands first with 20.5 per cent of the total scheduled caste population, followed by West Bengal with 10.7 per cent. Bihar with 8.2 per cent and Tamil Nadu with 7.2 per cent come third and fourth, so over all Scheduled Castes form around 16.6 per cent of India's population.[31]

The 2011 census recorded nearly 20.14 crore people belonging to various scheduled castes in the country. As per the 2001 census, the number was 16.66 crore. The scheduled castes population showed a decadal growth of 20.8 per cent, whereas India's population grew 17.7 per cent during the same period. Though there is an increase in the population of Dalits in the country, many states with a considerable number of Dalits don't have any legislation to protect the interests of the community.

It is also reported that the scheduled castes empowerment is very poor in many states. Many scheduled caste families don't own land or any other property. They are landless and efforts to empower them by giving free land have not been successful in many of the states.[32]

There are around 9.79 crore women among the total SC population, and the sex ratio works out to 946 females per 1000 males. Nagaland, Lakshwadeep and Andaman and Nicobar islands have no scheduled castes among their population. Though UP has the largest chunk of the total scheduled castes population, Punjab has the largest share of Dalits in its population at 31.9 per cent. Himachal Pradesh and West Bengal follow Punjab with 25.2 per cent and 23.5 per cent. In Tamil Nadu, Dalits account for about 18 per cent of the population.

The state budget should also allocate funds for creation of assets for scheduled castes but instead of distributing freebies, the state governments can set aside a portion of the total allocation for scheduled castes. In many cases, funds are being diverted and scheduled castes lose whatever is due to them. The states with considerable number of scheduled castes in their population must pass a separate legislation on the lines of Andhra Pradesh, which has passed the SC/ST Sub Plan Act.[33]

As we all know that Indian reservation/quota system is an old cup of tea. Issue of *'reservation'* day by day is gaining its ground. It is mainly shifting its space from Scheduled Caste, Scheduled Tribe and Other Backward Caste to other sections of the society. The very basic question comes in mind why today people are more concerned about reservation. Why they are rushing towards the *'lollipop of reservation'* in the era of globalisation, liberalisation so on so forth. Why they are now more concerned about their rights. The only reason is the absence of inclusion in various fields like economy, education, politics, employment and etc. Giving reservation to all the section of the society is no doubt a very debatable issue within the bureaucrats, political leaders, academic world, particularly to the privileged caste who were the beneficiaries for centuries. It is almost very clear that now every one desiring their share according to the proportion of their population.[34]

For the first time reservation was introduced in India legally after independence by the Constitution which created a big hue and cry. The reason for this was nothing but the shifting of representation from privileged sections to the marginalised/ excluded sections. Second time it created hue and cry at the time of OBC reservation particularly the *Mandal* issue and the third time again it fuelled the fire of reservation by *Arjun Singh*[35] when he proposed twenty seven per cent reservations to the OBC's in the higher educational institutions particularly in the top institutes[36] like AIIMS, IIT's, Management and other academic institutes etc.[37]

Reservations in favour of *Backward Castes* were introduced long before independence in a large area, comprising the Presidency areas and the Princely States of south of the Vindhyas. *Chatrapati Sahuji Maharaj*, Maharaja of Kolhapur in Maharashtra introduced reservation in favour of backward classes as early as 1902 to eradicate poverty from amongst them and to give them their due share in the state administration. The notification of 1902 created 50 per cent reservation in services for backward classes/communities in the state of Kolhapur. This notification is the first government order providing reservation for the welfare of depressed classes in India.

India is not only a union of states; it is also a union of castes, tribes and communities. The Constitution of India has recognised and continued the personal laws, of each and every caste, community and tribe, which were in force prior to the coming into force of the Constitution of India. We also have matriarchal and patriarchal systems. Even the communities which believe in equality by birth, unlike the graded caste system, have come to be divided on the lines comparable to the Hindu caste divisions. In India, the caste system represents not only a social division, but also a political and occupational division of the society. Therefore, for planning and development, collection of details about each and every caste and tribe in the country is a must. This position was recognised by the Government of India itself in the household schedule pertaining to the socio-demographic study of villages.[38]

> *"If people have no idea of the magnitude of the problem (of the Shudras) it is because they have not cared to know what the population of Shudras is. Unfortunately, the census does not show their population separately. But there is no doubt that*

excluding the untouchables, the Shudras form 75 to 80 per cent of the population of Hindus".[39]

Constitutionally the facility of reservation provided to the SC, ST, OBC's in the field of education, government jobs and other sectors was happened due to the untiring efforts of Dr B.R. Ambedkar. But because of the anti-reservation as well as various level of opposition to this provisions the full benefits of reservation policies is not reaching to the people belongs to excluded groups of the society.[40] Significantly, Article 15, which prohibits discrimination, also contains a clause allowing the Union and State Governments to make *"any special provision for the advancement of any socially and educationally backward classes of citizens or for the SC's and ST's, OBC's and Religious Minorities"*. This language was added in 1951 within weeks of a Supreme Court decision outlawing quotas in school admissions. Similarly, Article 16, calling for *"equality of opportunity in matters of public employment,"* contains clauses permitting the *"reservation of appointments or posts in favour of any backward class of citizens which, in the opinion of the State, is not adequately represented in the services under the State"* and another allowing *"reservation in matters of promotion"* for SC's and ST's. A separate section of the Constitution, *"special provisions relating to certain classes,"* requires the reservation of seats in the *"House of the People,"* or Lok Sabha, and the Legislative Assemblies of the states for the SC's and ST's.

Gautama Buddha in 2500 years ago in India thought that all people are equal. Equality was one of the most important ideas of Buddha. He says there are no differences of any meaningful kind between different people of any social class or race. It was thought that although people have different occupations, there should be no discrimination depending on occupation.[41] Amartya Sen in his writing emphasised on *'capabilities to function'* which means if any country wants to process for development or it wants to grow, it should have fair representation. All the section of the society should have equal representation and resources should be allocated equally.[42] John Rawls on the other hand have same understanding who also emphasis on the *'justice as fairness'* means equal representation to all. He also points that equal competition only gives equal development.[43] *Ronald Dworkin's* views the equality of resources is all examples of conceptualising the remedies of the socio-economic injustice through redistribution. In his book sovereign virtue he advocates a theory of *'equality of resources'*. He says that human beings are responsible for the life choices they make. Natural endowments of intelligence and talent are morality arbitrary and ought not to affect the distribution of resources in society. Every person is entitled to equal concern and respect in the design of the structure of the society.[44] Dr Ambedkar champion of social rights says that the inequality can be minimise only through the policy of re-distribution not on the basis of caste domination but on the basis of proportionate of the population and it is possible through reservation for weaker section.[45] For equality he says might be it a kind fiction but nonetheless one must accept it as a governing principle.

The SC's of the India's north-eastern states are suffering from multiple backwardness and exclusion viz.

(a) General caste discrimination.

(b) Regional backwardness/isolation.

(c) Language as a tool to discriminate by the state insurgents.

A total 30,36,603 scheduled castes have been denied their basic fundamental rights in the Northeastern region of India. They are suffering from huge discrimination and exclusion by both the state government as well as the local population of the state. In the recent judgement Supreme Court has ruled that the SC's, ST's and OBC's cannot claim the benefits of reservation if they migrate from one state to another if the caste/tribe to which they belong are not recognised as a reserved community in the adopted state. Further, a migrant SC or ST also cannot claim a reserved status in OBC quota in another state. Persons belonging to a particular caste or tribe may suffer disadvantages in one state but may not suffer the same disadvantages in the other. Our Constitutional scheme, therefore, seeks to identify the social and economic backwardness of people having regard to the State or Union Territory as a unit.[46]

Table 4.1: Condition once Migrate to other State

Category	*Socio- Political Condition*	*Economic Condition*	*Once Migrate*
*GEN	GEN (Citizen) Always Better	Best in all Cases	Remain Same
*OBC	OBC (Citizen) Little Better	Better in few Cases	Lost Rights/Status
*SC/ST	SC/ST (Citizens) Worse	Good in rare Cases	Lost Rights/Status

*GEN- Brahmin, Kshytriya and Vaisyas, *OBC- all recognised backward castes other than scheduled castes and scheduled tribes, *SC/ST- Dalits and Adivasis in all parts of India.

In 2009, Assam burnt on the issue of tribal status to nearly fourteen tribes who are being excluded and discriminated by centuries. They were aware and more conscious to be the part of the scheduled of the Constitution to get at least the basic benefit for survival as human being. In case of SC's Assam took some initiative to constitute commission to study the condition of SC's in the state and recommend necessary inclusive policies and laws to tackle the problem. Accept Assam none of the states of Northeast took any concrete step to see the problems seriously even after so many decades. In case of migrant tribes there is no response from the ruling regime. It is very difficult to understand why one person is SC in his or her state and general in another state. It is nothing but a Constitutional discrimination. These people are being denied various facilities and such anomalies are also there in many states.

The Central as well as State Government initiated lots of developmental activities to strengthen the political economy of the state and the people in Northeast, but none of the policies and programmes have any inclusive provisions for SC's of these states. These populations largely engaged with the jobs like sweeping, stitching shoes, washing dirty cloths, cleaning toilets, engaged in burial grounds, and all other dirty jobs. Even after getting good education they are not getting jobs. They are socially compelled to do their traditional dirty works as they are doing in other parts of India from centuries or to migrate back to other places. Governments of these states have all information regarding their social, economic, educational and political condition but they are behaving unaware. This is a kind of inhuman act and largely a human rights violation. Even after knowing that the SC's condition is so worse more than any other communities in the region, regimes are not showing any interest to bring any inclusive policy for their upliftmen. In place of bringing some concrete solution as well as policy and programme to the problems regimes of these states, cancelling trading licenses, charging taxes on different occupations, which is creating problem to earn their livelihood fairly. The States Government of India's Northeast, Government of India come together to bring something concrete inclusive policies on this line to solve the problems facing today by the SC's in the region.

The very important issue of having the right to reservation for certain people who are in India's northeast have habitually and by their nature, lived in a very backward condition. They are living in a socially isolated life and are not at all accepted in any other jobs. These people are totally dependent on dirty jobs and they have got no world outside.[47] They also don't have the economic status to raise their status to come forward and have more opportunities in outside the world.

Largely SC's are landless and constitutionally they cannot claim over domicile. They are just an '*unwanted denizen*'. In case of OBC once they migrate they improve but this is not the case with the SC's. They still denied their economic, educational and political rights. There should be a legal solution to the problems of the SC's who are facing multiple discrimination and exclusion in India's northeast. Caste should not be the criteria for dignity, every one those who born in this universe have natural rights to be a human being either he or she may belong to any caste, creed, language, sex, religion, tradition and so on so forth. The historical injustice should be removed by giving their due share so that they live with dignity.

India is one and her Constitution is one for all of us. It is not only the question of economic status but something else. These lots of people who migrated from other eastern, northern as well as southern states seventy years back actually belongs to the SC communities but deprived of SC status in origin. The Government should consider appointing a new commission to revise the status and study the status of all these backward, poor, under-developed and under-privileged community. If we confer the SC status to a certain community, by that alone, the community will not come up but get an opportunity to improve further. Even after seven decades, we find that the position of the SC people is much lower in the society. They are backward socially, economically, politically and educationally. The reason for it is not only the lack of education but also the question of representation. Education is the key part of our progress, and it is required for development and for social empowerment also. The people belonging to the SC's are being looked down upon even today by the society. To uplift the community every state should be given directions by the centre to amend Article 341 and provide reservation on the basis of socially, economically and educationally backward people.[48]

The biggest amendment in the list of SC's took place during the year 1977. Since Independence, Government of India is struggling for the inclusion of certain SC's in the list of respective states. A SC person in one State cannot be a non-SC in another state. It is unfortunate that even today regimes and its privileged sections still discriminate people on the line of caste and race.[49] Government should look into it and identify such type of categories in the country and incorporate these categories in the scheduled lists of SC's at the earliest so that they can get their Constitutional human rights and dignity.[50]

Table 4.2: Caste in Real Life Situation (in percentage points)

Items	*Brahmins*	*Kshatriya*	*Vaishya*	*Shudra*	*SC*	*Minorities*
Population	3.6	6.6	6.0	55.79	16.73	11.28
Reservation	-	-	-	27.0	15.0	-
Pristhood	100.0	-	-	-	-	-
Party Leadership	41.0	16.0	10.0	10.0	10.0	13.0
Business	10.0	20.0	60.0	7.08	0.02	2.0
Land	6.0	70.0	8.0	14.0	1.0	1.0
Education	54.0	16.0	12.0	8.0	6.0	4.0
Government Jobs	64.0	10.0	10.0	8.0	7.0	1.0

Source: Prakash, Louis, 2007, Caste-Based Discrimination and Atrocities on Dalit Christians and the Need for Reservations, Working Paper Series, Indian Institute of Dalit Studies, Vol. II, No. 04, New Delhi, p. 15.

Reservation is the operational form of the special Constitutional provisions. Reservation is of threefold in the legislatures, in the education and in the jobs.[51] The rationale for granting special privileges was that the founding fathers of the Constitution felt that mere granting of equal rights would not be sufficient for depressed classes.[52] As these people had remained deprived of education, political power, economic and social benefits for centuries, they were in no way competent to compete with the members of the privileged castes.[53] In Indian society mainly their are three kind of section whose freedom, equality, justice, human rights, livelihood, dignity and public space largely control by the caste, religion, sex, custom or tradition.

A. (Privileged Caste) Freedom from inside/outside

One feels equal and just in the society and free to participate in public sphere. Brahmins, Kshatriyas and Vaisyas have all kinds of freedom in every sphere to participate without any exclusion and fear.

B. (OBC) Freedom through physical

One feels unequal in the society but have muscle/economic power to participate in the public sphere. Sudras (OBC) more or less economically and politically stronger but excluded in social and educational sphere. They are physically strong enough to participate in the public sphere to minimise the level of exclusion.

C. (SC/ST) Freedom of society or community

One feels unequal and unjust in the society and has no participation in public sphere due to exclusion and discrimination. Dalits (SC) and Adivasis (ST) are socially, economically, educationally and politically backward and excluded in such a way even they do not think to participate in the public sphere anyway. This is the reason why they are called the second class citizen of India. Constitutionally, they have many rights and protection but in practical they denied to get basic human rights in almost all the parts of India.

Issue of reservation might confuse sometime when we think of representation. It would be very difficult to understand whether it is representation or limiting representation when it comes to the proportion of Indian social population is concerned. In Indian reservation/quata system 50:50 ratio is followed. 50 per cent is for general category (Brahmina, Kshatriyas and Vaisyas) who represent not more that 15 per cent of the total population and on the other side the 85 per cent population (Scheduled Castes, Scheduled Tribes, Other Backward Castes and Person with Disability) restricted to the 50 per cent reservation/quata policy.

One thing is clear that there are some fundamental mistakes and one has to think very seriously on this. India is a country based on equality, justice and fraternity. Her Constitution also starts with these three words but in reality it is opposite. Indian society is one of the most divided and "casteist society" in the world. India works on the principles of "excluded representation" and in this minority gets more shares than the majority. Might be people think Indian Constitution is not good and that is why it is so, but this is not correct. The reason is that, the forefathers who framed Constitution worked very hard to bring a Constitution which has a very strong inclusive policy. But they also said that, if this Constitution would be in wrong hand then it works reverse. In place of benefiting majority it benefit minority more. This is happening in case of reservation. The original habitants of "Jambudeepa" are fighting for their status and representation in the society. They are struggling to get equal representation in education, job and public sphere.[54]

Now let it put like this and question, is reservation really for the benefit of the larger section of the society who comes like 85 per cent or for the protection of some privileged section who have 50 per cent reservation in over all. India is the country where in the name of democracy minority ruled majority. So far Indian democracy is concerned it is "Marginal Democracy" not a functional democracy. If Dalits and Adivasis are Indian then why there is a duel policy. Why they had been placed as a second class citizen and treated as an excluded community with their caste and tribe stigma. India is a country where humanity is completely absent. Due to huge exclusion in hte society many social groups adopting means of violence for change which is at all not the right way of doing things in their favour. The solution can only be through education, unity and peaceful agitation and participation in the political affairs of the state.[55] The fight should be with the ballots and not with the bullets. Unless and until they remain divided minority get opportunity to rule year over year as they are doing since time immemorial.[56]

In Indian society SC's and ST's are considered to be the second class citizens[57] and are among the poorest of citizens, generally do not own land, and often are illiterate. They face significant discrimination despite the laws that exist to protect them, and often are prohibited from using the same wells and from attending the same temples as dominant caste Hindus, and from marrying persons from privileged castes. In addition they face segregation in housing, in land ownership, on roads, and on buses. Dalits tend to be malnourished, lack access to healthcare, work in poor conditions, and face continuing and severe social ostracism.

Social justice is an important policy objective of any government. The survey on employment-unemployment captures the status of the sample individuals on the basis of commonly classified social groups and sex. It is necessary for the policy makers to assess the extent of parity in employment without any discrimination based on caste, religion or sex in order to frame appropriate policies to achieve the objective of social justice. The present report is based on second annual employment-unemployment survey conducted by labour bureau.[58]

It could argued, that the Indian reservation policy is not the policy of representation rather it is a policy of "representative exclusion" by the minority over majority. If it is representative inclusive policy then it should have to have representative access to its "marginalised citizens" even if they migrate to any of the Indian states so far.[59] Like general category candidate the SC/ST/OBC's should have equal rights to work and earn their livelihoods and participate in public sphere. Indian way of reservation policy is another way to exclude SC/ST/OBC through inclusion. The minority regimes taking help of the Indian Constitution to exclude majority people through various inclusive policies. They are limiting representation through reservation. Over all one has to think deeply the arithmetic of the minority over majority.[60]

The present reservation policy is not enough. No doubt it is playing useful role but will likely be a diminishing part for the solution of SC and ST in particular and OBC problem in general.[61] There are major flaws in which reservation policy apply to the public sector but not the private sector in the probable growth area of the Indian economy.[62] There are more than twenty millions of SC's and ST's living in rural areas and not part of the '*organised*' economy. On the other hand, states like Rajasthan blocked promotions for SC's and ST's and said those who would get job through reservation unable to enjoy benefits of promotion and seniority.[63]

To minimise the conflict like situation in future the 50 per cent *'reservation frontier'* need to be break and increase because of the increase in population of all social groups time to time. It also needs to identify for those who are needy so that it could reach to all the social groups to minimise the conflict within. Reservation policy should be centralised so that any SC, ST and OBC once migrate should have freedom to get job for his/her livelihood. No doubt preference has to be given for the concerned states SC, ST and OBC then it moves to other states social groups. Overall, if the real representation and distribution of resources should be made according to the proportion of their population then it would be equal and just society for all.[64]

Casteism is the Indian species of Apartheid and Dalits, known as the Blacks of India as well as exiled citizens and facing atrocities and oppression of all kinds, seeking fundamental freedom.[65] Caste is a historical problem and needs a historical moment and effort to solve it and as for Dalit Muslims and Dalit Christians are concerned they are still in the making of history for freedom, dignity, equality and development. Problem of Dalit Muslims and Dalit Christians cannot be solved by mere theological reflections and choicest verbal gestures.[66] Various policies, administrative and structural changes have to be implemented to radically and rapidly change the structured inequalities. All these have to be seen in concrete action.[67]

Now few questions comes in mind rhetorically, Is this India we proud of and talk about her rich culture, belief in humanity? Further to extend this question it is also necessary to ask simply that, who is responsible for it, we ourself, or our for-fathers or some one else who are trying to be superior among one human over others. So far answer is concerned it is very difficult to answer. India is the motherland of each and every individual who born and become the citizen. Overall we need to focus on the issue of caste more than any other issues because everything is revolving around it and destroying the basic tenants of humanity, culture, identity for whom India known as the country of peace, non-violence, brotherhood, equality among all. We have to think very deeply to find out the solution to the problem deeply and work together which bring equality and brotherhood among all as well for equal and just society.

Dr Ambedkar for the whole issues rightly pointed that the *Rights, Liberty, Equality* and *Fraternity* is one of the most important principles which not only allow the citizen to live freely but to live with dignity.[68] He further questions, what we must do is not to content ourselves with mere political democracy. We must make our political democracy a social democracy as well.[69] Political democracy cannot last unless there is at the base of it, a social democracy. What does social democracy mean? It means a way of life which recognises liberty, equality and fraternity as the principles of life. These principles of liberty, equality and fraternity are not to be treated as separate items. They form a union in the sense that, to divorce one from the other is to defeat the very purpose of democracy. Liberty cannot be divorced from equality, nor can liberty and equality be divorced from fraternity. Rights are real only if they are accompanied by remedies.[70] It is no use giving rights if the aggrieved person has no legal remedy to which he can resort when his rights are invaded. Lost rights are never regained by appeals to the conscience of the usurpers, but by relentless struggle.... Goats are used for sacrificial offerings and not lions.[71] What are we having this liberty for? We are having this liberty in order to reform our social system, which is full of inequality, discrimination and other things, which conflict with our fundamental rights. It is your claim to equality which hurts them. They want to maintain the status quo. If you continue to accept your lowly status ungrudgingly, continue to remain dirty, filthy, backward, ignorant, poor and disunited, they will allow you to live in peace. The moment you start to raise your level, the conflict starts. Untouchability is not transitory or temporary feature; it is eternal, it is lasting. Frankly it can be said that the struggle between the Hindus and the Untouchables is a never-ending conflict. It is eternal because the religion which assigns you the lowest status in society is itself divine and eternal according to the belief of the so-called dominant caste Hindus. No change warranted by change of time and circumstances is possible. Equality may be a fiction but nonetheless one must accept it as a governing principle.[72] What does fraternity mean? Fraternity means a sense of common brotherhood of all Indians, all Indians being one people. It is a principle that gives solidarity to social life. It is difficult thing to achieve. It seems that there lies a heavy duty to see that democracy does not vanish from the earth as a governing principle of human relationship. If we believe in it, we must both be true and loyal to it. We must not only be staunch in our faith in democracy but we must resolve to see that whatever we do, we do not help the enemies of democracy to uproot the principles of liberty, equality and fraternity.[73] It follows that we must strive along with other democratic countries to maintain the basis of democratic civilisation. If democracy lives we are sure to reap the benefit of it. If democracy dies it will be our doom. On that there can be no doubt.[74]

Even after seven decade a travesty of justice that scheduled castes communities in a significant number of regions are unable to exercise their right of franchise in a free and fair manner as envisaged in the Constitution. Violent strategies are deployed by non- Scheduled Castes communities' vested interests to either prevent SC's from voting or to force them to vote for candidates against their wish or separate queues. As per the survey done by different organisations, it has been reported that in more than 18 per cent of villages Scheduled Castes were prevented to vote.[75] Dominant castes forcing the Scheduled Castes to vote for candidates against their choice is prevailing in more than 50 per cent of villages. In more than eight per cent villages' practice of separate queues at polling booths exists. In 18 per cent of villages Dalits are permitted to vote only after dominant castes. We are all known nature and extent of violence and the threat of violence before, during or after elections. Fourteen per cent of atrocities are related to political participation and out of which 80 per cent are happening during elections. All this, in spite of the fact that Indian Constitution guarantees equality before law, right of franchise to all citizens regardless of caste, creed, sex or religion; and in spite of the fact that we have excellent provisions against electoral offences in the Representation of the People Act, Cr. P.C. and the SC/ST (Prevention of Atrocities) Act. Now it is a time to get a legal solution to the durable problem within a time bound period and fulfil the legal requirements of the scheduled castes who are facing duel backwardness in the Indian state of Northeast. Their historical injustice should be removed by giving their due share so that they can live a dignified life as human being. They should be included in the job, education, State Assembly, Governmental agencies and Non-Governmental Organisations etc. State should frame strong inclusive policies and protect the rights and lifes of SC's in the region, so that they could earn their livelihood and get all the opportunities in the region which other scheduled castes of India so far availing.

Notes

1. Plato's Republic 4.427d.
2. Valerain, Rodrigues, "Ambedkar on Modernity and Religion", Voices for Equity: Minority and Majority in South Asia, RINDAS International Symposium Series, Ryukoku University, The Centre for the Study of Contemporary India, 2011, pp.3-18.
3. Valerain, Rodrigues, Justice as the Lens: "Interrogating Rawls through Sen and Ambedkar", Indian Journal of Human Development, Vol. V, No. 1, Jan.-June 2011.
4. Rawls, Justice as Fairness: a Restatement, p. 97.
5. Amartya Sen (2009). The Idea of Justice. Belknap Press (Harvard University Press). pp. 52–74.
6. Kennedy, D. (1912). St. Thomas Aquinas. In The Catholic Encyclopaedia. New York: Robert Appleton Company. Retrieved December 12, 2014 from New Advent: http://www.newadvent.org/cathen/14663b.htm
7. http://www.iep.utm.edu/aquinas/
8. Condition of the Untouchables or the Dalits (http://www.dalitchristians.com/html/condition.htm), See more in St. Thomas Aquinas", London and New York, 1911, p. 61
9. Locke, John, 1991. A Letter Concerning Toleration Routledge, New York. p. 5.
10. Immanuel Kant, 1797. The Metaphysics of Morals, abbreviated (MM), and translated by Mary Gregor (Cambridge, 1991) and included in Practical Philosophy (Cambridge Edition of the works of Imanuel Kant, 1996). Parenthetical references will be provided for this work as well as Kant's Groundwork of the Metaphysics of Morals, abbreviation (GMM), trans.
11. http://www.iep.utm.edu/bentham/, See more on the book: *The Classical Utilitarians: Bentham and Mill*, author: John Troyer, Professor of Philosophy at the University of Connecticut.
12. Rawls, Justice as Fairness: a Restatement, p. 97.
13. Rawls, John, 2007. Justice as Fairness: A Restatement, Rutledge, New York, p. 97
14. *Ibid.*

15. See details in Kumar, Vivek. 2006, 'Political and Civil Institution of Governance: Contradiction of Exclusion and Inclusion of Dalits in Contemporary India' in R B S Verma (eds.) Empowerment of Weaker Sections in India, New Delhi: Serials Publications.
16. *Egalitarianism*, First published Fri Aug 16, 2002; substantive revision Wed Apr 24, 2013, http://plato.stanford.edu/entries/egalitarianism/
17. Valerain, Rodrigues, Justice as the Lens: Interrogating Rawls through Sen and Ambedkar", Indian Journal of Human Development, Vol. V, No. 1, Jan.-June 2011.
18. *Ibid.*
19. http://lawmin.nic.in/coi/coiason29july08.pdf See more details in The Constitution of India, Government of India, Ministry of Law and Justice.
20. See Preamble of the Constitution of India (http://lawmin.nic.in/coi/coiason29july08.pdf (See more details in The Constitution of India, Government of India, Ministry of Law and Justice)
21. http://lawmin.nic.in/coi/coiason29july08.pdf See more details in The Constitution of India, Government of India, Ministry of Law and Justice.
22. http://lawmin.nic.in/coi/coiason29july08.pdf See more details in The Constitution of India, Government of India, Ministry of Law and Justice.
23. *Ibid.*
24. *Ibid.*
25. *Ibid.*
26. http://lawmin.nic.in/coi/coiason29july08.pdf See more details in The Constitution of India, Government of India, Ministry of Law and Justice.
27. *Ibid.*
28. http://lawmin.nic.in/coi/coiason29july08.pdf See more details in The Constitution of India, Government of India, Ministry of Law and Justice
29. http://lawmin.nic.in/coi/coiason29july08.pdf See more details in The Constitution of India, Government of India, Ministry of Law and Justice
30. Christophe Jaffrelot, 2009, Dr Ambedkar's Strategies Against Untouchability and the Caste System, Indian Institute of Dalit Studies, Volume III, No. 04, New Delhi, pp. 2-16.

31. See detail in Constitution of India (http://lawmin.nic.in/coi/coiason29july08.pdf (See more details in The Constitution of India, Government of India, Ministry of Law and Justice)

32. See details in K.C. Das, Indian Dalits – Voice, Vision and Politics, Global Vision Publishing House, Delhi, 2004, p. 5.

33. The Times of India, May 2, 2013.

34. Chunnu Prasad, 2014. "Understanding Census of India in Reference to the Scheduled Caste Populations of North East India Region", The Voice: An International Multidisciplinary Referred Research Journal, Gautam Buddha Kalyan Sansthan, Deoria, India, Vol. I, No. I, January - March, pp. 20-34

35. S.S. Gill, S.S. Gill, What the Mandal Commission wanted, Thursday May 11 2006, http://archive.indianexpress.com/news/what-the-mandal-commission-wanted/2343/, http://retributions.nationalinterest.in/arjun-singh-does-another-mandal/, http://indiatoday.intoday.in/story/arjun-singh-successful-in-securing-quota-for-obcs-implementation-matters/1/181520.html

36. SC pulls up government on quota in IITs, IIMs, New Delhi, October 16, http://www.liveindia.com/news/zzq.html

37. Prasad, Chunnu and Sudhakara, Karakoti, 2007. "Issue of Reservation and Quota: A Critical Perspective", Social Action, Vol. 42:3 July-September: 242-258.

38. Ambedkar, Dr B.R. 1946. Who were the Shudras, Government of Maharashtra Publication, Bombay: 9.

39. *Ibid.*

40. The Indian Express, 17 August 2009.

41. Ambedkar, Dr B.R. 1957. The Buddha and His Dhamma, Buddha Bhumi Publication, Nagpur: 25.

42. Sen, Amartya, 2000. Social Exclusion: Concept, Application and Scrutiny, Social development paper-1, Asian Development Bank, Philippines, pp. 30-38.

43. Rawls, John. 2007. Justice as Fairness: A Restatement, Rutledge, New York: 97.

44. Dworkin, Ronald. 2000. Sovereign Virtue: The Theory and Practice of Equality, Haward University Press, Cambridge: 157-190.

45. V. Rao, Didla and Pulla, Lakshmi. 2007. Ambedkar's thrust on Education and Reservation: Its Impact on Emancipation of Dalit, OBC and Minorities, Eastern Book Corporation, Delhi.

46. *Ibid.*

47. Chunnu Prasad, 2006. "Arunachal Pradesh Denies the Rights to Scheduled Caste in the State", Radical Humanist, Vol. 433, April: pp. 33-34.
48. Chunnu Prasad, 2008. Caste, Social Exclusion and the Question of Livelihood: A Case of Scheduled Castes of Assam and Arunachal Pradesh, Paper presented in a National Seminar organised by Dr B.R. Ambedkar Open University under VII Andhra Pradesh Sociological Society Conference, Hyderabad on 27th to 29th November.
49. See Rajya Sabha. 2006. (India) Synopsis of debates, Friday, July 28/Sravana 6, 1928 (Saka), http://164.10047.5/synopsis/208/28072006.html.
50. Satyanarayana, P. 1992. Reservation and Attitudes of Political Parties in B.A.V. Sharma and K. Madhusudan Reddy (ed.), Reservation Policy in India, Light and Life Publishers, New Delhi: p. 122.
51. Prasad, Chunnu. 2010. "Looking for Whose Identity; A Critical Overview of the Concept Dalit and Social Justice", Third World Impact, January-March: pp. 29-32.
52. Anant, S.S. 1972. The changing concept of caste in India, Vikas Publication, New Delhi: 23.
53. Sharma, B.A.V. and, Reddy, K. Madhusudan, 1982. ed. Reservation Policy in India, Light and Life Publishers, New Delhi: p. 62.
54. Chunnu Prasad, 2009. Dalits Struggle for Democratic Space: Bahujan Samaj Party and the Democratisation of Indian Politics, in an edited book by Vivek Kumar, G. Stanley, Jaya Kumar and Tenepali Hari in The Dynamics of Change and Community in the era of Globalisation: Voices of the Margins, Sunrise Publication, New Delhi: pp. 336-367.
55. Chunnu Prasad, 2010. Democracy, Dalits and Exclusive Policies: A Case of Scheduled Castes in Arunachal Pradesh, in an edited book by Yagati Chinna Rao and Karakoti Sudhakara in Exclusion and Discrimination; Concepts, Perspectives and Challenges, Kanishka Publishes and Distributors, New Delhi: pp. 120-144.
56. Chunnu Prasad, 2010. Naxalism Fighting for what: Question of Exclusion, Dignity and Livelihood, in an edited book by Pradeep Basu in Discourse on Naxalite Movement (1967-2009); Insights into Radical Left Politics, Setu Prakasan, Kolkatta: pp. 238-251.
57. Guru, Gopal, 2005. Citizenship in Exile: A Dalit Case in edited book by Rajiv Bhargava and Helmut Reifeld, Civil Society, Public Sphere and Citizenship, Dialogues and Perceptions, Sage Publication, New Delhi: pp. 260-276.

58. Report on employment and unemployment survey 2011-12, Ministry of Labour and Employment, Government of India, Chandigarh, pp. i-v.

59. Chunnu Prasad, 2010. "Contextualising Marginalisation and Reservation: An Overview of India's Northeast", National Conference on Movements for Equity in Reservations on 21st to 22nd February by Centre for the Study of Social Systems, Jawaharlal Nehru University, New Delhi and Dalit Information and Education Trust, Hyderabad.

60. Chunnu Prasad, 2014. "Understanding Census of India in Reference to the Scheduled Caste Populations of North East India Region", The Voice: An International Multidisciplinary Referred Research Journal, Gautam Buddha Kalyan Sansthan, Deoria, India, Vol. I, No. I, January - March, pp. 20-34.

61. See detail in SC pulls up government on quota in IITs, IIMs, New Delhi, October 16, http://www.liveindia.com/news/zzq.html

62. Sukhadeo Thorat, Prasant Negi and Aryama, 2006. Reservation in the Private Sector-Issues, Concerns and Prospects, Indian Institute of Dalit Studies, Working Paper Series, Vol. 1, No. 1, New Delhi, pp. 2-52.

63. Times of India, 8 December, 2010.

64. Chunnu Prasad, 2010. Mapping Caste, Social Exclusion and the Question of Livelihood in Manipur", National Seminar on Public Action and Inclusive Policy: Taking Stock of the Reality and Exploring the Road Ahead on 22nd to 24th March by Centre for Study of Social Exclusion and Inclusive Policy, Pondicherry University, Poducherry.

65. Chunnu Prasad, 2009. Social Exclusion and Caste Based Discrimination on Dalit Christians in South India, National Conference, Social Mobility in South India, on 24th and 25th September, by Department of Sociology, Pondicherry University, Puducherry.

66. Prakash, Louis, 2007. Caste-Based Discrimination and Atrocities on Dalit Christians and the Need for Reservations, Working Paper Series, Indian Institute of Dalit Studies, Vol. II, No. 04, New Delhi, pp. 4-40.

67. See website, http://www.Dalitchristians.com, article related to Dalit Christians in India. Also see Prakash, Louis, 2007. Caste-Based Discrimination and Atrocities on Dalit Christians and the Need for Reservations, Working Paper Series, Indian Institute of Dalit Studies, Vol. II, No. 04, New Delhi, pp. 4-40.

68. See detail in Constitution of India (http://lawmin.nic.in/coi/coiason29july08.pdf (See more details in The Constitution of India, Government of India, Ministry of Law and Justice).
69. See details http://www.achhikhabar.com/2012/05/31/dr-b-r-ambedkar-quotes-in-hindi/
70. *Ibid.*
71. *Ibid.*
72. See detail in J. Michael Mahar (ed.), 1972. The Untouchables in Contemporary India, University of Arizona Press, Tucson.
73. See details http://www.achhikhabar.com/2012/05/31/dr-b-r-ambedkar-quotes-in-hindi/
74. See more quotations of Babasaheb Dr Bhim Rao Ramji Ambedkar.
75. See details in Pushpendra, 2002. "Dalit Assertion through Electoral Politics", Economic and Political Weekly, Vol. XXXIV, No. 36, September 4, 1999, Sudha Pai, Dalit Assertion and Unfinished Democratic Revolution: The BSP in Uttar Pradesh, Sage Publication, New Delhi, Vivek Kumar, 2002. "Caste Mobilisation in UP and its Impact on Assembly Election", Mainstream, Vol. XXXX, No. 10, February 23.

APPENDICES

Appendix A

In the Gauhati High Court

(THE HIGH COURT OF ASSAM: NAGALAND: MEHGALAYA: MANIPUR: TRIPURA: MIZORAM AND ARUNACHAL PRADESH) IMPHAL BENCH

WRIT PETITION(C).No. 1347/2002

1. Shri Yumnam Ibobi Singh, aged about 53 yrs. S/o Y. Bira Singh, a resident of Langmeidong, PO Kakching, PS-Waikhong, District Thoubal, Manipur.
2. Shri Thokchom Biren Singh, aged about 44 yrs. S/o Th. Pishak Singh, a resident of Kaboleikai, Dewlahland, PO Imphal, PS-Porompat, Imphal East District, Manipur.

..... Petitioners

-Vs-

1. The State of Manipur represented by The Commissioner (Hills) Govt. of Manipur, Imphal.
2. Sadar Hills Autonomous District Council, Kangpokpi, Manipur, represented by the Chief Executive Officer.
3. Smt. Nengboi Haokip, promoted as Assistant Inspector of Schools under Sadar Hills Autonomous District Council, Kangpokpi.
4. Smt. Avei Chongloi, promoted as Assistant Inspector of Schools under Sadar Hills Autonomous District Council, Kangpokpi.

5. Shri Puni Losii, promoted as Assistant Inspector of Schools under Sadar Hills Autonomous District Council, Kangpokpi.
6. Shri S.T. Janglet Haokip, promoted as Assistant Inspector of Schools under Sadar Hills Autonomous District Council, Kangpokpi.
7. Smt Chinnu Kipgen, promoted as Assistant Inspector of Schools under Sadar Hills Autonomous District Council, Kangpokpi.
8. Smt Lhingkhonei, promoted as Deputy Inspector of Schools under Sadar Hills Autonomous District Council, Kangpokpi.

.... Respondents....

- BEFORE-

THE HON'BLE MR JUSTICE M.B.K. SINGH for the petitioners: Mr. N. Kotiswar, Advocate For the respondents :: Mr L. Shyamkishore Singh, Sr. Advt. Mr. S.T. Kom, Advt. Dates of Hearing: 12.5.2005 and 16.5.2005 Date of Judgment and order. :: 07.07.2005

JUDGMENT AND ORDER

This writ petition has been filed by two petitioners, who are serving as Head Masters under Sadar Hills Autonomous District Council, Kangpokpi and whose services have been utilised as Assistant Inspector of Schools from time to time, challenging the orders being No. 2/6/98-CHA, dated 13.9.2002 and No. 2/6/98-CHA, dated 16.9.2002 by which the respondents No. 4 to 8 and the respondent No. 9 were promoted as Assistant Inspector of Schools and Deputy Inspector of School respectively under Sadar Hills Autonomous District Council, Kangpokpi, Manipur. The petitioners are aggrieved by the said promotion orders on the grounds that without considering their seniority, merits, their services during the period of ethnic clashes and their services as Assistant Inspector of Schools on in-charge basis, the said respondents 4 to 8 were promoted as Assistant Inspector of Schools and that the respondent No. 3, who was not eligible for promotion to the post of Deputy Inspector of School as per the Hill District Council (Deputy Inspector of Schools) Recruitment Rules, 1995 at the relevant time was promoted to the said post. It is also alleged that the said promotions, having been made only in favour of the Scheduled Tribes are violative of the provisions of Manipur Reservation of Vacancies in Posts and Services (for Scheduled Castes and Scheduled Tribes) Act, 1975. Further, the petitioners are challenging the legality and propriety of the proceedings of the DPC leading to the issuance of the said promotion orders.

2. I have heard Mr N. Kotiswar, learned counsel appearing on behalf of the petitioners Mr L. Shyamkishore Singh, learned senior counsel appearing on behalf of the respondents No. 1 and 2 and 3

Mr S.T. Kom, learned counsel appearing on behalf of the remaining respondents.

3. There is no dispute that as per relevant recruitment rules, the posts of Assistant Inspector of Schools and Deputy Inspector of Schools under the said Hills Autonomous District Council, Kangpokpi are selection posts. It is also ascertained that the two petitioners and the respondents No. 4 to 8 were holding the feeder posts and are eligible for promotion to the post of Assistant Inspectors of Schools at the relevant time. Regarding the alleged violation of the provisions of Manipur Reservation of Vacancies in Posts and Services (for Scheduled Caste and Scheduled Tribe) Act, 1975, it is ascertained that none of the private respondents was promoted to a reserved post for Scheduled Caste and Scheduled Tribe. Merely on the basis of the fact that all the promotees to the said posts are found to be Scheduled Tribes, it cannot be concluded that the said promotions were made in violation of the provisions of the said Act. There is nothing to show that there was cent per cent reservation in favour of the Scheduled Tribes by issuing any formal order in connection with the filling up of the said post by way of promotion. On the basis of the materials before the court, it cannot be concluded that the said promotions were made in violation of the provisions of the said Act.

4. The post of Assistant Inspector of Schools under Sadar Hills Autonomous District Council, Kangpokpi is a selection post. It is ascertained that the two petitioners and the respondents No. 4 to 8 were holding the feeder posts and are eligible for promotion to the posts of Assistant Inspectors of Schools at the relevant time. The impugned promotion order dated 13.9.2002 in favour of the respondents No. 4 to 8 was issued purportedly

accepting the recommendation of the DPC held on 11.9.2002. As per the records produced by the Deputy Secretary (Hills), Govt. of Manipur, the respondents No. 4 to 8 were recommended by the DPC held on 11.9.2002 for filling up five vacant posts of Assistant Inspectors of Schools under Sadar Hills Autonomous District Council, Kangpokpi. On perusal of the records produced before the court, it is ascertained that no seniority list of those employees holding the feeder post was placed before the DPC. No reason is given as to why no such seniority list was produced. In the facts and circumstances, the only reasonable conclusion is that no such seniority list was prepared at that time. However, the list of eligible Headmasters for the posts of Assistant Inspector of Schools was before the DPC. Nothing is disclosed as to how and on what basis the said list of eligible Headmasters was prepared. In the relevant recruitment rules of Assistant Inspector of Schools, nothing is provided as to how the selection for filling in the post of Inspector of Schools is to be made. In view of the omission on the part of the concerned authority to specify as to how the selection is to be made, it was necessary on the part of the concerned DPC to proceed in accordance with the Government instructions issued by way of Office Memorandum dated 29.4.1999 which was published in Manipur Gazette, Extraordinary being No. 137 dated 9.6.1999. The said memorandum will have binding effect in the absence of any inconsistency or contradictions in between the provisions of the relevant recruitment rules and the said memorandum. In my considered opinion, the said office memorandum which was issued for guidance of all the departments in the State on the principles of promotions to higher posts to be followed by the Departmental Promotion Committees, in the absence of any alternative instructions or rules meant for Autonomous District Council, was applicable at the time of holding the DPC for filling up the posts under the Autonomous District Council. It is to be noted that as per Rule 53 of Manipur (Hill Areas) District Council Rules, 1972, all rules prevailing under the Manipur Government governing the conditions of service for Government servant are applicable to all officers and other employees of the Council in respect of matters except where the Rules, 1972 provide otherwise. The fact that the District Council had followed and acted purportedly in accordance with the Government instructions issued in the form of office memorandum while making appointment, can be seen from the fact of referring to Government Order No. 18/55/96-Adhoc-DP dated 26.7.1996 in the appointment order issued in favour of the respondent No. 9 on 15.8.1997 (Annexure –R/2 of the affidavit-in-opposition of the respondent No. 4 to 9). The said office memorandum are in the nature of instructions given in the interest of all to prevent DPCs from proceeding at their sweet-will or in an arbitrary or discriminatory manner at the time of consideration for giving promotion to higher posts. Any deviation from the instructions in the office memorandum will have to be examined if such deviation is permissible under any law or statutory rules.

5. On perusal of the records, it is ascertained that while proceeding for making recommendation for giving promotion to the vacant posts of Assistant Inspectors of Schools, the DPC did not proceed in accordance with the said office memorandum. As per the said office memorandum, where promotions are to be made by selection, the DPC shall fix zone of consideration from among the eligible officers in the feeder grade having regard to the number of vacancies proposed to be filled up in the year. For 5 (five) vacant posts, the normal zone of consideration should have been limited to 14 officers. When I examine the said list of eligible Headmasters for promotion, it is ascertained that there are 8 (eight) Scheduled Tribe Headmasters in between Sl.No. 1 to 14 of the list. However, the said DPC held on 11.9.2002 considered the cases of all the eligible 26 Headmasters submitted to it instead of restricting the zone of consideration as per instructions contained in the said office memorandum. As a result of not restricting the zone of consideration, the said DPC completely ignored the seniority position of the said Headmasters. Mr L. Shyamkishore learned senior counsel appearing on behalf of the respondents 1 and 2 submits that the said list of eligible Headmasters is not the one prepared according to seniority. It has not been disclosed as to why the seniority list of eligible Headmasters is not produced. The possibility that it has not yet been prepared is not rule out. The question of seniority of any of the eligible Headmasters was not considered by the DPC at the time of making recommendation. As per instruction No. 5.3.1 of the said office memorandum, while preparing the penal for promotion in respect of Class-II posts on selection basis, the DPC cannot

ignore the inter-se seniority inasmuch as all Headmasters whose overall grading is equal to or better than the bench mark "good" are to be included in the penal for promotion to the extent of number of vacancies in order of their inter-se seniority in the feeder post. On perusal of the relevant records of the DPC, it is ascertained that the said prescribed instructions were not followed. The DPC made their selection ignoring the question of inter-se seniority completely and thereby in violation of the said instruction. The selection process that was followed by the said DPC is contrary to the one followed by all the Departments of the State in respect of the giving of appointment by way of promotion to a Class-II selection post. The post of Assistant Inspector of Schools being a selection post, the concerned DPC should have adopted the process of choosing carefully from among the eligible Headmasters by adopting the same process prescribed to be followed by all Departments of the State instead of the proceeding in the manner not adopted by other Departments. In the facts and circumstances, by not adopting the said instructions contained in the office memorandum, the said DPC adopted an arbitrary or discriminatory procedure in making recommendation for the said selection post of Assistant Inspector of Schools. The impugned orders of promotion issued in favour of the respondents No. 4 to 8 on the basis of the recommendation made by the said DPC is not sustainable in the eye of law. It violates Article 14 of the Constitution.

6. The post of Deputy Inspector of Schools is also a selection post. Though there is dispute regarding the question if the respondent No. 9 was eligible for consideration for giving promotion to the post of Deputy Inspector of Schools at the relevant time, having regards to fact that she was having the educational qualification of B.A. with B.Ed. and that she had served regularly in the post of Headmaster of UJB school for more than 11 years in consequence of promotion order being No. 2/17/SH-ADC/81 dated 2.5.1987 before she was promoted to the post of Assistant Inspector of Schools on 21.1.1999. It is ascertained that though she had not rendered regular service of 5 years as Assistant Inspector of Schools, she was eligible for promotion to the post of Deputy Inspector of Schools as per relevant recruitment rule of Deputy Inspector of Schools when the DPC was held on 12.9.2002. On perusal of the relevant

records, it is ascertained that the DPC, after due consideration of all eligible persons, recommended the respondent No. 9 for promotion to the vacant post of Deputy Inspector of Schools. As per records, the respondent No. 9 was given promotion to the post of Assistant Inspector of Schools on the recommendation of the DPC held on 21.1.1999 on consideration of her being the senior most Headmasters. A copy of the promotion order is at Annexure-A/17. There is nothing to show that any of the petitioners challenged the said promotion order promoting the respondent No. 9 to the post of Assistant Inspector of Schools. On the basis of the materials before the court, I do not find any valid ground for interfering with the order dated 16.9.2002 by which the respondent No. 9 was promoted to the post of Deputy Inspector of Schools.

7. Keeping in view all the relevant considerations including the need for not disturbing the settled position to the possible extent, this writ petition is disposed of with the following directions:-

(i) A review DPC in respect of the DPC held on 11.9.2002 in connection with the promotion to the post of Assistant Inspector of Schools under the Sadar Hills Autonomous District Council, Kangpokpi is to be held in accordance with the said office memorandum dated 29.4.1999. On the basis of the result of the said review DPC, no promotion is to be disturbed as far as possible and if any of the private respondents 4 to 8 is found to have been not fit for selection as on 29.4.1999, he is to be pushed back so far as seniority position is concerned below the position of the petitioners who may be found to have been fit for promotion at the relevant time of the DPC.

(ii) The present direction will not cover the cases of private respondents who may have been promoted to the next higher post or who may have retired in the meantime.

8. This writ petition stands allowed to the extent as indicated above.

JUDGE

Appendix B
History of Exploitation

The history of the migration of tea and ex-tea garden communities to Assam is a long one, characterised by exploitation, deprivation and treachery. After the annexation of Assam from Burma (Myanmar), the British colonial administration started tea plantations on a large scale in the region. The first tea committee was formed in 1834, and the first tea garden was established in 1837. By 1900, there were 804 tea gardens covering an area of 337,000 acres (1 hectare = 2.47 acres). The industry soon began facing a shortage of labourers. With the native people of Assam engaged in independent farming, a labour class seeking wage employment on a regular basis was not available locally. It therefore became imperative for the planters to import labourers from outside Assam. The Tea District Labour Association, constituted under the Tea District Emigrant Labour Act of 1932, started recruiting labour from six labour-surplus provinces – Bengal, Bihar, Orissa, Central Provinces, United Provinces and Madras. The first batch of tea garden labourers were recruited from the Chotanagpur division of Bihar by the Assam Company in 1841. The industry continued to import labourers until 1960.

The labourers thus brought into Assam had a trying time. The agents, known as free contractors, enticed them with secure employment, good wages and healthy habitation. But what the labourers got was a raw deal. The mortality rate among them became high. The abuse of the free contractors was so grave that it met with protests from various quarters.

Some of the recruits did not stay in the tea gardens. They settled in government khas land or unused tea garden land in the vicinity of the tea estates so that they could earn their living as casual labourers in the tea gardens and also by cultivating land. This led to the creation of the Ex-Tea garden tribe.

In 1995, the Director of the Assam Institute of Research for Tribals and Scheduled Castes recommended to the Government of Assam, after conducting a detailed study of the status of Oraons, Santhals, Mundas, Kharias and so on, known as Tea and Ex-Tea garden communities of Assam, that these tribes be included in the list of S.T. (Plains). In the same year, the Hiteswar Saikia government also recommended the same to the Central Government. On August 5, 2004, the Assam Legislative Assembly adopted a unanimous resolution urging the Government of India to include Tea and Ex-Tea tribes/Adivasis and five other major communities (Koch Rajbongshi, Tai-Ahom, Moran, Mottak and Chutia) in the list of S.T. (Plains). The report submitted by the Amar Rai Pradhani Committee also made the recommendation.

Union Minister for Tribal Affairs P.R. Kyndiah told Parliament that the Assam government had sent a report regarding the social status of the six communities, recommending their inclusion in the S.T. list for Assam. He informed the House that in 1993 the then Assam government recommended the specification of Koch Rajbongshi as an S.T. but the report appended to the State government's recommendation was found contradictory and the RGI rejected the claim. Later, the State government sent a revised report, on the basis of which in 1995 the RGI supported its inclusion in the list, without connecting it with the earlier report. On January 27, 1996, an ordinance effecting the inclusion of Koch Rajbongshis in the list of S.Ts. of Assam (excluding the autonomous districts of Assam) was promulgated. The ordinance was re-promulgated thrice, on March 27, 1996; June 27, 1996 and January 1, 1997. It lapsed on April 2, 1997, prompting the organisations of Koch-Rajbongshis to revive their movement.

The Constitution (Scheduled Tribes) Order (Amendment) Bill, 1996, was introduced in the Lok Sabha on July 12, 1996. The Bill was referred to the Select Committee of the Lok Sabha on August 2, 1996. The Select Committee submitted its report on August 14, 1997. This report was circulated among the Assam government, the RGI, and the National Commission for Scheduled Castes and Scheduled Tribes. "The government of Assam and the Registrar General of India had recommended the inclusion of Koch Rajbongshi in the list of Scheduled Tribe of Assam (though in March 1997, the Government of Assam had stated that Koch Rajbongshi have benefited like other sections of the society by the process of development and it will not be correct to say that they have become backward during this period so as to claim status of Scheduled Tribe). But the National Commission for Scheduled Castes and Scheduled Tribes did not favour its specifications as Scheduled Tribe. However, in 2002, the National Commission changed its stand and recommended the inclusion. It also referred the case to the RGI for the justification, but the RGI rejected the claim of Koch-Rajbongshi community. The RGI has commented eight times (1981, 1992, 1995, 1997, 2000, 2003, 2005 and 20.3.2006) on the proposal for inclusion of Koch Rajbongshi including the above referred reference of 2005 (on 20.3.2006). Similarly in the case of other aforesaid communities, the RGI has rejected the claim for their inclusion in the list of Scheduled Tribes of Assam several times," the report said.

Kyndiah also stated that the modalities required the consent of the State government concerned, the RGI and the National Commission for Scheduled Castes and Scheduled Tribes for modification in the list of Scheduled Tribes. That would take time, and therefore, no specific time frame can be mentioned, he said.

New Delhi's stand on the issue has added to the worries of the Congress government in Assam, which fears that it will lose its traditional vote-bank in the tea belt. And with only a month left for the panchayat elections, State Congress leaders are now under pressure to go on an overdrive to hold on to this vote-bank. The Gogoi government is also worried about the armed outfits among the Adivasis throwing their weight behind the overground organisations. Local newspapers published a statement purported to have been issued by the All Adivasi National Liberation Army (AANLA), a new militant outfit active in the tea garden areas in Privileged Assam, which threatened to target "civilians and the Gogoi government's men" to avenge the brutalities on Adivasi protesters in Guwahati. In the coming weeks, the Gogoi government will be under pressure to convince New Delhi to concede the communities' demand.

A large number of people from Orissa, Jharkhand, Bihar, Chhattisgarh and Madhya Pradesh were migrated to Assam in search of jobs in tea estates hundred years ago. Out of them a sufficient number of people belong to Scheduled Caste categories. These people were provided Scheduled Caste status in their respective States. But these labourers are being denied to the status of Scheduled Caste in Assam. Such types of labourers are spread all over the country, originally belongs to Scheduled Caste categories in their respective States but they are yet being deprived of their Constitutional rights. The economic conditions of tea estate labourers, working in tea gardens are living here from generation are very pitiable. A person belongs to Scheduled Caste, deprived of their rights since long, and could get their rights. (Susanta Talukdar, Tribal Turmoil in Assam).

Appendix C

Rajya Sabha

SYNOPSIS OF DEBATES

(Proceedings other than Questions and Answers) Friday, July 28, 2006 / Sravana 6, 1928 (Saka)

THE CONSTITUTION (AMENDMENT) BILL, 2004 (AMENDMENT OF ARTICLES 341 AND 342) – *Contd*.................

DR E.M. SUDARSANA NATCHIAPPAN, continuing his unfinished speech dated 12th May, 2006, said: This Bill attracts a very important issue of having the right to reservation for certain people who are employed as tea garden workers, who have habitually and by their nature, lived in a very backward condition. They are living a socially isolated life. Especially in Assam, these people are not at all accepted in any other job. That is why, this community has come forward with this request of declaring them as Scheduled Tribes. These people are totally dependent on tea gardens and they have got no world outside. They also don't have the economic status to raise their status to come forward and have more education in colleges of universities.

These people should be protected and they should be given more concessions. They should be included in the Scheduled tribe list so that attention can be paid and the Government can have more measures for their benefits. The capacities of the

Scheduled Tribe or such people is not at all lower when you compare them with other people who have got opportunities of having better education for generations. For these types of people who have been identified and who have already been recommended, necessary steps should be taken.

I request that the Government of India should consider this Bill seriously. I support this Bill and expect that the Government of India will take personal interest in this matter and see that these communities are included in the Scheduled Tribe list.

SHRI SURENDRA LATH: A large number of people from Orissa, Jharkhand, Bihar, Chhattisgarh and Madhya Pradesh were migrated to Assam in search of jobs in tea estates hundred years ago. Out of them a sufficient number of people belongs to Scheduled Caste and Scheduled Tribe categories. These people were provided Scheduled Castes and Scheduled Tribes status in their respective States. But these labourers are being denied to the status of Scheduled Caste and Scheduled Tribe in Assam. Such type of labourers are spread all over the country, who originally belongs to Scheduled Caste and Scheduled Tribe categories in their respective States but they are yet being deprived of their Constitutional rights.

The economic conditions of tea estate labourers, working in tea gardens who are living here from generation are very pitiable. The Bill seeks uniform policy for whole of the country. In Orissa, some tribal people come under Scheduled Tribes category but in Assam, they are still being kept in OBC category. As a result, they are being deprived the facilities, being given to Scheduled Tribes.

This Bill is very important. People belongs to Scheduled Castes/Scheduled Tribes, which are deprived of their rights since long, could get their rights through enactment of this Bill. Government should look into it and identify such type of categories in the country and incorporate these categories in the scheduled lists of Scheduled Caste and Scheduled Tribe at the earliest so that they can get their Constitutional rights.

PROF P.J. KURIEN: I support this Bill. It is discrimination that the same caste of people or same group of people is considered Scheduled Caste or Scheduled Tribe in one State and as non-Scheduled Caste in other States. India is one and our Constitution is one for all of us. Of all the labour class, this tea garden labourers are the most deprived lot. In Kerala, the workers in tea gardens have no work because most of the tea gardens are closed. They are not getting wages; they are starving.

It is not only the question of economic status. Why do they demand the Scheduled Castes status? Because social empowerment will be possible only by giving them this Scheduled Castes status. This lot of people who are originally from other States like Bihar, Andhra Pradesh, Madhya Pradesh or West Bengal they are enjoying the status of Scheduled Castes in those States. I am of the view that the Government should have brought forward this Bill to correct this anomaly or correct this distortion in our Constitutional provisions. Not only that these communities are to be considered, there are other communities also in our country who actually belong to the Scheduled Castes communities but they are deprived of this Scheduled Castes status.

There are such other people also in our country who should be considered for inclusion in the list of Scheduled Castes. The Government should consider appointing a new Commission to study the status of all these backward, poor, under-developed and under-privileged people. All those who were untouchables once upon a time and who were not included in the list of Scheduled Castes should be included in the list and for that, the Government should appoint a Commission to study and revise the list of the Scheduled Castes.

If we confer the Scheduled Caste status to a certain community, by that alone, the community will not come up. Even after 50 years, we find that the position of the Scheduled Caste people is much lower in the society. They are backward - socially, economically and educationally. The reason for it is lack of education. Education is the key part of our progress, and it is required for development and for social empowerment also. So, special emphasis should be laid on the education of these communities, and also of those workers who are in the plantation field.

The percentage of drop-outs is more in the children of plantation workers. I suggest that the Government should come forward with a programme to help these Scheduled Castes and backward class people in furthering their education, and reducing the drop-outs from schools. With these words, I support the Bill.

SHRI MATILAL SARKAR: I support the Bill. This is a case of anomalies in the list of Scheduled Castes and Scheduled Tribes to be rectified and executed uniformly all over the country. The Munda community, the Urang community are treated as the Scheduled Tribes in our State. Similar to these communities, there are communities, viz. Rupini and Reang, which belong to a Scheduled Tribe in our State, but in our neighbouring States like Mizoram and West Bengal, these communities are not equally treated as Scheduled Tribe. Apart from Rupini and Reang, there are some other communities also in the same category. So, these anomalies exist all over the country. The Namasudra community is in the list of Scheduled Castes in our State. It is in the list of Scheduled Castes in West Bengal. But in most other States of the country, the Namasudra community is not included in the list of Scheduled Castes.

In case of OBCs, there are two Commissions. One is the National Commission, and the other is the State Commission. In our State, there are 46 communities in the State List, but in the Central List, there are only 42 communities included in the list of OBCs. In reply to a question the Hon'ble Minister has replied that there are eight States in the country, where there is no reservation for OBCs, because in all those eight States, the reservation has exceeded 50 per cent. The OBCs are not getting reservation in those States. It is a social torture. It is painful that in many parts of the country the atrocities are still going on Scheduled Castes. I suggest that not only Munda, Urang, Khana and all other communities that have been referred to by Members from different States but Namasudra Reang and Rupini communities should also be included in the list of Scheduled Castes. With these words I support the Bill.

SHRI DHARAM PAL SABHARWAL: This Bill has given a voice to those people who are trying for a long time to be included in the list of Scheduled Castes and Scheduled Tribes. The labourers from Odisha, West Bengal, Madhya Pradesh, Bihar and Andhra Pradesh were rehabilitated in Assam to flourish the tea industry. The castes, to which these labourers belong, were recognised as Scheduled Castes or Scheduled Tribes and they were availing the benefit of their caste in their respective native States. But in Assam they did not find place in Scheduled Castes and Scheduled Tribes. In this way, they are being deprived of the benefits available to them. That is why Articles 341 and 342 needs to be amended. A few concessions has been given to them by making certain provisions in the Constitution. Even today, we talk of giving reservation to their children, though it should have been ended 20 years before. The people belonging to the Scheduled Castes are being looked down upon even today by the society. There are also two groups in the Scheduled Castes. A few people from SC community got education and reached on higher posts and the others are earning their bread by doing odd jobs in the villages. We should concentrate on such people who have lagged much behind. Separate provision should be made for them so that they may get a chance to live keeping their heads high. Every state should be given the right by amending Article 341 so that it can provide reservation on the basis of population of socially, economically and educationally backward people. I support this Bill.

PROF RAM DEO BHANDARY: I support this Bill. This Bill has been brought to end the Constitutional discrimination being done with the community of Scheduled Castes and Scheduled Tribes in Assam. They have been put in the category of Scheduled Castes and Scheduled Tribes in Tripura and West Bengal but in Assam they have been put in the category of Other Backward Class. Several Commissions, after studying their condition, has said that these people should be put in the category of Scheduled Castes and Scheduled Tribes. What is the reason for keeping them so far in the category of backward class? It is a very big Constitutional discrimination. These people are being denied various facilities. Such anomalies are also there in many states. Various recommendations have come from many castes from Bihar to the effect that they should be put in the category of Scheduled Castes. Central Government should take decision soon on the pending recommendations received from states. There is no representation of such people in the Supreme Court and High Court.

Which people were there in the Anti-reservation campaign in AIIMS? 15-20 per cent people want that backward people should not progress. There is Constitution to protect the rights of such people.

DR PRABHA THAKUR: Congress Governments had taken the first ever initiative of providing equal participation through reservation for the community of Scheduled Castes and Scheduled Tribes. I am happy at this fact. If it comes to our knowledge that some categories of these communities have been left out and injustice has been done with them, then full social justice should be provided to them. The castes of labourers are getting benefits and facilities under the category of Scheduled Castes and Scheduled Tribes in Bihar, Orissa and Madhya Pradesh. But the workers working in Tripura, West Bengal and Assam should also be put in this category. It is the responsibility of the people of the society that the socially and economically neglected people are provided justice.

There are talented people in the community of Scheduled Castes and Scheduled Tribes also but they do not get the opportunity to prove their talent. Wherever they get the opportunity, they have proved their talent. Reservation should be provided according to the percentage proportion of Scheduled Castes and Scheduled Tribes in the states so that all their communities get benefits. Such an arrangement should also be made that priority is given in the benefit of reservation to the people of those families of Scheduled Castes and Tribes who have never got the benefit of SC/ST quota. Some special effort should be made for providing free education upto the highest level to the girls of these communities. There should be such arrangements in Government Schools so that the children of weaker section, if they want to get education in the English medium, should get opportunity to get education, free of charge, in English medium there. I support this Bill.

SHRI PRAVEEN RASHTRAPAL: It is very clear that the issue pertains to the Eastern sector of the country. I am also in possession of a Resolution passed by the Assam Legislative Assembly. The Government of Assam has requested the Central Government to take appropriate action in connection with the resolution passed by the Assembly.

The issue regarding the list of the Scheduled Castes and the Scheduled Tribes is a very complex issue. When we want to amend the Article 341 and Article 342 of the Constitution, we have to be very careful because once you make an amendment in Articles 341 and 342; it will not be applicable to a particular State. It will be applicable to the whole of India.

This list was prepared in the year 1930. It was adopted in the Government of India Act 1935 and when we became free in the year 1947 and the Constituent Assembly finally approved this list. The list of the Scheduled Castes and the Scheduled Tribes cannot be amended and should not be amended by any State Government. It has to be amended only by the Parliament. The list as prepared by various State Governments in those days was adopted as the national list. The initiative has to be taken by the respective State Governments.

A particular sub-caste was Scheduled Caste only for a particular district and when the area restriction was removed, they became Scheduled Caste all over the State. I am very sorry to inform you that all the Ministries told us that they are not the Nodal Ministry as far as the matters concerning Scheduled Castes and Scheduled Tribes are concerned. I will request the Government to first appoint a Ministry as a Modal Ministry for the affairs of Scheduled Castes, for the affairs to Scheduled Tribes, so that Ministry will be fully in charge as far as the matter concerned Scheduled Castes and Scheduled Tribes are concerned. Uttar Pradesh made certain amendments in the list of Scheduled Castes without permission from the Central Government, without obtaining approval from the Registrar General, without obtaining approval from the National Commission for the Scheduled Castes and the Scheduled Tribes, and the matter is pending in the Supreme Court or High Court in Delhi.

I would like to become a Brahmin. But will you give me the right of Brahmins? And, if I don't get, will you protect me? But thousands and thousands of people belonging to different religions other than Hindu religion are demanding before the learned Supreme Court that we may be treated as Scheduled Castes. There cannot be Scheduled Castes among Islam; there cannot be Scheduled Castes among Christianity. I fully agree with the mover of the Bill. The issue is very serious as far as Assam, West Bengal and Tripura is concerned. The issue of Eastern sector requires specific attention.

The biggest amendment in the list of Scheduled Castes took place during the year 1977. I have got information pertaining to one particular department and the Hon. Minister is also present here. According to this information available with me, as on

1st January, 2006, for the Department of Legal Affairs, there are 358 officers in Group B and the percentage of total employees is only 0.84 as far as Scheduled Tribe is concerned.

I will request the present Government of India to pay appropriate attention so that justice is done to the Scheduled Castes and the Scheduled Tribes as far as the correction of the list and issues concerning their welfare are concerned. Since it is a Constitutional Amendment, the Government may kindly give an assurance that the Bill will be introduced by the Government in due course.

SHRI N. JOTHI: I thank Shri Condappan for having brought this Bill. Since Independence, we are struggling for the inclusion of certain SCs and STs in the list of respective States. A Scheduled Caste person in one State cannot be a Scheduled Caste person in another State. It is shame in this 21st Century that we still discriminate people on the basis of caste and community, especially the Scheduled Castes and the Scheduled Tribes. It is a legacy of the Vedic concept. It is very unfortunate.

Pondicherry and Tamil Nadu are Tamil speaking States. The list prepared in Pondicherry is not applicable to Tamil Nadu. If a person obtains a certificate by false means, he should be prosecuted and put to jail. A judgment of the Supreme Court about three years ago has said that a State Government cannot include any community either in the Scheduled Caste List or the Scheduled Tribe List. It should be only by a Presidential Order with the concurrence of the State Government. The order of the day now is that they must bring an Amendment in the Constitution to remedy the problems of our own brothers.

I have no caste feelings. We feel shy in adding our community name with us. Whereas I see in very many States, next to their name, the community name automatically comes. But for all the social reforms, the term 'social justice' was coined by Dravidian Party. We are for social justice for the whole of India. We must have a social vision. The Parliament should have a social vision in uplifting our brothers who have been suppressed continuously for the past 3,000 years. By joining the issue with my friend, Mr Selvius Condappan I would go one step forward. We must make it a Constitutional burden. If a former community boy marriages a Scheduled Caste or a Scheduled Tribe girl, he should be given preference in employment. He should be given cash awards. Then only the untouchability will go. A lawyer enrolled in any State can go and practise anywhere in India. Nobody can question it. Whereas, a Scheduled Caste person in one State, cannot be a Scheduled Caste person in another State Even now, the Scheduled Caste people or the Scheduled Tribe people have no independence. They have to struggle for their livelihood. Why should these inequalities be there? Why should there be castes being further recognised? Why should there be religion being further recognised. I feel it very shameful in this country to continue this caste system. We must abolish this. We must have one India and we must have one kind of citizen and to avoid any inequalities, we must approve this Bill. I am for this Bill and I am supporting it.

MISS ANUSUIYA UIKEY: I support this Bill to bring about the amendment in the Constitution of India. The reservation should be provided to the Scheduled Castes and Scheduled Tribes in the whole country on the equal basis. In one State one tribe has got the status of Scheduled Tribe but in the other State the same tribe has been decided the same status. Because they are not recognised any Scheduled Tribes, they are economically and socially very backward. If the reservation is provided to the people belonging to Scheduled Castes and Scheduled Tribes one equal basis, the all people of this backward and poor section will be benefitted.

SHRI SANTOSH BAGRODIA: Today, people belonging to Scheduled Castes and Scheduled Tribes have become rich. This the only country in the world where people fight with each other to get themselves declared as backward.

(Speech unfinished). Discussion not concluded.

YOGENDRA NARAIN,

*Secretary-General.*rssynop@sansad.nic.in

Bibliography

REPORTS

Annual Report, Ministry of Personnel, Public Grievances and Pensions, Government of India, New Delhi, 2002-2003, Chapter 5, Paragraph 5.2.

Annual Reports, National Commission for the Scheduled Castes and Scheduled Tribes, Government of India, New Delhi, 1956-2001.

Annual Reports, Ministry of Personnel, Public Grievances and Pensions, Government of India, New Delhi, 1956-2003.

Annual Reports, Public Enterprises Survey Volume 1, Ministry of Heavy Industries and Public Enterprises, New Delhi, 1978-2005.

Census of India Report 2011, Government of India.

Census of India, Governement of India, Ministry of Home Affairs, Office of the Registrar General and Census Commissioner, India.

Report of the Commissions for SC/ST, Commission for SC/ST, Delhi, 1998.

Report of the speeches of S.C. Jamir, Chief Minister of Nagaland, Nagaland, 1999.

Report on Millennium Development Goals and Dalits A Status Report April 2006 National Conference of Dalit Organisations (NACDOR).

The Corporate Body of the Buddha Educational Foundation, Taiwan (1994), What is Buddhism? Published by Dallas Buddhist Association, Texas, USA.

Towards Equality, Report of the Committee on Status of Women in India, New Delhi: Ministry of India Publication.

Report of the Commissioner for Scheduled Caste and Scheduled Tribes. 1978-79. New Delhi: Government of India.

Desai, I. P. 1973. Water Facilities for the Untouchables in Rural Gujarat: A Report.

Government of Karnataka. Report of the Second Backward Classes Commission, Vol. 1. Bangalore, 1986, p. 26.

Government of India. 1957. Report of the Advisory Committee on the Revision of the Lists of Scheduled Castes and Scheduled Tribes.

Government of India. 1969. Report of the Committee on Untouchability, Economic and Educational Development of the Scheduled Castes and Connected Documents (Elayaperumal Report).

Shaw, P. G. 1955. Report on the Seminar on Casteism and Removal of Untouchability. Bombay: Indian Conference of Social Work.

Various reports of the Constitutent Assembly Debates on the Issue of Caste, Reservation, Quota, Migration etc.

The Constitution of India, Government of India, Ministry of Law and Justice, Annual Report on the Scheduled Castes and Scheduled Tribes (Prevention of Atrocities) Act, 1989 for the Year 2002.

Primary Census Abstract for Total population, Scheduled Castes, 2011, Office of the Registrar General and Census Commissioner, India.

Primary Census Abstract for Total population, Scheduled Castes, 2011, Office of the Registrar General and Census Commissioner, India.

Government of India, NSSO, Primary data (2009-10), Rural Development Statistics, Scheduled Castes and Scheduled Tribes.

Government of India, Planning Commission, Eleventh Five Year Plan, 2007-2012, Volume I, Inclusive Growth.

B.P. Mandal Commission Report Submitted to the Government of India on OBC, 1990.

Report on employment and unemployment survey 2011-12, Ministry of Labour and Employment, Government of India, Chandigarh, p. 37.

Fifth Schedule [Article 244(1)] – This provides for the administration and control of Scheduled Areas and Scheduled Tribes (areas and tribes needing special protection due to disadvantageous conditions). Sixth Schedule [Articles 244(2) and 275(1)]— Provisions for the administration of tribal areas in Assam, Meghalaya, Tripura, and Mizoram.

Government of India, NSSO, Report No. 516, Employment and Unemployment Situation among Social Groups in India, 61st Round, (July 2004 – June 2005), October 2006 and NSSO, Primary Data (2009-10).

BOOKS

Abbasayulu, Y. B. 1978. Scheduled Caste Elite. Hyderabad: Centre for Harijan Studies. Osmania University.

Abbasayulu, Y. B. 1979. Sociology of Depressed Groups. Hyderabad: Centre for Harijan Studies. Osmania University.

Abbi, B. L. 1984. ed. Northeast Region: Problems and Prospects of Development, Chandigarh: Centre for Research in Rural and Industrial Development, 1984.

Adhikari, O. S. 1988. Four Immigrants Tribes of Tripura. Tripura: Directorate of Research. Government of Tripura.

Agarwal, Partap C. and Ashraf, M. Siddiq. 1976. Equality Through Privilege: A Study of Special Privileges of Scheduled Castes in Haryana. New Delhi: Shri Ram Centre for Industrial Relations and Human Resources.

Aggarwal, L. B. 1934. The Harijans in Rebellion. Bombay: Taraporewala and Sons.

Aggarwal, S. Kailash. 1999. ed. Dynamics of Identity and Inter-group Relations in North-East India. Shimla: Indian Institute of Advanced Studies.

Aggarwal, Yash; Sibou, Sarika; Kumar, Ashok. 1992. Educating Scheduled Castes. New Delhi: NIEPA.

Agrawal, M.M. 1996. Ethnicity, Culture and Nationalism in North East India. New Delhi: Indus Publishing Company.

Agrawal, S. P. and Aggarwal, J. C. 1991. Educational and Social Uplift of Backward Classes: At What Cost and How? Mandal Commission and After. Part I. New Delhi: Concept Publishing Co.

Ahir, D.C. 1991. Buddhism in Modern India. Delhi: Sri Satguru Publications.

Ahmad, Imtiaj. 1978. ed. Caste and Social Stratification among Muslims in India. New Delhi: Manohar Publication.

Ainapur, L. S. 1986. Dynamics of Caste Relations in Rural India. Jaipur: Rawat Publications.

Aiyappan, A. 1965. Social Revolution in a Kerala Village: A Study in Cultural Change. Bombay: Asia Publishing House.

Allen, B. C. 1905. Gazetteer of Naga Hills and Manipur. New Delhi: Mittal Publications.

Aloysius, G. 1998. Religion as Emancipatory Identity: The Buddhist Movement among the Tamils under Colonialism. New Delhi: New Age Publishers.

Ambedkar, B. R. 1925. What Congress and Gandhi Have Done to the Untouchables? Bombay: Thacker and Co.

Ambedkar, B. R. 1943. Mr Gandhi and the Emancipation of the Untouchables. Bombay: Thacker and Co.

Ambedkar, B. R. 1946. Who Were The Sudras? How They Came To Be The Fourth Varna in Indo-Aryan Society. Bombay: Thacker and Co.

Ambedkar, B. R. 1948. The Untouchables: Who Were They and Why They Became Untouchables. New Delhi: Amrit Book Co.

Ambedkar, B. R. 1957. The Buddha and His Dhamma. Bombay: Siddharth College Publications.

Ambedkar, B. R. 1990. Annihilation of Caste: An Undelivered Speech. Edited by Mulk Raj Anand. New Delhi: Arnold Publishers.

Ambedkar, B.R. 1957. The Buddha and His Dhamma. Nagpur: Buddha Bhumi Publication.

Anand, J. H. 1995. Dalit Literature is the Literature of Protest in Bhagwan Das and James Massey edited Dalit Solidarity. Delhi: ISPCK.

Anand, Mulk Raj. 1953. Untouchable: A Novel. Bombay.

Anand, Mulk Raj; and Zelliot, Eleanor. 1992. ed. An Anthology of Dalit Literature. New Delhi: Gyan Publishing House.

Anant, S. S. 1979. Changing Caste Hindu Attitudes Towards Harijans: A Follow Up After Four Years in G. R. Gupta in edited Main Currents in Indian Sociology - III: Cohesion and Conflict in Modern India. New Delhi: Vikas.

Anwar, Ali. 2001. Masavaat Ki Jang. Delhi: Vani Prakashan.

Ao, Lanunungsang. A. 2002. From Phizo to Muivah: The Naga National Question in North-East India. New Delhi: Mittal Publications.

Aranha, Celine; Fernando, Peter; and Mahale, Prabha. 1991. Beyond The Fire Line: Perceptions of Eight Tribal Women. New Delhi: Indian Social Institute.

Atal, Yogesh. 1968. The Changing Frontiers of Caste. Delhi: National Publishing House.

Ayrookuzhiel, A. M. Abraham. 1990. ed. The Dalit Desiyata: The Kerala Experience in Development and Class Struggle. Delhi: ISPCK.

B.L. Shankar and Valerain Rodrigues. 2011. eds. The Indian Parliament: A Democracy at Work. New Delhi: Oxford University Press.

Bailey, F. G. 1957. Caste and the Economic Frontier: A Village in Highland Orissa. Manchester: University of Manchester.

Bailey, F. G. 1960. Tribe, Caste and the Nation. Bombay: Oxford University Press.

Bailey, F. G. 1963. Politics and Social Change in Orissa. Berkeley: University of California Press.

Balwally, Darshan. 2003. Growth of Totalitarianism in Arunachal Pradesh, Mizoram and Nagaland. Delhi: Spectrum Publications, 2003.

Bandyopadhyay, Sekhar. 1994. Caste, Class and Politics in Colonial Bengal: A Case Study of the Namasudra Movement of 1872-1937 in K. L. Sharma edited Caste and Class in India. New Delhi: Rawat Publications.

Baneerjee, Amalesh. 2004. ed. Decentralised Planning and Development. Delhi: Kanishka Publishers.

Barman, Debapriya Deb. 1983. Treatise on Traditional Social Institutions of the Tripuri Community. Tripura: Directorate of Research. Government of Tripura.

Barpujari, H. K. 1996. Assam in the Days of the Company. Shillong: North Eastern Hill University Publications.

Barua, Hem. 1954. The Red River and the Blue Hill. Guwahati: Lawyer's Book Stall.

Baruah, Sanjib. 1999. India against Itself: Assam and the Politics of Nationality. New Delhi: Oxford University Press.

Baruah, Sanjiv. 2005. Durable Disorder, Understanding the Politics of Northeast India. Delhi: Oxford University Press.

Basu, Pradip Kumar. 1996. The Communist Movement in Tripura. Calcutta: Progressive Publishers.

Battacharji, Romesh. 2002. Lands of Early Dawn. New Delhi: Rupa and Co.

Benjamin, Joseph. 1989. Scheduled Castes in Indian Politics and Society. New Delhi: Ess Ess Publications.

Berremen, Gerald D. 1979. ed. Self, Situation and Escape from Stigmatised Identity in Caste and Other Inequities. Meerut Folklore Institute.

Beteille, Andre. 1965. ed. Caste, Class and Power: Changing Patterns of Stratification in a Tanjore Village. Berkeley: University of California Press.

Beteille, Andre. 1969. ed. Caste: Old and New. Bombay: Asia Publishing House.

Beteille, Andre. 1969. ed. Social Inequality. New Delhi: Penguin Books.

Beteille, Andre. 1972. Inequality and Social Change. Delhi: Oxford University Press.

Beteille, Andre. 1981. The Backward Classes and the New Social Order. Delhi: Oxford University Press.

Bhagabati, K. Abani and Kar, K. Bimal. 1999. Survey of Research in Geography on North-East India 1970-1990. New Delhi: Regency Publication.

Bhagwat, Vidyut. 1995. Dalit Women in India: Issues and Perspectives - Some Critical Reflections in P. G. Jogdand, edited Dalit Women in India: Issues and Perspectives. New Delhi: Gyan Publishing House, in collaboration with University of Poona, Pune.

Bhai, P. N. 1986. Harijan Women in Independent India. New Delhi: B. R. Publishing.

Bhan, Susheela. 1999. Impact of Ethnic Violence on Youth: A Study of Tribal-Nontribal Violence in Kokrajhar, Assam. New Delhi: Shipra Publications.

Bharat Sewak Samaj. 1958. Slums of Old Delhi. Delhi: Atma Ram and Sons.

Bhargava, Rajeev. 2008. Politics and Philosophy of Indian Constitution. Delhi: Oxford University Press.

Bhatt, Anil. 1970. Caste and Political Mobilisation in Gujarat District in Rajni Kothari, edited Caste in Indian Politics. Delhi: Orient Longman.

Bhatt, Anil. 1975. Caste, Class and Politics: An Emperical Profile of Social Stratification in Modern India. Delhi: Manhohar Book Service.

Bhattacharjee, Chandana. 1996. Ethnicity and Autonomy Movement. New Delhi: Vikas Publishing House.

Bhattacharjee, J.B. 1995. North East Indian Perspectives in History. New Delhi: Vikas Publishing House.

Bhattacharjee, Pravas Ranjan. 1993. Economic Transition in Tripura. New Delhi: Vikas Publishing House.

Bhattacharjee, Prodip Nath. 1983. The Jamatiyas of Tripura. Tripura: Directorate of Research. Government of Tripura.

Bhattacharjee, Prodip Nath. 1987. The Garos of Tripura. Agartala: Directorate of Research Tribal Welfare Department. Government of Tripura.

Bhattacharya, Sabhyasachi. 2007. History, Political thought in Modern India and Social Science. New Delhi: Oxford University Press.

Bhattacharya, Suchintya. 1992. From Jhuming to Tapping. Tripura: Directorate of Research.

Bhattacharyya, Hiranya Kumar. 2001. The Silent Invasion: Assam versus Infiltration. Delhi: Spectrum Publications.

Bhattacharyya, N.N.1995. Religious Culture of North-Eastern India. New Delhi: Manohar Publishers and Distributors.

Bhattacherjee, P. A. and Singh, R. S. 1995. Tea Plantation and the Tribes of Tripura. Tripura: Tripura State Tribal Cultural Research Institute and Museum.

Bhaumik, Subir. 1996. Insurgent Cross Fire: North-East India. New Delhi: Lancer Publishers.

Bhuyan, Arun Chandan and De, Sibopada. 1999. ed. Political History of Assam Vol. I 1926-1919. Guwahati: Publication Board Assam.

Bhuyan, Arun Chandan and De, Sibopada. 1999. ed. Political History of Assam, Vol. II, 1920-1939. Guwahati: Publication Board Assam.

Bhuyan, B. C. 1989. Political Development of the North East. New Delhi: Omsons Publications.

Blunt, E. A. H. 1931. Caste System of Northern India. London: Oxford University Press.

Bordoloi, B. N. 1972. District Handbook: United Mikir and North Cachar Hills. Shillong: Tribal Research Institute.

Bordoloi, B. N. 1981. Tribes of Assam Part-III. Guwahati: Assam Institute of Research for Tribals and Scheduled Castes.

Bordoloi, B. N. 1984. The Dimasa Kacharis of Assam. Assam: Tribal Research Institute.

Bordoloi, B. N. Thakur, G. and Sharmah C. 1988. Tribes of Assam Part-II. Guwahati: Tribal Research Institute.

Bordoloi, B. N; Thakur, G. Sharmah C. and Saikia, M. C. 1987. Tribes of Assam Part-I. Guwahati: Tribal Research Institute.

Bose, Manilal. 1979. ed. Historical and Constitutional Documents of Northeast India, 1824-1973, Delhi: Concept Publishing House.

Bose, Pradip Kumar. 1985. Social Mobility and Caste Violence: A Study of the Gujarat Riots in I. P. Desai. (ed.) Caste, Caste Conflict and Reservations. Centre for Social Studies. Delhi: Ajanta Publications.

Bougle, C. 1971. Essays on the Caste System. Cambridge: University of Cambridge.

Briggs, G. W. 1920. The Chamars. Calcutta: Association Press.

Briggs, G. W. 1993. Doms and Their Near Relations. Mysore: The Wesley Press and Publishing House.

Brown, R. 2001. Statistical Account of Manipur. New Delhi: Mittal Publications.

Bujra, A. 1971. Politics of Stratification. Oxford: Oxford University Press.

Carsten, F. L. 1967. The Rise of Fascism. London: Methuen and Co.

Chakravarty, L. N. 1995. Glimpses of the Early History of Arunachal. Itanagar: Directorate of Research. Government of Arunachal Pradesh.

Chamanlal, B. 1962. Gypsies: Forgotten Children of India. New Delhi: Government of India Publications Division.

Chasie, Charles. 1999. The Naga Imbroglio: A Personal Perspective. Kohima: Standard Printers and Publishers.

Chatterjee, Partha. 1994. Caste and Subaltern Consciousness in Ranajit Guha, edited Subaltern Studies VI: Writings on South Asian History and Society. Delhi: Oxford Unviersity Press.

Chatterjee, Suhas. 1994. Making of Mizoram: Role of Laldenga Vol. I. and Vol. II, New Delhi: M D Publications Pvt Ltd.

Chaube, S. K. 1973. Hill Politics in Northeast India. Patna: Orient Longman Limited.

Chaudhuri, Dipak Kumar. 1991. Northeast: A Study of Mobility and Political Behaviour. Guwahati: New Delhi: Omsons Publications.

Chaudhuri, Dipak Kumar. 1993. Autonomy Movements in Assam. New Delhi: Omsons Publications.

Chaudhuri, Dipak Kumar. 1994. North East as I See It. New Delhi: Omsons Publications.

Chaudhuri, Dipak Kumar. 1995. ed. Administration Report of the Political Agency. Hill Tipperah 1872-1878, Vol. 1. Agartala: Tripura State Cultural Research Institute and Museum.

Chaudhuri, Dipak Kumar. 1996. Administration Report of the Political Agency, Hill Tipperah 1872-1878, Vol. 11. Agartala: Tripura State Cultural Research Institute and Museum.

Chaudhuri, Jagadis Gan. 1983. The Riangs of Tripura. Agartala: Directorate of Research.

Chitnis, Suma. 1981. Identity: Scheduled Caste Students, NCERT, New Delhi.

Chubey, S.K. 1985. Electoral Politics in northeast India. Madras: Madras University Press.

Cohan, B. N. 1955. The Changing Status of a Depressed Class in McKim Marriott edited Village India: Studies in the Little Community. Chicago: The University of Chicago Press.

D'Souza, Victor. 1980. Educational Inequalities Among the Scheduled Castes: A Case Study of Punjab. Chandigarh: Punjab University.

Dalit Panthers. 1973. Dalit Panthers Manifesto in Joshi, R. Barbara edited. 1986. Untouchable! Voices of the Dalit Liberation Movement. London: Zed Books.

Damle, Y. B. and Karve, I. 1963. Note on the Position of Scheduled Castes and Their Position in the Village in Group Relations in a Village Community. Poona: Deccan College. Post-Graduate and Research Institute.

Dangle, Arjun. 1992. ed. No Room for the New Sun. New Delhi: Orient Longman.

Dangle, Arjun. 1992. ed. Poisoned Bread: Translations from Modern Marathi Dalit Literature. New Delhi: Orient Longman.

Darlong, Letthuama. 1995. The Darlongs of Tripura. Agartala: Directorate of Tribal Research Institute. Government of Tripura.

Das, Amiya Kumar. 1982. Assam's Agony: A Socio-Economic and Political Analysis. New Delhi: Lancers Publishers.

Das, Bhagwan. 1969. Thus Spoke Ambedkar, Selected Speeches, Vol. II. Jullandar: Bheem Patrika Publications.

Das, Bhagwan. 1995. Socio-Economic Problems of Dalits in Bhagwan Das and James Massey edited Dalit Solidarity. Delhi: Indian Society for Promoting Christian Knowledge.

Das, Bhagwan. 1998. Revival of Buddhism in India. Role of Dr Baba Saheb B.R. Ambedkar. Lucknow: Dalit Today Prakashan.

Das, Gurudas and Purkayastha, R. K. 2000. ed. Border Trade: North-East India and Neighbouring Countries. New Delhi: Akansha Publishing House.

Das, Gurudas. 2002. Research Priorities in North-East India: With Special Reference to Arunachal Pradesh. New Delhi: Regency Publications.

Das, Kalyan. 2002. Labour Contracts and Work Agreements in Tea Plantations of Assam. Noida: V. V. Giri National Labour Institute.

Das, M. N.; Manpong, C. M. 1993. District Administration in Arunachal Pradesh. New Delhi: Omsons Publications.

Das, Ratna. 1997. Art and Architecture of Tripura. Agartala: Tribal Research Institute, Government of Tripura.

Das, S. K. 1989. Spotlight on Assam. Chanderpur: Premier Book Service.

Das, S. K. 1994. ULFA: A Political Analysis. New Delhi: Ajanta Publications.

Das, Samir Kumar. 1997. Regionalism in Power. New Delhi: Omsons Publications.

Datta, A. M. 1987. A Study on the Lushais of Jampui Hills in Tripura. Tripura: Directorate of Research. Government of Tripura.

Datta, P.S. 1995. ed. North East and the Indian State: Paradoxes of a Periphery. New Delhi: Vikas Publishing House.

Deepak, Lal. 1988. The Hindu Equilibrium. Clarendon: Oxford University Press.

Deka, Kanak Sen. 1991. Youths in Turmoil: Assam. Calcutta: Gurupada Chaudhury.

Deka, Kanak Sen. 1993. Assam's Crisis: Myth and Reality. New Delhi: Mittal Publications.

Dena, Lal. 1991. ed. History of Modern Manipur 1826-1949. New Delhi: Orbit Publishers-Distributors.

Department of Social Security. 1967. Report of the Advisory Committee on the Revision of Lists of Scheduled Castes and Scheduled Tribes. Government of India.

Desai, I. P. 1976. Untouchability in Rural Gujarat. Bombay: Popular Prakashan.

Desai, I. P. 1985. Anti-reservation Agitation and Struggle of Gujarat Society in Centre for Social Studies edited Caste, Caste Conflict and Reservations. Delhi: Ajanta Publications.

Deshpande, Vasant. 1978. Towards Social Integration: Problems of Adjustment of SC Elites. Pune: Shubhada- Saraswat.

Deshpande, Vasant. 1983. The Mhaisal Untouchables. Pune: Dastane Ramchandra and Co.

Deva, Naoroibam. 1998. Urban Settlement System of Manipur. Imphal: R. K. Sachirani.

Dewan, R. P. 1979. How to Erase Untouchability. New Delhi: R. P. Bookwala.

Dietrich, Gabriele. 1992. Dalit Movements and Women's Movement in Reflection on the Women's Movement in India. New Delhi: Horizons India Books.

Dube, S. C. 1955. Indian Village Ithaca, New York: Cornell University Press.

Dube, S. C. 1955. Ranking of Caste in Telangana Villages in D. N. Majumdar edited Rural Profiles. Lucknow: The Ethnographic and Folk-Culture Society.

Dubois, Abbe. 1983. Hindu Manners, Customs and Ceremonies. New Delhi: AES. Reprint.

Dumont, Louis. 1970. Homo Hierarchicus: The Caste System and Its Implications. London: Paladin, Granada Pub. Ltd.

Dutta, Ajit Kumar. 1990. Maniram Dewan and the Contemporary Assamese Society. Guwahati: Author Publication.

Dutta, Arup Kumar. 1996. Hammer Blow. Assam: Paloma Publications.

Dutta, Arup Kumar. 2001. The Brahmaputra. New Delhi: National Book Trust.

Dutta, N.C. 1997. ed. Politics of Identity and Nation Building in North-East India. New Delhi: South Asian Press.

Dutta, S. 1998. Student Movement in Arunachal Pradesh. Delhi: Himalayan Publication.

Elwin, Verrier. 1957. A Philosophy for NEFA. Itanagar: Directorate of Research. Government of Arunachal Pradesh.

Elwin, Verrier. 1970. A New Book of Tribal Fiction. Itanagar: Directorate of Research. Government of Arunachal Pradesh.

Endle, S.1990. The Kacharis. New Delhi: Low Price Publications.

Engineer, Asghar Ali. 1991. ed. Mandal Commission Controversy. Delhi: Ajanta Publications.

Epstein, T. S. 1962. Economic Development and Social Change in South India. Manchester: Manchester University Press.

Epstein, T. S. 1973. South India: Yesterday, Today and Tomorrow. London: Macmillan Press.

Esqr, Asok Bose. 1995. Geological Survey of Hill Tippera 1909-10: A Notes on the Geological and Economic Resources of the Southern Area of Hill Tippera. Tripura: Tripura State Tribal Cultural Research Institute and Museum.

Fisherman, A. T. 1941. Cultural Change and Underprivileged: A Study of Madigas in South India. Madras: Under Christian Guidance.

Freeman, James M. 1979. Untouchable: An Indian Life History. California: Stanford University Press.

Fuchs, Martin. 2001. A Religion for Civil Society? Ambedkar's Buddhism, the Dalit Issue and the Imagination of Emergent Possibilities in: Dalmia, Vasudha; Malinar, Angelika; Christof, Martin edited Charisma and Canon Essays on the Religious History of the Indian Sub-continent. New Delhi: Oxford University Press.

Fuchs, S. 1951. The Children of Hari: A Study of the Nihar Balahis in Madhya Pradesh. Ahmedabad: Navjivan Publishing House.

Fuchs, S. 1981. At the Bottom of Indian Society. New Delhi: Munshiram Manoharlal Pub. Pvt. Ltd.

Furer-Haimendorf, Christoph von. 1976. Return to the Naked Nagas. New Delhi: Vikas Publishing House.

G.G., Wankhede. 1999. Social Mobility and Scheduled Castes. Delhi: Rawat Publications.

Gait, Edward. 1925. A History of Assam. Guwahati: Lawyers' Book Stall.

Galanter, Marc. 1984. Competing Inequalities: Law and the Backward Classes in India. California: University of California Press.

Gandhi, M. K. 1954. For Workers against Untouchability. Ahmedabad: Navjivan Publishing House.

Gandhi, M. K. 1954. The Removal of Untouchability. Ahmedabad: Navjivan Publishing House.

Ganesan, L. 1991. Relevance of Reservation. Madras: Valentina Publications.

Gangadharan, K. K. 1970. Sociology of Revivalism: A Study of Indianisation, Sanskritisation and Golwalkarism. New Delhi: Kalmakar Prakashan.

Ganggopadhyay, D. K. 1990. Revenue Administration in Assam. Assam: Revenue Department. Government of Assam.

Gangopadhyay, Niladri Sekhar. 2002. Insurgency and Media: A study on Tripura. Agartala: Nabankur.

Gangrade, K.D. 1974. Educational Problems of Scheduled Castes in Haryana. ICSSR.

Gassah, L. S. 1992. ed. Regional Political Parties in North East India. New Delhi: Omsons Publications.

Gassah, L. S. 1997. ed. Autonomous District Council. New Delhi: Omsons Publications.

Gassah, L. S. 1998. Traditional Institutions of Meghalaya: A Study of Doloi and his Administration. New Delhi: Regency Publications.

Gassah, L. S. 1999. Survey of Research in Political Science on North-East India 1970-1990. New Delhi: Regency Publication.

Gassah, L. S. 2001. Research Priorities in North East India: With Special Reference to Mizoram. New Delhi: Regency Publications.

Ghose, Sumita. 1998. ed. Sanjoy's Assam: Diaries and Writings of Sanjoy Ghose. New Delhi: Penguin Books.

Ghosh, Subir. 2001. Frontier Travails: Northeast the Politics of a Mess. New Delhi: Macmillan.

Ghurye, G. S. 1950. Caste and Class in India. Bombay: Popular Books.

Ghurye, G. S. 1961. Caste, Class and Occupation. Bombay: Popular Prakashan.

Glen, M. and Johnson, S. B. 1979. Social Mobility Among Untouchables in G. R. Gupta edited Main Currents in Indian Sociology- III: Cohesion and Conflict in Modern India. New Delhi: Vikas Publication.

Gnanadason, Aruna. 1990. Dalit Women-The Dalit of the Dalit in Arvind P. Nirmal edited Towards A Common Dalit Ideology. Madras: Gurukul Lutheran Theological College and Research Institute.

Gohain, Hiren. 1985. Assam: A Burning Question. Guwahati: Spectrum Publications.

Gohain, U. N. 1942. Assam under the Ahoms. Guwahati: Spectrum Publications.

Gokhale, Nitin A. 1998. The Hot Brew: The Assam Tea Industry's most Turbulent Decade 1987-1997. Guwahati: Delhi: Spectrum Publications.

Gopalkrishnan, R.; Jhunjhunwala, K. K. and Nongkinrih, A. K. 2001. Voluntary Organisations and Sustainable Rural Development in Meghalaya. New Delhi: Regency Publications.

Gopalkrishnan, R. 1995. Insurgent North-Eastern Region of India. New Delhi: Vikas Publishing House.

Gopalkrishnan, R. 2001. Research Priorities in North-East India: With Special Reference to Assam. New Delhi: Regency Publication.

Gordon, Childe V. 1926. The Aryans. Reprinted 1970. New York.

Gorhe, Neelam. 1995. Social Development and Dalit Women in P. G. Jogdand edited Dalit Women in India: Issues and Perspectives. New Delhi: Gyan Publishing House.

Goswami, Debabrata. 1996. Military History of Tripura: 1490 to 1947. Agartala: Tripura State Tribal Cultural Research Institute and Museum.

Goswami, Indira. 2001. The Shadow of Kamakhya. New Delhi: Rupa and Co.

Gough, Kathleen. 1955. The Social Structure of a Tanjore Village in Mckim Marriot edited Village India. Chicago: University of Chicago Press.

Gough, Kathleen. 1973. Harijans in Thanjavur in Kathleen Gough and Hari P. Sharma edited Imperialism and Revolution in South Asia. New York: Monthly Review Press.

Goyal, Bhagat Ram. 1981. Educating Harijans. Haryana: Academic Press.

Gupta, S. K. 1985. Scheduled Castes in Modern Indian Politics: Their Emergence as a Political Power. New Delhi: Munshiram Manoharlal Publishers.

Gupta, Shanti S. 1991. Varna, Castes and Scheduled Castes: Documentation in Historical Perspective with a Classified Index to

Scholarly Writings in Indian Journals (1890-1990). New Delhi: Concept Pub Co.

Gurdon, P. R. 1990. The Khasis. New Delhi: Low Price Publications.

Guru, Gopal. 2009. Humiliation: Claims and Context. New Delhi: Oxford University Press.

Gurukal, Rajan. 1994. The Formation of Caste Society in Kerala in K. L. Sharms edited Caste and Class in India. New Delhi: Rawat Publications.

Gusfield, Joseph R. 1970. ed. Protest, Reform and Revolt: A reader in social movements, New York.

Halbar, B. G. 1986. Lamani Economy and Society in Change: Socio-Cultural Aspects of Economic Change among the Lamani of North Karnataka. Delhi: Mittal Publications.

Hall, Tarquin. 2000. To the Elephant Graveyard. London: Hohn Murray Publishers.

Hardgrave, Robert L. Jr. 1965. The Dravidian Movement. Bombay: Popular Book Depot.

Hardgrave, Robert L. Jr. 1969. The Nadars of Tamilnad. Bombay: Oxford University Press.

Harper, Edward B. 1968. Social Consequences of an Unsuccessful Low Caste Movement in James Silverberg edited Social Mobility in the Caste System in India. The Hague: Mouton Publishers.

Hazarika, Niru 1998. Profile of Youth Organisations in North East India. Assam: V. V. Rao Institute of Micro Studies and Research.

Hazarika, Sanjoy. 1995. Strangers of the Mist: Tales of War and Peace from India's Northeast. New Delhi: Penguin Books.

Hazarika, Sanjoy. 2000. Rites Passage: Border Crossings, Imagined Homelands, India's East and Bangladesh. New Delhi: Penguin Books.

Henry D'Souza and Valerian Rodrigues. 2006. eds. Catholic Communications: India. New Delhi: Media Centre.

Hocart, A. M. 1950. Caste. London: Mathew and Co.

Hudson, T. C. 1908. The Meitheis. New Delhi: Low Price Publications.

Hudson, T. C. 1911. The Naga Tribes of Manipur. New Delhi: Low Price Publications.

Hunter, W. W. 1879. A Statistical Account of Assam Vol. I. and
298

Vol. II. Guwahati: Delhi: Spectrum Publications.

Hussain, M. 1993. The Assam Movement: Class, Ideology and Identity.

New Delhi: Manak Publications Pvt. Ltd. and Har-Anand Publications.

Hutton, J. H. 1922. The Angami Nagas, with Some Notes on Neighbouring Tribes. London: Macmillan and Company.

Hutton, J. H. 1946. Caste in India: Its Nature, Function and Origins. London: Cambridge University Press.

Hutton, J. H. 2003. The Angami Nagas. Nagaland: Directorate of Art and Culture.

Ilaiah, Kancha. 2004. Buffalo Nationalism: A Critique of Spiritual Fascism. Mumbai: Samya; Distributed by Popular Prakashan.

Ilaiah, Kancha. 2005. Why I Am Not a Hindu: A Sudra Critique of Hindutva Philosophy, Culture and Political Economy. Mumbai: Samya Publication.

Ilaiah, Kancha. 2009. Post Hindu India: A Discourse on Dalit Bahujan, Socio Spiritual and Scientific Revolution. New Delhi: Sage Publications.

Iralu, Kaka. D. 2000. Nagaland and India: The Blood and the Kohima: Kaka D. Iralu Publication.

Iralu, Kaka. D. 2001. How Then Shall We Live: Reflections on the Political, Economic and Religious Implications of Naga Nationhood? Kohima: Kaka D. Iralu Publication.

Irschick, Eugene T. 1969. Politics and Social Conflict in South India. Loas Angelies: University of California Press.

Isaacs, Harold R. 1965. India's Ex-Untouchables. Bombay: Asia Publishing House.

Ishwaran, K. 1966. Tradition and Economy in Village India. Bombay: Allied Publications.

Ishwaran, K. 1968. Shivpur: A South Indian Village. London: Routledge.

Jacobs, Julian; Alan MacFarlane; Sarah Harrison and Anita Herle. 1990. The agas: The Hill People of Northeast India: Society, Culture and the Colonial Encounter, London: Thames and Hudson.

Jamir, S. C. 1998. Reminiscences of Correspondences with A. Z. Phizo. Kohima: Published by the Author.

Jayaraman, R. 1975. Caste Continuities in Ceylon. Bombay.

Jeevaratanam, A.G. 1973. Political Implications of Untouchability. Hyderabad: Kondaveedu Press.

Jeferlot, Cristoper. 2004. Dr Ambedkar and Untouchability: Fighting and Analysing Caste. New Delhi: Sage Publication.

Jenkins, Nigel. 2001. Through the Green Door: Travels Among the Khasis. New Delhi: Penguin Books.

Jha, D. N. 1977. Temples as Landed Magnates in Early Medival South India (c. A.D. 700-1300) in R. S. Sharma edited Indian Society: Historical Probings. Second Edition. New Delhi.

Jivaka, Sramanere. 1986. Growing up into Buddhism. Calcutta: Maha Boddhi Society of India.

Jogdan, Prahlad G. 1991. Dalit Movement in Maharashtra. New Delhi: Kanak Publications.

Jogdand, P. G. 1995. ed. Dalit Women in India: Issues and Perspectives. New Delhi: Gyan Publishing House.

Johnson, Glen and Bose, Sipra. 1978. Social Mobility among Untouchables in G.R. Gupta edited Cohesion and Conflict in Modern India. New Delhi: Vilas.

Johnstone, James. 2002. Manipur and the Naga Hills. New Delhi: Gyan Publishing House.

Johnstone, James.1896. Manipur and the Naga Hills. Delhi: Vivek Publishing House.

Joshi, Barbara R. 1982. Democracy in Search of Equality: Untouchable Politics and Indian Social Change. Delhi: Hindustan Publishing Co.

Joshi, Barbara R. 1986. ed. Untouchable! Voices of the Dalit Liberation Movement. London: Zed Books.

Juergensmeyer, Mark. 1979. Religion as Social Vision: The Movement against Untouchability in Twentieth Century Punjab. Berkeley: University of California Press.

Juergensmeyer, Mark. 1988. Religion Rebels in the Punjab: The Social Vision of Untouchables. Delhi: Ajanta Publication.

Kabra, Lalita 1991. Scheduled Caste Girls, Mittal Publications, New Delhi.

Kakade, S. R. 1990. Scheduled Castes and National Integration: A Study of Marathwada. New Delhi: Radiant Pub.

Kakati, Banikanta, The Mother Goddess Kamakhya. Guwahati: Publication Board Assam.

Kamble, J.R. 1979. Rise and Awaking of Depressed Classes in India. New Delhi: National Publication.

Kamble, N. D. 1981. Atrocities on Scheduled Castes. New Delhi: Ashish Publishing House.

Kamble, N. D. 1982. The Scheduled Castes. New Delhi: Ashish Publishing House.

Kamble, N. D. 1983. Deprived Castes and their Struggle for Equality. New Delhi: Ashish Publishing House.

Kamei, Gangmumei. 2002. Ethnicity and Social Change: An Anthology of Essays. Imphal: Pouganglu Gangmei.

Kananaikil, Jose. 1984. Constitutional Provisions for the Scheduled Castes. New Delhi: Indian Social Institute.

Kanshi Ram. 1982. The Chamcha Age: An Era of the Stooges. New Delhi: Authors Publication.

Karlekar, Malvika. 1983. Education and Inequality in André Beteille edited Equality and Inequality. Delhi: Oxford University Press.

Karve, Irawati and Damle, Y. B. 1963. Group Relations in Village Community. Poona: Deccan College.

Karve, Irawati. 1961. Hindu Society: An Interpretation. Poona: Sangam Press.

Kaul, Rekha. 1993. Caste, Class and Education: Politics of the Capitation Fee Phenomenon in Karnataka. New Delhi: Sage Publications.

Kazi, Jigme N. 1993. Inside Sikkim Against the Tide. Gangtok: Hill Media Publications.

Khan, Mumtaz Ali. 1980. Scheduled Castes and their Status in India. New Delhi: Uppal Publishing House.

Khan, Mumtaz Ali. 1994. Identity Formation and Self Identity Among Harijan Elite. New Delhi: Uppal Publishing House.

Khan, Mumtaz Ali. 1994. Reservation for Scheduled Castes: Gaps between Policy and Implementation. New Delhi: Uppal Publishing House.

Khan, Mumtaz Ali. 1995. Human Rights and the Scheduled Castes. Delhi: Uppal Publishers.

Khare, R. S. 1984. The Untouchable as Himself: Ideology, Identity and Pragmatism among the Lucknow Chamars. London: Cambridge University Press.

Kilikdar, Bibhas Kanti. 1998. Customary Laws and Practices: Reangs of Tripura. Tripura: Tribal Research Institute.

Kosambi, D. D. 1956. Myth and Reality: Studies in the Formation of Indian Culture. Bombay: Popular Prakashan.

Kosambi, D. D. 1975. Introduction to the Study of Indian History. Bombay: Popular Prakashan.

Kshirsagar, R. K. 1994. Dalit Movement in India and Its Leaders (1857-1956). New Delhi: MD Pub. Pvt. Ltd.

Kumar, B.B. 1995. Tensions and Conflict in Northeast India. New Delhi: Cosmo Publications.

Kumar, Dharma. 1965. Land and Caste in South India: Agricultural Labour in Madras Presidency during the Nineteenth Century. London: Cambridge University Press.

Kumar, Narender and Rai, Manoj. 2006. Dalit Leadership in Panchayats: A Comparative Study of Four States, Jaipur: Rawat Publications.

Kumar, Narender. 2001. Scheduled Castes and Panchayat Elections in Haryana, New Delhi: Indian Social Institute.

Kumar, Narender. 2004. Dalit Policies, Politics and Parliament, New Delhi: Shipra Publishers.

Kumar, Narendra and Rai, Manoj. 2006. Dalit Leadership in Panchayats: A Comparative Study of Four States. Jaipur: IIDS and Rawat Publications.

Kumar, Nikhilesh. 1999. Survey of Research in Sociology and Social Anthropology in North-East India (1970-1990). New Delhi: Regency Publications.

Kumar, Vivek. 2003. Dalits, Alternative Economic Survey 2002-2003: Liberalisation Sans Social Justice. Noida: Rainbow Publisher.

Kumar, Vivek. 2004. Social Exclusion, Alternative Economic Survey: Magnifying Mal- Development. Noida: Rainbow Publisher and London: Zed Books.

Kumar, Vivek. 2002. Dalit Leadership in India, New Delhi: Kalpaz Publication.

Kumar, Vivek. 2004. Bahujan Samaj Party avm Sanrachnatmak Parivartan. New Delhi: Samyak Prakashan.

Kumar, Vivek. 2006, India's Roaring Revolution: Dalit Assertion and New Horizons, New Delhi: Gagan Deep Publications.

Kumar, Vivek. 2007. Dalit Samaj: Purani Samasyaen Nai Akanshayen. New Delhi: Samyak Prakashan.

Kumar, Vivek. 2009. Co-edited. Dynamics of Change and Continuity in the Era of Globalisation: Voices from the Margins. New Delhi: Sunrise Publication.

Kumar, Vivek. 2013. Dalit Assertion and Bahujan Samaj Party, New Delhi: Samyak Prakashan.

Kumar, Vivek. 2014. Caste and Democracy in India: Perspective from Below. New Delhi: Gyan Publishing House.

Kumar, Vivek. 2014. Prajatantra Mein Jati Arakshan aur Dalit. New Delhi: Samyak Prakashan.

Kyndiah, P. R. 1994. Mizo Freedom Fighter. New Delhi: Sanchar Publishing House.

Kyndiah, P. R. 1999. Pillars of Mizo Society and Thoughts to Share. Mizoram: Secretary Law and Parliamentary Affairs Department. Government of Mizoram.

Kynta, Hamlet Bareh Ngap. 2001. The Economy of Meghalaya: Tradition to Transition. Guwahati: Delhi: Spectrum Publications.

Lakshmanna, C. 1973. Caste Dynamics in Village India. Bombay: Nachiketa Publications.

Lakshmanna, C. 1974. The Study of Scheduled Caste and Scheduled Tribe High Students in Andhra Pradesh. ICSSR Report.

Lakshmanna, C. 1977. Harijans and the Social Discrimination: A Study of Some Telangana Villages. Hyderabad: Osmania Univeristy. Department of Sociology.

Lal, Sheo Kumar and Nahar, Umed Raj. 1990. Extent of Untouchability and Pattern of Discrimination. New Delhi: Mittal Publications.

Lal, Shyam. 1981. Caste and Political Mobilisation: The Bhangis. Jaipur: Panchsheel Prakashan.

Laloo, Minimon. 2001. Meghalaya Handbook: The Abode of Clouds Shillong: Laloo Brothers.

Lanithanga, P. 1997. State of Our Union: Mizoram. New Delhi: Publication Division. Government of India.

Lannoy, Richard. 1971. The Speaking Tree. London: Oxford University Press.

Leach, E. R. 1960. ed. Aspects of Caste in South India, Ceylon and North-West Pakistan. London: Cambridge University Press.

Liddle, J., and Joshi, R. 1986. Daughters of Independence: Gender, Caste, and Class in India. NJ: Rutgers University Press.

Lokanatha. 1936. Buddhism Will Make You Free. Panadura: The Harijan Publishing Society.

Luthra, P. N. 1971. Constitutional and Administrative Growth of the North-East Frontier Agency. Shillong: North-East Frontier Agency.

Luthra, P. N. 1974. Nagaland: From a District to a State. Shillong: Director of Information and Public Relations.

Luthra, P. N. 1993. Constitutional and Administrative Growth of the Arunachal Pradesh. Itanagar: Directorate of Research. Government of Arunachal Pradesh.

Lynch, Owen M. 1969. The Politics of Untouchability: Social Mobility and Social Change in a City of India. New York: Columbia University Press.

Mackenzie, Alexander. 1884. The North East Frontier of India. New Delhi: Mittal Publications.

Mackenzie, Alexander. 2001. The North East Frontier of India. New Delhi: Mittal Publications.

Mahar, Michael J. 1972. ed. The Untouchables in Contemporary India. Tucson, Arizona: University of Arizona Press.

Maitra, Kiranshankar. 2002. The Noxious Web: Insurgency in the Northeast. New Delhi: Kanishka Publishers and Distributors.

Majumdar, D. N. 1958. Caste and Communication in an Indian Village. Bombay: Asia Publishing House.

Mallik, Suneila. 1979. Social Integration of the Scheduled Castes. New Delhi: Abhinav.

Mann, K. 1987. Tribal Women in a Changing Society. Delhi: Mittal Publications.

Marriott, Mckim. 1955. ed. Village India: Studies in the Little Community. Chicago: The University of Chicago Press.

Marriott, Mckim. 1965. ed. Caste Ranking and Community in Five Religions of India and Pakistan. Poona: Deccan College.

Marwah, Ved. 1995. Uncivil Wars: Pathology of Terrorism in India. New Delhi: Harper Collins Publishers India.

Massey, James. 1994. ed. Indigenous People: Dalits - Dalit Issues in Today's Theological Debate. Delhi: Indian Society for Promoting Christian Knowledge.

Mathew, Joseph. 1986. Ideology, Protest and Social Mobility: Case Study of Mahars and Pulayas. New Delhi: Inter India Publications.

Mathew, P. D. 1983. The Law on Abolition of Untouchability: Theory and Practice in J. Kananaikil edited Scheduled Castes and Their Struggle Against Inequality. New Delhi: Indian Social Institute.

Mathew, Thomas. 1992. Caste and class dynamics: Radical Ambedkarite praxis. New Delhi: D.Tec Publication.

Maw, Martin. 1990. Visions of India. London: Vertag Perer Lang.

Mehta, Sushila. 1971. Social Conflicts in a Village Community. New Delhi: S. Chand and Co. (Pvt.) Ltd.

Menon, K. P. Subramanya. 1961. The Shame of Free India: A Study of the Social and Economic Disabilities of Scheduled Castes and Tribes. Communist Party of India Publication.

Meyer, Mark J. 1982. Religion as Social Vision: The Movement Against Untouchability in Twentieth Century in Punjab. Berkeley: University of California Press.

Mills, J. P. 1982. The Rengma Nagas. Nagaland: Directorate of Art and Culture. Government of Nagaland.

Mills, J. P. 2003. The Ao Nagas. Nagaland: Directorate of Art and Culture.

Minz, Nirmal. 1990. Dalit-Tribal: A Search for Common Ideology in Arvind P. Nirmal edited Towards a Common Dalit Ideology. Madras: Gurukul Lutheran Theological College and Research Institute.

Mishra, Narayan. 2001. Scheduled Castes Education: Issues and Aspects. New Delhi: Kalpaz Publications.

Misra, Udayon. 1988. North East India: Quest for Identity. Guwahati: Omsons Publications.

Misra, Udayon. 2000. The Periphery Strikes Back: Challenges to the Nation-State in Assam and Nagaland, Shimla: Indian Institute of Advanced Studies.

Mitter, Sara S. 1991. Dharma's Daughters: Contemporary Indian Women and Hindu Culture. NJ: Rutgers University Press.

Moffatt, Michael. 1979. An Untouchable Community in South India: Structure and Consensus. NJ: Princeton University Press.

Mohan, P.E. 1993. Scheduled Castes: History of Elevation, Tamil Nadu, 1900-1955. Madras: New Era Publication.

Moon, Vasant. 1979. ed. Writing and Speeches of Dr Babasaheb Ambedkar, Bombay: Education Department. Government of Maharashtra. Vol. I, XXVI.

Moore, P. H. 1901. ed. Twenty Years in Assam. Guwahati: Ramesh Kumar Omsons Publications.

Mukherjee, B. N. 2001. Nationhood and Statehood in India: A Historical Survey. New Delhi: Regency Publications.

Mukherjee, Prabhati. 1988. Beyond the Four Varnas. Shimla: Indian Institute of Advanced Studies.

Muller, F. Max and Oldenberg, H. 1891-97. Vedic Hymns. 2 Vols. Sacred Books of the East, Vols. 32 and 46. Oxford: Oxford University Press.

Muller, F. Max. 1921. Thirteen Principal Upanishads. Oxford: Oxford University Press.

Murthy, B. S. 1969. The Glimmer in Darkness. Secunderabad: Lakshmi and Co.

Murthy, B. S. 1971. Depressed and Oppressed-For Ever in Agony. New Delhi.

Murugkar, Lata. 1991. Dalit Panther Movement in Maharashtra: A Sociological Appraisal. Bombay: Popular Prakashan.

Nag, Chitta Ranjan. 1998. Mixo Polity and Political Modernisation. New Delhi: Vikas Publishing House Pvt. Ltd.

Nag, Sajal. 1998. India and North-East India: Mind, Politics and the Process of Integration 1946-1950. New Delhi: Regency Publications.

Nag, Sajal. 2002. Contesting Marginality: Ethnicity, Insurgency and Subnationalism in North-East India. New Delhi: Manohar.

Nagaraj, D. R. 1993. The Flaming Feet: A Study of the Dalit Movement. Bangalore: South Forum Press.

Naidu, A. Nagaraja. 1994. Caste and Land in Colonial South India in K. L. Sharma edited Caste and Class in India. New Delhi: Rawat Publications.

Namo, Dalle. 1987. The Prisoner from Nagaland. Nagaland: United Publisher.

Narain A.K. and Ahir, D.C. 1994. Dr Ambedkar and Buddhism and Social Change. Delhi: B.R. Publishing Corporation.

Nataraj, V. K. 1990. Backward Classes and Minorities in Karnataka Politics in Ramashray Roy and Richard Sisson edited Diversity and Dominance in Indian Politics: Division, Deprivation and the Congress. Vol. II. New Delhi: Sage Publications.

Nath, Trilok. 1987. Politics of the Depressed Classes. Delhi: Deputy Publications.

Nepram, Binalakshmi. 2002. South Asia's Fractured Frontier: Armed Conflict, Narcotics and Small Arms Proliferation in India's North East. New Delhi: Mittal Publications.

Nesfield, J. C. 1885. Brief View of the Caste System of the North-Western Provinces and Oudh. Allahabad: Author Publication.

Nibedon, Nirmal. 1978. Nagaland the Night of the Guerrillas. New Delhi: Lancers Publishers.

Nibedon, Nirmal. 1980. Mizoram: The Dagger Brigade. New Delhi: Lancers Publications.

Nibedon, Nirmal. 1981. North-East India: The Ethnic Explosion. New Delhi: Lancers Publishers.

Nirmal, Arvind P. 1990. ed. Towards A Common Dalit Ideology. Madras: Gurukul Lutheran Theological College and Research Institute.

Nuh, V. K. 1986. Nagaland Church and Politics. Nagaland: V. Nuh and Bro.

Nuh, V. K. 1996. Crusade on Naga Morality. Kohima: Council of Naga Baptist Churches.

Nuh, V. K. 1998. Revive Us Again. Calcutta: Research Department. CNBC.

Nuh, V. K. 2001. Struggle for Identity in North-east India: A Theological Response. Guwahati: New Delhi: Spectrum Publications.

Nuh, V. K. 2002. My Native Country: The Land of the Nagas. Guwahati: Delhi: Spectrum Publications.

Nuh, V. K. 2002. The Origin of Naga. Kohima: Vision Press.

Nye, Robert. 1973. Conflict Among Harijans. New York: Springer Publications.

O'Malley, L. S. S. 1974. Indian Caste Customs. Delhi: Vikas Publishing House.

Omprakash, S. 1989. Development of the Weaker Section: Problems, Policies and Issues. New Delhi: Uppal Publishing House.

Omvedt, Gail. 1976. Cultural Revolt in a Colonial Society: The Non-Brahmin Movement in Western India - 1873 to 1930. Bombay: Scientific Socialist Education Trust.

Omvedt, Gail. 1982. Land, Caste and Politics in Indian States. Delhi: Authors Guild Publications.

Omvedt, Gail. 1991. Theories of Violence. New Delhi: Kali for Women.

Omvedt, Gail. 1994. Dalits and the Democratic Revolution: Dr Ambedkar and the Dalit Movement in Colonial India. New Delhi: Sage Publication.

Omvedt, Gail. 1995. Dalit Visions: The Anti-Caste Movement and the Construction of an Indian Identity. New Hyderabad: Orient Longman Ltd.

Omvedt, Gail. 1995. Dalit Women and Communalism in P. G. Jogdand edited 1995. Dalit Women in India: Issues and Perspectives. New Delhi: Gyan Publishing House.

Pai, Sudha and Kumar, Avinash. 2014. Revisiting 1956: B. R. Ambedkar and States Reorganisation. New Delhi: Orient Black Swan.

Pakem, B. 1997. Insurgency in North-East India. New Delhi: Om Sons Publications.

Pandey, B. B. 1997. Status of Women in Tribal Society: Arunachal Pradesh. Itanagar: Directorate of Research. Government of Arunachal Pradesh.

Pandey, B. B. 2001. Wander Land: Arunachal Pradesh. Itanagar: Directorate of Tourism. Government of Arunachal Pradesh.

Pandey, B. B; Duarah, D. K. and Sarkar, N. 1999. Tribal Village Councils of Arunachal Pradesh. Itanagar: Directorate of Research. Government of Arunachal.

Pandey, Gyan. 1983. Rallying Roung the Cow: Sectarian Strife in the Bhojpuri Region, c. 1888-1917 in Ranajit Guha, edited Subaltern Studies II. Delhi: Oxford University Press.

Pandey, R. S. 1991. Social Profiles of Scheduled Castes-Perspective of Development Programmes in R.S. Tripathi and P.D. Tiwari edited Dimensions of Scheduled Castes Development in India. New Delhi: Uppal Publications.

Paranjpe, A. C. 1970. Caste, Prejudice and the Individual. New Delhi: Lalvani Publishing House.

Parmaji, S. 1985. Caste Reservations and Performance. Warangal: Mamata Publications.

Parvathamma, C. 1984. Scheduled Castes and Scheduled Tribes: A Socio-Economic Survey. New Delhi: Ashish Publishing House.

Parvathamma, C. 1986. New Horizons and Scheduled Castes. New Delhi: Ashish Publishing House.

Parvathamma, C. 1989. Scheduled Castes At the Cross Roads. New Delhi: Ashish Publishing House.

Patankar, Bharat and Omvedt, Gail. 2004. The Dalit Liberation Movement in Colonial Period. New Delhi: Critical Quest Publication.

Pathy, Jaganath. 1982. "Politics of Reservation in India: Case Study of Political Agitation in Bihar and Gujarat," Philosophy and Social Action, Vol. 8, No. 2.

Patnaik, Nitayananda. 1969. Caste and Social Change: An Anthropological Study of Three Orissa Villages. Hyderabad: National Institute of Community Development.

Patwardhan, Sunanda. 1973. Change Among India's Harijans: Maharashtra a Case Study. New Delhi: Orient Longmans.

Phanjoubam, Tarapot. 1983. Insurgency Movement in North East India. Delhi: Vikas.

Philip, P. T. 1976. The Growth of Baptist Churches in Nahgaland. Guwahati: Christian Literature Centre.

Phukon, Girin. 1996. Politics of Regionalism in Northeast India. Guwahati: New Delhi: Spectrum Publications.

Phule, Jotiba. 1990. Samagra Wanghmay. Bombay: Government of Maharashtra.

Piyadassi, Nayaka Thera. 1994. The Buddhist Doctrine of life after Death. Colombo: Vajirana Srilanka.

Poliakov, Leon. The Aryan Myth. New Yeork: New American Library.

Prabhakar, M. E. 1995. Dalit Education and Youth in Bhagwan Das and James Massey edited Dalit Solidarity. Delhi: ISPCK.

Prabhavathi, M. 1995. Dalit Women in Contemporary Indian Situation in P. G. Jogdand edited Dalit Women in India: Issues and Perspectives. New Delhi: Gyan Publishing House.

Prabhu, P. N. 1955. Report of the Seminar on Casteism and Removal of Untouchability. Bombay: Indian Conference of Social Work.

Pradhan, A. C. 1986. The Emergence of the Depressed Classes. Bhubaneswar: Bookland International.

Prasad, Chunnu, 2013. India's Refugee Regime and Resettlement Policy: Chakmas and the Politics of Nationality in Arunachal Pradesh, New Delhi, Kalpaz Publications.

Prasad, R. N. and Agarwal, A. K. 2001. Administrative Review: Special Issue on Judicial Administration in Mizoram Vol. VI. Mizoram: The Indian Institute of Public Administration Mizoram Regional Branch.

Pratap Bhanu Mehata and Niraja Gopal Jayal. 2010. ed. Companion to Indian Politics. Delhi: Oxford University Press.

Programme for Scheduled Castes. 1994. Dalit Organisations: A Directory. Second Edition. New Delhi: Indian Social Institute.

Pulloppillil, Thomas and Aluckal, Jacob. 1997. ed. The Bodos Children of Bhullumbutter. Guwahati: Delhi: Spectrum Publications.

Punalekar, S. P. 1980. Aspects of Class and Caste in Social Tensions: A Study of Marathwada Riots. Surat: Centre for Social Studies.

Punalekar, S. P. 1986. Social Situation and Development Perceptions of Rural Poor in Western India. Surat: Centre for Social Studies.

Punalekar, S. P. 1995. On Dalitism and Gender in P. G. Jogdand edited Dalit Women in India: Issues and Perspectives. New Delhi: Gyan Publishing House.

Purandare, C. K. 1995. People of India: Some Prima Facie Inferences with Reference to Secheduled Castes and Scheduled Tribes in P. G. Jogdand edited Dalit Women in India: Issues and Perspectives. New Delhi: Gyan Publishing House.

Rafiabadi, H. N. 1988. Assam from Agitation to Accord. New Delhi: Genuine Publications and Media Pvt Ltd.

Rajshekar, V. T. 1994. Brahminism: Father of Fascism, Racism, Nazism. Bangalore: Dalit Sahitya Akademy.

Ram, Jagivan. 1980. Caste Challenge in India. New Delhi: Vision Books.

Ram, Nandu. 1995. Beyond Ambedkar: Essays on Daits in India. New Delhi: Har-Anand Publications.

Rao, Hanumantha G. 1977. Caste and Poverty: A Case Study of Scheduled Castes in a Delta Village. Mulikipuram: Savithri Publication.

Rao, Hemlata and Babu, M. Devendra. 1994. Scheduled Castes and Tribes: Socio-Economic Upliftment Programmes. New Delhi: Ashish Publishing House.

Rao, M. S. A. 1978. Social Movement and Social Transformation: A Study of Backward Class Movement. New Delhi: Macmillian Press.

Rao, M.S.A. 1979. ed. Social movement in India. Delhi: Sage Publication.

Rao, V.Venkata. 1976. A Century of Tribal Politics in North- East India 1874-1974. New Delhi: S. Chand and Company.

Rathnaiah, K. 1991. Social Change among the Malas: An Ex-Untouchable Caste in South India. New Delhi: Discovery Publishing House.

Rawls, John. 1971. A Theory of Justice, Oxford: Oxford University Press.

Ray, A. C. 1972. States of Our Union Mizoram. New Delhi: Publication Division. Ministry of Information and Broadcasting. Government of India.

Ray, Animesh. 1993. India-The Land and the People: Mizoram. New Delhi: National Book Trust of India.

Rayappa, P. Hanumantha and Grover, Deepak. 1980. Employment Planning for the Rural Poor: The Case of Scheduled Castes and Scheduled Tribes. New Delhi: Sterling Press.

Reddy, D. N. 1984. Women in Economic Development: The Scheduled Caste Female Agricultural Labourers in India - A Target Group Approach in Manohare edited Women's Status and Development in India. Warangal: Society for Women's Studies and Development.

Rege, Sharmila. 1989. Sati: A Critical Analysis. Poona: Women Studies Centre. Department of Sociology. University of Poona.

Rege, Sharmila. 1995. Caste and Gender: The Violence against Women in India in P. G. Jogdand edited Dalit Women in India: Issues and Perspectives. New Delhi: Gyan Publishing House.

Risley, Herbert. 1908. The People of India. Calcutta: Thacker Spink and Co.

Robb, Peter. 1993. Dalit Movements and the Meanings of Labour in India. New Delhi: Oxford University Press.

Rodrigues, Valerian and Shankar, B.L. 2011. The Indian Parliament: Democracy at Work. New Delhi: Oxford University Press.

Rodrigues, Valerian. 2002. ed. The Essential writings of Dr B.R.

Ambedkar. New Delhi: Oxford University Press.

Rodrigues, Valerien. 1993. Buddhism, Marxism and the Conception of Emancipation in Ambedkar in Robb Peter edited Dalit Movements and the Meanings of Labour in India. Delhi: Oxford University Press.

Roy Burman, B. K. 1970. ed. Social Mobility Movement Among Scheduled Castes and Scheduled Tribes of India. New Delhi: Registrar-General of India. Ministry of Home Affairs. Government of India.

Rustomji, Nari. 1971. Enchanted Frontiers. Delhi: Oxford University Press.

Rustomji, Nari. 1989. ed. Verrier Elwin: Philanthropologist Selected Writings. New Delhi: Oxford University Press.

Rustomji, Nari. 1989. Imperiled Frontiers. Delhi: Oxford University Press.

S.K. Chatterjee. 2000. Educational Development of Scheduled Castes: Looking Ahead. New Delhi: Gyan Publishing House.

S. Radha and Kumari, Ranjana. 1989. Impact of Education on Scheduled Caste Youth in India. New Delhi: Radiant Publications.

S. Ram Sharma. 1996. Education of Women of Scheduled Castes. New Delhi: Discovery Publishing House.

Sachchidananda and Sinha, R. P. 1989. Education and the Disadvantaged: A Study of Scheduled Castes and Tribes. New Delhi: Uppal Publishing House.

Sachchidananda. 1974. Research on Scheduled Castes with Special Reference to Change. Trend Report in Survey of Research in Sociology and Social Anthropology. New Delhi: ICSSR.

Sachchidananda. 1976. The Harijan Elite: A Study of their Status, Networks, Mobility and Role in Social Transformation. Haryana: Thompson Press.

Sachdeva, Gulshan. 2000. Economy of the North-East: Policy, Present Conditions and Future Possibilities. Delhi: Konark Publishers.

Sachdeva, Rajesh. 2001. ed. Language Education in Nagaland: Sociolinguistic Dimensions. New Delhi: Regency Publications.

Saha, S. B. 1986. Socio-Economic Survey of the Noatia Tribes. Agartala: Tribal Welfare Department. Government of Tripura.

Saigal Omesh. 1978. Tripura. New Delhi: Concept Publishing Company.

Saikia, Anil; Goswami, Homeswar and Goswami, Atul. 2003. Population Growth in Assam 1951-1991: With Focus on Migration. New Delhi: Akansha Publishing House.

Saikia, Mrinal Kr. 1995. Assam towards Islamisation. Guwahati. Authors Publication.

Sanajaoba, N. 1990. Manipur: Past and Present. Delhi: Mittal Publication.

Sanajaoba, N. 1992. Manipur: Treaty and Documents. 2 Vols., Delhi: Mittal Publication.

Sangma, Jangsan. 1973. Principles of Garo Law. Tura: Jangsan Sangma.

Sarin, V. I. K. 1982. India's North-East in Flames. Uttar Pradesh: Vikash Publishing House.

Sarkar, J. 1984. Caste, Occupation and Change. Delhi: B. R. Publishing Co.

Schweitzer, Albert. 1980. Indian Though and Its Development. Bombay: Wilco Publishers.

Searle-Chatterjee, Mary; and Sharma, Ursula. 1994. Contextualising Caste: Post-Dumontian Approaches. Oxford: Blackwell Publishers.

Sema, Piketo. 1992. British Policy and Administration in Nagaland 1881-1947. New Delhi: Scholar Publishing House.

Sen, Amartya K. 1970. Collective choice and social welfare. California: Holden Day Publication.

Seth, Mahendra Kumar. 2006. SC/ST Students Access to Education: Challanges and Opportunities. Delhi: Abhijeet Publications.

Shah, Ghanshyam. 1975. Caste Association and Political Processes in Gujarat. Bombay: Popular Prakashan.

Shah, Ghanshyam. 1975. Politics of Scheduled Castes and Scheduled Tribes. Bombay: Vora and Co. Pvt. Ltd.

Shah, Ghanshyam. 2002. ed. Dalit and the State. New Delhi: Concept Publication Co.

Shah, Ghanshyam; and Chaturvedi, H. R. 1985. Caste in Contemporary India in Centre for Social Studies edited Caste, Caste Conflict and Reservations. Delhi: Ajanta Publications.

Shand, Mark. 2002. River Dog: A Journey down the Brahmaputra. London: Little Brown.

Shankar, Jogan. 1990. Devadasi Cult: A Sociological Analysis. New Delhi: Ashish Publishing House.

Sharma, B. D. 1994. Dalits Betrayed. New Delhi: Har-Anand Publications.

Sharma, G. S. 1975. Legislation and Cases of Untouchability and Scheduled Castes in India. Bombay: Allied Publishers.

Sharma, K. L. 1974. The Changing Rural Stratification System. New Delhi: Orient Longman.

Sharma, K. L. 1980. The Harijans and Class Stratification in Essays on Social Stratification. Jaipur: Rawat Publications.

Sharma, K. L. 1986. Caste, Class and Social Movements. Jaipur: Rawat Publications.

Sharma, Rama. 1995. Bhangi: Scavenger in Indian Society-Marginality, Identity and Politicisation of the Community. New Delhi: M.D. Publications Pvt. Ltd.

Sharma, S. K. and Sharma, Usha. 1998. ed. Documents on Sikkim and Bhutan. New Delhi: Anmol Publications Pvt. Ltd.

Shetty, V. T. Rajshekar. 1978. Dalit Movement in Karnataka. Madras: Christian Literatuure Society.

Shivaraman, Mythily. 1973. Thanjavur: Rumblings of Class Struggle in Tamil Nadu in Kathleen Gough and Hari P. Sharma edited Imperialism and Revolution in South Asia. New York: Monthly Review Press.

Shukla, K. S. and Verma, B. M. 1993. Development of Scheduled Castes and Administration. New Delhi: Uppal Publishing House.

Shyamala. 1981. Caste and Political Mobilisation: The Bhangis. Jaipur: Panchshil Prakashan.

Silverberg, James. 1968. ed. Social Mobility in the Caste System in India. The Hague: Mouton Publishers.

Silversen, Dagfinn. 1963. When Caste Barriors Fall: A Study of Social and Economic Change in a South Indian Village. London: Allen and Urwin.

Simone, Holzwarth; Soumya Kanthy and Rosarie Tucci. 2006. Untouchable in Schools, Experiences of Dalit Children in Schools in Gujarat. Gujarat: UNICEF.

Singh, B.P. 1987. The Problem of Change: A Study of North- East India. Delhi: Oxford University Press.

Singh, Bhupinder. 2002. Autonomy Movements and Federal India. Jaipur and New Delhi: Rawat Publications.

Singh, Harjinder. 1967. ed. Caste among Non-Hindus in India, New Delhi: National Publishing House.

Singh, K. K. 1967. Patterns of Caste Tensions. Bombay: Asia Publishing House.

Singh, K. S. 1977. A Study in State-Formation among Tribal Communities in R. S. Sharma edited Indian Society: Historical Probings. Second Edition. New Delhi.

Singh, K. S. 1993. ed. People of India: Sikkim Vol. XXXIX Calcutta: Seagull Books.

Singh, K. S. 1994. ed. People of India: Meghalaya Vol. XXX11 Calcutta: Seagull Books.

Singh, K. S. 1994. ed. People of India: Nagaland Vol. XXXIV Calcutta: Seagull Books.

Singh, K. S. 1995. ed. People of India: Arunachal Pradesh Vol. XIV. Calcutta: Seagull Books.

Singh, K. S. 1995. ed. People of India: Mizoram Vol. XXXIII Calcutta: Seagull Books.

Singh, K. S. 1996. ed. People of Tripura Vol. XLI Calcutta: Seagull Books.

Singh, K. S. 2003. ed. People of India: Assam Volume XV Part Two Calcutta: Seagull Books.

Singh, K.M. 1989. Hijam Irabot and Political Movement in Manipur. Delhi: B.R. Publishing.

Singh, Mohinder. 1947. The Depressed Classes. Bombay: Hind Kitab Ltd.

Singh, N. Bisheshwar. 1987. Battle of Waterloo. Imphal: Pax Publications.

Singh, N. Joykumar. 1992. Social Movements in Manipur. Delhi: Mittal Publications.

Singh, Prakash. 2001. Kohima to Kashmir: On the Terrorist Trail. New Delhi: Rupa and Co.

Singh, Puran. 1989. Problem of Education among Scheduled Castes. New Delhi: Mittal Publications.

Singh, R. G. and Barma, Arun Deb. 1915. ed. History of Tripura. Tripura: Tripura State Tribal Cultural Research Institute and Museum.

Singh, Rajkumar Manisana. 2000. A Short Constitutional History of Manipur 1891-1971. Imphal: Smt Usha Devi Publication.

Singh, Rajkumar Manisana. 2001. Customs of Manipuri Hindus. Manipur: Smt Usha Devi Publication.

Singh, S. N. 1987. Reservation: Problems and Prospects. New Delhi: Uppal Publishing House.

Singh, T. R. 1969. The Madiga: A Study of Social Structure and Change. Lucknow: Ethnographic and Folk Culture Society.

Sinha, A.C. 1994. ed. Youth Movements in North-East India: Structural Imperatives and Aspects of Change. New Delhi: Indus Publishing Company.

Smith, W. C. 2002. The Ao Naga Tribe of Assam. New Delhi: Mittal Publications.

Soran, Singh. 1987. Scheduled Castes in India: Dimensions of Social Change. New Delhi: Gyan Publications.

Srinivas, M. N. 1952. Religion and Society among the Coorga of South India. London: Oxford University Press.

Srinivas, M. N. 1962. Caste in Modern India and Other Essays. Bombay: Asia Publishing House.

Srinivas, M. N. 1966. Social Change in Modern India. New Delhi: Allied Publishers.

Srivastav, Nirankar. 2000. Survey of Research in Economics on North East India 1970-1990. New Delhi: Regency Publications.

Srivastava, S.N. 1980. Harijans in Indian Society: A Cultural Study of the Status of Harijans and Other Backward Classes from the Earliest Times to the Present Day. Lucknow: The Privileged India Publishing House Pvt. Ltd.

Stevenson, Margaret S. 1930. Without the Pale: The Life Story of an Outcaste. Calcutta: Association Press (Y.M.C.A.).

Sukhadeo, Thorat and Kumar, Narender. 2008. ed. In Search of Inclusive Policy: Addressing Graded Inequality, Jaipur: Rawat Publications.

Sukhadeo, Thorat and Kumar, Narender. 2009. ed. B.R. Ambedkar: Perspective on Social Exclusion and Inclusive Policies, New Delhi: Oxford University Press.

Sumitra. 1988. Pan on Fire: Eight Dalit Women Tell Their Story. New Delhi: Indian Social Institute.

Swaris, Nalin. 2006. Buddhism, Human Rights and Social Renewal. New Delhi: Critical Quest Publication.

Syiemlieh, David. 1990. A Brief History of the Catholic Church in Nagaland. Shillong: Vendrame Institute Publications.

Syiemlieh, R. David. 2000. Survey of Research in History on North-East India 1970-1990. New Delhi: Regency Publication.

Tarapot, Phanjoubam. 1997. Drug Abuse and Illicit Trafficking in North Eastern India. New Delhi: Vikash Publishing House.

Tartakov, Gary Michael. 2012. ed. Dalit Art and Visual Imagery. New Delhi: Oxford University Press.

Thag, Bhagwan. 1991. ed. Dalit Poetry Today: An Anthology of Dalit Poems Rendered into English. Maharashtra: Jansahitya Prakashan.

Thakur, G. C. Sharma. 1972. The Plains of Tribes of Lakhimpur,

Dibrugargh, Sibsagar and Nowgong. Assam: Tribal Research Institute.

Thakurta, S. N. Guha. 1986. India-The Land of the People: Tripura. New Delhi: National Book Trust.

Thapar, Romila. 2000. ed. India another Millennium. New Delhi: Penguin-Viking.

Thomas, C. Joshua and Das, Gurudas. 2002. Dimensions of Development in Nagaland. New Delhi: Regency Publications.

Thomas, C. Joshua. 2002. Dimensions of Displaced People in North-East India. New Delhi: Regency Publications.

Thomas, C. Joshua; Gopalakrishnan, R. and Singh, R. K. 2001. Constraints in Development of Manipur. New Delhi: Regency Publications.

Thorat, S.K. 1996. Ambedkar on Economics of Hindu Social Order: Understanding its Orthodoxy and Legacy in Walter Fernandes The Emerging Dalit Identity. New Delhi: Indian Social Institute.

Thorat, Sukhadeo and Aryama. 2007. Ambedkar in Retrospect - Essays on Economics, Politics and Society. Jaipur: IIDS and Rawat Publications.

Thorat, Sukhadeo and Newman Katherine S. 2009. ed. Blocked by Caste: Economic Discrimination and Social Exclusion in Modern India. New Delhi: Oxford University Press.

Thorat, Sukhadeo and Sabharwa Nidhi, Sadana. 2014. Bridging the Social Gap: Perspectives on Dalit Empowerment. New Delhi: Sage Publications.

Thorat, Sukhadeo, Macwan, Martin and Omvedt, Gail. 2009. Social Justice Philanthrophy: Approaches and Strategies of Funding Organisation Jaipur: IIDS and Rawat Publications.

Thorat, Sukhadeo. 2009. Dalits in India: Search for a Common Destiny New Delhi: Sage Publications.

Thurston, Edgar and Rangachari, K. 1987. Castes and Tribes of Southern India, Volume IV – K to M. New Delhi: Asian Educational Services.

Tripathi, R. S. and Tiwari, P. O. 1991. Dimensions of Scheduled Caste Development in India. New Delhi: Uppal Publishing House.

Tripathy, R. B. 1994. Dalits: A Sub-Human Society. New Delhi: Ashish Publishing House.

Tripathy, R.B. 1994. Scheduled Castes: A Sub-Human Society. Delhi: Ashish.

Trivedi, H. R. 1990. Scheduled Caste Women: Studies in Exploitation

- With Reference to Superstition, Ignorance and Poverty. Delhi: Concept Publishing House.

Trivedi, V. R. 1997. Important Events of Assam, New Delhi: Omsons Publications.

Tucker, Helby. 2000. Among Insurgents: Walking Through Burma. New Delhi: Pengiun Books.

Tyson, Geoffrey. 1992. Forgotten Frontier. New Delhi: Spectrum Publications.

Uadri, Safdar and Kumar Sanjay. 2003. Marginalisation of Dalit Muslims in Indian Democracy. Delhi: Deskhal Publication.

Valerain Rodrigues. 1997. B.R. Ambedkar: Sources and Traditions. Hyderabad: Osmania University.

Varman, S. B. K. Dev. 1986. The Tribes of Tripura: A Dissertation. Agartala: Directorate of Research. Government of Tripura.

Varman, S. B. K. Dev. 1999. A Study Over the Jhum and Jhumia Rehabilitation in the Union Territory of Tripura. Agartala: Directorate of Research.

Varman, S. B. K. Dev. 2001. Young, Gavin, Indo-Naga War: A Journalist Account (1961). Viphuora: Gase Publications.

Vasu, Nagendra Nath. 1983. The Social History of Kamarupa Volume I, II, III. New Delhi: Northern Book Centre.

Venkateswarlu, D. 1990. Harijan-Privileged Caste Conflict: A Study in Andhra Pradesh. New Delhi: Discovery Publishing House.

Verghese, B G. and Thanzawna, R. L. 1997. A History of the Mizos Vol. II. New Delhi: Vikas Publishing House Pvt. Ltd.

Verghese, B. George. 1996. India's Northeast Resurgent: Ethnicity, Insurgency, Governance, Development. Delhi: Konark Publishers.

Verghese, B.G. 1997. India's Northeast Resurgent: Ethnicity, Insurgency, Governance, and Development. New Delhi: Konark Publishers.

Verghese, B.G. 2001. Reorienting India: The New Geo-Politics of Asia. New Delhi: Konark Publishers Pvt. Ltd.

Verma, D. N. and Dixit, R. S. 1988. Place of Women in Occupational Structure of Scheduled Caste Population in UP in D. Maurya edited Women in India. Delhi: Chugh Publications.

Verma, Vidhu. 2000. Justice, Equality and Community; An Essay on Marxist Political Theory. New Delhi: Sage Publishers. India.

Verma, Vidhu. 2002. Malaysia: State and Civil Society in Transition. Colorado, USA: Lynne Rienner Publishers.

Verma, Vidhu. 2011. Non-discrimination and Equality; Contesting Boundaries of Social Justice in India. London: Routledge.

Vidyarthi, L. P. and Mishra, N. 1977. Harijan Today: Sociological, Economic, Political, Religious and Cultural Analysis. New Delhi: Classical Publications.

Viswanadhaam and Reddy, Narashima. 1985. Scheduled Castes: A Study in Educational Achievement. Hyderabad: Scientific Services.

Webster Jhon. 1994. The Christian Dalits: A History, Indian Society for promoting Christian Knowledge. Delhi: ISPCK.

Webster, John. 1994. The Christian Dalits: A History. Delhi: Indian Society for Promoting Christian Knowledge.

Weid, Denis von der. and Poitevin, Guy. 1981. Roots of a Peasant Movement: Appraisal of the Movement Initiated by Rural Community Development Association. Pune: Shubhada-Sarswat Publications Pvt. Ltd.

Yadav, S.K. 1986. Educational Schemes for Scheduled Castes. New Delhi: Shree Publications.

Zairema. 1978. God's Miracle in Mizoram. Mizoram: Synod Press and Bookworm.

Zehol, Lucy. 1998. Ethnicity in Manipur: Experience, Issues and Perspectives New Delhi: Regency Publications.

Zehol, Lucy. 2001. Research Priorities in North-East India: With Special Reference to Manipur. New Delhi: Regency Publications.

Zelliot, Eleanor. 1970. Learning the Use of Political Means: The Mahars of Maharashtra in Rajni Kothari edited Caste in Indian Politics. Delhi: Orient Longman.

Zelliot, Eleanor. 1992. From Untouchable to Dalit: Essays on the Ambedkar Movement. New Delhi: Manohar.

Zelliot, Eleanor. 2005. Ambedkar's Conversion. New Delhi: Critical Quest Publication.

JOURNALS/MAGAZINE/NEWS-PAPERS/MONOGRAPHS/ SEMINAR-PAPERS/ RESEARCH PAPERS

A.K. Narain and D.C. Ahir, eds., *Dr Ambedkar, Buddhism and Social Change,* Delhi, B.R. Publishing, 1994, pp. 137-162.

Ahmad, Imtiaj, 1971. Social Stratification among Muslims, *The Economic Weekly,* Vol. 10, pp. 1093-96.

Ahmad, Imtiaj. 1966. The Ashraf-Ajlaf Dichotomy in Muslim Social Structure in India, IESHR, Vol. 3, No. 3, pp. 268-78.

Alexander, K. C. 1968. Changing Status of Pulaya Harijans of Kerala. *Economic and Political Weekly.* July, Special Number, pp. 1071-75.

Anon. 1986. Scheduled Castes and Marginalisation. *Social Action*. Vol. 36, No. 2, pp. 137-194.

Barik, R. 1985. Caste System and Economic Backwardness of Orissa. *Social Science Probings*. Vol. 2, No. 2, pp. 254-62.

Basu, S. K. 1968. Agrarian Problems of Scheduled Castes and Tribes of West Bengal. *Bulletin of Cultural Research Institute*. Vol. 7, Nos. 1-2.

Bernard, Jessie. 1965. The Future of the Backward Classes: The Competing Demands of Status and Power. *Journal of Public Administration*. Vol. 11, No. 1, pp. 1-39.

Berremen, Gerald D. 1962. Caste in India and the United States. *American Journal of Sociology*. Vol. 10, pp. 386- 394.

Bhattacharya, Amit. 1982-83. Tanning and Leather Workers in the Providence of Bengal. *The Quarterly Review of Historical Studies*. Vol. xxii, No. 2.

Bhattacharya, S. and Almeida, Fleur. 1986. The Caste System and Discrimination in Historical Perspective. *New Frontiers in Education*. Vol. 16, No. 2, pp. 25-32.

Bose, N. K. 1951. Caste in India. *Man in India*. 31: 107-123.

Bose, N. K. 1969. The Scheduled Castes and Tribes and Their Present Conditions. B. C. Mazumdar Memorial Lectures. Calcutta: University of Calcutta.

Breman, Jan. 1974. Mobilisation of Landless Labourers: Halpatis of South Gujarat. *Economic and Political Weekly*, Vol. 9, No. 6-8, Feb.

Chanana, Karuna. 1993. Accessing Higher Education: The Dilemma of Schooling Women, Minorities, Scheduled Castes and Scheduled Tribes in Contemporary India. *Higher Education*. Vol. 26, No. 1, p 69-92.

Chaudhary, Kameshwar. 1998. The Policy of Reservation: Need to Continue and Transcend. *Social Action*. April-June.

Chauhan, B. R. 1969. Scheduled Castes and Scheduled Tribes. *Economic and Political Weekly*. January, pp. 257-63.

Choudhary, K. 1990. Reservation: A Systematic Compulsion. *Mainstream*. Vol. 28, No. 19, pp. 23-25.

Christophe Jaffrelot, 2009, Dr Ambedkar's Strategies Against Untouchability and the Caste System, Indian Institute of Dalit Studies, Volume III, No. 04, New Delhi, pp. 2-16.

Chunnu, Prasad and Sudhakara, Karakoti. 2007. Issue of Reservation and Quota: A Critical Perspective. *Social Action*. 42:3 July-September, 2007, pp. 242-258.

Cohan, B. N. Changing Conditions of a Low Caste in Traditional India. *Journal of American Folklore*. Vol. 21.

Cohen, S. P. 1969. The Untouchable Solider: Centre, Politics and the Indian Army. *Journal of Asian Studies.* Vol. 18, No. 3, pp. 453-68.

Cohn, Bernard S. 1958. Changing Tradition of a Low Caste. *Journal of American Folklore.* Vol. 21, July.

Cohn, Bernard S. 1961. Chamar Family in a North Indian Village: A Structural Contingent. *Economic Weekly.* Vol. 13, Nos. 27, 28 and 29, pp. 1051-55.

Cohn, Bernard S. 1962. Review of M. Marriott. Caste Ranking and Community Structure in Five Regions of India and Pakistan. *Journal of the American Oriental Society.* Vol. 82: 425-430.

D'Souza, Victor S. 1962. Changing Status of Scheduled Castes. *Economic and Political Weekly.* Vol. 16, No. 48.

D'Souza, Victor S. 1967. Caste and Class - A Reinterpretation. *Journal of Asian and African Studies.* Vol. 2, No. 3-4.

D'Souza, Victor S. 1975. Scheduled Castes and Urbanisation in Punjab: An Explanation. *Sociological Bulletin.* Vol. 24, No. 1.

D'Souza, Victor S. 1977. Does Urbanism Desegregate Scheduled Castes: Evidence From a District in Punjab, *Contributions to Indian Sociology,* New Series. Vol. 2, No. 1, pp. 219-39.

Das, Man Singh. 1976. A Cross-National Study of Inter-Caste Conflict in India and the United States. *International Journal of Contemporary Sociology.* Vol. 13, nos. 3 - 4, pp. 261-77.

Desai, Haribhai G. and Uchat, D.A. 1981. Self Concept of Harijan Students and Attitudes of Other Students towards Them. *Indian Educational Review.* Vol. 16, No. 3, pp. 44-50.

Deshi, A.K. and H. Singh. 1995. Education, Labour Market Distortions and Relative Earning of Different Religious - Caste Categories in India. *Canadian Journal of Development of Studies.* December 21.

Dietrich, Gabriele. 1988. Women, Ecology and Culture. Paper for the IV National Conference on Women's Studies. Hyderabad: Andhra University.

Doshi, Harish. 1974. Use of Public Places and Facilities by Bhangis in Surat. *Journal of Social and Economic Studies.* Vol. 2, No. 1.

Dunn, Dana. 1993. Gender Inequity in Education and Employment in the Scheduled Castes and Tribes of India. *Population Research and Policy Review.* Vol. 12, No. 1, p. 53-71.

Dushkin, Lelah. 1979. Backward Class Benefits and Social Class in India, 1920-1970. *Economic and Political Weekly.* April 7th.

Dworkin, Ronald. 1981. What is equality? Part-I, Equality of welfare and part-2, Equality of Resources. *Philosophy and public affairs.* Vol. 10, pp. 283-385.

Galanter, Marc. 1961. Equality and Protective Discrimination in India. *Rutge's Law Review.* 16: pp. 42-74.

Galanter, Marc. 1963. Law and Caste in Modern India. *Asian Review.* Vol. 3, No. 2: pp. 3544-59.

Galanter, Marc. 1969. Untouchability and the Law. *Economic and Political Weekly.* Annual, January: 131-70.

Gangrade, K. D. 1975. Social Mobility in India: A Study of Depressed Class. *Man in India.* Vol. 55, No. 3:248-72.

Gangrade, K. D. 1976. Adult Suffrage and Social Change: Changing Status of a Depressed Caste. *Social Change.* Vol. 7, nos. 1 and 2.

Geetha B. Nambissan, 2009, Exclusion and Discrimination in Schools: Experiences of Dalit Children, Working Paper Series Indian Institute of Dalit Studies and UNICEF, New Delhi.

Gough, Aberle E. K. 1959. Criteria of Caste Ranking in South India. *Man in India.* Vol. 39, pp. 115-26.

Gupta, Dipankar. 1979. Understanding the Maharashtra Riots-A Repridiation of Eclectic Marxism. *Social Scientist.* Vol. 7, No. 10.

Gupta, Dipankar. 1984. Continuous Hierarchies and Discrete Castes. *Economic and Political Weekly.* Vol. 19, Nos. 46-47, 48. pp. 1955-58; 2003-2005; and 2049-53.

Gupta, Shiva K. 1980. Harijan Legislation: Their Alienation and Activism: A Case Study of Harijan Power. *Indian Journal of Political Science.* Vol. 41, No. 3, pp. 457-70.

Guru, Gopal, 1985. Casteism in the South. *Mainstream.* Vol. 23, No. 47, pp. 20-22.

Guru, Gopal, Archaeology of Untouchability', *Economic and Political Weekly,* September 2009.

Guru, Gopal, Dalit Movement in Mainstream Sociology', *Economic and Political Weekly,* No. 14, April, 3, 1993.

Guru, Gopal, How Egalitarian are Social Sciences in India?' *Economic and Political Weekly,* Dec. 14, 2002.

Guru, Gopal, Liberal Democracy in India and the Dalit Critique', Social Research, 78:1, *Spring,* 2011, pp. 99-122.

Guru, Gopal, The Idea of India: Desi, Derivative and Beyond', *Economic and Political Weekly,* Vol. XXXXVI, No. 37, 10 September 2011.

Hardgrave, Robert L. Jr. 1966. Varieties of Political Behaviour among Nadars of Tamil Nadu. *Asia Survey.* Vol. 6, pp. 614-621.

Harrison, Selig S. 1956. Caste and the Andhra Communists, *The American Political Science Review,* Vol. 1, No. 2, pp. 378-404

Heredia, Rudi. 1986. Minority Rights and Reservation Policy: Towards Coherence and Consistence. *New Frontiers in Education.* Vol. 16, No. 2, pp. 60-63.

Horsey, Anita. 1981. Conditions of Scheduled Castes and Tribes. *New Frontiers in Education.* Vol. 11, No. 2, pp. 1-36.

Iman, Mohammed. 1966. Reservation of Seats for Backward Classes in Public Services and Educational Institutions. *Journal of Indian Law Institute.* Vol. 16: pp. 441-49.

Jayagopal, R. 1986. Occupational Mobility among a Special Group of Scheduled Castes in Tamil Nadu: A Survey. *Indian Journal of Adult Education.* Vol. 47, No. 1, pp. 8-12.

Joshi, Barbara, R. 1977. The Buddhist Movement of Uttar Pradesh. *Mimeographed Paper.* March 27.

Joshi, Barbara. R. 1977. The Buddhist Movement of Western Uttar Pradesh. *Mimeographed Paper.* March 27.

Joshi, Barbara. R. 1987. Recent Developments of Inter-Regional Mobilisation of Dalit Protest in India. *South Asia Bulletin.* Vol. 7.

Kamila, Banu Behari. 1985. A Study of Attitude of Students towards School of Harijans and Tribal Welfare Department High School of Orissa. *Journal of Education and Psychology,* Vol. 43, pp. 187-92.

Kannibaran, V. and Kannibaran, K. 1991. Caste and Gender: Understanding Dynamics of Power and Violence. *Economic and Political Weekly.* Sept. 14.

Karlekar, M. 1982. Some Perspectives on the Employment of Scheduled Castes Women. *Social Action.* Vol. 32, pp. 292-302.

Khalid Khan and Nidhi Sadana Sabharwal, 2012, Access and Equity in Higher Education: Aspects of Gender, Caste, Ethnicity, Religion, Occupation and Economic Groups in Rural and Urban Areas During Pre and Post Reform Periods, Indian Institute of Dalit Studies, New Delhi, pp. 7-149.

Khan, Zillor. 1968. Caste and Muslim Peasantry in India and Pakistan. *Man in India.* Vol. 48, pp. 133-148.

Khurana, G. 1979. Education Facilities for Scheduled Castes. *Education Quarterly.* Vol. 31, Nos. 3 and 4, pp. 31-35.

Kriesberg, Louis. 1968. Abolition of Untouchability in Andhra Pradesh. *Social Welfare.* Vol. 15, No. 2.

Kumar, Vivek, 1999 a. 'Nature and Crisis of Dalit Leadership: A Brief Socio-Historical Profile' in Ashish Ghosh (eds.), Dalit and Peasants the Emerging Caste-Class Dynamics, New Delhi: Gyan Sagar Publications.

Kumar, Vivek, 1999. 'Deconstruction and Reconstruction of Identities in UP' in Ambrose Pinto (eds.) Dalit Assertion for Identity, New Delhi: Indian Social Institute.

Kumar, Vivek, 2001, 'Globalisation and Empowerment of Dalits in India', Indian Anthropologist, Volume 31, No. 2, December, New Delhi, pp. 15-25.

Kumar, Vivek, 2001. 'Untouchability in Uttaranchal', *Economic and Political Weekly*, Volume XXXVI, No. 49, December 8, Mumbai, pp. 4536-37.

Kumar, Vivek, 2002. 'Ambedkar's Vision of Social Justice: Quest for Unification, Empowerment and Differentiation', Jagriti, Journal of History, Culture, Art and Social Justice, Kashi Hindu University, Varanasi.

Kumar, Vivek, 2002. 'Globalisation and Empowerment of Dalits in India', *Guru Nanak Journal of Sociology*, Guru Nanak Dev University, Amritsar, Punjab.

Kumar, Vivek, 2002. 'Socio-Political Mobilisation and Empowerment of Dalits in Uttar Pradesh', Contemporary Social Work, Volume XIX, April 2002., Department of Social Work, Lucknow University, Lucknow, pp. 57-72.

Kumar, Vivek, 2002. 'The Power of Strategy, The Dalit, Dalit Media Network, Chennai, Tamil Nadu, May-June, pp. 13-16.

Kumar, Vivek, 2003. 'Dalit Movement and Dalit International Conferences', *Economic and Political Weekly*, Volume XXXVIII, No. 27, July 5-11, Mumbai.

Kumar, Vivek, 2003. 'Emergence of Dalit Youth: Some Sociological Reflections' in Vinod Chandra (eds.) Construction and Reconstruction of Indian Youth, Lucknow: J N Postgraduate College.

Kumar, Vivek, 2003. 'From Social Reform to Political Mobilisation: Changing Trajectory of Dalit Assertion in UP', Social Action: A Quarterly Review of Social Trends, Volume 53, No. 2, April-June, New Delhi, pp. 115-31.

Kumar, Vivek, 2003. 'Uttar Pradesh: Politics of Change', *Economic and Political Weekly*, Volume XXXVIII, No. 37, September 13-19, Mumbai, pp. 3869-3871.

Kumar, Vivek, 2004. 'Ambedkar's Vision of Social Justice: Quest for Unification, Empowerment and Differentiation' in M H Makwana (eds.) Dr Babasaheb Ambedkar's Vision and Social Justice, Ahemdabad: Dr Babasaheb Ambedkar Chair, School of Social Sciences, Gujarat University.

Kumar, Vivek, 2004. 'BSP and Dalit Aspirations', *Economic and Political Weekly*, Volume XXIX, No. 18, May 1-7, Mumbai, pp. 1778-1781.

Kumar, Vivek, 2004. 'Reformist's Role' in Renuka Singh (eds.) The Path of Buddha: Writings on Contemporary Buddhism, New Delhi: Penguin Books.

Kumar, Vivek, 2004. 'Understanding Dalit Diaspora', *Economic and Political Weekly*, Volume XXXIX, No. 1, January 3-9, Mumbai, pp. 114-116.

Kumar, Vivek, 2005, 'Understanding the Politics of Reservation', *Economic and Political Weekly*, Volume XL, No. 9, February 26 March 4, Mumbai, pp. 803-806.

Kumar, Vivek, 2005. 'Situating Dalits in Indian Sociology', Sociological Bulletin (Special issue of South Asia: The State of Sociology, Issues of Relevance and Rigour), Volume 54, No. 3, September-December, New Delhi, pp. 514-532.

Kumar, Vivek, 2005. 'Violence and Youth: Carving Out an Independent Agenda for Youth', Indian Journal of Youth Affairs, Vol. 9, No. 2, July-December, Vishva Yuvak Kendra, New Delhi, pp. 55-62.

Kumar, Vivek, 2006 'Education: A Perspective from Below: Viewing Social Sciences from a Dalit Perspective', Biblio, September-October, New Delhi, pp. 35-36.

Kumar, Vivek, 2006. 'Dalit Sahitya Ka Samajshastra' in Devendra Chaube (eds.) Sahitya Ka Naya Saundryasastra, New Delhi: Raj Kamal Prakashan.

Kumar, Vivek, 2006. 'Political and Civil Institution of Governance: Contradiction of Exclusion and Inclusion of Dalits in Contemporary India' in R B S Verma (eds.) Empowerment of Weaker Sections in India, New Delhi: Serials Publications.

Kumar, Vivek, 2006. 'Sociology of Indian Minorities' in Joseph Benjamin (eds.) Minorities in Indian Social System, New Delhi: Gyan Publishing House.

Kumar, Vivek, 2007. 'Babasaheb Ambedkar's Ideas of Social Justice and Just Society', Dialogue, Volume 9, No. 2, October-December, New Delhi, pp. 117-126.

Kumar, Vivek, 2007. 'Behind the BSP Victory', *Economic and Political Weekly*, Volume XLII, No. 24, June 1-7, Mumbai, pp. 2237-2239.

Kumar, Vivek, 2007. 'Governance and Development in the Era of Globalisation: Understanding Exclusion and Assertion of Dalits in India' in Kameshwar Chaudhary (eds.) Globalisation Governance Reform and Development in India, New Delhi: Sage Publications

Kumar, Vivek, 2007. 'Literary Representation of Ambedkar: A Survey from Hindi Literature', Creative Forum: Journal of Literary and Critical Writings, Volume 20, No. 2, July-December, New Delhi: Bahri Publications, pp. 45-54.

Kumar, Vivek, 2007. 'When the Marginalised Mobilise: A Case Study of the Bahujan Samaj Party', Indian Journal of Social Work, Volume 68, No. 1, January 2007, Tata Institute of Social Sciences, Mumbai, pp. 88-100.

Kumar, Vivek, 2007. Bahujan Samaj Partya: Some Issues of Democracy and Governance in Sudha Pai (eds.) Political Process in Uttar

Pradesh: Identity, Economic Reform and Governance, New Delhi: Pearson Longman.

Kumar, Vivek, 2008. 'Babasaheb Ambedkar: Conceptualisation and Operationalisation of Social Justice' in P G Jogdand (eds.) Globalisation and Social Justice: Perspectives, Challenges and Praxis, New Delhi: Rawat Publications.

Kumar, Vivek, 2008. 'Changing Trajectory of Dalit Assertion in Uttar Pradesh' in Nandu Ram (eds.) Dalits in Contemporary India: Discrimination and Discontent, New Delhi: Siddhant Publications.

Kumar, Vivek, 2008. 'Democracy and Self-Representation', Mainstream, Volume XLVI, No. 42, October 4, New Delhi.

Kumar, Vivek, 2009. 'Dalit Diaspora: Invisible Existence', Diaspora Studies, Volume 2, No. 1, January-June, Journal of the Organisation for Diaspora Initiatives, New Delhi, pp. 53-74.

Kumar, Vivek, 2009. 'Indian Media and its Role in the Empowerment of Dalits', Communicator: A Journal of the Institute of Mass Communication, Volume XLI, No. 1, January-December, Indian Institute of Mass Communication, New Delhi, pp. 73-97.

Kumar, Vivek, 2009. 'Locating Dalit Women in the Indian Caste System, Media and Women's Movement', Social Change: Journal of the Council for Social Development, Volume 39, No. 1, March, New Delhi, pp. 64-84.

Kumar, Vivek, 2010. 'Ambedkar's Idea of Nation and Nation Building', Human Rights Global Focus (published by the International Human Rights Foundation), Volume 5, No. 3 and 4, July-December, pp. 69-85.

Kumar, Vivek, 2010a. Different Shades of Dalit Mobilisation, in T.K. Oommen (eds.) Social Movements I: Issues of Identities, New Delhi: Oxford University Press.

Kumar, Vivek, 2010b. 'Teaching Caste and the Hindu Social Order: Dalits in Indian Sociology' in Maitrayee Chaudhuri (eds.), Sociology in India: Intellectual and Institutional Practices, New Delhi: Rawat Publications.

Kumar, Vivek, 2012. 'Dalit Diaspora: Invisible Existence' in S.K. Jain (eds.) Indian Diaspora in the Era of Globalisation, New Delhi: Kalpaz Publications.

Kumar, Vivek, 2013. 'Recognising Structures of Corruption and Understanding the Nature of Mobilisation Against It in Thakur M.N. and D Rai (eds.) Democracy on the Move? Reflections on Moments, Promises and Contradictions, New Delhi: Aakar Publications.

Kumar, Vivek, 2013. 'Representation of Marginalised Sections and Indian Political Parties' in A K Mehra (eds.) Party System in India: Emerging Trajectories, New Delhi: Lancer Publications.

Kumar, Vivek, 2013. 'Social Development and Planning in Developing Countries in Shewta Singh (eds.) Social Work and Social Development: Perspectives from India and the Unites States, Chicago: Lyceum Books INC, USA.

Kumar, Vivek, 2013. Ambedkarism and Future of Dalits in Sukant K Chaudhury (eds.) Ambedkar and Future of Dalits, New Delhi: Serials Publications.

Kumar, Vivek, 2013. Towards Epistemology of Social .Exclusion' in Ashish Saxena (eds.), Marginality, Exclusion, and Social Justice, New Delhi and Jaipur: Rawat Publications.

Kumar, Vivek, 2013f. 'The New Dalit Diaspora: A Sociological Analysis' in Sharma K L and Renuka Singh (eds.), Dual Identity: Indian Diaspora and Other Essays, New Delhi: Orient Black Swan.

Kumar, Vivek, 2014, 'Dalit Studies: Continuities and Change' in Yogendra Singh (eds.), Indian Sociology (Volume 3): Identity, Communication and Culture (ICSSR Research Surveys and Explorations), New Delhi: Oxford University Press.

Kumar, Vivek, 2014. *'B R Ambedkar aur Rashtra Nirman Ki Avdharna', Bhartiya Samajshastra Sameeksha* (*Bhartiya Samajshatra Parishad Ki Shodh Patrika*), Volume 1, No. 1, January-June, New Delhi, pp. 22-31.

Kurien, C. T. 1982. Economic Conditions of Scheduled Castes. *Yojana.* Vol. 26, No. 19: 13-17.

Leopold, Joan. 1970. The Aryan Theory of Race. *IESHR.* pp. 270-97.

Lynch, Owen M. 1970. Political Mobilisation and Ethnicity among Adi-Dravidas in a Bombay Slum. *Economic and Political Weekly.* Vol. 9, No. 39, pp. 1657-68.

Mahar, Pauline M. 1960. Changing Religious Practices of an Untouchable Caste. *Economic Development and Culture Change.* Vol. 7, No. 3, pp. 279-87.

Mankidy, Aruna. 1979. Inter-generational Mobility among the Scheduled Castes. *Social Change.* Vol. 9, Nos. 1-2, pp. 10-17.

Marriott, Mckim. 1959. Interactional and Attributional Theories of Caste Ranking. *Man in India.* Vol. 39, No. 2, pp. 92-107.

Marulasiddaish, H.M. 1971. Caste, Consolidation, Social Mobility and Ambivalence: A Case Study of Caste Hostels in Mysore State. *Indian Journal of Social Work.* Vol. 31, No. 4, pp. 391-399.

Mayer, Adrian C. 1956. Some Hierarchical Aspects of Caste. *South Western Journal of Anthropology.* Vol. 12, No. 2, pp. 144-45.

Meillassoux, Claude. 1973. Are There Castes in India? *Economy and Society*. Vol. 2.

Mishra, Ajay M. 1983. A Study of Attitude towards Learning of Science among Scheduled Caste Students. *Journal of Education and Psychology*. Vol. 43, No. 3, pp. 112-116.

Mishra, N. 1978. Studies on the Scheduled Castes in Bihar. *Journal of Social Research*. Vol. 21, No. 2, pp. 47-70.

Moffatt, Michael. 1975. Untouchables and the Caste System: A Tamil Case Study. *Contributions to Indian Sociology*. New Series. Vol. 9, No. 1.

Mohanty, Manoranjan. 1984. Social Roots of Backwardness in Orissa: A Study of Class. *Caste and Power in Social Science Probings*. Vol. 1, No. 2, June, pp. 184-228.

Mohanty, Manoranjan. 1985. Arguing with Bailey by Proxy. *Social Science Probings*. Vol. 2, No. 2, June, pp. 263-67.

Monga, Veena. 1967. Social Mobility among the Potters: Report of a Caste Conference. *Economic and Political Weekly*. Vol. 2, pp. 1047-1055.

Naidu, A. Nagaraja. 1985. Harijans in Semi-fedual Set-up: A Case Study of Karamchedu. *Social Science Probings*. Vol. 2, No. 4, pp. 450-58.

Nair, Janaki. 1986. Fighting for Backwardness: Venkataswammy Commission Report and After. *Economic and Political Weekly*. Vol. XXI, No. 42, pp. 1837-38.

Narayana, C. 1974. Emerging Elite in Scheduled Castes. *Secular Democracy*. Vol. 7, No. 9.

Narayanan, R. 1978. False Concern for the Harijans. *Mainstream*. Vol. 16, No. 24.

Nargolkar, V. S. 1969. Removal of Untouchability: Goals and Attainments. *Indian Journal of Social Work*. Vol. 30, No. 3.

Omvedt, Gail. 1978. Class Struggle or Caste War. *Frontier*. Calcutta. Vol. 2, No. 8-11, Sept. 30, pp. 30-40.

Oommen, T. K. 1968. Strategy for Social Change: A Study of Untouchability. *Economic and Political Weekly*. June 22, pp. 933-36.

Oommen, T. K. 1970. The Concept of Dominant Caste: Some Queries. *Contribution to Indian Sociology*. Vol. 4, December, pp. 73-83.

Oommen, T. K. 1980. Sources of Deprivation and Styles of Protest: The Case of Dalits in India. *Contributions to Indian Sociology*. New Series, Vol. 18, No. 1, January-June.

Pandya, B. V. 1959. Trends and Patterns of Indebtedness among Harijans. *Journal of the Cultural Research Society*. Vol. 21, pp. 99-115.

Parvathamma, C. 1968. The Case for the Indian Untouchable. *United Asia.* Vol. 20, No. 5, pp. 279-86.

Parvathamma, C. 1973. Ambedkar and After: The Position and Future of Indian SC Masses. *Eastern Anthropology.* Vol. 26.

Pathy, Suguna. 1985. The Untouchables - Protectors Fail. State and Society. Vol. 5, No. 3, July-September, pp. 37-44.

Patil, Sharad. 1979. Dialectics of Caste and Class Conflict. *Economic and Political Weekly*, February.

Patil, Sharad. 1989. Mobilising Scheduled Castes and Scheduled Tribes. *Economic and Political Weekly.* Vol. 24, No. 35-36, pp. 2002-06.

Patwardhan, Sunanda. 1968. Social Mobility and Conversion of Mahars. *Sociological Bulletin.* Vol. 17, No. 2, pp. 187-202.

Pimpley, Prakash N. 1976. Politisation among the Scheduled Castes Students of Punjab. Social Action. Vol. 30, No. 2, pp. 138-61.

Pinto, Ambrose. 1992. Caste Conflict in Karnataka. *Economic and Political Weekly.* July 11, Vol. XXVII, No. 28.

Prasad, Chunnu, "Apatani Tribal Culture", *Habitus*, Vol. 3, No. 3, Issue. 10, July-September 2006, pp. 23-25.

Prasad, Chunnu, "Arunachal Pradesh and the Inner-Outer Line Regulation of 1873-1874 of North East Frontier Agency", *Third World Impact,* Vol. XVIII, No. 173, January-March, 2007, pp. 15-19.

Prasad, Chunnu, "Arunachal Pradesh as the Factor in Indo-China Relation", *Third Concept*, April 2006, Vol. 331, pp. 51-55.

Prasad, Chunnu, "Arunachal Pradesh Denies the Rights to Scheduled Caste in the State", *Radical Humanist,* Vol. 433, April 2006, pp. 33-34.

Prasad, Chunnu, "Between two Nations: Arunachal Pradesh and the Politics of Nationality in India's North East", International Seminar on Sitting Law (Second law and Social Science Research Network) Conference on 27th to 30th December, 2010 by FLAME, Pune, Maharastra.

Prasad, Chunnu, "Between two Nations", *Dialogue Quarterly,* Vol. 13, No. 3, January-March 2012, New Delhi, pp. 167-182.

Prasad, Chunnu, "Buddhism and Buddhist Heritage of India's North East: A Study in Arunachal Pradesh", International Seminar on Buddhism and Buddhist Heritage of Gujarat and India on 15th and 16th January, 2010 by Maharaja Sayajirao University of Baroda, Vadodra, Gujarat.

Prasad, Chunnu, "Buddhism and its Relevance Today", *Third Concept,* January 2006, Vol. 227, pp. 51-55.

Prasad, Chunnu, "Caste and the Question of Dignity in Tripura", National Conference on Socially Excluded People in India: Towards an inclusive Socio-Economic Policy on 20th and 21st February, 2009 by *Gokhale Institute of Politics and Economics*, Pune, Maharastra.

Prasad, Chunnu, "Caste, Exclusion and the Question of Livelihood in Sikkim: An Overview", National Seminar on Democratic Governance and Human Development: Stocking and Future Strategies on 28th and 29th January, 2010 by *Madhya Pradesh Institute of Social Science Research*, Ujjain, Madhya Pradesh.

Prasad, Chunnu, "Caste, Social Exclusion and the Question of Livelihood: A Case of Scheduled Castes of Assam and Arunachal Pradesh", National Conference on Economic Reforms in India: Social Exclusion and Social Justice, on 27th to 29th November, 2008, Dr B.R. Ambedkar Open University, Hyderabad, Andhra Pradesh.

Prasad, Chunnu, "Chakma Refugees in Arunachal Pradesh: Question of Identity and Citizenship", *Eastern Anthropologist*, Vol. 61, No. 1, January-March, 2008, pp. 95-104.

Prasad, Chunnu, "Chakma-Hajong Refugee Problem and Politics of their Settlement in Arunachal Pradesh (1947 to 2004)", *South Asia Politics*, Vol. 5, No. 1, May 2006, pp. 46-50.

Prasad, Chunnu, "Citizenship Rights in North East: The Case of Chakmas and Hajongs in Arunachal Pradesh", *Journal of Peace Studies*, Vol. 13, Issue 4, October-December 2006, pp. 49-55.

Prasad, Chunnu, "Comparative Context of Discrimination, Social Exclusion and Religion: A Study of Dalit Muslims in India", National Seminar on Socio-Economic and Educational Status of Muslims in Maharashtra on 21st to 23rd December, 2009 by *Tata Institute of Social Sciences*, Mumbai, Maharashtra.

Prasad, Chunnu, "Conceptualising Migration in the Era of Globalisation: A Brief Overview of the Problems and Challenges in an edited book by Hokip in *Migration*, New Wave, New Delhi, 2012, pp. 1-16.

Prasad, Chunnu, "Contextualising Marginalisation and Reservation: An Overview of India's Northeast", National Conference on Movements for Equity in Reservations on 21st to 22nd February, 2010 by *Centre for the Study of Social Systems, Jawaharlal Nehru University*, New Delhi and *Dalit Information and Education Trust*, Hyderabad.

Prasad, Chunnu, "Dalit-Muslim Unity and Reservation: An Overview", Lecture given in a National Workshop on "Dalit-Muslim Unity", on 22nd October, 2009 organised by Dr K. R. Narayanan Centre for Dalit and Minorities Studies, *Jamia Millia Islamia*, New Delhi.

Prasad, Chunnu, "Dalits Struggle for Democratic Space: Bahujan Samaj Party and the Democratisation of Indian Politics", in an edited book by Vivek Kumar, G. Stanley, Jaya Kumar and Tenepali Hari in *The*

Dynamics of Change and Community in the Era of Globalisation: Voices of the Margins, Sunrise Publication, New Delhi, 2009, pp. 336-367.

Prasad, Chunnu, "Democracy, Dalits and Exclusive Policies: A Case of Scheduled Castes in Arunachal Pradesh", in an edited book by Yagati Chinna Rao and Karakoti Sudhakara in *Exclusion and Discrimination; Concepts, Perspectives and Challenges*, Kanishka Publishes and Distributors, New Delhi, 2010, pp. 120-144.

Prasad, Chunnu, "Dial Marx for Murder", *Frontier*, Vol. 39, No. 43, May 13-19, 2007.

Prasad, Chunnu, "Dr B.R.Ambedkar and the Revival of Buddhism in India After 1956", *Journal of Humanities and Social Sciences*, Contemporary Issue-2, No. 5, September, 2009, Scottish Church College, University of Calcutta, pp. 28-39.

Prasad, Chunnu, "Ecology and Tribal Society in Arunachal Pradesh", *The India Economic Review*, Volume VIII, Quarterly, Indian Institute of Public Management, February-May, 2011, pp. 154-161.

Prasad, Chunnu, "Ecology and Tribal Society in Arunachal Pradesh", in an edited book by George T. Haokip in *Human Rights and Social Security in Northeast India*, Mittal Publication, New Delhi, 2012, pp. 160-174.

Prasad, Chunnu, "Exclusion and the Question of Livelihood: A Case of SC's in Arunachal Pradesh", Young Scholar Programme on Human Development under UNDP, on 10th to 22nd November, 2008, *Indira Gandhi Institute of Development Research* (Reserve Bank of India), Goregao, Mumbai, Maharastra.

Prasad, Chunnu, "Exclusion of Excluded Dalits in Nepal: A Case of Hill, Madhesi and Terai Region", in an edited book by B.C. Upreti and Uddhab Pd. Pyakurel in *Contemporary Nepal: Reflections on Emerging Political and Social Issues and Trends*, Kalinga Publications, New Delhi, 2012, pp. 81-90.

Prasad, Chunnu, "Exile and Belongingness: Embattled Chakma Refugees in Arunachal Pradesh", *Journal of Humanities and Social Sciences*, Contemporary, No.8, July, 2011, Scottish Church College, University of Calcutta, pp. 22-34.

Prasad, Chunnu, "Illegal Immigration in North-East", Published in the editorial page of *Daily Excelsior*, Jammu and Kashmir, 2007 (http://www.dailyexcelsior.com).

Prasad, Chunnu, "India Pakistan: Man who Divided", *Third World Impact*", April-June, Vol. XIX, No. 178, 2008, pp. 23-29.

Prasad, Chunnu, "India's Refugee Problem and Acceptability: A Case of Chakmas in Arunachal Pradesh", National Conference, by Indian Social Science Congress on 17th to 22nd December, 2008, *Jamia Milia Islamia*, New Delhi.

Prasad, Chunnu, "India's Refugee Regime and the Chakma's of Arunachal Pradesh Reclaiming Lost Identity", in an edited book by A.K. Agarwal and Bhartendu Singh in *Understanding India's North East*, DAV Publishers, Guwahati, 2011, pp. 203-216.

Prasad, Chunnu, "Ithihas Kea Dabe Panno Mea Jalkari Bai", *Hasieo Kee Awaaj*, No. 9, March 2008, pp. 2-4.

Prasad, Chunnu, "Karl Popper: Critical Rationalism, Falsification and Open Society", in an edited book by Pradeep Basu in *Modern Social Thinkers*, Setu Prakasan, New Delhi, 2012, pp. 302-318.

Prasad, Chunnu, "Looking for Whose Identity; A Critical Overview of the Concept Dalit and Social Justice", *Third World Impact*, January-March, 2010, pp. 29-32.

Prasad, Chunnu, "Mapping Caste, Social Exclusion and the Question of Livelihood in Manipur", National Seminar on Public Action and Inclusive Policy: Taking Stock of the Reality and Exploring the Road Ahead on 22nd to 24th March, 2010 by *Centre for Study of Social Exclusion and Inclusive Policy, Pondicherry University*, Poducherry.

Prasad, Chunnu, "Migration and the Question of Citizenship: People of Chittagong Hill Tract in Arunachal Pradesh", *Indian Journal of Political Science*, Vol. LXVII, No. 3, July-September, 2006, pp. 471-490.

Prasad, Chunnu, "Natural Resource Management and Sustainable Development: A Study in Arunachal Pradesh", *Social Action*, Vol. 58, April-June, 2008, pp. 200-207.

Prasad, Chunnu, "Naxalism Fighting for what: Question of Exclusion, Dignity and Livelihood", in an edited book by Pradeep Basu in *Discourse on Naxalite Movement (1967-2009); Insights into Radical Left Politics*, Setu Prakasan, Kolkata, 2010, pp. 238-251.

Prasad, Chunnu, "Pakistani Dalit Auur Unke Halat", *Ham Dalit*, No. 8, August 2006, pp. 17-19.

Prasad, Chunnu, "Political Economy and Social Exclusion: A Case of Scheduled Castes in Arunachal Pradesh", *South India Journal of Social Sciences*, Vol. vi, No. 2, December, 2008, pp. 47-58.

Prasad, Chunnu, "Political Structure of Apatanis' Buliang System in Arunachal Pradesh", *Third Concept*, November 2005, Vol. 225, pp. 30-33.

Prasad, Chunnu, "Possibility and Challenges of Tourism in Arunachal Pradesh", National Seminar on Creativity and Innovation in Indian Entrepreneurship: Contemporary Trends on 19th to 20th March, 2010, by *Department of Tourism Studies, Pondicherry University*, Poducherry.

Prasad, Chunnu, "Question of Equity and Social Justice in India's Northeast: A Case of Excluded Chakmas in Arunachal Pradesh", National Conference on Indigenous Technology, Livelihood Option and Habitat Utilisation: Concepts and Perspectives of Development, on 23rd to 22nd November, 2009 by *Northeast Centre for Research and Development* (NECRD), Guwahati, Assam.

Prasad, Chunnu, "Refugees and Human Rights Violation in Arunachal Pradesh", in an edited book by M.R.Biju in *The Dynamics of Modern Democracy: The Indian Experience*, Concept Publishing Company Pvt. Ltd., New Delhi 2009, pp. 255-270.

Prasad, Chunnu, "Refugees and Human Rights: Comparative Studies Between Chakmas in India and Biharis in Bangladesh", in an edited book by M. R. Biju in *Development Issues in Contemporary India*, Concept Publishing Company Pvt. Ltd., New Delhi 2010, pp. 238-262.

Prasad, Chunnu, "Reservation: Exclusion Through Inclusion", Lecture given in a Symposium on Reservation; The State and the Constitution of India, on 30th October, 2010 organised by Bahujan Teacher's Front, *University of Delhi*, New Delhi.

Prasad, Chunnu, "Rights and the Question of Livelihood: A Case of Scheduled Castes of Arunachal Pradesh", National Seminar on Social Exclusion, Poverty and Livelihood of Marginalized Groups in India-need for effective Inclusive Strategies, on 24th and 25th September, 2008, *Centre for Study of Social Exclusion and Inclusive Policy Mangalore University*, Karnataka.

Prasad, Chunnu, "Sexuality versus Equality: Issue of Human Rights and Identity", *Journal of Humanities and Social Sciences*, Contemporary Issue-1, No.5, September, 2008, Scottish Church College, University of Calcutta, pp. 53-69.

Prasad, Chunnu, "Social Exclusion and Caste Based Discrimination on Dalit Christians in South India", National Conference, Social Mobility in South India, on 24th and 25th September, 2009 by Department of Sociology, Pondicherry University, Puducherry.

Prasad, Chunnu, "Social Security of Social Groups in Assam", *The India Economic Review*, Volume VII, Quarterly, Indian Institute of Public Management, January, 2011, pp. 130-139.

Prasad, Chunnu, "Student Movement in Arunachal Pradesh: A Case of Chakma-Hajong Refugee Problem", *Economic and Political Weekly*, Vol. XLII, No. 15, April 14-20, 2007, pp. 1373-1379.

Prasad, Chunnu, "Sustainable Development in Zero (Arunachal Pradesh)", *Third Concept*, No. 234, August 2006, pp. 55-58.

Prasad, Chunnu, "The Nagas in North-East India: Historical Perspectives", *Third Concept*, March 2006, Vol. 229, pp. 51-57.

Prasad, Chunnu, "Tourism in Arunachal Pradesh: Changes and Challenges", in an edited book by Y.Venkata Rao and G. Anjaneya Swamy in *Tourism Entrepreneurship*, Excel Books Publication, Department of Tourism, Pondicherry University, 2011, pp. 185-190.

Prasad, Chunnu, "Traditional Knowledge and Sustainable Agriculture: A Study of Apatani Tribes in Arunachal Pradesh", National

Conference on 26th to 28th December, 2008 by *Head, Department of Anthropology, University of Delhi*, Delhi.

Prasad, Chunnu, "Understanding the Political Economy of Arunachal Pradesh", *Political Economy Journal of India*, Vol. 18, Issue 3 and 4, July-December 2009, pp. 86-93.

Prasad, Chunnu, "Victims of Partition: A Case of Chakma and Hajong Refugees of Arunachal Pradesh", *Think India*, Vol. 9, No. 4, October-December, 2006, pp. 59-71.

Prasad, Chunnu, 2006. Pakistani Dalit Auur Unke Halat. *Ham Dalit*. No. 8, August, pp. 17-19.

Prasad, Chunnu, Understanding Census of India in Reference to Scheduled Caste Population of North East India Region, *The Voice: An International Multidisciplinary Revised Research Journal*, Jan-March 2014, pp. 20-34.

Premi, Kusum K. 1976. Scheduled Castes and Educational Opportunities. *The Indian Journal of Social Work*. Vol. 37, No. 3.

Premi, Kusum K. 1984. Education Equality and Economic Opportunities: A Comparative Study of Scheduled Castes and Non-Scheduled Castes. *Journal of Higher Education*. Vol. 9, No. 3, pp. 363-72.

Pullapilly, C. K. 1976. The Izhavas of Kerala and Their Historic Struggle for Acceptance in the Hindu Society. *Journal of Asian and African Studies*. Vol. 2, nos. 1 and 2, pp. 24-46.

Punalekar, S. P. 1975. Harijans of Eastern U.P. Region: A Profile on Marginality. *The North-Eastern Research Bulletin*. Vol. 6, pp. 30-40.

Puri, Balraj. 1971. Caste and Class and Party Polarisation. *Economic and Political Weekly*. 6 (27), pp. 1317-18.

Radetotad, N.K. 1966. Caste Hierarchy among the Untouchables of Dharwar. *Eastern Anthropologist*. Vol. 19, No. 3, pp. 205-214.

Ramaswamy, Uma. 1984. Preference and Progress: The Scheduled Castes. *Economic and Political Weekly*. Vol. 19, pp. 1214-17.

Ramaswamy, Uma. 1986. Protection and Inequality Among Backward Groups. *Economic and Political Weekly*. Vol. 31, No. 9, pp. 399-403.

Ramu, G. N. 1968. Untouchability in Rural Areas. *Indian Journal of Social Work*. Vol. 25, No. 2.

Rao, N. V. Kameswara and Raju, M. V. T. 1975. Malas and Madigas: An Ethnographic Study of Two Scheduled Castes of Telangana. *Journal of Social Research*. Vol. 18, No. 2, pp. 59-68.

Ravindranatha, M.N. 1981. Educational Problems of Scheduled Castes. *Educational Review*. Vol. 87, No. 4, pp. 69-74.

Reddy, Subha N. 1950. Community Conflict Among the Depressed Castes of Andhra. *Man in India*. Vol. 30, No. 4, pp. 1- 12.

Romila Thapar, The Aryan Question Revisited Transcript of lecture delivered on 11th October 1999, at the Academic Staff College, JNU (http://ascjnu.tripod.com/aryan.html).

Rudolph, Lloyd I. 1965. The Modernity of Tradition: The Democratic Incarnation of Caste in India. *American Political Science Review*. Vol.59, No. 4, pp. 975-89.

Saberwal, Satish. 1972. The Reserved Constituency: Candidates and Consequences. *Economic and Political Weekly*. Vol. 7, No. 2, pp. 71-80.

Sachchidananda and Iyer, Gopal G. 1969. Caste Tension in India. *Eastern Anthropologist*. Vol. 22, No. 3, pp. 327-48.

Sachchidananda. 1967. Caste and Conflict in Bihar Village. *Eastern Anthropologist*. Vol. 20, No. 2, pp. 143-50.

Sachchidananda. 1974. Emergent of Scheduled Castes Elite in Bihar. *Religion and Society*. Vol. 21, No. 3, pp. 55-61.

Sahay, K. N. 1975. Eradication of Untouchability and the Caste System. *Journal of Social Research*. Vol. 18, No. 2, pp. 1-8.

Saradomoni, K. 1973. Agrestic Slavery in Kerala in the Nineteenth Century. *The Indian Economic and Social History Review*. Vol. X, No. 4, December.

Satyanarayana. 1982. Educational Problems of Scheduled Caste College Students in Karnataka. *Journal of Higher Education*. Vol. 7, No. 3, pp. 253-60.

Senapati, Chitranjan "Poverty and Rural Employment of Scheduled Castes in Era of Economic Reforms" in (ed) Wahab, Abdul and Abdul W. Economic Reforms and Growth in India: Introspection and Future Agenda, Lap Lambert Academic Publishing, Germany (April, 2012).

Senapati, Chitranjan "Social Exclusion in Service Sectors: A Study of SCs in Indian Banking", Labour File (abimonthly journal of labour and economic affairs) Vol. 6, No. 1, pp. 20-23 (Jan-Feb 2008).

Senapati, Chitranjan, "Political Exclusion in South Asia: India's Role as a Model of Inclusive Policy" in R.G Dandge, Social Exclusion and Inclusive Policies in South Asia, Sivaji University Seminar Proceeding, 2008.

Senapati, Chitranjan, "Public Sector Reservations in the Era of Globalisation" in Dr B.R. Ambedkar's Vision of Dalit Uplift and its Contemporary Relevance, Dr Ambedkar Studies Centre, Kakatiya University, Warangal, Sree Bhagavan Publications, Hyderabad 2007.

Senapati, Chitranjan, "Social Exclusion and Poverty in Era of Economic Reforms: A Case of Scheduled Caste in Rural India" in (Eds) B.V. Murlidhar, G. Stanley and others, The Dynamics of Change and Continuity in the era of Globalisation: Voices from the Margins, Sunrise Publications, New Delhi, 2009.

Senapati, Chitranjan. "Applicability of Social Exclusion Frame Work and Poverty: A Case of Scheduled Castes andScheduled Tribes in India" Anvesak, (*Journal of Sardar Patel Institute of Economic and Social Research*, Ahmedabad) Vol. 41, No. 2 (Dec-2011).

Sharma, Satya P. 1983. A Materialistic Thesis on the Origin and Continuity of the Caste System in South Asia: A Review Article. *Eastern Anthropologist*. Vol. 36, No. 1, pp. 55-77.

Sharma, Ursula M. 1976. Status Striving and Striving to Abolish Status: The Arya Samaj and the Low Castes. *Social Action*, Vol. 26, July-September.

Sheth, D.L. 1986. The Problems of Reservations: Economic Backwardness or Social Injustice. *Indian Journal of Adult Education*. Vol. 47, No. 5, pp. 9-15.

Singh, N. C. 1981. State Politics in Bihar: A Crisis of Political Institution. *Indian Journal of Political Science*. Vol. XLII, No. 4, pp. 45-64.

Singh, Pratap. 1983. Caste as a Determinant of Rural Leadership: A Case Study of Haryana. *The Indian Political Science Review*. Vol. 17, No. 2, pp. 157-62.

Singh, Soran. 1977. The Scheduled Castes and New Dimensions of Social Change. *Indian Journal of Comparative Sociology*. Vol. 3, pp. 28-38.

Singh, T. R. 1967. The Harijan Leather Worker: Some Aspects of Untouchability in Andhra Pradesh. *Voluntary Action*. Vol. 9, No. 2.

Singh, Yogendra. 1968. Caste and Class: Some Aspects of Continuity and Change. *Sociological Bulletin*. Vol. 17, No. 2, pp. 165-86.

Sinha, Arun. 1977. Class War, Not 'Atrocities' Against Harijans. *Economic and Political Weekly*. Vol. 12, No. 50, pp. 2037-40.

Sinha, Arun. 1986. Caste and Faction in Bihar Politics. *Times of India*. July 9.

Srinivas, M. N. 1959. The Caste of the Potter and the Priest. *Man in India*. Vol. 39, No. 3, pp. 109-209.

Srinivas, M. N. 1959. The Dominant Caste in Rampura. *American Anthropologist*. Vol. 61, No. 1.

Subrahmanyam, S. 1986. Problems of School Dropouts: A Study with a Special Reference to Scheduled Castes and Scheduled Tribes in Andhra Pradesh. *Education Quarterly*. Vol. 38, No. 3, pp. 28-32.

Subramhamanyam, S. 1986. Problems of School Dropouts with a Special Reference to the Scheduled Castes. *Educational Quarterly*, p. 28.

Sukhadeo Thorat and Nidhi Sadana Sabharwal, 2006, Rural Non-Farm Employment of the Scheduled Castes - A Comparative Study, Indian Institute of Dalit Studies, Vol. I, No. 05, New Delhi, pp. 2-31.

Sukhadeo Thorat, Paul Attewell and Firdaus Fatima Rizvi, 2009, Urban Labour Market Discrimination, Indian Institute of Dalit Studies, Volume III, No. 01, New Delhi, pp. 2-15.

Sundaresh, Aruna. 1986. Constitution Law and Reservations. *New Frontiers in Education*. Vol. 16, No. 2, pp. 33-40.

Surinder S. Jodhka and Tanvi Sirari, 2012, In the Footsteps of Ambedkar: Mobility, Identity and Dalit Initiatives for Change Mobility, Indian Institute of Dalit Studies, New Delhi, pp. 2-39.

Swaminathan, M.S. 1982. Educational Development of the Scheduled Castes. *Journal of Indian Education*. Vol. 8, No. 1, pp. 40-55.

Thiagarajan, A.P. 1981. A Study of the Scheduled Caste Students in Some Secondary Schools of Tamil Nadu. *Indian Education*. Vol. 11, No. 5, pp. 22-26.

Thorat S.K, Ambedkar on Economics of the Hindu Social Order – Understanding its Orthodoxy and Legacy in Fernandes, The Emerging Dalit Identity, Indian Social Institute, New Delhi, 1996.

Thorat S.K, Oppression and Denial - Dalit Discrimination in the 1990s, *Economic and Political Weekly*, February 9, 2002.

Thorat, S.K and Deshpande, R.S., Caste and Labour Market Discrimination, Indian Journal of Labour Economics, Conference Issue, November 1999.

Valerain, Rodrigues, 'Ambedkar's Sources and Traditions,'Osmania University, 1997, (U.G.C. instituted Memorial lecture, 1996).

Valerain, Rodrigues, "A Note on the Indian State" in Somen Chakravarthy and R.M. Pal, eds., *State And Civil Rights, Revisiting Contemporary India*, New Delhi, Indian Social Institute, 2002.

Valerain, Rodrigues, "Ambedkar on Modernity and Religion", *Voices for Equity: Minority and Majority in South Asia*, RINDAS International Symposium Series, Ryukoku University, The Centre for the Study of Contemporary India, 2011, pp. 3-18.

Valerain, Rodrigues, "Ambedkar on Preferential Treatment," *Seminar*, 549-May 2005, pp. 55-61.

Valerain, Rodrigues, "Ambedkar, Gandhi and the Marxists," *Shudra*, Vol. 12, October 1993.

Valerain, Rodrigues, "B. R. Ambedkar and Civil Society," *The Radical Humanist*, Vol. 68, No. 8, November, 2004, pp. 3-7.

Valerain, Rodrigues, "Caste among Muslims and Christians in India", *One India One People*, August, 2001.

Valerain, Rodrigues, "Citizenship and the Indian Constitution," in Rajeev Bhargava eds. *Politics and Ethics of the Indian Constitution*, Delhi, Oxford University Press, 2008.

Valerain, Rodrigues, "Citizenship and the Indian Constitution," in Rajeev Bhargava and Helmut Reifeld, eds., *Civil Society, Public Sphere and Citizenship*, New Delhi, Sage, 2005.

Valerain, Rodrigues, "Dalit-Bahujan Discourse in Modern India" in V.R. Mehta and Thomas Pantham ed., *Political Thought in Modern India*, New Delhi, Sage, 2005, Chapter 4.

Valerain, Rodrigues, "Dalits and Cultural Identity: Ambedkar's Prevarications on Culture," *Social Action*, Volume 50, No. 1.

Valerain, Rodrigues, "Dalits and representation", in Sandeep Pendse, ed., *Dalit Movement Today*, Bombay, Vikas, 1993.

Valerain, Rodrigues, "Good Society: Rights, Democracy and Socialism," in Sukhdeo Thorat and Aryama, eds. *Ambedkar in Retrospect, Essays on Economics, Politics and Society*, Jaipur, Rawat, 2007.

Valerain, Rodrigues, "In Search of An Anchor: Muslim Thought in Modern India", *Economic and Political Weekly*, Vol. XLVI, No 49, December 3, 2011, pp. 43-58.

Valerain, Rodrigues, "Indian Democracy: Retrospect and Prospects," *Chair of Christianity Journal*, Mangalore University, 1998.

Valerain, Rodrigues, "Indian Democracy" in Prof K.S. Acharya, et al (eds.), *Freedom and Development*, Udupi, M.G.M. College, 1998.

Valerain, Rodrigues, "Religion as an ideological apparatus: The role of the Catholic Church in Dakshina" in Moin Sakir, ed., *Religion, State and Politics*, New Delhi, Ajanta, 1988.

Valerain, Rodrigues, "Social Inequality and Democracy", Munich, *Proceedings of the German Sociological Congress*, Munich University, 2006.

Valerain, Rodrigues, "Two Discourses on Democracy in India", In Rajesh Basrur, ed., *Challenges to Democracy in India*, New Delhi, Oxford University Press, 2009.

Valerain, Rodrigues, "Untouchability, Filth and the Public Domain", in Gopal Guru, ed, *Humiliation: Claims and Context*, New Delhi, Oxford University Press, 2009.

Valerain, Rodrigues, Contentions on Human Rights : The Divide between Theory and Advocacy" in R.M. Pal, ed., *Protection of Human Rights – A Critique*, New Delhi, Indian Social Institute, 1999.

Valerain, Rodrigues, Justice as the Lens: "Interrogating Rawls through Sen and Ambedkar", *Indian Journal of Human Development*, Vol. V, No. 1, Jan.-June 2011.

Varma, R.P. 1984. Education and the Disadvantaged: A Few Suggestions. *National Journal of Education*. Vol. 6, No. 2, pp. 1-6.

Velaskar, Padma and G.G. Wankhede. 1998. From Old Stigma to New Exploring the Changing Identity of Urban Scheduled Castes. *Indian Journal of Social Work.* Vol. 57.

Verghese, Alexander V. 1984. Education, Earning and Occupation of Weaker Castes. *Journal of Higher Education.* Vol. 9, No. 3, pp. 373-81.

Verma, Vidhu, 1998. Exploitation and Justice: Should we be interested in a theory of exploitation?' *Economic and Political Weekly*, 17 January - 23 January, Vol. 33, No. 3, 115-121.

Verma, Vidhu, 1999. Colonialism and Liberation: Ambedkar's Quest for Distributive Justice, *Economic and Political Weekly*, 25 September – 1 October, Vol. 34, No. 39, pp. 2804-2810.

Verma, Vidhu, 2007. Caste and Caste Systems : Varna and Jati. An Overview. *Encyclopaedia of Women in World History.* OUP, New York.

Verma, Vidhu, 2008. Class Democracy and Conceptions of Justice in India in Rajeev Bhargava, Michael Deusche and Helmut Reifeld. eds. *Justice. Political, Social and Juridical* Sage, New Delhi.

Verma, Vidhu, 2010. Reinterpreting Buddhism: Ambedkar on the Politics of Social Action. *EPW*, Vol. XLV, No. 49, December 4. pp. 56-65.

Verma, Vidhu, 2011a. Conceptualising Social Exclusion: New Rhetoric or Transformative Politics? *EPW*, Vol. VLVI, No. 9, December 10, pp. 89-97.

Wiebe, P. D. and Ramu, G. N. 1975. Christian and Hindu Harijans: A Study of the Effects of Christian Programmes in India. *Eastern Anthropologists.* Vol. 28, No.3, pp. 215-30.

Yadav, S.K. 1982. A Study of the Scheduled Castes Awareness about the Schemes for their Educational Progress. *Indian Educational Review.* Vol. 17, No. 1, pp. 85-93.

Yadav, S.K. 1983. Research Review on Implementation of Educational Schemes of Scheduled Castes. *Indian Educational Review.* Vol. 18, No. 3, pp. 112-22.

Zachariah, Mathew. 1986. Policy Isssues in the Educatiion of Minorities: A Worldwide View. *Education and Urban Society.* Vol. 18, No. 4, pp. 487-499.

Index